The War for Mexico's West

Other titles in the Diálogos series available
from the University of New Mexico Press:

SERIES ADVISORY EDITOR:
LYMAN L. JOHNSON,
UNIVERSITY OF NORTH CAROLINA AT CHARLOTTE

The War for Mexico's West

Indians and Spaniards in New Galicia, 1524-1550

IDA ALTMAN

University of New Mexico Press ❖ Albuquerque

LIBRARY OF CONGRESS CATALOGING-IN-PUBLICATION DATA

Altman, Ida.
The war for Mexico's west : Indians and Spaniards in New Galicia,
1524–1550 / Ida Altman.
p. cm. — (Diálogos)
Includes bibliographical references and index.
ISBN 978-0-8263-4493-9 (pbk. : alk. paper)
1. Nueva Galicia—History—16th century. 2. Mexico—History—Conquest,
1519–1540. 3. Spaniards—Mexico—Nueva Galicia—History—16th
century. 4. Indians of Mexico—Mexico—Nueva Galicia—History—
16th century. 5. Indians, Treatment of—Mexico—Nueva Galicia—
History—16th century. I. Title.
F1296.A558 2010
972'.02—dc22
2010005576

BOOK DESIGN
Composed in 10/13.5 Janson Text Lt Std
Display type is Bernhard Modern Std

To Richmond F. Brown, Judy Oppenheimer,

and Deborah Altman

Contents

Illustrations

Preface

My objective in this book is to tell the story of the prolonged struggle that took place in the early sixteenth century between Spaniards and the indigenous inhabitants of present-day western Mexico. After many years of contention, disorder, and a major insurrection, today known as the Mixton War, this struggle finally resulted in the definitive establishment of Spanish rule over most of the territory the Spaniards called the kingdom of New Galicia. This large region encompasses the modern-day Mexican states of Nayarit, Zacatecas, Aguascalientes, and much of Jalisco, a land area of some 180,000 square kilometers (or more than 100,000 square miles), stretching from the Pacific coast to the Sierra Madre Occidental and including much of the plains of north central Mexico east to the foothills of the Sierra Madre Oriental.[1] In 1540 a coalition of indigenous groups rose in rebellion against the tenuous Spanish regime established ten years earlier under Nuño de Guzmán's leadership. After that uprising was suppressed, the Crown recognized New Galicia as a quasi-independent jurisdiction within the viceroyalty of New Spain, and in 1548 it acquired its own high court, or *audiencia*. Most of the history recounted here took place while jurisdictional boundaries still were vague. Some of the events described occurred in, or directly affected parts of, Colima and Michoacan to the south, which never were considered to be part of New Galicia, as well as other areas where civil and ecclesiastical jurisdiction later would be disputed. Those jurisdictional disputes for the most part began after the events discussed in this book. In some cases place names have changed since the sixteenth century. For clarity and consistency, and because there often are variant spellings in the documents, I use contemporary forms for place names (Juchipila rather than Suchipila, Etzatlan rather than Izatlan, and the like).

xiii

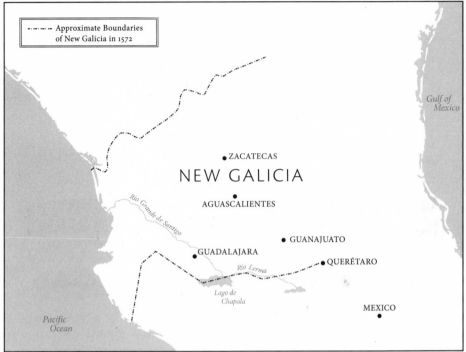

Source: From J. H. Parry, *The Audiencia of New Galicia in the Sixteenth Century*

MAP I. New Galicia in the sixteenth century

The story of the conquest and Spanish settlement of New Galicia has attracted the attention of historians going back to the time of the Franciscan fray Antonio Tello, who wrote his lengthy *Crónica miscelánea de la Sancta Provincia de Xalisco* in the late seventeenth century, emphasizing Franciscan endeavors but also devoting a great deal of attention to the early history of New Galicia more generally. No one who participated in or was a contemporary of the events examined here wrote a complete history. Given the existence of multiple accounts of the conquest of central Mexico and the number of early chroniclers who wrote about early New Spain from both Spanish and indigenous perspectives, the absence of a full contemporary account of the conquest and early settlement of New Galicia is notable. The explanation might lie in the perceived poverty and marginality of the region and its people, together with the aura of failure and discord that surrounded early Spanish activity in the West.

The first Spanish foray into the region, sponsored by Hernando Cortés, the conqueror of central Mexico, took place in 1524. Led by Cortés's kinsman Francisco Cortés, it was relatively inconsequential for the Spaniards. Their next significant move into the West, the expedition organized by the president of the first audiencia of Mexico, Nuño de Guzmán, produced controversy and scandal and contributed to Guzmán's political downfall. It yielded neither glory nor riches and perhaps for that reason failed to attract the attention of any chronicler. Although a number of accounts of the expedition were compiled, the people from whom they were solicited most likely dictated their recollections of the campaign in the course of an inquiry conducted by the high court in Mexico City. While of great value as eyewitness reports, these narratives are uneven and inconsistent, and not one of them offers a complete account of the expedition. Although the campaign that the first viceroy of New Spain, don Antonio de Mendoza, conducted to suppress the indigenous rebellion that engulfed much of New Galicia in 1540–41 garnered more general recognition as a significant victory, it too failed to yield any bonanza of wealth and perhaps again for that reason never found its chronicler.

I decided to write this history for several reasons, perhaps the foremost being my curiosity about the virtually unknown peoples of the West and a long-term interest in early Mexico and the consequences of Spanish enslavement of Indians in the early Caribbean and Mexico. I began by looking at the Mixton War of 1540–41 in connection with a possible broader inquiry into Spanish responses to early rebellions in the rapidly growing empire. It quickly became apparent that it would be impossible to make sense of the war without understanding conditions in New Galicia in the 1530s, which in turn led me to the accounts of Guzmán's expedition of conquest. It then became obvious that the only place to begin was at the beginning, with the first episode of Spanish-indigenous contact in the West, the expedition of Francisco Cortés. As I learned more about this history, I became aware that even before the major mining strikes of the late 1540s, the region played a surprisingly important role in the early politics of New Spain, notwithstanding the remoteness of the West and (to Spaniards) the seeming poverty of its peoples. In the 1530s the ambitions and activities of such leading figures of early Mexican history as Cortés, Guzmán, don Antonio de Mendoza, Pedro de Alvarado, and Francisco Vázquez de Coronado all involved the West. Thus, a detailed examination of the early history of New Galicia in a sense became a way to look at the complex forces and politics that shaped postconquest society in early New Spain.

The history of early New Galicia proved to be considerably richer and more interesting than expected, given how little is known about it among scholars and students of Mexican history in the United States—and perhaps in much of Mexico as well, outside of the western states. Although notable progress has been made in the history of Mesoamerican peoples through the use of indigenous language records, many groups that did not produce records in their own languages remain lesser known. Scholars such as Cynthia Radding, Susan M. Deeds, and others have used Spanish and missionary records quite effectively to study indigenous groups in the North and Northwest.[2] The earliness of the Spanish conquest of New Galicia and the drastic disruption of indigenous life that occurred there as a result of the attempt to impose Spanish rule, however, resulted in great dislocations and high mortality. Given the rapidity of change in the region, using descriptions and histories written in later periods as guides to understanding the varied peoples of the West in the era of contact with Europeans can be problematic. As a result many questions regarding society and culture in the region remain unanswered here.

Yet if much about the indigenous peoples of the West is still unknown, it is possible nonetheless to derive a sense of their world and perspective on events from the existing documentation. We know that the autonomous communities of the region were ethnically and linguistically diverse and that their ways of life varied, although they also had much in common with one another and with other Mesoamericans. Although often in conflict, they maintained ties of trade and alliance and perhaps participated in religious cults that encompassed multiple communities. It did not take the people of the West long to understand the profound threat to their world that the Spaniards and Christianity posed and to make common cause against the hated newcomers, notwithstanding their diversity.

My hopes for this book are modest: to make known to an English-speaking audience a dramatic, complex episode in the early history of New Spain that stands as an instructive counterpoint to the much more familiar, triumphalist narrative of Spanish daring, resilience, and victory embodied in the oft-told tale of the conquest of central Mexico led by Hernando Cortés. The story of early New Galicia is characterized by violence—extreme at times—brutal exploitation, and stark polarization between Spaniards and the people they intended to make their subjects.

If graphic descriptions of cruelty and abuse make some readers uncomfortable, they appear here because it is partly through such details that we appreciate the true dimensions of the disaster that befell the people of New Galicia. This history is indeed bleak in many respects. Nonetheless it underscores the vitality of the Western peoples and their determination to maintain their way of life in their own lands. For me, at least, their courage and tenacity, not their victimization, resonate most strongly.

I hope also that this book will encourage others to pursue the study of indigenous groups in early Mexico that did not leave records in their own languages. The careful consideration and analysis even of sources that are well known and have been readily available for quite some time can yield substantial benefits, and the enforced reliance on Spanish records at the least provides insight into the nature and functioning of Spanish-indigenous relations. It is my hope, finally, that this book contributes to our knowledge and understanding of early Mexico—not only of how the West was won but of how it was lost as well.

Acknowledgments

The assistance and generosity of a number of people and institutions helped me to complete this project. I am grateful for research support provided by a fellowship from the National Endowment for the Humanities in 2004–5 and sabbatical leave from the University of New Orleans, as well as a semester's leave from the University of Florida. A number of people shared with me their knowledge, insights, and even their research. Special thanks go to Sarah Cline, who read and commented on the entire manuscript twice, and to Lyman Johnson, who is as distinguished an editor as he is a scholar. Without their guidance and assistance this book would not exist in the form it does. James Boyden, James Lockhart, and Michael Polushin read the manuscript and made invaluable suggestions. I greatly benefited from insights and advice on early New Galicia and the ethnohistory of Mesoamerica from James Lockhart and Phil C. Weigand; Phil C. Weigand also provided the photos of Teuchitlan. I thank Clark Whitehorn for his support and Susan Silver for her excellent copy editing.

I also wish to express my appreciation to Judith Reynolds for her encouragement and generous gift of books; Donald Chipman for the loan of some useful material and his interest in this project; and Thomas Hillerkuss of the University of Zacatecas for sharing so generously his extensive knowledge of the geography and early history of New Galicia, as well as books, photos, and the results of his research. Clarence L. Mohr allowed me to use the facilities of the history department of the University of South Alabama when, after Katrina, for a time I had no institutional "home." I also thank Barbara Tenenbaum and David Dressing for assistance at the Library of Congress and the Latin American Library of Tulane University, respectively; John Chuchiak IV, Camilla Townsend, and José Cuello for helpful references; Susan M. Deeds for her comments on a paper on enslavement of Indians in New Galicia; Linda Arnold for advice regarding the Archivo General de la Nación; the knowledgeable staff of the Archivo General de Indias, where much of the research for this project was conducted; and Randall Renner of the University of Florida Library, Bill Modrow of the Florida State University Libraries, and Bonnie Coles of the Library of Congress for assistance in obtaining and producing digitized images for illustrations.

In the midst of this project, which details the calamitous disruption of the lives of the people who lived in the once flourishing but today little-known societies of western Mesoamerica, the city of New Orleans, where I lived for nearly twenty-five years, suffered massive destruction and upheaval following hurricane Katrina and the collapse of the levee system. Thus, around the time that I was completing research on dislocation and destruction in a remote place and time I gained unimagined insights into how such events change lives and communities. That experience deepened my grasp of the profound and lasting consequences of disasters, whether their causes are of natural or human origin. This book is my tribute to the long-vanished people of New Galicia, who lived at the wrong time. I dedicate it with love and deep gratitude to Richmond F. Brown, my companion through Katrina and so much else, and to Deborah Altman and Judy Oppenheimer, my constant support and inspiration.

CHAPTER I

Prelude to Conquest

> At the time that the said Marqués del Valle [Hernando Cortés], being governor of this New Spain, sent Francisco Cortés to the town of Colima [and] sent him on the conquest . . . this witness was in the said town and saw Francisco Cortés as captain in the name of the Marqués del Valle summon the people in the town of Colima and leave on the said conquest. . . . This witness saw [them] pacify and conquer many pueblos and provinces of diverse names and differing qualities of people and different languages which had not been seen or pacified or conquered by any other Spaniards.
>
> —Testimony of Jerónimo López in the lawsuit brought by Hernando Cortés against Nuño de Guzmán over claims to New Galicia (western Mexico), 1531[1]

FOR MOST PEOPLE THE CONQUEST OF MEXICO, LED BY THE AUDACIOUS and ambitious Hernando Cortés, epitomizes Spanish achievements in the Americas. During a campaign lasting a year and a half (1519–21) and penetrating the densely-populated heart of Mesoamerica, Cortés maintained his supreme confidence and determination despite a dramatic series of challenges and setbacks. By marching into the interior he far exceeded the mission that Diego Velázquez, the governor of Cuba, had authorized.

Cortés was living in Cuba, which served as the base for organizing his expedition, or *entrada*, into Mexico. Spaniards had reconnoitered and landed on the coast of Yucatan, where they gained a sense of what might be found farther inland. When Velázquez authorized Cortés's entrada, however, it was in hopes of extending his own jurisdiction to include new territory and thus reap the benefits of any significant windfalls. He tried to limit his potential rival's field of action by stipulating that the expedition should do no more than reconnoiter the Gulf coast, with an eye toward establishing trade relations. Anticipating the consequences of his illegal actions, Cortés devised an alternative legal framework by orchestrating the founding of a new municipality, Veracruz, on the Gulf coast, the citizens of which (his own men) then endorsed a plan to march inland. They made their way into the interior, acquiring key allies, the Tlaxcalans, along the way. When they finally reached Tenochtitlan, the dazzling island capital of what today is usually called the Aztec Empire, the ruler Moctezoma greeted them, and they entered the city unopposed.[2]

Subsequently, Cortés faced down a challenge from a rival group of Spaniards led by Pánfilo de Narváez, who arrived on the Gulf coast with another sizable contingent of men, arms, and horses after Cortés reached Tenochtitlan. Cortés succeeded in persuading most of the newcomers to join him, but on returning to Tenochtitlan he confronted a situation that even his audacity and rhetorical skills could not rectify. During his absence from the city the actions of his second-in-command, the daring but reckless Pedro de Alvarado, produced turmoil when he launched a bloody massacre of an unarmed group of Mexica (Aztec) warriors and nobles celebrating a religious festival. In the ensuing disorder Moctezoma, who had been held hostage by Cortés, died. The city's population having turned against them, the Spaniards had no alternative but to flee with considerable losses. They regrouped successfully, thanks in large measure to the support they enjoyed from the Mexica's longtime enemy, Tlaxcala. In February 1521 they finally overcame Tenochtitlan's defenses and its residents, who continued to resist even as they died by the thousands from disease and starvation. The Spaniards by then had attracted the support of a number of other provinces, including even Texcoco, a longtime ally of Tenochtitlan. After nearly thirty years of Spanish activity in the Caribbean and adjacent mainland, Hernando Cortés finally took the greatest prize conceivable: he seized a populous, wealthy empire.

Yet Cortés, along with many other Spaniards, was not content to settle down to enjoy the fruits of this accomplishment, notwithstanding the rewards he received from the Crown: rich agricultural and grazing lands and extensive *encomiendas* (grants of rights to indigenous labor and tribute) that allowed him to exploit thousands of people who lived in specified communities. He continued to search for new opportunities to gain wealth and assert his dominance. Notwithstanding the fall of Tenochtitlan, since most of the communities in the south, west, and north of the very large territory that the Spanish named New Spain were independent of the Aztec Empire, the lands and peoples of those areas remained unconquered. They quickly drew the attention of Cortés and other Spaniards. In the summer of 1522 Cortés sent Cristóbal de Olid to occupy Michoacan to the west.[3] Cortés himself pushed northeast into Pánuco and then led a disappointing expedition south into Honduras to confront Cristóbal de Olid, who had become his rival. Pedro de Alvarado set off for the conquest of Guatemala in 1524, and in 1527 Francisco de Montejo undertook his first expedition into Yucatan. The Spaniards' expansion into these other areas, often fiercely opposed, to a large degree depended on their ability to use the indigenous personnel now available to them in central Mexico as fighters, auxiliaries, and sometimes colonists for new territories they had conquered.[4] In this regard the conquest of western Mexico, which would become the kingdom of New Galicia, was no exception. The speed with which Spaniards undertook these entradas suggests complex responses to what we usually today assume to have been a great triumph, the conquest of central Mexico. Cortés worried about being outflanked by potential rivals and coveted greater recognition from the Crown in the form of high office that ultimately was not forthcoming. Men like Pedro de Alvarado hoped to gain greater power and wealth for themselves. Perhaps equally important, central Mexico, for all its impressive productivity, failed to yield the immediate riches that Spaniards found ten years later when Francisco Pizarro and his men toppled the Andean Empire of the Incas and seized the spectacular treasure of Atahualpa. The shares from what remained of Tenochtitlan's treasure proved disappointing to the conquistadors, and many men who participated in the conquest did not receive encomiendas, or found that their grants were small or located at some remove from central Mexico. Such men often were willing to join expeditions into still unconquered areas. Until his final departure from Mexico in 1539 Cortés himself never abandoned the quest for new lands, mines, wealthy peoples, and lucrative trade.

Even before occupying Michoacan, Cortés became interested in establishing a port and shipyards in Zacatula on the Pacific coast (south of present-day Acapulco). From Zacatula he dispatched a fairly substantial group of 50 horsemen and 150 footmen, who took over the province of Colima in 1523.[5] By 1524 Spaniards were poised to move farther into the unknown western lands that lay north of Colima and Michoacan. In this very large region they would find scores of autonomous communities. Among these loosely organized, ethnically and linguistically diverse societies neither the Spaniards' usual stratagems of conquest—such as seizing a principal leader or allying with groups that might welcome the assistance of the newcomers in confronting their traditional rivals—nor their attempts to impose their institutions met with much success. Later, in the 1530s, Spaniards in New Galicia complained that the Indians there would not serve them, nor would they furnish tribute.[6] Christianization made no progress. When an uprising against Spanish rule erupted in 1540 and attracted thousands of people from many different indigenous communities, it brought Spanish failure in the region into sharp relief.

The challenges that Spaniards faced in their attempts to govern New Galicia suggest much about the limitations on their capabilities and their dealings with different native groups. Their relative success in central Mexico owed a great deal to the nature of the indigenous societies there. Alliance with the Mexica's rivals was crucial in bringing down the Aztec Empire. After that conquest the Spanish usually left the sociopolitical structures and arrangements of the indigenous states in place and used native rulers as their intermediaries. In this fashion they were able to maintain existing systems for collecting tribute and organizing public labor in central Mexico and redirect them for their own profit and use. In New Galicia, where sociopolitical power was not centralized and mechanisms for funneling tribute and organizing labor were weak to nonexistent, Spanish efforts to exploit the labor and productivity of the indigenous population produced more frustration than success.

The early history of New Galicia shows that the process of bringing territory and native peoples under Spanish control could be prolonged, strongly contested, and ambiguous. New Galicia was not, of course, unique in the obstacles it posed to the extension of Spanish rule. The occupation of Yucatan, for example, required a series of campaigns spanning nearly twenty years.[7] In parts of Spanish America where Spaniards failed to find organized societies and met with violent opposition—the Río de la Plata region, southern Chile, Texas, and other parts of the southwestern United States—they experienced similar difficulties in asserting control over native groups and avoided or deferred committing men and resources to lengthy campaigns that seemed unlikely to bear fruit. In contrast to these other situations, however, New Galicia exerted a strong pull because of its proximity to central Mexico, potential mineral wealth, and coastline and harbors on the "South Sea" (the Pacific), which beckoned ambitious men like Cortés, Alvarado, and even the first viceroy of New Spain, don Antonio de Mendoza, to further efforts of exploration. Added to these attractions were persistent tales that the mythical island of the Amazons or the fabulous seven golden cities might be found in the west or north.[8] Thus, the region attracted those who were looking to carve out new domains, gain advantage over political rivals, and discover new sources of wealth. Yet despite the keen interest of several powerful individuals, and the relative earliness of the first Spanish foray into the area (1524), the West stubbornly rejected Spanish rule. It took two major military campaigns and twenty years to establish effective control, and even then Spaniards continued to be vulnerable to indigenous violence and resistance. As Spanish mining, stock raising, and settlement spread progressively northward, indigenous groups in the west and north continued to challenge Spaniards' determination to pursue their economic interests and establish their political and religious authority.[9] Indeed, significant parts of New Galicia remained virtually independent of Spanish rule until well into the eighteenth century.

The tremendous destruction, mortality, disruption, and dislocation occasioned by Spanish efforts to extend control over the region very early produced such enormous changes that it is not possible to reconstruct with assurance many aspects of life in the West before the arrival of Europeans. The uncertainties include vital questions, such as what languages some groups spoke (many languages in use at the time of the conquest no longer exist); the nature of sociopolitical organization, kinship, and gender roles; family or household size and population numbers; and religious beliefs and practices. Archaeological work in western Mexico has made significant strides in recent years, but it sheds little light on the nature and circumstances of indigenous societies in New Galicia at the time of contact.[10] Thus, our principal source of information comes from contemporary written records, produced mainly by Spaniards and therefore reflecting their interests, priorities, biases, and misunderstandings.[11]

Into the West: The Expedition of Francisco Cortés

Following the conquest of Colima, Hernando Cortés sent his kinsman Francisco Cortés to serve as its lieutenant governor. Little is known about the "other" Cortés. Although he was called a relative of Hernando Cortés, who after the conquest of Tenochtitlan in 1521 received from Charles V the title of Marqués del Valle (by which he became commonly known), the nature and degree of the relationship between the two men is not clear.[12] Nonetheless Francisco must have had fairly close ties with the Marqués, who trusted him to act as his proxy in the West when the latter headed south on his ill-fated expedition to Honduras.[13] The Marqués issued ambitious—and doubtless unrealistic—instructions to his lieutenant, directing him to expand Colima's jurisdiction by acquiring additional lands, take control over Michoacan and distribute encomiendas there, continue to develop the shipyards at Zacatula where the vessels that Cortés hoped would allow him to explore the South Sea were being built, and then move on to further conquests.[14] He was especially interested in finding an island near the coast supposedly inhabited exclusively by women, thought to be similar to the mythical Amazons.[15]

Francisco Cortés left Mexico City at the very end of 1523 or early in 1524, accompanied by *vecinos* (householders or citizens) of Colima, as well as men recruited in the new capital that had been built on the ruins of Tenochtitlan. The very recent Spanish occupation of Colima probably hampered recruitment for the expedition; Spaniards who went to live there were involved in establishing new enterprises and control over their encomiendas and probably not inclined to venture further. In all likelihood, most of the men who participated in the entrada accompanied Cortés from the capital. He managed to gather some twenty or twenty-five horsemen and perhaps a similar number of men on foot, along with an unknown number of local Indians to serve as bearers and scouts and, with luck, as interpreters who could mediate between the Spaniards and the peoples they encountered as they moved north.[16] The Marqués directed his lieutenant to try to maintain peace with the communities they found and forge friendly relations, avoiding confrontations if possible. If it proved necessary to counter violence with violence, he urged that they do so with restraint and limit hostilities.[17] Given the relatively small size of the party, these instructions probably described the most practical course to pursue. As had been the case in central Mexico and elsewhere, however, the Spaniards' horses and firearms usually assured their military superiority over the local residents, who probably were taken by surprise.

Who were the people Francisco Cortés and his men found when they ventured north of Colima? The fertile river valleys, lakes, and marshes of western Mexico for centuries had attracted waves of settlers who probably arrived mainly from the north.[18] The groups that lived in the West at the time that Spaniards entered the region—among them Coras, Tecuexes, Tecuales, and, perhaps the latest arrivals, Cazcanes, who settled north of the Río Grande de Santiago and probably at least partially displaced other groups—had much in common with other Mesoamericans.[19] Internal social distinctions and possibly hierarchies that in some measure separated the majority of people, the commoners, from smaller ruling groups were characteristic of many Western communities. Their diet was based on maize, beans, squash, and chilis; they wove their clothing from cotton and maguey fiber; the weapons they used included bows and arrows, clubs, round shields, and *macanas* (wooden swords edged with obsidian); and they were heirs to traditions of mining and metallurgy.[20] They held regular markets and engaged in local and longer-distance trade.[21] The construction of large-scale structures long predated the period of European contact and conquest.[22] Although their material culture and sociopolitical organization for the most part were less elaborate than those of groups living in central and southern Mexico, the "Westerners" differed from other Mesoamericans more in degree than in kind. Many of the languages spoken in the West bore a close relationship to Nahuatl, the main language of central Mexico. Given their proximity to central Mexico and Michoacan and their cultural and linguistic affinities, people living in the West maintained direct and indirect contacts with other Mesoamericans, mainly through trade (and sometimes warfare).

The West attracted outsiders in part because of its rich resources. Minerals that could be used to fashion weapons, tools, and ornaments, as well as for trade—salt, obsidian, quartz crystals, malachite, azurite, opals, copper, silver, and gold—were abundant. Cotton, maguey (a cactus that yields fiber from which clothes could be fashioned, as well as edible flesh and sap), and fruit trees were plentiful, and cacao grew in some places. Indications of intensive forms of cultivation such as terracing and

FIGURE I. Circular, stepped structures, today known as
guachimontones, were characteristic of the Teuchitlan tradition and
date to around 400–700 CE. Photo courtesy of Phil C. Weigand.

irrigation further attest to the productivity of labor-intensive agriculture
and the substantial populations the land could support, at least in some
areas.[23] Forests of pine and oak covered much of the land, creating humid
microclimates and providing additional resources of game animals that
furnished meat, skins, sinews, and fur.[24] In the warmest zones of the
South and Pacific coast especially, exotic birds yielded highly desirable
plumage for feather work and trade.

Despite many similarities, the Western groups were diverse in language and custom, and lifestyles could vary even within ethnic groups.
In some cases people apparently of the same ethnicity occupied different
ecological zones, with some communities cultivating crops in the river
valleys and others living in the foothills and mountainous regions that
were less hospitable to agriculture. The latter probably depended more
heavily on hunting than did the valley dwellers. In some settlements,
residents lived dispersed over a fairly large area, while other communities were compact, and still others seemed to combine aspects of the
two patterns. Communities varied considerably in size and organization.

People of differing language and ethnicity sometimes lived together in the same place, probably as distinct sociopolitical entities. Even where one group predominated, the presence of more than one ruler suggests the existence of distinct subunits.[25]

As in the rest of Mesoamerica, migration and conflict left their mark on the human landscape. Conquest could mean the displacement and relocation of older populations, with the result that the West resembled an ethnic and linguistic kaleidoscope, densely populated in some areas, sparsely peopled in others. The men of the West were warriors, almost by definition, capable of defending themselves from outsiders, as they did against the invaders from the South, the Purépecha (or Tarascans) of Michoacan, who themselves developed one of the strongest military states in Mesoamerica before the arrival of the Spaniards and remained independent of the Triple Alliance of central Mexico.[26] The political fragmentation, fierce independence, and formidable fighting skills of the Western natives presented considerable challenges to the latest newcomers to the region, the Spaniards.

In the summer or early fall of 1524 Francisco Cortés and his expeditionary party entered this little-known world, a land of dramatic contrasts, parts of which today still possess a wild beauty belying centuries and

FIGURE 2. View of area around Teuchitlan. Photo courtesy of Phil C. Weigand.

millennia of human occupation. They headed north along the coast, reaching a small, protected bay later known as the Puerto de la Navidad.[27] From there they continued north and northeast into the valley of Espuchimilco, where, despite the Marqués's cautions, they came into conflict with the local people, causing substantial damage and dislocation. During the year following the expedition, two Spaniards, Gonzalo Cerezo and Francisco de Vargas, conducted an official tour of inspection (*visitación* or *visita*) of the area and observed firsthand the destruction the Cortés party left in its wake. The lord of the pueblo of Xalipanga, a man named Aupipiluli, reported to the inspectors that only twenty-one houses remained there "because it was very destroyed, and that they killed many people and burned all of the pueblo, and people died of hunger in the mountains with the war that the Spaniards waged when they conquered them, and not a single house remained undamaged." If he explained to the inspectors the reason for the hostilities, the officials did not record it. Francisco de Vargas, who made the report, guessed that there remained perhaps sixty men from the community who were living "among the trees, and because of the war they were not peaceful, [and] fearing that they [the Spaniards] would return to destroy, they did not sow their maize, although they have good land for it." The inspectors who visited the Espuchimilco Valley in 1525 found that in another pueblo, Iustlichanga, there were no houses left standing "because when they [the Spaniards] conquered it [they] did not remain peaceful, and with the fear [they had] they had been in the mountains until now."[28] This statement suggests that the Cortés party either approached or was received belligerently—in the latter case, most likely because the people of Iustlichanga knew of the hostilities that already had occurred elsewhere in the valley.

Leaving behind this trail of destruction in the valley of Espuchimilco, Cortés led the party east to Autlan and the populous valley of Milpa, where his encounter with the indigenous pueblos apparently was less violent, although Autlan and Milpa were intermittently at war with each other. Autlan, the only settlement large enough to be described in the visitación as a *ciudad* (city), was located four leagues from Espuchimilco. As was not unusual in the West, Autlan had two rulers, an "old man" named Milpanecatetle and a "boy" around fifteen years of age named Opuchel. Between them they governed some 1,200 to 1,400 households with an estimated 4,000 men.[29] In nearby Epetlan, set "in a very beautiful valley among groves of fruit trees," the ruler also was very young, in this

MAP 2. Area contacted by Francisco Cortés

case a twelve-year-old boy named Uoalo, who together with his *principales* (leaders, members of the upper class), reported that his pueblo and an *estancia* (or subject community) had 330 houses with 660 men.[30] Apparently there were two other estancias a quarter league distant that also were subject to Epetlan's rule. Although in 1525 one of the inspectors reported that there were another 178 houses there, he noted that "these estancias were destroyed," suggesting that the area did not altogether escape the violence that the Spaniards brought to the valley of Espuchimilco.[31]

Francisco Cortés and his men also left considerable devastation in the valley of Ayutla, where two men named Melindoque and Aquytapil governed the main settlement; after the entrada passed through there, only 23 houses remained undamaged. One of the rulers later told the inspectors that the pueblo "was very destroyed, and he said that they killed the people of the said pueblo when they conquered it." The visitors of 1525 judged that there were 30 dispersed houses with 60 men. They observed that the people dressed in clothing made of maguey fiber and described them as being poor. The subject community of Tepetitlan, a quarter of a league away, experienced similar destruction, and the people there also were characterized as poor.[32]

From Ayutla, Francisco Cortés and his party went on to Etzatlan, which bordered a large freshwater lake, where the inspectors later would report seeing houses with stone walls and straw rooftops built along the lakeshore. The pueblo's ruler informed the inspectors that his people traded salt, maize, some cotton, and fish that they caught in the lake, where the visitors observed numerous well-built canoes made of reeds. On a rocky island in the lake there were people said to be "from the *cabecera* [main pueblo] that fled for fear of the wars . . . and they have their fields on the land." The ambiguous wording of the report makes it impossible to know if the "wars" to which the informants referred were conflicts among local groups or with the Cortés party. The houses on the island also had walls of carved stone and straw roofs.[33]

After the expedition left Ayutla, it crossed to the valley of Aguacatlan and skirted the volcano Ceboruco to reach Xalisco and Tepic, two communities located close to each other but belonging to different ethnic groups. These two pueblos would play an important role in Nuño de Guzmán's conquest in 1530 and during the subsequent Spanish settlement of the region. Although Xalisco was one of the larger communities in the region—in 1525 the inspectors recorded it as having 400 houses with 800 men—nonetheless, it was somewhat isolated. Its ruler told the inspectors that they had no market and conducted no trade, and Xalisco apparently lacked subject communities. Even so, it came to occupy such a key place in the Spaniards' understanding of the region that very soon the core of New Galicia became known as the province of Jalisco.[34] To distinguish the pueblo from the Spanish notion of a larger province of Jalisco, here the name of the indigenous community itself will be spelled Xalisco. The nearby community of Tepic, located on a river and closer to the coast, apparently had about half the population of Xalisco, also distributed in a dispersed pattern. Unlike Xalisco, however, Tepic had a market, and its people traded cotton and maize. The visitors of 1525 reported that the two pueblos waged war on each other.[35]

An unusual document that originated in the community of Xalisco later in the sixteenth century provides an account of Xalisco's experiences from the time that Spaniards first appeared. It briefly mentioned the arrival of the entrada: "Our lord Martín [*sic* for Francisco?] Cortés came to our home Xalisco. . . . He did not conquer us; he was received on the road, in the field of the ruling lord. . . . Then they went to Tepic. Then his messenger came. . . . Seven people greeted him, each with a jar of gold." The so-called messenger probably was one of the inspectors who visited there in 1525.[36] The testimony of a participant in the Cortés entrada, Alonso Quintero, however, suggests that a complicated series of events took place when the expedition reached Xalisco. Quintero stated that the people of Xalisco

> greeted them in war, and that they fought with them until they threw them out of the pueblo. And being in the said Xalisco for three or four hours thinking they would come in peace, and they did not, that same day they [the Spaniards] went to sleep in Tepic, which was a league from there. And the next day those from Xalisco came in peace and got back the women who had been taken. And they [people from Xalisco] went with them and were there for three or four days, and Tepic met them in peace. And from there they [the Spaniards] went seven leagues to another pueblo, and all the people of Xalisco and Tepic went in their aid, and from that same pueblo they returned to Colima, conquering along the coast.[37]

Quintero's testimony indicates not only that there was conflict with Xalisco and that the Spaniards took women from the pueblo, perhaps as hostages, but that people from both Xalisco and Tepic, who were unfriendly toward each other, joined the expedition as allies of the Spanish, apparently participating in the conquest of at least one other pueblo. The word that Quintero used for the recovery of the women, *rescatar*, implies some kind of exchange; perhaps the people of Xalisco agreed to accompany Cortés in return for his letting the women go free. Whatever the terms of the agreement, the much more extensive violence and destruction that took place when Nuño de Guzmán's expedition arrived in Xalisco in 1530 might have occurred because the pueblo's people thought that they already had established an alliance with the Spaniards, symbolized and solidified by the gold they gave to the inspectors in 1525. They might have seen Guzmán's aggression as a betrayal of what they thought was an alliance forged with Francisco Cortés; alternatively, they might have thought that Guzmán had nothing to do with the earlier party of Spaniards, meaning that there was no agreement with him. For his part Guzmán could have concluded that the people of Xalisco had reneged on an earlier unqualified acceptance of Spanish rule.[38] Although, as will be discussed, the linguistic situation of the area through which the Cortés expedition moved is poorly understood, neither the few participants in the expedition who testified later nor the visitors of 1525 mentioned any difficulties in communicating with the local residents. That omission, however, does not mean that the Spaniards and the indigenous people with whom they dealt necessarily understood each other entirely or very well.

From Tepic the expedition passed through pueblos from the valley of the Río Grande de Santiago to the coast, apparently not crossing the river, which formed the northernmost limit of their trajectory.[39] The party then headed south to Colima, "making war" and "conquering" along the coast, as Quintero and one other participant testified.[40] Little is known about the return journey, and indeed we lack detailed information for most of the expedition. Jerónimo López, the conquistador of Mexico who participated in the entrada, testified that it lasted about nine months and that he wrote a detailed report for Hernando Cortés, which unfortunately has not been found.[41] López might have exaggerated the duration of the expedition, and there is little indication that the party stayed anywhere for any significant length of time.[42]

The Visitación of 1525 and the Aftermath of the Cortés Expedition

Because there is no account of the expedition and only very scant subsequent testimony from participants, most of what is known about it and the area it traversed comes from the aforementioned official visitación that took place in 1525. The purpose of the inspection was to record information about the pueblos that the expedition contacted and presumably brought to submission. With that information Francisco Cortés could assign encomiendas to Spaniards who participated in the expedition and perhaps to others as well whom either he or Hernando Cortés wished to reward (or confirm assignments possibly made during the expedition itself). These encomiendas stretched northward from Colima, from Autlan to Tepic; but, apart from the men who received grants located close to Colima, it does not appear that the Spaniards to whom they were assigned had much luck in claiming them.[43]

Francisco de Vargas and Gonzalo Cerezo, a *criado* (retainer) of Hernando Cortés, conducted the inspection of the pueblos, accompanied by Diego de Coria, also Cortés's criado, who acted as notary. Departing from Colima in January 1525, they did not follow the same route as the entrada itself and most likely did not visit every community that Francisco Cortés contacted. Nonetheless, the account includes information on more than eighty pueblos and attached estancias and offers the most detailed survey of any part of New Galicia until the 1540s.[44]

The visitors followed a standard format in gathering information about the communities, inquiring about local rulers, numbers of houses and men, types of crops grown, clothing worn, the kind of trade conducted, and whether or not there was a market (*tiánguiz*). They apparently questioned their informants, who seem mainly to have been the local rulers, as to whether their communities had dependent settlements or were subject to another, what and with whom they traded, and whether they were at war with any other group. Additional information—especially comments on geographic features (rivers, lakes, mountains); the location and nature of settlements (in valleys or on mountainsides, dispersed or compact); and the quality of the communities (poor, very poor); and (probably) languages spoken—more likely derived from their own observations. The document omits any reference to interpreters, although surely they were present.

The information elicited about the local rulers shows that, despite the absence of large political units, political organization entailed a degree of complexity that probably reflected in part the multiethnic composition of the region. *Calpixques* (administrators), for example, governed the settlements listed as part of Aguacatlan.[45] The province itself had two rulers: Procoal, said to be a Naguatato, and Suchipil, an Otomí. One of the dependent communities, Xalpa, had two calpixques, one Naguatato and the other Otomí. Although there are considerable uncertainties about what these linguistic or ethnic designations meant, at the least they suggest that these communities encompassed more than one ethnic group. The existence in Aguacatlan of Naguatato and Otomí corulers implies a more complex kind of accommodation than a simple dichotomy of conqueror and conquered. In a few other places as well rulership was split between two people; in Ixtlan (spelled Ispan in the report) an old man named Coal governed jointly with his son Coautlatla.[46]

The question of language and ethnicity remains murky. The largest number of communities were said to be Otomí, but in many of them the residents were called Naguatatos, and in a number of cases people from the two ethnic or language groups lived together. Thus, in Aguacatlan and Xalpa, where one ruler was a Naguatato and the other Otomí, the majority of people were said to be Naguatatos, while in Ixtlan "part of them are Naguatatos."[47] Spaniards adopted the term *naguatato* (which also appears in documents of the period as *nahuatato* and *nahuatlato*) from Nahuatl, in which the word meant someone who could "speak clearly" in interpreting between two languages.[48] In its most prevalent usage in Spanish the word referred to someone who understood and spoke Nahuatl and by implication could act as an interpreter, but the term took on additional meanings in the West. In New Galicia a number of languages, as mentioned previously, were related to one another and to Nahuatl, one or more of them very likely being mutually intelligible with Nahuatl.[49]

In New Galicia, Spaniards seem to have used the term naguatato to refer to people whose languages resembled Nahuatl and who perhaps were closely related to the Nahuatl speakers of central Mexico in other respects as well. Since there is no information on the interpreters who accompanied the visitors in 1525, we cannot judge what role they might have played in making linguistic or ethnic determinations. Their absence from the records is frustrating, as presumably their input was crucial, given that only four years after the conquest of central Mexico few Spaniards would have had the linguistic knowledge and sophistication to identify and distinguish among different languages, especially ones that were closely related. It is also possible, given the existence of trade networks that connected the West with other regions, that there were actual enclaves of Nahuatl speakers in some communities. In Teutlichanga in the province of Milpa, for example, the inspectors recorded the existence of "a neighborhood [*barrio*] of Naguatatos called Yzcaentlan."[50] Several years later, during Nuño de Guzmán's conquest, one author of the accounts of that expedition mentioned that in Tonala "a group [*un barrio*] of Naguatatos were in their houses."[51]

The term "Otomí" also presents problems, as there is no conclusive evidence that Otomís lived in the area to any extent at the time of contact. There are almost no mentions of Otomís in the numerous accounts of the Nuño de Guzmán expedition of 1530–31. Historical geographer Peter Gerhard suggests that "it seems probable that the 'Otomíes' found in 1525 in Xalisco and elsewhere as far as Chacala were Tecual (Huichol) speakers, and that 'Naguatatos' who lived beyond there (often side-by-side with the Otomíes) spoke a variety of Cora (Pinome, Totorame, Temurete)."[52] María de los Dolores Soto de Arechavaleta argues that the apparent extent of Otomís in the region may be a reflection of Spaniards' linguistic and ethnic misconceptions. She notes the consistent association of the word "*pobre*" (poor) with "Otomí" in the *Suma de visitas* of 1545–50.[53] In this usage Spaniards probably followed the lead of the Nahuas of central Mexico, who viewed the Otomís as poor and backward. Thus the term Otomí as used in the mid-1520s visitación could indicate a cultural or social category rather than an ethnic or linguistic one, similar to the generic use of the word "Chichimeca" for the more mobile groups of the North (and sometimes of the West as well). Indeed, in one case the inspector noted that the people of Guatechico, a dependency of Aguacatlan, were Otomís "and they are even said to be *teules chichimecas*, who are like beasts."[54]

The figures given for *casas* (houses) and *hombres* (men) also call for explanation, but here again interpretation can be only tentative. In many cases the inspectors revised upward the number of houses that the local rulers reported, the disparities at times being considerable. Coyulan, the ruler of Etzatlan, said there were one hundred houses, but the visitor tripled the count to three hundred. The visitor almost doubled the number of houses recorded for Tequecistlan in the valley of Espuchimilco, from fifty-five to one hundred, and he increased the number of Teuzaqualpa's houses from four hundred to six hundred.

In almost all cases the number of men recorded was double that of the houses. Presumably *hombres* referred to adult men. Could this method of calculating the number of adult men imply that these communities had compound households, where fathers and adult sons or perhaps adult male siblings coresided? Although this might well have been the case, there is insufficient evidence to support such a conjecture.[55] Perhaps the officials assumed that on average each house would include, in addition to the male head of household, at least one son old enough to work—or to fight. Both of these would have been relevant considerations for Spaniards who were in the process of assigning encomiendas and probably were interested in the military capacities of these communities as well. Despite the inscrutable

quality of the figures for adult men, scholars have used them to make
rough population estimates. At the least the figures provide some basis for
assessing the relative sizes of different communities, which clearly varied
from the low hundreds to the thousands.[56]

What do and can we know about the people who lived in the West when
Spaniards first entered the region? As was true in many other situations,
Spaniards' interest in the local inhabitants concentrated on those aspects
of indigenous life that they hoped would serve their objectives. Intending
to assign the local communities in encomienda, Spanish authorities tried
to estimate the numbers of potential tributaries and assess the nature
of the local economy—what was produced, whether communities were
flourishing or poor, what items were traded. The inspectors of 1525 did
not include descriptions of other aspects of local life in their report, and
indeed they might not have spent enough time in any one place to form
more than sketchy impressions of the communities and their people. Some
years later, during and following the conquest of New Galicia led by Nuño
de Guzmán, Spaniards commented on the military skills and weapons
of the warriors and focused on behavior that seemed to pose the greatest challenges to establishing Spanish rule and Christianity, such as the
mobility of local residents, who often were absent from their homes. From
initial appreciations of the bravery and tenacity of their adversaries, they
increasingly came to view local people as brutal, uncivilized, and incom-
prehensible, given to drunken revels and violent physical contests that
could end in serious injury and even death. Spaniards frequently accused
the Indians of acts of human sacrifice and cannibalism, although most
likely it was the more mobile groups of the sierras rather than the farmers
of the valleys who engaged in these practices.[57]

There is a general if erroneous impression in the historical literature on early Mexico that Francisco Cortés's expedition was essentially
peaceful. That assumption, clearly contradicted by the reports that the
inspectors made in the visitación of 1525, might stem from the scarcity
of direct evidence regarding the expeditionary party's actions. Certainly
the visitación attests that the Spaniards with Cortés brought violence and
destruction to at least part of the area they traversed. Yet this first entrada
into New Galicia also might have offered a precedent for establishing
peaceful relations between native residents of the West and European
newcomers that would allow some measure of coexistence. The temporary
alliance that the communities of Xalisco and Tepic formed with Cortés

suggests that at least in this one episode Spanish violence was fairly limited in scale, perhaps intended to convince the pueblos of the advisability
of allying with them rather than risking subjugation or destruction. In
contrast, Nuño de Guzmán never forged a comparable alliance with any
community, nor did he seem interested in doing so. If, following Cortés's
entrada, few Spaniards laid effective claim to encomiendas or settled much
farther north than the Pueblos de Avalos, neither did they experience
serious problems in the area.[58]

Very possibly the lives of people in the West began to change before
any organized group of Spaniards arrived. These transformations would
have accelerated, first with Cortés's entrada and then, much more rapidly
and drastically, with the arrival of Guzmán and his forces. Disease might
have spread into the region in advance of the Spaniards' actual arrival,
as occurred elsewhere. The conquest of central Mexico itself probably
initiated a breakdown in the long-distance trade networks that long played
a vital role in the economy and society of the West, a change that could
have undermined significantly local socioeconomic arrangements and the
bases for political authority.[59] Compounding these changes, Guzmán's
conquest brought widespread violence and dislocation to the region and all
but guaranteed the impossibility of achieving an accommodation between
conquerors and conquered. Years of bitter and brutal conflict and, ultimately, the near destruction of many communities were the result.

CHAPTER 2

Taking the West

Because it is a new country and one of faithless idolaters, where so much service to God may be done, it seemed [well] to me to compose an account of all that would be done on this journey and everything that occurred in conquering this land, as well as declaring the quality of the land and its peoples and customs. From Michoacan I wrote to Your Majesty . . . how I came with 150 horsemen and an equal number of infantry, well armed with a dozen pieces of light artillery and with seven or eight thousand [native] allies well provided with supplies, to discover the country and conquer the province of the Teules-Chichimecas, which borders on New Spain, and those lands that lie beyond.

—Nuño de Guzmán, letter to the Crown
from Omitlan, July 8, 1530[1]

✝ DESPITE FRANCISCO CORTÉS'S ENTRADA FROM COLIMA INTO NEW Galicia, the subsequent 1525 visitación of the pueblos, and the assignment of some encomiendas, almost no Spanish settlement took place in the region in the late 1520s. In those years New Galicia was territory that Spaniards partly had reconnoitered and claimed but with few exceptions had not occupied. This situation afforded an open invitation to an enterprising person who could commit the time and energy and marshal the resources needed to bring the peoples and lands of the West effectively under Spanish control, especially in the absence from Mexico of the Marqués del Valle. As it happened not only was such a man already living in New Spain in the late 1520s, he had become—if briefly—the most powerful political authority in the kingdom. This man was Nuño Beltrán de Guzmán.

Guzmán was born sometime between 1485 and 1490, the second son in a noble family of Guadalajara in Castile that had close ties to the Crown. On the basis of that connection he became a *continuo*, one of Charles V's personal guards. His services to the Crown earned him an appointment in 1525 to the governorship of the somewhat vaguely defined region of northeastern New Spain known as Pánuco, which Hernando Cortés conquered in 1523. Delayed by illness for many months in Hispaniola and Cuba, Guzmán took up the position of governor of Pánuco in May 1527.[2] The following year the Crown appointed him to an even more important office: he became the president, or presiding official, of the first audiencia of Mexico, established by the Crown to assert greater royal authority.[3] Although he might have spent some time studying at a university in Spain, Guzmán lacked a degree and was not a *letrado* (university-trained lawyer), meaning he could not vote in the court's judicial decisions. Nonetheless, he dominated the first audiencia—still a weak institution—and took advantage of his dual position, as both governor of Pánuco and president, to undercut his rival Cortés and use his leverage as New Spain's most powerful appointed official for his own ends. Although as governor he sponsored further campaigns in Pánuco and the export of thousands of enslaved Indians to the Caribbean islands in exchange for livestock, as president of the audiencia his attention soon turned to the West and North. He convinced the judges of the audiencia to support an expedition into the West.

Nuño de Guzmán's historical reputation is the darkest of any of the early leaders and conquistadors of New Spain. J. H. Parry calls him a "natural gangster."[4] He was ambitious, ruthless, and unyielding. Like most of his contemporaries who viewed the Indies as offering rich opportunities to someone who knew how to take advantage of them, he was determined and self-serving, even as he affirmed his loyalty, and the value of his services, to the Crown. He was envious of Cortés and driven to outdo him, yet the animosity that developed between the two leaders perhaps was not personal in its origins (although it rapidly became so). The Crown itself virtually guaranteed the enmity between them (it was not uncommon for the king to play one man off against another as a check on the power and independence of both). Charles V sent Guzmán to New Spain at the same time as Luis Ponce de León, who was to conduct the *residencia* (investigation of an official's conduct in office) of Cortés's term as governor and whom Guzmán was instructed to assist as needed.[5] Guzmán received further instructions to investigate Cortés's activities in Pánuco and to reassign encomiendas as he saw fit.[6] This second directive was certain to infuriate and undermine Cortés, as many of those who lost their grants were his supporters. Guzmán also made an enemy of the first bishop of Mexico, the Franciscan fray Juan de Zumárraga, also an ally of Cortés. In general Guzmán's relations with the Franciscans, the most influential religious order in early Mexico, were troubled, probably in some measure because of the order's association with Cortés.[7] Yet Guzmán, much like his archrival, was pious and placed a high priority on the veneration of the Virgin Mary and the holy cross, establishment of churches in New Galicia, and extirpation of what he saw as idolatrous practices. He was, in short, a complex but unsympathetic man, legalistic in his thoughts and writing, endlessly self-promoting, fiercely dedicated to his grandiose objectives. His actions often were destructive, sometimes ruinous and self-defeating, his behavior frequently arrogant and callous.

Guzmán's short but intense career in New Spain is well documented, in part because of the controversy that his various offices and enterprises generated. The extensive documentation includes Guzmán's own letters; "Memoria"; the records of the lawsuit between him and Cortés; and the residencias that were conducted of his governorships of Pánuco and New Galicia and presidency of the first audiencia. Officials of the second audiencia, which replaced the first while Guzmán still was campaigning in the West, very early initiated an inquiry into the conduct of the entrada in New Galicia. Since it took place before Guzmán became governor of New Galicia but at least in part after he was removed as president, the conquest itself did not fall within the legal purview of the residencias. Nonetheless the complex politics and rivalries of early New Spain, together with Guzmán's increasingly controversial tactics in dealing with the Indians, both the peoples of the West and the thousands of indigenous troops and auxiliaries that he recruited in central Mexico and Michoacan for his expedition, guaranteed there would be considerable scrutiny of his actions during the two-year campaign. The result was a series of accounts, nearly all firsthand and mostly solicited by the second audiencia, describing the events of the conquest from rather distinct points of view.

There are eight full or partial accounts of Nuño de Guzmán's 1530–31 campaign, as well as Guzmán's letter to the Crown and the later "Memoria." The accounts vary considerably in length, detail, bias, and emphasis and sometimes offer contradictory information and perspectives.[8] Some display obvious biases. Cristóbal Flores wrote a chronicle that was highly critical of Guzmán's actions and those of some of his officers.[9] The interpreter García del Pilar also cast Guzmán's behavior in very negative light, as did Pedro de Carranza, who was an unwilling participant.[10] In contrast, Gonzalo López, one of Guzmán's closest associates who served as his field marshal in the second half of the campaign, was a consistent supporter of the captain general. López himself was directly responsible for one of the most controversial episodes of the entrada, the taking of large numbers of slaves in Xalisco and other nearby communities and the apparently forcible recruitment of additional native troops or auxiliaries when he returned to Michoacan halfway through the campaign to find reinforcements for Guzmán's decimated expedition. His report is one of the longest and most detailed and as such is quite useful despite his unquestioning support of Guzmán. The long letter Guzmán wrote from Omitlan to the king, covering only the first six months of the campaign, emphasized his efforts to initiate peaceful contacts and to bring Christianity and the divinely sanctioned rule of the Castilian monarchy to the peoples he tried to subjugate. He described how he also tried to inculcate discipline and Christian behavior among his indigenous troops as they marched through New Galicia. His report to the king, predictably, cast his accomplishments in the best possible light.

The tone of the other accounts for the most part is neutral, and they can be considered mainly pro-Guzmán. Juan de Sámano's is fairly detailed. The "Primera relación anónima" includes quite a lot of ethnographic and topographical information, mainly for Culiacan (present-day Sinaloa).[11] Perhaps the least accurate account is one written by historian Gonzalo Fernández de Oviedo, based mainly on an interview with Francisco de Arceo, although it is not without interest.[12] Taken together, these *relaciones*, or narrative accounts, offer quite a full picture of the campaign, notwithstanding significant discrepancies and some notable silences.

Organizing an Expedition

On May 15, 1529, the audiencia formally authorized Guzmán's proposed expedition to the West.[13] He borrowed ten thousand pesos (*de tepuzque*, a unit of currency worth 272 maravedís, less valuable than *pesos de minas*, worth 450 maravedís) from the royal treasury to pay for supplies, arms, and horses and then began recruiting—or conscripting—Spaniards and Indians in central Mexico for the campaign. This entrada was to be organized on a far grander scale than Francisco Cortés's relatively modest one. In his "Memoria" Guzmán later wrote that

> I got together about four hundred Spanish foot soldiers and cavalry to go to discover and conquer that land of the South Sea . . . and they were well outfitted with arms and change of horses, besides the thirty that I took at my own expense to assist those who might need them or whose horses might die; and I did this, going to the war with seventy crossbows and fifty muskets and twelve small bronze cannons with their stands and many lances and a large supply of bolts [for the crossbows] and arrowheads and bowstrings and powder, fiber sandals and leather armor for the foot soldiers and Indians, and cloth for bartering and other things for gifts and two bellows and much iron and hardware and tools and nails in order to build a brigantine if necessary, and wine, vinegar, oil and flour, and a store of medicines, and three thousand head of my pigs and sheep besides another six or seven thousand head that went with the army and besides other extensive provisions of bacon, cheese, conserves, and things necessary for the sick.[14]

Having made himself unpopular in Mexico City, Guzmán had considerable difficulty recruiting sufficient numbers of volunteers and resorted to forced conscription of both Spaniards and Indians. Many residents were said to have fled the capital or taken refuge in monasteries to avoid Guzmán's draft, although he rounded up and pressed into service some men such as Pedro de Carranza, who in a lawsuit that he later brought against Guzmán claimed that he was arrested and jailed in Mexico City and then carried in shackles to Michoacan. There Guzmán promised to hang him if he did not agree to participate in the expedition. Guzmán ostensibly also threatened other recalcitrant *encomenderos* (holders of encomienda grants) with the loss of their tributes if they did not participate in or support the entrada, and he commandeered arms, horses, and equipment.[15] Some Spaniards in the capital wondered about the necessity of conquering and pacifying a region that apparently was peaceful, while others questioned whether Guzmán, who lacked much prior military experience, was the right person to undertake such a campaign.[16] The use of coercive tactics and the contentiousness that characterized the organization of the entrada set the tone for a campaign that itself would be arduous, divisive, and violent, extremely costly in terms of human and other resources, and severely disruptive and destructive for the peoples of the West. If the outcome of Francisco Cortés's entrada of 1524 had been inconclusive, Guzmán's campaign, in contrast, established a permanent—if tenuous—Spanish presence in the region. The simultaneously brutal and insecure nature of that presence reflected the character of the campaign itself—and indeed that of its leader.

While many reluctant Spaniards were forced into participation, Guzmán also had his close associates. Guzmán's captains included Cristóbal de Oñate, who subsequently would become the most important official and encomendero in early New Galicia and one of the first mining entrepreneurs in Zacatecas; Francisco Verdugo, who was accompanied by his ensign Francisco de Arceo; Lope de Samaniego, whose ensign Cristóbal Flores would become one of Guzmán's critics; and Cristóbal de Barrios, with his ensign Francisco Barrón. In addition, Guzmán brought a personal entourage of forty men who "ate at his table and were continuously by his side," which most likely included men who were with him in Pánuco. Pedro de Guzmán, a relative of the captain general from his hometown of Guadalajara in Spain, was in charge of the banner with the image of the Virgin Mary made by the people of Huejotzinco. Diego Vázquez, also from Guadalajara, and Diego de Proaño were captains of infantry.[17]

Guzmán conscripted several thousand native warriors and demanded supplies from indigenous communities in central Mexico. Very likely the communities responded to Guzmán's exactions under duress. He mainly recruited men in Tlaxcala, nearby Huejotzinco, and Mexico City. These provinces were logical targets for recruitment. Mexico City was solidly under Guzmán's control—in addition to dominating the audiencia, he and the judges also attended meetings of the city council against the express

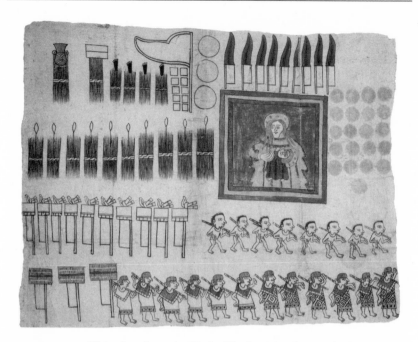

FIGURE 3. This plate from the Codex Huejotzinco depicts the banner
made of gold and silver, trimmed with feathers and featuring an image
of the Virgin Mary and Child, which Nuño de Guzmán commissioned
in 1529 for his campaign in the West. Also shown are tributes that
Huejotzinco furnished, including slaves, possibly sold to acquire the gold
needed to fashion the banner. Courtesy of the Library of Congress.

wishes of the *regidores* (city councilmen)—so he readily could tap it for
manpower.[18] Tlaxcala famously forged an alliance with the Spaniards
during Cortés's conquest of central Mexico, as did Huejotzinco; during
Cortés's absence from Mexico, Huejotzinco came under Guzmán's sway.
Probably smaller numbers of recruits came from other places as well. Two
accounts, for example, mention the execution of Indians from Toluca who
were accused of sacrificing a child during the campaign; the expedition
would have passed through Toluca en route to Michoacan, so Guzmán
probably picked up more recruits along the way.

The actual numbers of people conscripted are hard to fix. According
to Oviedo, Francisco de Arceo reported that fifteen thousand "*indios
de guerra*" (warriors) left Mexico City with the captain general. In his

testimony to the second audiencia in 1531, Cristóbal de Barrios, who participated in the first half of the entrada, claimed that ten or twelve thousand *"naturales de la tierra"* (natives of the land) accompanied Guzmán, while bishop Zumárraga thought that Guzmán took with him as many as twenty thousand Indians from central Mexico.[19] Guzmán himself stated that he took seven or eight thousand Indian troops from central Mexico, and this might be the most accurate estimate.[20]

In 1531 Hernando Cortés brought lawsuits against Nuño de Guzmán and the other members of the first audiencia, accusing Guzmán of usurping his rights to Huejotzinco and contesting Guzmán's claims to New Galicia on the basis of Cortés's own claims to the region that he argued were established by Francisco Cortés's earlier expedition. Witnesses from Huejotzinco testified regarding the men that the province sent to the war, but they offered varying estimates of the numbers actually recruited. One man referred to the "thousand Indian men whom the said Nuño de Guzmán took from the said town to the war." Another witness, however, stated that "Nuño de Guzmán said to the lord of Huejotzingo that he should give him men to go to the war with him—six hundred men outfitted for war. . . . And among the said men whom he took to the war there were eleven leading men of eleven houses of Huejotzingo." The painted codex (indigenous pictorial record) that accompanied the lawsuit indicated only 320 warriors.[21] The native witnesses from Huejotzinco also referred to items that the town supplied, most famously the banner fashioned of silver, gold, and feathers that displayed an image of the Virgin Mary and child, reproduced in the Codex Huejotzinco. One vecino attested to the town's contributions to the campaign as follows:

> A Christian Spaniard who was at the time overseer in the said town of Huejotzingo asked the lord and leading men of the said town to give him gold to buy a horse so that don Tomé, the lord of the said town, could go to the war on horseback. . . . The said Nuño de Guzmán asked them for ten painted banners to take to the war, and they gave them to them. And he also asked them for a thousand and six hundred pairs of the shoes which they wear, which are called *cutaras*, and also four hundred small awnings [*toldillos*] . . . and four thousand arrows, and another four thousand breeches and blankets . . . and also six leather-covered chests and also another two thousand eight hundred blankets.[22]

In all, Guzmán initially might have conscripted ten to fifteen thousand natives if the recruits from Michoacan are added to those from central Mexico. Guzmán departed from the capital just before Christmas in 1529. He took with him the native ruler, or Cazonci, of Michoacan, whom he was holding prisoner in Mexico City. Once they reached Michoacan, Guzmán pressured the Cazonci to provide thousands of additional troops, bearers, and supplies. García del Pilar, an interpreter who earlier was associated with Cortés and later became Guzmán's bitter enemy, reported that Guzmán ordered the Cazonci to provide eight thousand men in Michoacan, although he admitted that he did not know how many men he actually produced.[23]

In addition to warriors, large numbers of Indians would have accompanied the expedition as servants and porters. The Spaniards called the native troops their *indios amigos* (literally, Indian friends or friendly Indians), an ironic term given the manner in which they were recruited and the treatment they received during the campaign. In addition, however, the accounts refer to the presence of *naborías*, or servants. Some of the Purépechas might have been employed more in this capacity than as fighters, although their roles probably varied over time. Confusingly, however, the accounts also mention instances in which Spaniards were assigned Indians, implying they were servants or bearers. J. Benedict Warren writes that "the Relacion [de Michoacan] indicates the 8,000 men did assemble but that when the Spaniards began distributing them among themselves, without any account or order, many of them fled. The Spaniards then used chains to make sure that no more of them ran away."[24] Pedro de Carranza probably was referring to this incident when he noted that the Cazonci gave to the Spaniards "*muchos tamemes*" (many native porters), who were divided among the Spaniards on the expedition.[25] The chronicle that is credited to Cristóbal Flores gives perhaps the most detailed account of the recruitment and treatment of the Purépecha:

> Each ruler of a town came with the portion of his subjects that had been assigned by the *repartimiento* [allotment of labor], all of whom were divided up by the Spaniards who went to war so that they would carry their goods, and for security that these Indians would not flee and leave their belongings, the lords and nobles marched with chains around their necks, and many of them died prisoners.[26]

guzmā. michvacā.

FIGURE 4. This image from the Lienzo de Tlaxcala shows Guzmán in Michoacan (plate 52). It is one of a series of depictions of Spaniards fighting alongside their Tlaxcalan allies against Indian warriors in the West. The original Lienzo, commissioned by the second viceroy of New Spain, don Luis de Velasco, is missing, but reliable copies were made. Because the Lienzo dates to the 1550s, it is not always clear whether the battles depicted took place during Guzmán's entrada or during Viceroy Antonio de Mendoza's campaign in New Galicia in the early 1540s. Alfredo Chavero, *El Lienzo de Tlaxcala*, 1892 (facsimile, Mexico City. Cosmos, 1979).

Flores also claimed that Guzmán treated the Purépecha as if they were "rebels" (that is, people who merited punishment) rather than allies and noted that many men "told him how badly this was done."[27]

The expedition must have included native women as well as male servants, slaves, and captives, although women are mostly missing from the accounts. Their failure to appear in the accounts does not mean that they were absent in reality. Francisco de Arceo claimed that the Cazonci, in addition to supplies, provided for each Spaniard "an Indian woman to cook food" as well as a total of ten thousand men "to carry the packs of the Christians."[28] If true, this would imply that at least several hundred women participated in the expedition. Of the other accounts only Carranza's alludes to the presence of women, mentioning that when they left Chiametla (on the Pacific coast, during the second part of the campaign) many "indios e indias" remained there ill.[29] In the preconquest period women did not accompany Aztec armies, but large numbers of porters and young men did. Thus when Guzmán called on indigenous communities to send men to war, native rulers in central Mexico might have followed preconquest tradition, sending both fighting men and porters and young men to accompany them. The practice might have been different in Michoacan, however; Warren notes that Purépecha women had carried burdens for the Spaniards during Gonzalo de Sandoval's campaign of 1523 in Colima.[30]

Certainly the Spaniards used the indios amigos to carry loads and haul equipment. Although Francisco de Arceo claimed that when the warriors recruited in Mexico City departed the capital, "they did not carry any burdens for the Christians, only those things they needed for themselves," there is plenty of evidence that later, if not at the very outset, they would do exactly that.[31] Cristóbal Flores noted that as they left for Tonala there were always "many of the *amigos* in chains, with Nuño de Guzmán's consent, so they wouldn't flee and leave the packs."[32] The author of the third anonymous chronicle wrote that later, when the expedition reached the Sierra Madre Occidental near Culiacan in the north, many of the indios amigos "left their loads, their own as well as those of the Spaniards," because of the harsh conditions.[33]

There were military advantages in leading these large forces into mostly unfamiliar territory, where Guzmán must have anticipated conflict and hostilities. The sheer numerical superiority of the Spaniards with their indigenous forces certainly played a role in overcoming the able fighters of the West, perhaps as much as (or even more than) did the horses, artillery, and dogs the Spaniards brought. Given the relatively small size, ethnic diversity, and number of autonomous communities in the region, it seems fair to assume that virtually all men—and this very likely included youths in their teens—were skilled and experienced in the use of weapons for both warfare and hunting, which remained an important feature of life in much of the West even though most communities were agricultural. Guzmán described the bravery and expertise of the people who fought at Tonala, a substantial community where the Spaniards fought a battle during the first half of the campaign. Guzmán noted that some of the men with him who were involved in campaigns elsewhere in New Spain "swear not to have seen more daring or brave Indians than these. The arms they bore were bows and arrows and *macanas* and two-handed wooden swords and some slingshots and round shields."[34] Widespread expertise in the use of the bow and arrow especially meant that even relatively small communities could field fairly large numbers of warriors. At least during the first half of the campaign, however, most of the pueblos confronted the Spaniards and their native allies alone, meaning that the numbers of fighters that individual communities could muster were usually far smaller than the invading forces.[35] Ten years later, during the Mixton War, the emergence of large coalitions that drew on many communities, combined with the mobility and guerrilla tactics of the skilled warriors of the West, would alter the balance of military power in favor of the indigenous forces.

In addition to fighting for the Spaniards, the Indian troops and other auxiliaries recruited in central Mexico and Michoacan performed all the heaviest physical labor, including building bridges and rafts to cross the region's numerous rivers, constructing churches and temporary housing, moving artillery and other heavy equipment, and, of course, carrying loads. The Spaniards in command did not spare the indigenous rulers and elites from these labors, from which they would have been exempt by virtue of their rank in preconquest times. In his narrative Gonzalo López described the construction of bridges made of earth and branches, commenting that "on these bridges the indios amigos of this city [Mexico] worked a great deal and with much good will."[36] According to Cristóbal Flores, however, when Guzmán instructed field marshal Antonio de Villarroel to have rafts made to cross a river, the latter "ordered the cacique Tapia, lord of Mexico, to bring wood and equipment for them, which his *macehuales* [commoners] made. And because the said cacique, because he was ill, did not enter the water to help them, the field marshal treated him in such a way, putting his hands on him, that he never again was well until he died."[37] Much later, when Guzmán himself became ill, he ordered that a litter be made on which "the lords, Indians of this city [Mexico], would carry him up into the sierra."[38] Being physically abused and forced to perform menial labor would have been deeply offensive to the indigenous lords. The humiliation and mistreatment that the indios amigos, including their elite leaders, suffered at the hands of Guzmán and his officers are one of several dark motifs of the expedition. Few if any of the indigenous rulers would survive the miserable conditions of the entrada and the harsh and demeaning treatment they received from the Spaniards.

The logistical challenges of moving, controlling, and maintaining these large armies were enormous and at times proved overwhelming. The need to supply the expedition was a constant concern and one for which the indios amigos became primarily responsible when local groups were unable or unwilling to provision the conquerors.[39] Guzmán did make considerable effort to outfit the expedition adequately with supplies and equipment in central Mexico and Michoacan. Notwithstanding his planning, however, shortages of food arose early on. By the time they left Michoacan in February 1530, Guzmán noted the abundance of food at Cuinao, of which they were already in need.[40] The Spaniards relied on the indios amigos to forage for food and to loot and plunder the local communities of New Galicia. The livestock that Guzmán brought did not fare well in the face of bad weather, rough terrain, and a local populace that might have welcomed the fresh meat that arrived with the Spaniards. As was the case for many of the early Spanish expeditions into northern New Spain and what is today the southwestern United States, the search for food was a constant preoccupation and challenge and could result in violence when Spaniards attempted to force local communities to supply provisions.

Supplying the expedition remained a problem because, with only rare exceptions, the Spaniards failed to form alliances with local groups in New Galicia. Probably many of the groups that Guzmán encountered in the West were aware of earlier Spanish conquests in Michoacan and Colima, and some of them already had clashed with Francisco Cortés's expedition. The typical response to the reappearance in their midst of the Spaniards with their alien host was to fight or else to flee. Guzmán found that few local people were willing to offer either material or military support. Indeed, the Spaniards almost entirely failed to forge workable relations with the peoples of the West. In the absence of an established state exercising political authority such as existed in central Mexico, Western communities had little incentive to ally with the newcomers to challenge a long-standing, more powerful rival or oppressive authority. The region certainly was not free of conflict, either when Spaniards arrived or later, but warfare generally was limited in scope; raiding other communities, taking captives, and engaging in small skirmishes probably constituted the norm. Since local people did not welcome the intruders as potential allies, Guzmán and his troops found themselves isolated in hostile territory, able to rely only on those groups that they could intimidate into acquiescence. As conditions deteriorated during the entrada, both Spaniards and their Indian allies attempted to desert. These people must have known that they faced almost certain death if they tried to make their way south unaided—and yet, as will be seen, some did try, a sure indicator of their desperation to escape the miserable circumstances in which they found themselves.

The expedition also faced linguistic difficulties. Despite the presence of people in the West who spoke and understood either Nahuatl or languages that were similar enough to Nahuatl possibly to be mutually intelligible, Spaniards at times could not communicate with the local people. They constantly had to seek guides and interpreters and sometimes came up short. No sooner did Guzmán's entrada leave Michoacan than they encountered people described as wearing "beards of straw" "whose language no one understood." Soon afterward they found another group speaking yet another language. Once again they were stymied. They had no interpreter and the Indians began to flee, so Guzmán's party returned to the previous pueblo.[41] These problems recurred throughout the expedition.

Guzmán brought interpreters with him, but the Spanish interpreters who accompanied the expedition—García del Pilar (who previously worked for Cortés), Juan Pascual, and Rodrigo Simón—knew Nahuatl or possibly Purépecha but none of the local languages. Pascual and Simón were with Guzmán in Michoacan, and both remained in New Galicia after the conquest and probably became proficient in at least one of the local languages. Simón especially might have picked up one of them quickly. One of the accounts of the expedition noted that he dealt with the "señores de Xalisco" (who initially capitulated to the Spaniards but later resisted) and was responsible for transmitting Guzmán's orders to them. Although the people of Xalisco were Tecuales, there might have been residents of the community who were bilingual; Simón could have communicated with the people of Xalisco through someone who knew Nahuatl and Tecual.[42]

The Campaign Gets Underway

By the time Guzmán departed Mexico City with his expedition at the end of December 1529, he already had begun to suspect that the native ruler of Michoacan, the Cazonci, was concealing treasure. He also was convinced that the Cazonci was aware of—and possibly authorized— the murders of some Spaniards living in rural areas in Michoacan. After Guzmán arrived in Michoacan, he tarried for more than a month while he tried to extract confessions regarding treasure from the Cazonci and his family and retainers, subjecting the ruler and others, including two native interpreters, to extended torture. These extreme measures yielded no additional information. Still frustrated but having, as noted earlier, obtained extensive additional forces and supplies, Guzmán took the ruler with him when he left Michoacan and subsequently tried and executed him on charges of treason.[43] The violent conquest of New Galicia thus began with an act of judicial murder, but the decision to get rid of the Cazonci was pragmatic. Since Michoacan was the staging ground for an entrada into an only partially known and potentially hostile region, Guzmán needed to ensure that the former Purépecha kingdom would remain securely under Spanish control.[44]

The conquest finally got underway in early February 1530 when Guzmán led the expedition across the Lerma River. Having crossed into what Guzmán termed "enemy territory," he memorialized the occasion by erecting three large crosses that he and his captains and others carried on their shoulders. They placed one by the river, another by a church dedicated to the Virgin Mary that they began to build, and the third "on the route where we were going."[45] People from some friendly pueblos arrived, and within a few days they completed the church, surrounding it with a fortified wall that provided sufficient room inside for fifteen or twenty horsemen, its purpose clearly defensive. They celebrated Mass in the new church and the priest delivered his sermon, following which "some ordinances for the good order that the army should maintain were read"—a reminder of the close link between piety and military ventures that often characterized Spanish entradas.[46]

FIGURE 5. This image from the Codex Telleriano-Remensis shows Guzmán on a white horse (plate 44r). The figure on the lower left is an Indian lord, possibly don Andrés de Tapia Motelchiuhtzin, the Indian governor of Tenochtitlan who accompanied Guzmán and died during the entrada. The two figures to his right may represent the oidores of the first audiencia. The codex was compiled by 1563; see the excellent study and facsimile by Eliose Quiñones Keber, *Codex Telleriano-Remensis. Ritual, Divination, and History in a Pictorial Aztec Manuscript* (Austin. University of Texas Press, 1995). In this plate the Spanish gloss on the lower left reads, "Year of Eleven Houses and 1529, Nuño de Guzmán departed for Jalisco, going to conquer that country. Note the serpent that comes out of the sky, saying that trouble would come to the natives [with] the Christians going there." Reproduced by permission of the Bibliothèque Nationale de France.

On February 14, for the first of many times, the Spaniards pronounced to the assembled people the *requerimiento*, a statement that explained Spain's claims to their allegiance and called on the Indians to acknowledge the sovereignty of the Spanish Crown and the Roman Catholic Church or to suffer the consequences of their refusal.[47] Guzmán then dispatched two of his captains to proceed ahead to reconnoiter the territory. Thus commenced his ambitious enterprise of laying claim to the western lands that he provisionally—and unsuccessfully, in view of the Crown's terse disapproval—would call "La Mayor España," or Greater Spain. Some of the Spaniards stayed behind to see that the church and fortifications were completed.[48]

About a week later, the main party reached Coyna. Pedro de Carranza reported that as they marched, Guzmán began to put in order his battalions of Spaniards and Indian allies; the allies with their colorful feathered head-gear (*penachos*) and devices "were a sight to see." Gonzalo López described Coyna as a "cheerful and abundant" place, despite being relatively arid, with some fruit trees and good supplies of maize and beans.[49] Juan de Sámano remarked on the plentiful maguey plants and fruit trees, as well as game animals and birds.[50] They found Coyna deserted, however, and the indios amigos began to burn the houses. Pedro Carranza noted that this burning of the pueblos continued wherever they went. After a few days they returned to Coyna, where the local ruler submitted to them and handed over some porters (*tameme*) when the expedition left.[51] Cristóbal Flores was certain that while they were there, messengers arrived at night from Michoacan bringing gold and silver in even larger amounts than Guzmán already had obtained.[52] That last donation of treasure, however, apparently was not sufficient to save the Cazonci.[53]

The expedition's route from that point does not suggest that Guzmán collected reliable intelligence. Instead of continuing along the Lerma and Santiago (Rio Grande) river system, they headed north and then doubled back. The first substantial battle took place in Cuiseo near Lake Chapala, where, according to García del Pilar, "we had war with the natives. . . . And after seven or eight days that we were there . . . a fat man said to be a lord came peacefully, and because he didn't bring *tamemes* or gold or silver, which it was said that he [Guzmán] asked him for, a dog was set on him, and [he was] thus mauled and bitten all over; we departed and left him there at the door to his house, setting fire to it and to the entire pueblo."[54] Clearly the basically peaceful approach that Hernando Cortés (however unrealistically) urged his relative Francisco to take had no place in Guzmán's plans.

According to Guzmán, fighting began before they reached the main pueblo. Although he omits the incident that Pilar described, he wrote that a naguatato, "one of their interpreters," sought him out to ask why they had come and what they were looking for. If it were food that they needed, the cacique would send it to them. In the end, however, they fought a two-hour-long engagement with the local warriors. The infantry captain Diego Vázquez received three arrow wounds, one of them serious, and the local people defended themselves "with such effort and spirit as if they were Spaniards." The Spaniards initially took one of the most impressive fighters to be a woman but later discovered he was a man wearing women's clothing. They took him captive and Guzmán ordered him burned; despite the man's valor in battle, his feminine dress constituted a sin and inexcusable offense in Guzmán's eyes.[55] The confrontation with the invaders fomented panic among the local people. Some of them apparently fled from the Spaniards straight into the hands of their enemies, where they were captured and, according to the Spanish accounts, sacrificed and cannibalized. Pedro de Carranza reported that as they followed the river downstream they found it crowded with men, women, and children trying to escape the fighting, a pitiful sight in his eyes.[56]

The expedition headed north to the Tecuexe community of Tonala, southeast of present-day Guadalajara. Arceo, probably exaggerating, described Tonala as having at least six thousand houses located on a fertile plain with abundant crops and fruit trees.[57] The woman ruler greeted them peacefully but warned that some of the people on the opposite side of the river had begun to prepare for war.[58] García del Pilar added the interesting detail that those gearing for war were led by one of the *cacica*'s daughters, together "with other principales and pueblos subject to her that had risen up."[59] The cacica sent food, and although Guzmán prepared his forces for battle, he tried to prevent the Indian allies' inevitable burning of the pueblo, which had received the Spaniards peacefully.

Guzmán formed three squadrons to attack the war party. Cristóbal de Oñate led a company of horsemen, footmen, and some of the indios amigos to take one side of the lower slope of the hill near the river, where an estimated one thousand warriors had gathered.[60] Guzmán sent Captain Francisco Verdugo with more Indian troops to the other side of the hill, while he headed for the center with the artillery and infantry, taking

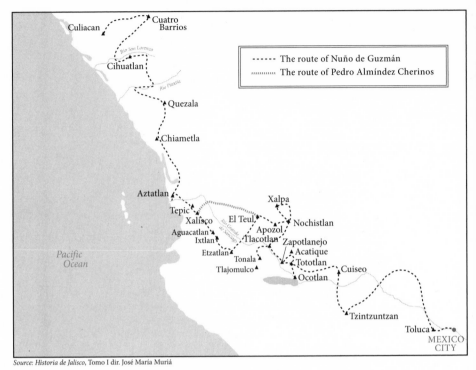

Source: *Historia de Jalisco*, Tomo I dir. José María Muriá

MAP 3. Route of Nuño de Guzmán's expedition

with him a notary who would pronounce the requerimiento, the response to which was "a great shout." Guzmán again remarked on the skill and daring of the Indians during the battle; he reported that a single warrior on his own sometimes would confront a man on horseback.[61] According to Carranza, Guzmán himself was injured when one of the native fighters grabbed his lance and beat him with it.[62] Having defeated the recalcitrant warriors, they returned to Tonala where "all the lords and all the country came to serve and give obedience and bring much food. . . . This is very good land, populous and with a great deal of sustenance."[63] They spent two or three weeks there, and Guzmán erected a shrine dedicated to the Virgin Mary, which, according to Gonzalo López, he ordered built on the hill where they confronted the warriors.[64]

Continuing north they reached Nochistlan and from there fanned out. Along the way they skirmished and burned pueblos, leaving Nochistlan

tonallan.

FIGURE 6. This image from the Lienzo de Tlaxcala shows the Battle
of Tonallan (Tonala) (plate 55). Note that the warriors of Tonala (on
the right) use round shields and are armed with double-edged swords
and bows and arrows, but their battle attire is much less elaborate
than that of the Tlaxcalan warriors. Chavero, *Lienzo de Tlaxcala*.

itself, according to Pilar, "destroyed and laid waste."[65] Guzmán described
Nochistlan as consisting of three barrios, lying within the space of about
a league, among *tunales* (nopal cacti), "the best settled that has been seen
and with a very good fashion of houses, and the best land and of the most
extensive cultivation so far encountered, where were found copper hoes
with which they work the land."[66] They stayed in Nochistlan nearly a
month, in part because it was nearly Semana Santa (Holy Week), for which
they needed to make preparations, and in part because "of not being able
to reach or find anyone who would give them information about large

pueblos and provinces. . . . Rather all the Indian natives that were asked said that there was nothing but rugged mountains that could not be passed; and for this and because they said that on the south coast they could go as far as Cihuatlan, and that there were many and very robust pueblos, it was decided to cross to the South Sea."[67]

From Nochistlan, Guzmán sent Pedro Almíndez Cherinos to Teul (on the other side of the Juchipila River, about twelve leagues away) with an infantry company and dispatched Verdugo and Barrios to another large settlement named Xalpa. He also put some miners to work looking for gold along the river. At this point the Spaniards had reached the heartland of the Cazcanes, the cradle of the great uprising that took place ten years later. As they moved through the area, they continued to skirmish with the local people. During one of these engagements Oñate and his company killed some 130 of the local people.

Guzmán's often dry but detailed report suggests the extent of disruption and alarm that the expedition's arrival occasioned. As the Indian allies spread out across the countryside, they followed their own bellicose customs—burning houses and possibly sacrificing captives. At one point when Guzmán rode out seeking a group that had attacked their camp, he stopped to "collect the allies, and two of my criados going to do this, ran into some Chichimecas who came following our allies."[68] They reached a stream where more than four thousand people—men, women, and children with all their belongings—had taken refuge. The people fled at their approach, and Guzmán reported that he found the remains of women and children, some of whom might have been sacrificed, apparently the work of his Indian allies. "There is no one who can prevent it however much punishment is inflicted, although some affirm that they are good Christians. . . . Today they sacrifice secretly just as they once did [openly]."[69] By this time everyone living in the region must have been all too aware of the thousands of invaders in their midst. For the indigenous residents choices were limited: retreat to the mountains, organize war parties, or attempt to propitiate the menacing strangers. In desperation some groups tried all three approaches to fend off the imminent threat. Catastrophe had overtaken them.

The people of Xalpa, not far from Nochistlan, chose capitulation, saying they wished for peace. They brought the Spaniards "an idol made of cotton cloth and full of blood with a large stone knife in the middle with which they sacrifice, which I think they thought would destroy us all."

Guzmán ordered it burned. He then decided they would celebrate Holy Week there; this would have been at the end of March 1530. In one day they constructed on top of a hill a "very pretty" church made of reeds and covered with straw, with a cross in front and shrines for five stations of the cross. The special altar for Holy Week was entirely covered with feathers. On Holy Thursday they conducted the procession and on Tuesday after Easter departed for Teul.[70]

By the time Guzmán's party arrived in Teul, Cherinos already had been there and the Indian allies had burned many of the buildings. There were few people to be found, but it was clear to all that Teul once was an important site. The invaders recognized its significance; the author of the third account stated that "from what was seen there and what some of the Indians said, it seems to be the head of all the land."[71]

> It appears to be something of much grandeur and authority, because most of it was very sumptuous buildings and temples . . . and the natives say that the greatest idol of all, made of gold, was there, and in earlier times it had been destroyed by warfare. They [the buildings] were of very well carved stone, and there were stones of eighteen palms, in which all with their steps and great stone figures of men, where they sacrificed, and other things, are much like those found in Mexico, and which the Mexicans say are like what they have. There were very good houses with patios; there are fountains with very good water.[72]

From Teul, Guzmán sent Verdugo to Tlaltenango, where they found few people, as apparently most had fled to the mountains. Verdugo heard that there were other large pueblos ahead but followed Guzmán's instructions to rejoin him.

Guzmán then decided to split his forces in two, sending Cherinos with Verdugo and another captain, Diego de Proaño, with some Spanish infantry and Indians from Tlaxcala and Huejotzinco, northeast, well into the mountains. From there they eventually circled back toward the coast. Most likely the Indian guide who told them they would find substantial pueblos in that direction misled them deliberately. Gonzalo López accompanied Cherinos and reported that they traveled through many canyons and rivers, finding little to eat. After two and a half weeks they finally got word of a large pueblo near the coast that turned out to be Tepic, which received Francisco Cortés and his party in 1524, and made their way there. Initially some archers shot at them, but then some naguatatos came out and shouted to them not to respond and they would not be hurt. Cherinos accompanied the naguatatos to the house of the ruler, who received them cordially.[73] Riding out one day not far from Tepic, López saw another large pueblo, Xalisco. Cherinos sent two principales from Tepic to summon the rulers of Xalisco, who refused to come and killed one of the messengers.[74] Despite the proximity of the two communities, Tepic and Xalisco belonged to different ethnic groups and were enemies. The visitación of 1525 reported that Tepic and Xalisco had been at war.[75] The people of Xalisco therefore would have seen Tepic's apparent alliance with the newcomers as a threat.

While Cherinos's party headed northeast and then turned back toward the coast, Guzmán also set out for the coast, marching for four days and finding very little in the way of food or settlements and experiencing such difficulty in crossing the gorge of the Río Grande that his party was delayed for another three days. Most of the cattle died on the difficult route through the canyon. Cherinos lost most of the fifteen hundred hogs that he had taken as well. By now it was the beginning of May 1530. Continuing to move through rough mountainous terrain, Guzmán reached Ixtlan, where the people provided food, and then Aguacatlan, described as a large pueblo located in a well-populated valley.[76] Although the local lords "came out to receive us and lodged us in their houses, giving us a plentiful supply of maize and all the necessities," this friendly reception did not ensure that they would be spared the conquerors' demands. Guzmán demanded gold and silver. They gave him some unspecified amount, as well as some women and close to a thousand porters. Guzmán ordered that the lords of Aguacatlan be taken captive and scoured their houses for treasure.[77] According to Cristóbal Flores, some of the lords later died in captivity.[78] Carranza reported that Guzmán threatened to set a dog on the four *señores* (lords, rulers) he detained if they did not supply any gold or silver, and in fact he did set a dog on one of the lords.[79] Guzmán glossed over these events in the letter he later wrote from Omitlan, simply noting that they departed Aguacatlan and then arrived at the pueblo of Tetitlan "with the caciques of all those pueblos accompanying me"— apparently his hostages.[80]

In another three days Guzmán and his force drew near to Xalisco. Cherinos rode out to meet them and they continued together to Tepic, about a league and a half from Xalisco.[81] The rulers of Xalisco brought food, but apparently the Spaniards tried to impose a more substantial tribute on them. Cristóbal Flores stated that "many of us believe—I do not know if it is so—that because they could not obey they rose up. . . . And for this offense [*enojo*] Nuño de Guzmán made war and he proclaimed it [to be] in fire and blood. And he ordered that they be made slaves, although later they did not brand most of them they took. The day that Nuño de Guzmán left with his company they burned the pueblo entirely."[82] Guzmán organized a large party to march on Xalisco, dividing the force in two. During his approach he pursued some people into the canyon, finding and burning many small settlements and taking captive or killing many warriors. The Spanish attack culminated in a horrific act of terror. Guzmán's men captured two Indians from Xalisco and on his orders cut off the hands of one and tied them to his hair and cut off his nose as well; they cut off the hands of the second man and hung them from his neck. Guzmán then told them "that is what they would do to all the others if they would not submit." Not surprisingly Guzmán omitted this incident from his report to the king.[83]

The region around Tepic, a moderately high plateau stretching to the coast, was rich in resources. Guzmán described it as a "temperate place with many pleasant springs, through which passes a good river; [it is] a place with many cultivated fields and cotton fields and with all manner of food and fruit trees." The pueblo of Martonchel had "much fish and oysters and all the rest of the food extremely abundant and honey and much cotton."[84] The Spaniards pacified most of the territory around Tepic. The two lords of Xalisco submitted to Guzmán, as did three other good-sized pueblos near the coast reputed to have gold mines. The expedition stayed in Tepic for more than a month, allowing the horses to rest and regain some of the weight they lost in the recent difficult journey.

While Guzmán waited in Tepic for some of his associates who were traveling from Mexico City to join him, he also appointed new officials: Francisco Verdugo as treasurer; Juan de Sámano, who was the cousin of the royal secretary of the same name, as *factor* (royal agent); Hernando Cherinos, nephew of Pedro Almíndez Cherinos, as *veedor* (inspector); and Cristóbal de Oñate as *contador* (accountant).[85] Although one or two priests accompanied the expedition, they seem to have had little to do with either the Spaniards' indigenous allies or the local people. Guzmán placed two crosses in Xalisco and two in Tepic, where he established a lodging for

x alixcco

FIGURE 7. This image from the Lienzo de Tlaxcala shows the
Battle of Xalisco (plate 53). The warriors of Xalisco are shown
without the band around the eyes that apparently was characteristic
of some other western groups. Chavero, *Lienzo de Tlaxcala.*

Spaniards who might come through the area. He formally named the river
Espíritu Santo and the whole territory "la conquista del Espiritu Santo
de la Mayor España," a name swiftly rejected by the king, who probably
was put off by Guzmán's grandiose pretensions and renamed the territory
New Galicia.[86] Pedro de Carranza reported that Guzmán "made a proclamation in which he titled himself president of New Spain and governor,
and named that land . . . Greater Spain and took his sword and began to
cut the trees that were there, taking possession."[87]

Crossing the river, Guzmán put his forces in order and at Tecomatlan
confronted a massed attack of several thousand warriors at whose prowess
Guzmán once again marveled: "They came at me before I could attack, with

so much force and audacity and with such skill as if they were Spaniards all their lives accustomed to war, knowing so well how to protect themselves from horse or lance as if they were soldiers used to that army." The battle lasted two hours, the warriors using bows and arrows and wielding lances, clubs, and large shields covered with caiman skins. The warriors "came well dressed in cotton mantles and feathers, carrying very beautifully worked quivers, although there did not appear the gold and silver that they said [they have]."[88] As the fighting raged, another squadron of about one thousand warriors swarmed around the expedition's baggage. Despite the Indians' fighting abilities, Guzmán's forces eventually prevailed, killing large numbers of warriors, whom he thought represented "the elite of the province and bravest." He also noted that many lords died there, suggesting that the communities north of Tepic were allied or at least joined forces temporarily to try to halt the advance of the invaders. The latter did not come away unscathed; some fifty horses were wounded and around ten of them died. Some Spaniards received serious wounds as well. Ten or twelve of the Indian allies died, and Tapia, the lord from Mexico, took an arrow in the stomach.[89]

From there they continued north to Omitlan, where they spent Corpus Christi and stayed for forty days "and all that province came in peace." Guzmán made Gonzalo López one of his field marshals and sent him to find a place where they could spend the winter. Traveling through rivers, lakes, and marshes, López's guides brought him to a large river, the Acaponeta, the flood plain of which was densely settled.[90] The residents of Aztatlan apparently built up artificial mounds along the river to escape flooding; Guzmán and his party soon would discover why.[91] The rains already had made moving the large host cumbersome and slow.

As they prepared to depart Omitlan, however, Guzmán was in a positive frame of mind and wrote his lengthy report to the king. From his point of view they had accomplished a great deal, pacifying much of the region along the Río Grande and the coast around Tepic, and he anticipated even greater achievements. He wrote that he had been told that the fabled Amazons lived only ten days' journey from Aztatlan. He described them as "wealthy and feared by the inhabitants of the land as gods and they are whiter than these others [women]. . . . And when a male child is born they kill him." He signed his letter on July 8, 1530, from "la Mayor España."[92] Notwithstanding Guzmán's optimism, from this point on the entrada began to assume a very different character, becoming nearly as

harrowing for the participants as it was for the residents of the West whom
they overwhelmed, brutalized, and exploited. Disaster was about to engulf
the expeditionary force itself.

Disaster and the March North

Aztatlan appeared to offer ideal conditions for a prolonged stay. In Gonzalo
López's words, "Here there was great abundance of provisions and fowl
. . . of which a large amount was collected, in such quantity that it should
have sufficed for two years if what later occurred had not happened. . . .
The countryside was full of cultivated plots. . . . Houses and huts having
been made for the Christians as well as the Indians, they rested."[93] How
long they were there before disaster struck is not clear; probably it was
a couple of months.[94] They made the usual forays into the surrounding
area. Suddenly in mid-September 1530 a hurricane swept through, knocking down most of the winter quarters that had been erected (with the
exception of Guzmán's house). Overnight the river swelled, overflowing
its banks; "when it dawned, all the land was sea."[95]

The water receded in a couple of days, but by then the expedition was
in complete disarray. The swollen river ruined or swept away supplies and
livestock. The dazed survivors were astonished to see scores of animals
caught in the flood rush past them. The bewildered horses could not
find their way out of the watery and treacherous swamps. Hundreds of
Indian allies and servants drowned or later died from illness and starvation. Nearly all the accounts that cover that period mention the hurricane
and flood, although they differ on the details. García del Pilar reported
that more than a thousand Indians "who were lying in their beds sick"
drowned and that "more than eight thousand Indians and *naborías* fell ill,
in such manner that there weren't two hundred of them who could walk
on their own two feet."[96]

It is difficult to judge accurately the extent of the damage. Gonzalo
López estimated that three thousand died in the flood itself. Cristóbal
Flores thought that perhaps only five hundred of the allies remained
unharmed. In addition to the shockingly high human mortality, much
of the remaining livestock also died.[97] The expedition unquestion-
ably had reached its nadir, and both Spaniards and Indians attempted to
flee. In the midst of the wreckage, Guzmán, struggling to control the
survivors, ordered would-be deserters hung; Pilar claimed there were

fifty such executions.[98] A number of the Indian lords pleaded with Guzmán to be allowed to retreat south. Cristóbal Flores described the scene as follows:

> Seeing the lord of this city of Mexico, who was named Tapia, and the lord of Tlatelolco, and the lord of Tlaxcala, and the lord of Huejotzinco and many other lords and principales from this province of Culhua how bad their health was, and that hardly a subject remained who wasn't dying (on them), and other necessities they experienced, they went to beg and ask mercy from Nuño de Guzmán for the love of God, since all their people had died, would he please take their jewels and ornaments of war and let them return to Xalisco, which was healthier country to spend the winter. . . . I know that not one of those lords who went to plead escaped, that they all died.[99]

Rather than retreat southward, Guzmán decided that the main part of the expedition, "the healthy as well as the ill," should continue north to Chiametla. They made their way through swamps as bodies accumulated along the banks of the river and on the road. Pedro de Carranza alleged that, recognizing the impossibility of rescuing most of those who suffered, Guzmán ordered that the remaining Indians be rounded up and distributed to "those who wanted to carry them so they could brand them, and those they didn't take away remained there, and he ordered them brought to a house where later I saw them all dead."[100] Gonzalo López, in contrast, insisted that both the sick Spaniards and the suffering Indians "were treated and helped by the captain general with such solicitude and care, as if they were his children."[101] Guzmán ordered that the dead be buried, but the sheer numbers of bodies and the stench defied the efforts of the survivors. They began throwing the dead into the river, but as the water already was receding, instead of being carried off by the current the corpses remained along the banks.[102]

The Indian lords were hardly the only ones desperate to abandon the expedition. Flores reported that before leaving Aztatlan, Guzmán hanged a Spaniard whom he conscripted in Michoacan and wanted to return home, and he started to hang another; he also allegedly detained and tortured "certain hidalgos" who wanted to leave.[103] Pedro de Carranza recounted a disturbing episode that took place after they reached Chiametla, in which

Guzmán ordered the hanging of another Spaniard who tried to desert. As the unfortunate man prayed to the Virgin Mary, they placed a rope around his neck. Somehow the rope broke when they threw it over the branch of a tree. The onlookers begged Guzmán on their knees not to carry out the execution, to no avail. The condemned man also fell to his knees and, with a cross in his hands, promised to become a friar, but at Guzmán's orders his constables threw another rope around the man's neck and dragged him off to be hanged.[104]

The tattered and severely weakened expeditionary force took nearly three weeks to reach Chiametla. More Indians died along the road and, according to García del Pilar, many hanged themselves to escape the misery. It is possible that local people rescued a few of the stragglers. Gonzalo López mentioned that during Semana Santa in a pueblo in the sierra near Culiacan he found "four Indians of our allies, of which two were mine, who had been brought there by the Indians of the country who had taken them from the rear guard that remained sick."[105] In view of his sharply reduced forces and with hardly anyone left to carry the baggage and equipment, Guzmán decided to send López south to Michoacan with a company of fifteen or twenty horsemen and an equal number of footmen. They were to obtain reinforcements, "Indians and cattle and Spaniards, by force or whatever means possible," in the words of Cristóbal Flores. Guzmán also sent Lope de Samaniego together with the interpreter García del Pilar ahead to deal with the rulers of Chiametla, who received them peacefully and offered them fowl and fish. The rulers came out to greet Guzmán and, in view of the pitiful state of the expedition, offered to provide people to carry the baggage. The weight and friction of the loads, however, produced severe sores on the backs and shoulders of people unaccustomed to carrying such burdens. "And because of this as well as for some offense that the Spaniards who were with the sick committed, they rose up and are at war today."[106]

After López had been absent about forty days, Guzmán sent García del Pilar with ten horsemen to look for him. Pilar found him in Aguacatlan "with up to one thousand Indians from the province of Michoacan, and many principales from there in chains, and with those Indians and the horsemen he had, he was patrolling this province and burning, and he had a large corral in which many women and Indian men and children were prisoners, the men with chains around their necks and the women tied with rope, ten by ten." Pilar also testified that one of the horsemen, Alcaraz, seized a principal of one of the pueblos subject to Aguacatlan and took him to López, who told him that if he brought people to carry the baggage he would release all the women and children. Weeping, the man agreed to comply, saying that the women and children "had never killed any Spaniard and always had served." He returned with one or two hundred men. Pilar claimed that López then put them all in chains and did not free the women or children, the latter tied together in groups of five.[107] He told Pedro de Carranza how pathetic it was to see the small children rounded up this way. Carranza also said that when López and his men headed to Zacualpa, the lords or naguatatos came out to meet them in an effort to demonstrate that they were peaceful and submissive.[108] Nonetheless, López seized many men and women and burned much of the pueblo.[109] Cristóbal Flores also testified regarding the episode. Although, like Carranza, he was not an eyewitness, he was careful to name his sources. He claimed that when the people of Xalisco realized what was happening they began to flee, and to punish the pueblo López seized the ruler and threw him in a fire and burned him alive. He also stated that the Indian allies killed more than two thousand people "for being their enemies," with the blessing of the Spaniards.[110]

This episode proved to be one of the most controversial of the entrada, since a large number of slaves were taken at Guzmán's orders (even though he was not present) at a time when enslavement of Indians for any reason was prohibited by the Crown.[111] It will be recalled that earlier Aguacatlan submitted peacefully to Guzmán; what had the people done in the interim to merit this severe punishment? Unfortunately, there is no testimony that reflects the indigenous perspective. Possibly the people of these communities already had discovered that capitulation and service to the Spaniards meant unanticipated obligations, and as a result they turned on the Spaniards who remained in the area. According to López, before the remnants of the expedition left Aztatlan for Chiametla, some Spaniards whom Guzmán sent to Tepic and Xalisco to retrieve cattle he had left there returned to complain that the people of Xalisco beat and robbed them and killed some of the pigs. They alleged that similar attacks occurred in Zacualpa and Aguacatlan. Hearing this, Guzmán determined that the people of those pueblos should be enslaved, and he sent López to "wage war by fire and blood" on them. Thus when López departed from Aztatlan

he went first to the Pueblos de Avalos in Michoacan to collect reinforcements and then headed back north via Xalisco and Aguacatlan, where
he carried out Guzmán's orders to punish the pueblos and take slaves.[112]

When López returned with his human bounty he found only Cristóbal
de Oñate still at Aztatlan. They then proceeded together to Chiametla to
rejoin Guzmán. By the time López reached Chiametla with his recruits
and prisoners, all "the little children of the women died and were killed
on the road, which was the greatest pity in the world," according to Flores.
He also testified that the Indians brought from the Pueblos de Avalos and
other areas to the south were divided up among the Spaniards "as one
rents beasts of burden, so the poor Indian allies were rented among some
of the Spaniards [in return?] for valuables." They divided up the slaves
as well.[113]

Probably thinking that a stronger presence was needed to secure
the south, Guzmán sent Francisco Verdugo and others back to establish
the town of Espíritu Santo near Tepic. The settlement became the city
of Compostela and first capital of New Galicia. In mid-January 1531
Guzmán prepared to continue north. Two Spaniards who were ill begged
to return south with Verdugo, but Guzmán would not allow them to leave;
they died in Quezala a few days after the expedition left Chiametla.[114]
A number of people too sick to travel were allowed to stay behind. By
this time there was considerable dissent in both Spanish and native ranks,
which Guzmán called mutiny. A number of the allies attempted to head
south from Piaxtla. Guzmán ordered one burned alive and others hanged,
but despite the double threat of Guzmán's brutal justice and hostile locals
some Indian auxiliaries escaped anyway, the majority apparently perishing
as they attempted to reach home.[115]

The expedition moved north through a large coastal plain. Quezala
was just south of the Presidio River and Piaxtla on what the Spaniards
called the Río de la Sal (today Elota). Here they saw a different style of
houses surrounded by palisades, which the author of the first anonymous
account took as an indication of the frequency of warfare in the area. He
described in detail the snakes kept "in a dark part of the house in a corner,
all of them mixed up in a large pile. And as all of them are in a large ball,
and one would take its head out above and another below and another in
the middle, it was a very frightening thing, because they're as thick as an
arm. . . . They do no harm at all, rather the Indians take them in their

hands and eat them." He noted the abundance of cotton and cotton cloth, the fine dress of the people, and the beauty of some of the women.[116] They also began to hear languages that were different from those to the south, meaning they again would have problems in communicating and in obtaining good information about the best routes to follow. Much of this area was heavily wooded, making it very difficult to move on horseback. Heading down to the coast provided no solution, as they found no water and had to turn inland again. When they reached a settlement called Pochotla they found abundant food and fish as well as parrots and some falcons in cages. The people there made alcohol from maguey and plums.[117]

As they continued north, Guzmán employed the same tactics he had used earlier, sending smaller companies off to patrol and reconnoiter the territory. Gonzalo López mentioned that on Ash Wednesday "we went to take ashes at a pretty pueblo, although it already was burned, as the Indian allies who had gone with Cristóbal de Oñate had burned it."[118] These smaller parties often engaged in minor skirmishes and, clearly, the Indian allies continued to burn the pueblos through which they passed. Guzmán sent Gonzalo López to find the ostensible province of the Amazons, which turned out to be large and densely populated. Numerous pueblos stretched down toward the sea. Although in one of the largest ones they found many women and few men, there was nothing unusual about the women; presumably the absent men were away preparing for war, as there were constant reports of warriors in the area.[119] They finally reached Cihuatlan, supposedly the town of women, "of which for a year there had been news that it was a very great thing, although it did not turn out that way."[120] García del Pilar said they could not find out anything about the situation of the women as language problems and lack of an interpreter once again stymied their inquiries. He also noted that "in these times the allies went with chains around their neck with the loads, and thus we departed, leaving it in a state of war."[121]

From there Guzmán sent his field marshal López in one direction with thirty-five horsemen and Lope de Samaniego in another with twenty-five. They found the area going north to the Cihuatlan River (today San Lorenzo) also densely populated, with abundant maize, vegetables, fruit, and fish. Ten or twelve days after leaving Cihuatlan, "still passing through very good pueblos, which we left destroyed," they reached the province of Culiacan "between some very large pueblos that are on one side and the other of the shores of a very beautiful river, where they waited for us ready for war."[122] From the pueblo of Colombo, located near the confluence of the Humaya and Culiacan rivers, the expeditionary force initiated a series of engagements with the warriors of the region. Cristóbal Flores reported that they took captive "a gang (*cuadrilla*) of women who by their appearance were principales, and a dwarf," and carried them off to Colombo.[123] They fought a day-long battle, reportedly with some twenty-five or thirty thousand men, and captured the lord of Colombo, said to be the brother of the ruler of Culiacan.[124]

The author of the first account clearly was impressed by the valley of Culiacan, which he described as "the best settled land that has been seen in the Indies." He noted that from the sea to the sierras there were nine leagues of land along the river with large pueblos of five or six hundred houses, "long and very well made, very skillfully covered with straw, and they had on the ridged roofs contrivances like those in Castilla of brightly painted clay." The Spaniards fought a major battle there. The writer of the first account explained that the local people came to terms with Guzmán "because the Indians of this valley were of great reason, and they greatly esteemed their caciques, and in their way of dress and comportment they were very courtly and in their trading very sharp, because in all those pueblos there were very great markets and exchange among them of fish and cloth and fruit and all the trifles [*menudencias*] as in Mexico, except they don't know what gold is, [although] there is some silver. There are many turquoises, which the men and women who are lords wear in bracelets on their legs and arms."[125] There was ample game as well. Flores commented that it was very hot country, "more than the island of Española," and that there was "no lack of mosquitoes."[126]

In this area they again experienced difficulties in obtaining information because of language problems and lack of interpreters. Torturing several Indians proved of no help in identifying the best route to follow. Guzmán sent Cristóbal de Oñate, Lope de Samaniego, and Gonzalo López in different directions to reconnoiter the surrounding territory.[127] Samaniego reached the Petatlan River in the north and Gonzalo López traveled east into the Sierra Madre, followed by Guzmán himself with a larger party, probably seeking a route that would lead them to Pánuco, a journey he made later but departing from a point much farther to the south.[128] He also subsequently sponsored another entrada in 1533 that went as far north as the Yaqui River.[129]

The Expedition Ends

The expeditionary party remained in Culiacan for four months, perhaps until some time in June 1531 or later. The area was rich in a variety of foodstuffs, with enormous fisheries on the river. Guzmán established a town named San Miguel on the Cihuatlan River. When he departed for the south he left behind not only a number of would-be Spanish settlers but also many of the allies who accompanied them and survived so much misery; "they remained in chains and other restraints."[130] Cristóbal Flores described the heartrending scene of their departure from San Miguel:

> Leaving in that town . . . a large number of the Indians from this country [i.e., central Mexico] that he had taken with him to help make war, in payment for their good service and work at the end of two years, in which they traveled the roads and mountains loaded down, every day making huts and looking for food for us, he [Guzmán] left them in that town among the vecinos, free men made slaves, chained by the neck or in stocks so that they would not follow us, shouting and weeping when they saw us leave because of the great wrong that was done to them in repayment for their work.[131]

Although it was not unusual for the Indian allies who participated in Spanish expeditions of conquest not to return home, the circumstances in which they were left behind varied a great deal. In some instances they were regarded as colonists and even recognized as having certain privileges, while in others they clearly were abandoned.[132] The apparently forcible detention of Guzmán's allies in San Miguel seems to have constituted a fairly extreme case.

The main party returned south along a trail of destruction and reached the burned remains of Chiametla, where they discovered that most of the Indians who had stayed on there because they were too ill to travel had been killed.[133] Before leaving Chiametla, one of the Indian lords from central Mexico, don Tomé of Huejotzinco, once again tried to bribe Guzmán into releasing him. He probably was sick, as he had to be carried on the back of another man, who led don Tomé's horse when he went to see Nuño de Guzmán. Guzmán later told some of the Spaniards that don Tomé offered him "all his jewels but they weren't any good" and gave him

his horse—presumably the same one that the town of Huejotzinco purchased for him when he went off to war. Within two or three days after
this meeting don Tomé was dead. Carranza wrote that he saw don Tomé's
horse in Guzmán's stable and that Guzmán kept the Indian ruler with his
pigs for two or three days.[134]

Indeed, almost none of the Indians who set off on the expedition
returned home. Referring to the departure from San Miguel (Culiacan),
García del Pilar reported that "of one thousand two hundred who went
from Tlaxcala, no more than twenty escaped, and these remained chained,
save perhaps two that Gonzalo López brings [with him]."[135] Flores stated
that of all the Indians brought from Tlaxcala, "I don't recall having
escaped more than two principales who went chained guarding Nuño de
Guzmán's pigs."[136] This aspect of Guzmán's conduct of the entrada drew
strong criticism, especially as the Tlaxcalans, who were the main indigenous supporters of Cortés during the conquest of central Mexico, were
supposed to enjoy certain privileges. Yet it was not only the fate of the
Tlaxcalans that caused concern. A letter to the Crown from the second
audiencia in late April 1532 mentioned a series of provisions that they sent
to Nuño de Guzmán, including one stating that "he should allow to come
to their houses and estates certain Indians of this city [Mexico City] and
its district who remain of those whom he took on his conquest, that there
were few who returned."[137]

Subject to the authority of a single-minded and callous leader and
isolated in hostile territory, the Indian allies had few options, although
occasionally local people were friendly to them. In Tonala, for example, a
"barrio de naguatatos" offered the amigos some fruit and water.[138] A small
number of deserters or refugees from the disaster at Aztatlan might have
found asylum among people in the sierra.[139] The residents of New Galicia
had little reason, however, to sympathize with the Spaniards' Indian allies.
Probably most of Nuño de Guzmán's indios amigos perished miserably—
from illness, starvation, drowning, or at the hands of their enemies or the
Spaniards themselves—or lived out the remainder of their lives far from
their homes and families.

Guzmán returned to the area of Tepic and Tonala in late 1531 to
find that, rather than having strengthened and consolidated his authority in New Spain by extending Spanish dominion over a huge territory
in the west and northwest, his political position had eroded considerably.
Although the Crown appointed him governor of New Galicia—he

remained governor of Pánuco also—a new audiencia replaced the first; he was no longer president, a development he was reluctant to acknowledge. Yet another threat loomed in the person of his archrival Cortés, who had returned from Spain with rekindled enthusiasm for the exploration of the South Sea. The second audiencia, in an unsuccessful bid to outflank Guzmán's claims to New Galicia, sent the recently arrived don Luis de Castilla, a relative of Cortés's second wife, to establish a settlement near Xalisco or Tonala (reports vary on this point), which would have brought it under the jurisdiction of New Spain.[140] Guzmán had Cristóbal de Oñate arrest Castilla, then (according to his account) treated him courteously and dispatched him back to Mexico City. By this act he helped to ensure New Galicia's administrative separation from New Spain. The creation in 1548 of the audiencia of New Galicia, with its capital in Compostela (moved to Guadalajara in 1560), in effect confirmed the quasi-independence of the West that Guzmán tried hard to establish.[141]

Was the expedition a success? It exacted an appallingly high toll on resources and people's lives and fomented turmoil, displacement, death, and deep-seated resentment among the societies of the West and Northwest. If the results of Francisco Cortés's entrada were ambiguous, there could be no question about the enduring consequences of this second expedition. As will be seen, however, Guzmán's conquest fell far short of being complete, and many people of the West resisted Spanish domination for years. Nonetheless, he established a permanent Spanish presence in New Galicia. The next several years would reveal the extent to which the conquest fostered both a new order and growing disorder in the land.

Was Guzmán a criminal? By the standards of his times he might have been exceptional, mainly in the speed of his meteoric rise and then definitive fall from power. He offended and alienated many; he did not have Cortés's ability to inspire and ingratiate himself with others. Despite the prominence of his brothers, he seems to have lacked the status and connections necessary to retain the Crown's support in the face of controversy, although their influence might have protected him from more severe punishment.[142] Guzmán spent the last twenty years of his life in a sort of legal limbo, once again a continuo but living in very modest circumstances, perhaps a quasi prisoner at court. Given his ruthlessness in dealing with his inferiors, whether Spanish or indigenous, it is ironic that he himself perhaps became Charles V's sacrificial lamb, struck down to propitiate Zumárraga and the Dominican fray Bartolomé de las

Casas, whose *An Account, Much Abbreviated, of the Destruction of the Indies* included a description and righteous denunciation of Spanish violence against the people of New Galicia.[143] Cortés's flagrant transgressions of legality in undertaking the conquest of central Mexico brought him the huge rewards of a noble title, lands, and encomiendas, if ultimately not the high political office of viceroy that he so desired; Guzmán's actions, which were not all that different from those of Cortés, landed him in the public jail of Mexico City for a year and a half, where to his disgust he lived among "blacks and thieves."[144] For a man of such great aspirations and energy his was, ultimately, a hard fate, if not nearly so hard as that of the people, Indian and Spaniard alike, who bore the brunt of his ambitions.

CHAPTER 3

Occupying New Galicia

Here we record what we suffered with the specified tribute. . . .
They caused us to fall down, they cleaved our heads, although
it was only a little that we were short in [meeting] the tribute;
but even if it were very little, for this we would have to work too
much [until] they made us fall down. And we went around with
fear and worry; in no moment were we happy. And for this reason
we lost much of our property, our gold, our turquoise, our cotton
mantles. . . . We paid not with the property of the commoners but
rather with our gold, that of the rulers: I, don Cristóbal, don Juan
Oñate, don Pedro, don Diego, don Francisco, don Alonso, don
Juan, don Rodrigo, don Gonzalo, don Francisco, we all suffered
greatly and lost our property.

—From an account written by the rulers of Xalisco[1]

✝ NUÑO DE GUZMÁN'S CONQUEST MARKED THE BEGINNING OF A
continuing, if tenuous, Spanish presence in the West and Northwest. The
settlements that he founded for the most part proved lasting. In accord
with Iberian municipal tradition, each of the four new Spanish towns—
Compostela, Guadalajara, Purificación, and San Miguel de Culiacan—
came into existence as a legal entity with its own municipal council and
other officials. Spaniards began to work mines in the region, and those

who remained to settle at the conclusion of the expedition attempted to impose their authority on the Indians assigned to them in encomienda in the countryside.

Yet all was far from well; indeed, for both Indians and many Spaniards, the new circumstances of their lives were difficult and dangerous. Guzmán's closest associates and supporters, whose mistreatment of both Indians and Spaniards alike fostered bitter complaints, generally dominated the towns in the early years and garnered the largest encomiendas. Some Spanish settlers left, and indigenous residents abandoned their homes to escape demands for precious metals, tribute, and labor. Spaniards who went to live in the countryside in hopes of being able to make their encomiendas the basis for productive enterprises found themselves isolated and vulnerable to attack. Disorder was almost constant and violence endemic, in all probability the product both of indigenous resentment and defiance of the new

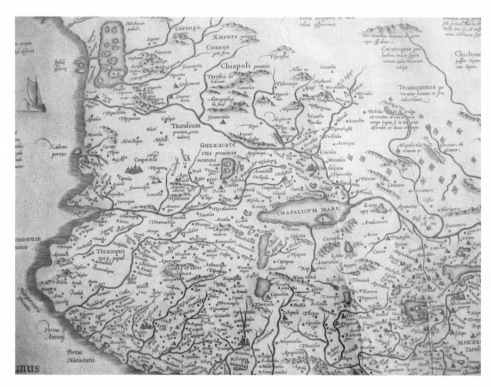

FIGURE 8. This map of New Spain and New Galicia is from the 1579 edition of Abraham Ortelius's *Theatrum Orbis Terrarum* (Antwerp: privately printed, 1579).

order and of older conflicts among local groups that predated the arrival of the Spaniards. Indeed, the Spanish presence might well have exacerbated existing patterns of local conflict. Members of groups that remained independent of Spanish rule targeted communities that appeared to have forged alliances with the hated newcomers. The goods and livestock that Spanish settlers imported into the region provided new incentives for raids and attacks. Spaniards in turn responded to what they characterized as "rebellion" by organizing further "conquests." In the mid-1530s slaving expeditions resulted in the capture of thousands of men, women, and even small children, leading to more disruption, violence, flight, and seething resentment.

Adding to the turmoil, Nuño de Guzmán himself was absent from the region for about a year in 1533–34. By then he already was approaching the end of his brief sway as the most powerful official in New Spain and aware that the tide of his political fortunes was turning. His decision to execute the native ruler of Michoacan proved one of the worst of his career, contributing to the erosion of the support he once enjoyed from the Crown—although in truth that process already was well under way by the time he left Mexico City at the end of 1529. Subsequent complaints about the funding, organization, and conduct of the campaign in New Galicia and possible illegalities in taking slaves further undercut royal confidence in him.[2] In 1533, having already been displaced by the appointment and arrival of the second audiencia and challenged by Hernando Cortés's ambitions in the Pacific, Guzmán left New Galicia in the hands of his associates to undertake an arduous journey over the Sierra Madre and back in an attempt to establish a route that would connect Pánuco with his new governorship in hopes of merging the two jurisdictions.[3] This ambitious but quixotic effort to offset the claims of both Cortés and the second audiencia by consolidating his hold over Pánuco and New Galicia would have little impact.[4]

In April 1535 the Crown appointed don Antonio de Mendoza viceroy and governor of New Spain in a move to strengthen and consolidate royal authority and reduce the power and influence of Cortés and his fellow conquerors and encomenderos. Mendoza, member of a high-ranking noble family with close ties to the former Muslim kingdom of Granada in southern Spain, arrived in Mexico to take up his position six months later. Guzmán left New Galicia for Mexico City to pay his respects to the viceroy, who received him cordially. The Crown, however, had ordered a residencia of Guzmán's conduct as governor of New Galicia. In March 1536 Lic. Diego Pérez de la Torre arrived in Mexico City to initiate the proceedings and take up the position of governor of New Galicia.[5] After arresting and jailing Guzmán in January 1537, he left the capital for New Galicia to begin his work there.[6] Guzmán spent many months in jail in Mexico City before being released. Subsequently, he left for Spain, probably in late 1538. Although he lived another two decades, he never returned to the Indies. His era of dominance in New Galicia and New Spain was at an end by 1537.[7]

The Establishment of Towns

Along with a few sites by new silver and gold mines, four towns came into existence in the early 1530s, becoming home to most of the Spaniards who remained in the West after Guzmán's entrada. They served as centers for the distribution of encomiendas and for what little in the way of Spanish society existed in early New Galicia.[8] Guzmán founded San Miguel in Culiacan (in the modern state of Sinaloa) in 1531, before he and his forces departed to return south. Although San Miguel probably was the most troubled of the settlements because of constant conflict, both within Spanish society and with local indigenous groups, Guzmán and others thought San Miguel had the most propitious location because of Culiacan's dense population, fertile lands, and rivers.

This same year Guzmán ordered Francisco Verdugo to establish the town of Espíritu Santo near the indigenous settlement of Tepic. In June 1532, however, the site was renamed Compostela in honor of the great pilgrimage site in Galicia in northwestern Spain. Compostela, the only early Spanish settlement to be called a ciudad, or city, served as the region's first capital. Its site moved southward to the valley of Cactlan in 1540.[9] Guadalajara, named for Guzmán's hometown, in the late 1540s became the seat of the bishopric and, eventually, New Galicia's permanent capital. Like Compostela it was founded in 1531, in the vicinity of some substantial indigenous communities on both sides of the Río Grande de Santiago. First located near Nochistlan, within two years it moved to Tonala, then to a site near Tlacotlan, and, following the Mixton War, to its final location south of the river in the Atemajac Valley.[10] The town of Purificación, which also moved once, was the southernmost of the settlements that Guzmán established, located close to the Pacific coast.

What were the early towns like? Lacking any detailed—or even general—descriptions, we must rely on partial impressions and inference. Most likely the founders would have tried to follow what in Spanish America became the standard municipal plan, laying out a central plaza and then marking off blocks and streets to form a gridiron pattern. The list of house lots distributed to the people who settled in Guadalajara, included in the *cabildo* (town council) records of 1532, suggests just this.[11] First on the list is a *cuadra*, or block, "in the middle of the whole town." Although the wording is less than clear, apparently they also set aside a block "toward where the sun rises" and "toward the church of San Pedro," another one on the left for public works, and one on the right for the governor's house.[12] The remaining blocks typically, although not invariably, were each divided among four vecinos, another indication that an effort was made to establish a rectilinear pattern of streets. There was no town hall yet, so the town council met in the lodgings of Juan de Oñate, the first *alcalde mayor*, or district governor. Nuño de Guzmán had a house in Compostela but probably never built one in Guadalajara. How many houses actually existed in Guadalajara before the town moved, and moved again, is not known. It seems safe to assume, however, that the construction of most houses in the early towns relied on such readily available materials as thatch, wooden poles, and mud, although in 1539 recently arrived governor Francisco Vázquez de Coronado wrote to the king that he would announce a royal order that houses be built of stone and adobe.[13] By the time of the Mixton War, when the town had moved to Tlacotlan, at least a few structures were considered strong enough to serve as a defensive enclosure for women and children and for the men who remained behind in the town to protect them.

Compostela was Guzmán's capital and main place of residence when he was in New Galicia. In its plaza he placed a gallows and pillory, the traditional symbols of municipal justice and autonomy.[14] In his response to the charges made against him in the residencia he described the church constructed by local Indians. Built of adobe, it had doors and a tabernacle made of brick and lime "for lack of a master [artisan] who knew how to do it," adorned with a cloth of silver and purple velvet. He also donated other fine fabrics and silver ornaments for the church service.[15] Although Guzmán took credit for the construction of the church in the city's main plaza, the first *protector de los naturales*, or Spanish official responsible for Indians' welfare, Lic. Cristóbal de Pedraza, who lived in Compostela for two years in the mid-1530s, apparently convinced Guzmán to build a church that was both larger and in a different location than Guzmán first planned.[16] In the early 1530s the town council used the church to convene its meetings. Guzmán put his own Indians to work sweeping the streets of Compostela, and men with encomiendas in the area began to build houses there.[17] Cristóbal de Oñate twice had the Indians of Xalisco build a house for him in Compostela, soon after the conquest at the first site and then again in 1540 when the city moved to its second location.

Little is known of domestic life. The inventory of Guzmán's house that was done in May 1537 leans heavily toward weapons, but at that time he had been absent from Compostela for some months. Apart from arms the inventory included medicines and a few other, mainly nonhousehold, items.[18] Guzmán claimed to have helped people build houses and plant vineyards and orchards, but despite his efforts the town failed to grow in the early years. When Francisco Vázquez arrived in Compostela at the end of 1538 he wrote to the king that although thirty encomiendas had been assigned to vecinos of Compostela, there were only ten houses in the town.[19] People were reluctant to build houses because they wanted to move the site. Furthermore, by the time that Vázquez arrived to begin his term as governor, it was becoming clear that at least some settlers preferred Guadalajara to Compostela as the kingdom's capital because of its more central location, greater proximity to Mexico City, and the density of the indigenous communities in its vicinity. In any case, the implications of Compostela's stagnation in the early years seem clear. Many settlers had opted to live in the countryside, or in the nearby indigenous pueblos that were granted to them in encomienda, where they mostly eked out a hardscrabble existence.

Because details relating to the factionalism and violence endemic in the early centers of Spanish settlement emerged during the residencia of 1537, we know more about the conflicts and confrontations that characterized the towns than about their physical appearance. It should be noted that these were towns only in a limited sense. As suggested, many people did not live full-time in the settlements, which in the early years lacked some of the elements associated even with small Iberian communities. While each had at least one church—tellingly, the adobe-built church in Compostela probably was the most impressive of these structures—they lacked some basic features of Iberian civic life, such as town halls and even jails. Both Spaniards and Indians who ran afoul of local authorities ended up in stocks, often for days at a time. There was little commercial life; the costs of transporting goods from central Mexico, together with the lack of wealth in the region, made obtaining supplies difficult and expensive.[20] Indigenous markets continued to function, however, and at least by 1537 in Guadalajara there was a weekly Saturday market, which the Spaniards called by the Nahuatl-derived term tiánguiz, where Spaniards and Indians mingled.[21]

To an extent the economy was a redistributional one, in which indigenous-produced goods supported Spanish households or mining operations and sometimes made their way to Mexico City—on the backs of indigenous porters—to be sold or exchanged for needed items. The constant exchange and redistribution of goods, together with the personal service that many encomenderos demanded and obtained from the people of "their" pueblos, meant that a strong indigenous presence characterized the towns, as Indians arrived and departed to deliver food and perform labor in Spanish households. In addition Africans, both slave and free, and Indians from other parts of New Spain lived with and worked for Spaniards in the towns and countryside. In the early years the numbers of Africans doubtless remained small because of the region's poverty.

Guzmán established councils for the towns, appointing six regidores (councilmen) each for San Miguel and Guadalajara and eight for Compostela since it was the "cabeza" (head town).[22] Notwithstanding these legally constituted councils, however, the strong-arm, even brutal tactics of some of Guzmán's captains and retainers in the early years fostered an atmosphere of lawlessness, fear, and disorder, especially in Guadalajara and San Miguel. The behavior of Juan de Oñate, Guzmán's choice for captain and alcalde mayor in Guadalajara, and of Diego de Proaño, who occupied the corresponding position in San Miguel, was so extreme in its brutality and divisiveness that Guzmán was shrewd enough not to try to defend them in his residencia. The actions of these two men and their cronies hastened the departure from the region, or at least relocation within it, of a number of would-be Spanish settlers.

Juan de Oñate, brother of the ultimately much better-known Cristóbal de Oñate (Cristóbal would become acting governor of New Galicia when Francisco Vázquez de Coronado left the province on his expedition to New Mexico), was one of Nuño de Guzmán's captains and closest associates.[23] Guzmán sent him to establish the first site of Guadalajara, assigning him one of the best encomiendas in the area. In great contrast to his brother

Cristóbal, who won the regard and admiration of virtually all the Spanish settlers and officials with whom he dealt, Juan quickly gained a reputation for arbitrary, vindictive, and even sadistic behavior that affected Spaniards and Indians alike. At one point he placed all of the town's regidores and *alcaldes* (magistrates) in stocks for two or three days. He was verbally and physically abusive. One vecino, Maximiano de Angulo, who served as *alcalde ordinario* (magistrate of the first instance) during the first year of the town's existence, complained that Oñate mistreated people and that "instead of keeping the vecinos at peace as a magistrate [instead] he stirred them up and . . . was very much the cause for their killing each other and . . . he was a great bandit . . . with little ability to serve as a judge." He went on to testify that Oñate favored those of his own clique (hardly surprising) while speaking badly of and dishonoring others, "saying very ugly words unsuitable for a judge" and that no one dared to speak to him because he was so foul-mouthed. Angulo also claimed that Oñate hanged the cacique of Nochistlan because the people of the pueblo refused to serve him.[24]

Diego Segler, whom Guzmán had appointed as Guadalajara's *teniente de gobernador* (lieutenant governor), echoed Angulo's testimony. He named some vecinos (including himself) who had been particular targets of abuse, whom Oñate had called "dirty scoundrels, fucked Jews, and other words" apparently so much worse that he would not repeat them. He alleged that Juan de Oñate on many occasions sent his cronies on secret, unauthorized slave raids and would then demand that Segler, who held the royal branding iron, hand it over to him. This Segler tried to refuse to do, not from humanitarian considerations but rather because Oñate's intention was to avoid paying the *quinto*, the royal fifth of the proceeds of the raids that was owed to the Crown, but Oñate bullied him into surrendering the branding iron on several occasions. Another witness, Juan Delgado, testified that he accompanied Oñate and others on a slaving expedition to Juchipila, where they were told that the Indians refused to serve the Spaniards. When they arrived some of the people of the pueblo came out to greet them peacefully on the road, offering food and drink. Allegedly Oñate captured and enslaved this welcome party and then entered the pueblo to take more slaves, nearly five hundred altogether.[25]

Although many settlers complained about Oñate to Guzmán, he did not remove him from office. There were people who spoke in Oñate's favor, but evidence for his abuse of office is strong. Perhaps most tellingly, he left New Galicia permanently shortly before Guzmán himself, thus avoiding the residencia proceedings; he was thought to have gone to Peru. A strong indication of the continuing favor that he enjoyed from the soon-to-be discredited Guzmán was that he was able to have his substantial encomienda grants reassigned to his nephew Juan de Zaldívar, newly arrived from the Basque country. This and other assignments of encomiendas to men who did not participate in the conquest provoked considerable anger among settlers who were in New Galicia from the outset but did not receive grants themselves, or at least not ones of any substance. Zaldívar, however, proved the equal of many conquistadors in his vigorous participation in slaving expeditions and the search for mines, and he served as a captain in the expedition to New Mexico.

In the early 1530s, well to the north in San Miguel, the rash and brutal conduct of Diego de Proaño engendered so much fear and divisiveness that even Guzmán, who appointed him alcalde mayor and captain, later condemned his behavior. Proaño already was a man of some experience in New Spain prior to Guzmán's expedition. According to his deposition of 1545 he arrived in New Spain in the mid-1520s with Luis Ponce de León, who was appointed to conduct the residencia of Cortés's term as governor. Ponce de León died in July 1526, and Proaño's cousin, Diego Hernández de Proaño, who was the *alguacil mayor* (chief constable), left New Spain to return to court. Proaño took his place as alguacil mayor but then joined Guzmán as one of his infantry captains.[26]

A long passage in the "Primera relación anónima" describes the rapid deterioration under the leadership of Diego de Proaño of relations between the vecinos of the new town of San Miguel and the local indigenous population:

> The Spaniards neglected to plant and began to buy maize from the Indians and to trade with them for it, as well as the other foods they needed, because what the Indians contributed was not enough to sustain them and their households. When the Christians had exhausted the maize as well as the things with which to buy it . . . [Proaño] allowed them to take it forcibly from the Indians' houses. After taking the maize they took blankets and . . . turquoise, and other things they had, in such way that the Indians . . . decided to rise up and hide in the forests and mountains and burn their own pueblos, which they did. Rather than try to make good this damage, the Christians began to pursue them and to

rob the land . . . and destroy it as it now is, and the Indians died of
hunger, because they stopped planting for two or three years. . . .
Now they have discovered rich mines, so the Christians can live
in that town. Because of this a captain who doesn't know how to
manage such a good land, as populous and extremely abundant as
it was, does not deserve what others merit who know how to do
it [properly].[27]

Proaño's partner in San Miguel was Sancho de Caniego, Guzmán's
cousin and also a native of Guadalajara in Spain and veteran of bloody
campaigns in Pánuco. Historian Donald E. Chipman writes that witnesses
in a secret inquiry into one of those campaigns agreed that "Sancho de
Caniego was a cruel, heartless commander, and he apparently lacked the
ability to establish harmonious relations with his men. . . . He was brutal
beyond reason to Indians and Spaniards alike. At the slightest provoca-
tion he would beat an Indian to death."[28] With such a man as his close
collaborator, it comes as no surprise that Proaño, like Juan de Oñate,
quickly gained a reputation for abusive behavior. Given the considerable
distance between San Miguel and the other Spanish settlements to the
south, aggrieved Spanish residents felt they had no legal recourse for their
complaints and perhaps that their lives were in danger, leaving flight as
their only option. In one instance a party of fifteen settlers left as a group
for Compostela.[29]

When Licenciado Pérez de la Torre conducted the residencia, he
received a petition from Cristóbal de Tapia and Diego de Alcaraz in the
name and with the power of attorney of the town of San Miguel regarding the abuses of Proaño and Caniego, "of which they have not been able
to complain to anyone because of being far away and the country being at
war."[30] By then, however, both Proaño and Caniego had left San Miguel.
Caniego actually took up the post of treasurer of New Galicia and was in
Compostela in 1535, and Proaño possibly planned to move on to Peru; he
apparently got as far as Oaxaca or Guatemala but no farther.[31] Although
Guzmán seemingly acknowledged the problems that Proaño caused in San
Miguel, according to his own testimony he also tried to persuade him to
come back with promises that he would be reinstated in his encomienda,
despite a nearly two-year absence. In the end he rewarded him handsomely
with a good encomienda near Guadalajara, where he became a vecino. In

1550 Proaño also had a residence, refinery, and sixteen houses for slaves near the mines of Zacatecas.[32]

Of Purificación in the early years we know little. Juan Hernández de Híjar, whom Guzmán sent south in early 1533 to establish a settlement in an area that had not been effectively occupied, seems to have functioned there largely on his own. In 1543 Francisco Vázquez retroactively approved all the measures that Hernández de Híjar had taken to lay out streets and distribute house plots, gardens, and other properties.[33] If early vecinos complained about the extreme poverty of their circumstances, which forced some to leave Purificación at least temporarily, in contrast to the situation in San Miguel none of them blamed Hernández de Híjar for their difficulties. Antonio de Aguayo, for example, testified in the residencia that before they were allowed to capture slaves he had left Purificación "to make a living, faced as he and the others were with dying of hunger and they didn't have the wherewithal for a pair of shoes. And after they took slaves and pacified the land he returned to it [the town of Purficación] and found that the vecinos had discovered mines, so with one thing and the other the situation improved and they were able to support themselves." Aguayo at one time was in Tehuantepec heading for Guatemala, so he probably traveled and worked as a trader.[34]

If men like Diego de Proaño and Juan Hernández de Híjar functioned for all intents and purposes on their own in isolated outposts of Spanish settlement, the latter seems to have behaved much more judiciously, at least in his dealings with fellow Spaniards. Many of the men whom historical geographer Peter Gerhard lists as holding encomiendas in Purificación in 1548 were among the original (or at least very early) vecinos who either remained there or returned at some point, as in the early 1530s there were as few as five vecinos in the town. Both Guzmán and later Vázquez seemed happy to leave Hernández de Híjar to run things, and both rewarded him with a series of grants—which in the early years probably were of no great worth, as most agreed that few people in the area would provide any tribute.[35] The area would be the scene of much violence and turmoil during the Mixton War.

In the decade following the conclusion of Guzmán's entrada, then, town life in New Galicia was rudimentary at best. Settlers spent much of their time in the countryside—dealing with their encomiendas, living at least part of the year in or near the Indian pueblos, working at the mines, or moving around as traders—and came into town only intermittently. Probably almost all the women in the early towns were indigenous, the domestic servants or partners of the Spanish settlers, some (or even many) of whom might have originated in central Mexico or Michoacan. Structures built of poles and straw reflected the tenuous nature of the early Spanish settlements, all of which shifted in site at least once. In all likelihood only the most prominent local men maintained establishments that approached the Spanish ideal of the *casa poblada*, a large household establishment. One such household was that of the first protector of the Indians, Lic. Cristóbal de Pedraza, who initiated an ambitious but short-lived campaign of religious instruction and conversion in which he urged the "Christians who have pueblos of natives commended to them by the king to order the caciques and principales of their pueblos to bring to the house of the said protector their young children." At least some of the children (probably boys, although the term *niños* could include girls as well) lived in Pedraza's house, where he provided food purchased with his salary and clothes fashioned from local cloth but in the Castilian style "to show them how to sew in civilized fashion and so they won't go around naked as they were accustomed to do." Because of the variety of native languages spoken in the area he taught the children in Castilian and devised a system by which he sent them in pairs "to the houses of the Spaniards to teach the naborías and slaves and criados of the said Spaniards." Several vecinos, including Cristóbal de Oñate, testified that Pedraza's young instructors came to their lodgings regularly in the evenings.[36] Pedraza's experiment ended abruptly with his departure in 1536, when Guzmán and the cabildo of Compostela sent him to Spain to report to the king on the difficult situation in New Galicia.[37] Although Pedraza's system of instruction did not last, at least for a brief time it provided another dimension to town life beyond the gambling, card games, and brawling that probably constituted the main leisure pursuits of most settlers.

Encomiendas

As in central Mexico the participants in the conquest of New Galicia expected to make stable and prosperous lives for themselves by exploiting the human and natural resources of the region—the labor and productivity of the indigenous people and whatever precious metals could be found. Nuño de Guzmán and his successors assigned encomiendas intended to yield labor and tribute, authorized the granting of urban and rural property, and searched for mines. Guzmán tried to coerce local indigenous leaders into handing over whatever gold or silver they might have accumulated, although the yields were limited. In terms of rural enterprise Spaniards in the region at first engaged mainly in ranching and raising pigs, relying on their encomiendas to supply them with other foodstuffs, although they also turned to commercial production of cotton and later of cacao. The coastline offered a number of good harbors. One of them, Puerto de la Navidad, through which Francisco Cortés passed and which Juan Hernández de Híjar later surveyed during his journey of exploration along the Pacific coast, became a site for shipbuilding as well as a port.[38] The early ports of Zacatula and Navidad, however, later lost out to Acapulco as New Spain's main Pacific outlet.

As usually was the case following the Spaniards' campaigns of conquest in the Indies, the expedition's leader became governor of the new jurisdiction and awarded the most substantial encomiendas to his captains and friends, reserving the largest and most productive for himself.[39] Not surprisingly, Nuño de Guzmán took some of the most populous pueblos near Compostela and Guadalajara. Those who received small grants, or none at all, or were assigned communities in areas that had not been brought under Spanish control, bitterly resented what they saw as the favoritism and partiality of Guzmán's assignments, particularly when substantial grants went to men like Juan del Camino and Pedro de Bobadilla, both of whom were Guzmán's criados but did not participate in the entrada (they arrived soon thereafter). Witnesses testified that Juan del Camino and Juan de Zaldívar, who received his uncle Juan de Oñate's encomiendas when the latter left for Peru, both had pueblos with a thousand households. Although such complaints about unfairness in the distribution of encomiendas characterized the process everywhere in the Indies, Guzmán's unyielding stance—he brooked no questioning of his policies and decisions—surely heightened resentment. When Juan Sánchez complained to Guzmán that he and others had received nothing, the governor allegedly responded that "he should wait with dignity, that from what he had he would give him nothing, even though his father Hernán Beltrán rose from the dead."[40] According to another conquistador, Martín de Castañeda, when he asked Guzmán for an allotment the latter said he had nothing to give and that anyone who asked would become his enemy. Guzmán most likely was trying to force some of the men who failed to receive grants to abandon

the area. Indeed, Juan de Villalba said that the increasingly desperate settlers would have left New Galicia; they stayed only because they heard a
judge was coming from Spain who would set things right.[41] While most of
Guzmán's captains and close associates—Cristóbal de Oñate, his brother
Juan de Oñate, Lope de Samaniego, Diego Vázquez, Diego de Proaño,
Francisco Barrón—remained in New Galicia, his most bitter critics during the entrada—Cristóbal Flores, Pedro de Carranza, García del Pilar
(who died soon after the conquest ended)—returned to Mexico City.

By contrast a number of people emphasized the generosity of Francisco
de Villegas (interestingly, the man Chipman believes was Guzmán's
closest friend) and Cristóbal de Oñate, the conquistador who became
Guzmán's accountant midway through the conquest.[42] Both Villegas and
Oñate were reputed to have fed people who lacked the means to support
themselves. Oñate in particular seems to have been building a strong base
of support among the settlers that in the future would serve him well.
The interpreter Rodrigo Simón, who knew Guzmán well having served
as his interpreter in Michoacan, testified that Oñate asked Guzmán to
allow him to divide up one of the repartimientos he received. According
to Martín Benítez, this was the pueblo of Xalisco, which Oñate requested
"be taken from him and given to the conquistadores so they can maintain themselves with it and the land won't be depopulated," but Guzmán
"never wanted to do it."[43] Although it is difficult to imagine that agreeing
to this would have undermined the governor's authority, Guzmán might
have begun to see Oñate's growing constituency as a potential threat to his
authority. Some of Guzmán's defenders, however, insisted that he showed
concern for both Spaniards and Indians in need.[44]

Regardless of whether grants were large or small, a key issue is
whether the communities of New Galicia offered the basis for establishing encomiendas similar to those that existed in central Mexico. This
question actually entails three related considerations. The first has to do
with the indigenous economy: did the inhabitants of New Galicia produce—or could they be persuaded or coerced into producing—food and
goods that Spaniards needed or desired? The answer to this question is
yes. Most communities consisted of farmers who cultivated maize, cotton,
and other staples, although in some areas, most notably near Purificación,
at least some of the people were fishers or hunters and gatherers. They, and
some of the pueblos near the lakes, could provide fish, which the Spaniards
demanded during Lent especially. Clearly, many communities produced

surpluses that allowed them to participate in the local and regional trade frequently mentioned in the 1525 visitación. After the conquest these surpluses would have made it possible for local residents to hand over some portion of what they produced in tribute or to obtain the goods the Spaniards required that they did not produce themselves, either through exchange or purchase.

The second consideration has to do with tribute: were the people of New Galicia accustomed to channeling some of what they produced to local authorities? This is a much more difficult question to answer. There is no consistent evidence that tribute was collected on a regular basis in the region at the time of contact. Juan Hernández de Híjar testified that when they settled in Purificación "he never saw that the natives gave [anything] to their masters" worth more than five pesos and that "they don't know how to give tribute, either to their masters or to their own principales, and this is true in the entire province of the town of Purificación."[45] In Guzmán's defense against charges brought against him, he suggested that "their custom and habit is to give tribute to their lesser rulers [*tributar a sus menores principales*] and their gods," but this ambiguous statement could imply that they did so on an irregular basis.[46]

Only very few Spaniards thought that the locals paid tribute systematically. Alonso Martín, who was the parish priest of Compostela at the time of the residencia and who accompanied Guzmán during the conquest, testified that "it is the use and custom among the natives to give tribute to their elders."[47] Santiago de Aguirre's statement—that "it is the custom among them to pay some tribute to their elders and principales according to the usage of each place, so that in some they are accustomed to provide wine in tribute and in others whatever they have"—also is ambiguous, but it points to the probable variability of such practices.[48] Possibly these statements imply only that some communities handed over a portion of surplus goods to their leaders (whether local elders, religious figures, or a recognized ruler or ruling group), reflecting traditions of redistribution and reciprocity and not necessarily taking place on a regular basis. Only Juan de Sosa, who at the time that Licenciado de la Torre was completing the residencia was a vecino of Puebla, temporarily staying in Mexico City, categorically claimed that the people of New Galicia were accustomed to paying tribute: "This witness knows that it is customary and public and notorious that in all the pueblos of Indians there are lords and caciques to whom those Indians are used to contributing with all the things that there are in their lands and also this witness knows . . . that those Indians offer and contribute to their idols and they sow fields from which their administrators eat."[49] Gonzalo Varela's assertion, that "the Indians of New Galicia are poor and unable and don't have or pay those tributes that those [native people] of New Spain are accustomed" to give, reflects the differences that settlers perceived between the peoples of the West and those of central Mexico, with regard to their capacity and willingness to participate in the encomienda.[50]

This, then, brings us to the last consideration: could local people be persuaded to furnish labor and tribute to the Spaniards, whether or not they had analogous practices predating the conquest? There is no single answer to this question. At least some encomenderos collected tribute and exacted items necessary for the maintenance of their households as well as labor service from their subject communities. The responses of a number of witnesses in the residencia, however, reflect the variability of the encomenderos' experience. Maximiano de Angulo, who held an encomienda near Guadalajara, noted that in the case of some settlers who "had nothing to eat, it was because the Indians that they had received in repartimiento refused to serve them and were of no benefit and didn't pay tribute and refused to . . . give anything at all."[51] Gonzalo Varela stated that "this witness's Indians that he has in encomienda have left so they don't have to serve him or plant a field for him or anything else, because they are not subject to any lord or principal or anyone else but rather all of them live for themselves."[52] Only with great difficulty could Spaniards exact labor and tribute from many of the people over whom they claimed authority. The (admittedly limited) available evidence suggests that only Guzmán and perhaps a few of the region's other powerful men succeeded in exploiting their encomiendas to their economic advantage—largely because they had been assigned the most productive and populous communities.

Nuño de Guzmán was one of the few who profited from his encomiendas in the early 1530s. Guzmán's success in collecting tribute from his subject communities likely hinged on the intimidating presence of his *mayordomos* (stewards or managers) and criados in "his" pueblos and their proximity to the main centers of Spanish settlement. The same might have been true for a handful of other men in the region, such as Cristóbal de Oñate, whose encomienda was the focus of the extraordinary report compiled by the indigenous leaders of Xalisco.[53] However, not only did most encomenderos lack the enforcement personnel that men like Guzmán and

Oñate could deploy but the communities that they were assigned did not offer a sound basis for systematic exploitation.

We can learn a fair amount about Guzmán's encomiendas from the residencia records. The tribute items that his encomiendas yielded were traditional Mesoamerican staples—maize, beans, and chili peppers—along with bolts of locally made cotton cloth, usually called *mantas de la tierra*.[54] All of these were standard tribute items in central Mexico as well. In addition Guzmán required local indigenous leaders to hand over slaves and possibly other workers who were put to work in the mines, and he attempted to exact gold and silver from the native rulers. The charges lodged against him in the residencia stated that in the four years since the conquest he had received over 1,800 mantas de la tierra, more than 12,000 *fanegas* (a fanega is equivalent to about one and a half bushels) of maize, and nearly 600 fanegas each of *ají* (chili peppers) and *frijoles* (beans).[55] These figures accord with the testimony of local indigenous leaders. Hernando, the cacique of Tonala, stated that his people provided 200 fanegas of maize each year, 30 of beans every two months, 40 bolts of cloth (also apparently handed over every two months, as he said they supplied a total of 240 mantas every year), and more than 300 fanegas of chilis "and beyond this they carried at their own cost all these supplies to the mines of Colima, which are thirty leagues from the town of Guadalajara, and to the mines of Compostela, which are twenty leagues from this town." At Guzmán's order they also brought him sixty or seventy Indians, including women, some of them younger than fourteen years old. Hernando went on to state that in addition his community provided salt, chilis, and all the maize, beans, firewood, water, chickens, fodder for the horses, and eggs needed "for all the people who are in the said town [of Guadalajara] on behalf of Nuño de Guzmán and the said Nuño de Guzmán when he was there, whether there were many people or few." Don Pedro testified that the annual tribute from Cuiseo, on the northern shore of Lake Chapala, came to 1,000 fanegas of maize and 100 fanegas of beans, also delivered to the mines; 600 mantas de la tierra delivered to Mexico City and other places; and all the supplies necessary for Guzmán's household "or for the other people who are there on his behalf in the said town." Tetlan provided 600 fanegas of maize and 360 mantas de la tierra, as well as 100 *cargas* (a carga equals three or four fanegas) each of chilis and beans.

The tributes that other encomenderos collected were similar in nature if generally much smaller in quantity. Diego Vázquez, cacique of

Tlaxomulco, named Cristóbal Romero as the "señor" of his pueblo and said that he and Romero had made an agreement that he would give him 70 mantas de la tierra in rent each year "and all the supplies of maize and chickens and other things that he needed for his household."[56] Oyequante and Quigua, caciques "del lugar de Cuitseo, lugar de Francisco Barrón," said that they had no agreement with Barrón other than "he asks for twenty mantas to be given to him if they have them and all the supplies for his house" and that "they haven't given him any other things."[57] The use of the term *contratar* (to contract or bargain) in reference to determining these tributes is interesting, suggesting the possibility that at least some communities negotiated the terms of tribute or service with their encomenderos. Probably only a very few encomenderos received more substantial tributes than these. The cacique of Tlacotlan, which had been Juan de Oñate's encomienda until it was reassigned to his nephew Juan de Zaldívar, maintained the household and supplied 240 mantas a year, as well as maize, chilis, and beans. Requirements or agreements to provide personal service and to provision households probably were standard in most encomiendas.

Guzmán claimed that he received very little in tribute during his four years as governor and that what he derived from Tonala "he spends for the salary of two or three or four Spaniards who have been and are there to maintain them and keep them at peace." He said that he received nothing from Senticpac apart from some cotton cloth and the things (unspecified) that they initially gave him in tribute. He stated that the only way in which they served him was by cultivating a field, the produce of which went to support the people of the pueblo along with some Spaniards that Guzmán maintained there. He also claimed that altogether the encomiendas he held in New Galicia might have comprised "three or four thousand men who serve"—a not insubstantial number.[58]

An Indigenous Perspective

The account compiled by a cacique and several other principales of Xalisco, quoted at the beginning of this chapter, provides a detailed look at the operation of an encomienda in the early years from an indigenous point of view. It was written down under unknown circumstances, and assigning exact dates to the events described is difficult. The narrative underscores both the high degree of coercion the Spaniards brought to bear on the local governing group and their likely (if unwilling) complicity that helped to sustain the new system of exploitation. Although Francisco Cortés reached Xalisco and assigned it in encomienda to one Pablos de Luzón, after Guzmán's entrada Cristóbal de Oñate became the encomendero of Xalisco, which also included the community of Tecomatlan north of Tepic, where the Spaniards fought a major battle during the campaign.[59]

The account that describes the operation of Oñate's encomienda in Xalisco incorporates multiple narrators, although the most prominent is don Cristóbal, one of the pueblo's two caciques. The other voices (the account varies among first-person singular, first-person plural, and third-person narration) belong to members of the upper tier of local society, which in this period included the traditional upper class as well as interpreters and *tequitlatos*, or overseers. In the postconquest milieu the latter two groups played a crucial role in mediating relations between Spaniards and indigenous societies and thus possibly came to form part of a new or expanded local elite.[60] All the caciques and "nobles" apparently had received baptism and Christian names. The narrators sometimes pointed out which individuals were not Christian and were still known by their indigenous names.[61] The practice by which local men took the names of prominent Spaniards might have reflected patron-client ties.

The narrative offers a tale of lies, broken promises, threats, and physical punishment administered by Oñate and his men as they strove to fashion the encomienda in Xalisco into an efficient unit of production and source of labor. Four hundred men harvested maize but received nothing of the payment promised by Oñate's mayordomo Domingo de Arteaga. After people from Xalisco built Oñate's house in Compostela—later they would be forced to build a second and larger house of wood and adobe when Compostela was relocated in 1540—Melchor Díaz, who was a regidor and later alcalde of San Miguel, asked for fifty men and fifty women to look for gold, probably in mines he held in partnership with Oñate. The community had to supply food and blankets for the people sent to the mines. Although they avoided mine labor, the señores themselves helped drag the wood to the site of Oñate's house; "we didn't do it with happiness but rather with suffering."[62]

Tributes included large amounts of maize, beans, cotton cloth, salt, and honey, as well as clay jars for carrying water. During Lent the Indians furnished fish and shellfish, which they were forced to purchase. They also handed over quantities of eggs, turkeys, rabbits, quail, ducks, and chickens. Arteaga and another Spaniard who worked for Oñate, Francisco Cornejo, beat and threatened the Indians constantly and required the nobles to use their own possessions to make up for any shortfall in tribute. The pueblo daily supplied Arteaga's house with five loads of firewood, eighty tamales, and a gourdful of salt and one of chilis. The cacique, don Cristóbal, was solely responsible for delivering eggs on meatless Fridays, and Arteaga helped himself freely to the native lords' flocks of domesticated turkeys. When Cortés passed through Tepic in the spring of 1535, Oñate authorized him to collect supplies from Xalisco, which was located not far south of Tepic.[63] The people of Xalisco also were responsible for helping with the upkeep of Oñate's pigs and sheep.

We see also the beginnings of commercial agriculture in connection with the encomienda in this region. Arteaga initiated the cultivation of cotton on a large scale. After workers harvested the cotton, they delivered it to Arteaga, who would then hand it over to the pueblo to be woven into cloth, a process in which the señores participated as well.[64] One of the cotton fields was located in Tecomatlan, which, since it lay at a lower elevation close to the coast, was much hotter than Xalisco.[65] Although the language in the account is confusing, Arteaga might have forced the señores themselves to purchase this field. Many of those forced to work in Tecomatlan became ill and died in the unaccustomed heat. Whether because of labor difficulties or other problems, cotton did not flourish in the new field: "it produced little [cotton]; in vain we died [and] sickened."[66] The mines were deadly as well, and many Indians tried to escape from the hard labor and mistreatment. Oñate held accountable and himself punished "all the nobles and our interpreters" for those who fled. As demands for tribute and labor escalated along with the scale of Oñate's enterprises, the native lords found it increasingly difficult to comply, and punishments and threats multiplied accordingly. Only much later, in 1545, did the visit from Mexico City of the *oidor* (judge) Lic. Lorenzo de Tejada offer the community the prospect of some relief. Although Oñate and Arteaga tried to bribe and intimidate the señores into silence, at least some of the truth emerged. Tejada attempted to institute measures of protection for the people of Xalisco against the extremes of exploitation, but enforcement remained minimal.[67]

Although the account does not tell us anything entirely new about how encomiendas functioned, certain details expand and perhaps modify our understanding both of its operation and its possible ramifications for New

Galicia's indigenous inhabitants. One aspect that emerges is the extensive involvement of women, not only in auxiliary or mainly domestic tasks but apparently in providing labor for mines and commercial agriculture as well. Young boys, possibly adolescents—"muchachos" in the Spanish text—also provided full-time labor for commercial enterprises. Another clear pattern is the high degree of vigilance exercised by Oñate's mayordomos and partners, as well as by Oñate himself. While they depended on the native lords to organize labor and the collection of tribute and forced the latter to act as intermediaries and even collaborators—patterns characteristic of the encomienda from the time it first appeared in the Caribbean Islands—the Spaniards left little to chance in imposing their harsh regimen. If in central Mexico the native ruling group at least at times seems to have gained certain advantages by collaborating with the new masters, the lords of Xalisco did not. Finally, the early commercialization of the encomienda, in this case at least, is noteworthy. Not only did the people of Xalisco provide labor for commercial enterprises, they themselves operated at least to some degree in a monetary or barter economy, as when they were forced to purchase fish outside their community.[68]

Was Xalisco especially vulnerable, possibly accounting for the effectiveness with which the encomienda functioned there in the early years? By 1531 the community already had suffered considerable losses and violence at Spanish hands. During the conquest Guzmán inflicted substantial damage on the pueblo, burning houses and horribly mutilating two men. Although in his letter of July 1530 Guzmán described Xalisco as having been pacified, when news later reached him in the north that the pueblo had attacked some Spaniards, he sent Gonzalo López with a company of men to punish the community. As noted in the previous chapter, López took as many as one thousand men, women, and children captive; branded them as slaves; and forced them north to Chiametla to be distributed to the Spaniards in the expeditionary party.[69] He also may have burned to death one of the local rulers. The impact of these calamitous early events perhaps accounts in some measure for the degree of compliance Xalisco's governing group exhibited in face of the demands and threats from Oñate and his associates. Communities that did not have such a violent experience of conquest might have been more successful in evading Spanish control.[70] Yet, as seen, from the very beginnings of the Spanish presence in the region, Xalisco attracted the Spaniards' interest, probably because of its location, productivity, and substantial population.

Resistance and Punishment

In various times and places the people of New Galicia resisted every aspect of the encomienda regimen. Flight from, or defiance of, Spanish demands was common. Juan Durán testified that the especially sadistic and brutal punishment meted out by Guzmán's mayordomo Francisco del Barco in Zacualpa came about not because the people refused to work but rather because they did not want to deliver tribute to the city of Compostela. A number of witnesses testified that Guzmán's mayordomo in Guadalajara, Diego Vázquez, frequently beat Indians and placed them in stocks for failing to meet their tribute quotas. The interpreter Juan Pascual stated that he noticed that a number of caciques had left their pueblos near Compostela, some of whom went to live in another pueblo that belonged to him.[71] When he saw them there and asked why they had left, the caciques told him that Guzmán and his mayordomos demanded tribute in gold and silver that they could not provide. Martín Benítez, who understood at least one of the local languages, reported a similar encounter and conversation on a mountain with some of the principales from Senticpac. Several of the caciques who testified in the residencia stated that substantial numbers of people had left their pueblos. Hernando, cacique of Tonala, said that forty households abandoned his pueblo and went to live in other communities; Guzmán, cacique of Tetlan, reported twenty households vacant as a result of mistreatment by Guzmán's mayordomo Diego Vázquez.

Although some of Nuño de Guzmán's supporters denied that Indians fled rather than serve the Spaniards, Antonio de Aguayo, vecino of Purificación, testified that "he has seen that some of the pueblos and farms of some vecinos were depopulated because [the Indians] would not serve and they go to the mountains and other places where Christians [i.e., Spaniards] can't go to see them, being as they are . . . the Indians with the least [capacity?] that exist in all the land, because they won't plant a grain of maize or cotton or anything else without their master compelling them"—which is what he himself did.[72] In a similar vein, Pedro de Castellón, the alcalde ordinario of Purificación in 1537, said that he could not stay in town to be deposed for the residencia because he was "about to leave to go to the Indians of his encomienda and deal with his property because every day he loses more." He did reiterate what others said, however, maintaining that the Indians never served anyone and that he knew this "because they themselves had told him and because . . . he deals with them every day. And many times he thinks he'll find them in their houses where he left them and he doesn't find them because they've departed and they tell him that they're going in order not to serve. . . . They are not subject to God nor king nor cacique."[73] The frequently reported temporary or permanent abandonment of homes almost certainly reflected both older patterns by which people moved around—perhaps in connection with seasonal activities, trade, religious ceremonials, or external threats—and new responses to the increasingly unbearable demands of the Spaniards. Because the outcome was the same, Spaniards explained the departure of people from their pueblos in varying and even contradictory terms.

The brutal conduct of Guzmán's associates and mayordomos—and occasionally of Guzmán himself, although generally he left the dirty work to others—might have succeeded at least temporarily in terrorizing people into submission and cooperation, but clearly these tactics had consequences that worked against the Spaniards' interests: some Indians resorted to flight or violence.[74] Guzmán's mayordomo Francisco del Barco exhibited the most extreme behavior reported during the residencia; but, given the violence that characterized the conquest and the heavy-handed imposition of Spanish demands for tribute and service, his actions were exceptional more in degree than in kind. Rodrigo Simón testified that he witnessed Barco kill sixteen people in Xalpa, a community subject to Zacualpa, "hanging them and cutting off their feet and hands and setting dogs on them that bit and killed them and then throwing the bodies into some trees" and that on another occasion he saw Barco kill two Indians in Chacala.[75] The same witness stated that he saw Barco summon some Indians of Chintla, a community subject to Senticpac, "and they didn't come as fast as he wanted. And then [when] two Indians came, one of them a naguatato, he threw one of them to a dog to kill him, which bit him, and he killed the other, pulling out his tongue which he cut out." In another pueblo subject to Senticpac, Simón saw that the cacique, who Barco claimed refused to follow his orders, died after being placed in the stocks. Barco then brought the cacique's women "to his house to make use of them and . . . he [Simón] saw them in his house and later heard it said that they had fled and were absent in other pueblos."[76]

A number of other witnesses testified to Francisco del Barco's homicidal actions. Juan Durán reported some of the same details that Rodrigo Simón supplied. He testified that Barco killed some forty Indians in the area of Zacualpa who were "serving and peaceful . . . because they didn't

want to bring the tributes and *servicios* [household supplies] they delivered
to the city of Compostela." Miguel Sánchez testified that Barco killed
sixteen people, burning some and setting dogs on others, for the same
reasons found in Durán's testimony. He was certain that although Nuño de
Guzmán himself was in Compostela at the time, he knew what happened
and indeed ordered Barco to punish the recalcitrant Indians; he claimed
that he saw and heard Guzmán authorize the action. Sánchez himself was
one of Guzmán's mayordomos, so it certainly is plausible that he could
have witnessed Guzmán order Barco to force the Indians into obedience.

Overall, the evidence against Barco, particularly testimony about his
sadistic punishments, was so strong—indeed, none of Guzmán's witnesses
refuted it—that Guzmán had to admit that such acts could have occurred
but, of course, without his knowledge or oversight.[77] He stated that while
on an expedition in the valley of Banderas he heard complaints against
Barco and would have initiated an inquiry, arrested, and punished him, but
he could not find him. Contradicting this alleged intention, however, was
another statement in which Guzmán sought to justify Barco's behavior as
having resulted from the hostilities perpetrated by the Indians of the coast
near Zacualpa.[78] By the time of the residencia Barco had left New Galicia,
possibly for Peru, although more likely he was in Mexico City. Martín
Benítez insisted that because Guzmán usually was only eight leagues away
in Compostela during the time of these incidents, he hardly could have
failed to know what Barco was doing. Benítez also noted that in addition
to the sixteen people killed in or near Zacualpa and four others executed
by burning, there were many other such instances, probably accounting
for the discrepancies in numbers that witnesses reported. Benítez testified
that because of Barco's mistreatment and homicidal rage "many pueblos
that at the time were peaceful, seeing how badly those Indians were treated
and thinking that they too would be mistreated, rebelled and did not want
to serve."[79]

Although clearly the degree to which encomiendas actually functioned
to supply labor and tribute varied a good deal, on the whole they apparently
did not do so consistently except in the case of the largest grants—which
would have been the best organized and most productive communities—
held by the most powerful men. The local people bitterly resented and
resisted the demands that the institution entailed. Furthermore, the uses
to which the Spaniards in the West put their grants of labor and tribute
deviated from legal and acceptable practice. As Francisco Vázquez noted

when he arrived there in 1538, continuous personal service frequently was the norm in New Galicia (as it was perhaps everywhere in the early post-conquest period despite its prohibition) rather than periodic labor duty or established tribute quotas. He expressed particular shock to discover that encomenderos were illegally sending their Indians as far away as Mexico City to deliver goods. He reported to the king that this prohibited practice had reached such proportions that when he traveled west from the capital he encountered people from New Galicia carrying loads "forty by forty and fifty by fifty, dying of hunger because they [the encomenderos] did not even feed them in return for their work. . . . [It is] in great detriment to the natives of this province that they should go thus loaded eighty leagues from their homes."[80] Indians from New Galicia also could find themselves laboring far from home. In 1531 Juan Bautista testified that he had seen natives of Tonala in Colima "who served Martín Jiménez at the command of Nuño de Guzmán." Jiménez apparently went to Tonala to bring the people back to Colima where "they served him there in his house."[81]

The Quest for Precious Metals

Guzmán attempted to extort gold and silver from the caciques under his control, an illegal although virtually universal practice during the conquest period. The first four charges that Licenciado Pérez de la Torre lodged against him in the residencia specifically concerned Guzmán's demands for precious metals from the cacique of Senticpac and the fatal aftermath of that dispute; the fifth charge mentioned similar demands he had made of other caciques. Juan Pascual, for example, testified that Guzmán's criado Juan Navarro imprisoned two "principales y señores" of Zupango in his house in Compostela and that he overheard Navarro telling the men that Guzmán was angry that they failed to bring any gold or silver. Navarro released them so they could bring back what was demanded; they returned with "three ingots of silver and one of gold . . . and they told him they did not have any more."[82] Juan Navarro replied that what they brought was insufficient and they would have to bring more or risk being further detained. Two days later Pascual heard that the men had been freed and that, when they returned to their pueblo, everyone there fled to the mountains "and they've never returned; nor has there been a single Indian in that pueblo; nor is there at present."[83] Licenciado Pérez de la Torre found Guzmán guilty of all the charges related to extortion, ordered him to repay what he had taken from the communities, and sentenced him to one year's exile.[84]

Another instance in which Guzmán tried to extort gold and silver placed the cacique of Senticpac in an untenable position vis-à-vis his own people. According to Rodrigo Simón, who offered the most complete account of the episode, soon after the Spanish began to settle the area, Guzmán's captain Francisco de Godoy brought the cacique to Guzmán.[85] The cacique handed over "many pieces of gold and silver that the said Indians wear in their ears and on their bodies," worth altogether perhaps five hundred pesos. Simón testified that he acted as interpreter for Guzmán, who asked for more gold and silver from the cacique and from another twenty principales who accompanied him. They promised to bring three or four thousand pesos' worth and departed. When he returned to Senticpac, the cacique summoned a number of principales and other Indians and told them that Guzmán required a certain quantity of gold and silver to be delivered within sixty days and that they needed to see that this was done. The Indians angrily "demanded to know who was he to ask for silver or gold from anyone, that they did not have it to give, and for this reason they surrounded the said cacique to kill him and the whole country rose up."[86]

The cacique then sent a messenger to Guzmán with a plea for help. According to this man, "the cacique, with his wife and children, was surrounded by the Indians of his pueblo and they had rebelled against him because of the gold that he had demanded." Guzmán instructed Simón and some other men to prepare to go to his aid, but as they were doing so another man arrived and reported that "they [the cacique's people] had killed the cacique and his wife and children and all his progeny," after which those responsible disappeared into the mountains. A month later Guzmán sent Simón and another man to find out what happened; two or three months after that the Indians of Senticpac began to bring gold to Guzmán.[87]

A man named Cristóbal de Oñate, who was cacique of Senticpac in April 1537, testified that Quiculin, the former cacique, "sent some gold to Nuño de Guzmán in such quantity that many of the principales and natives of the said pueblo killed him and all his progeny and descendants."[88] He further testified that he was the pueblo's naguatato at the time and saw Xoyl, who succeeded Quiculin as cacique, give Guzmán a gourd full of gold and silver. Xoyl died shortly thereafter, and the naguatato Cristóbal de Oñate succeeded him and also faced Guzmán's demands for precious metals. Support for his testimony came from Antonio Camacho, cacique of Chialmaloa, a pueblo subject to Senticpac. He stated that for the past four years the caciques of Senticpac had required all the "caciques, principales, and all the subjects of the said pueblo" to provide gold and silver for Guzmán.[89] They imposed this levy four times (presumably once a year).

Nuño de Guzmán offered a very different explanation of events. He said that, when asked what he could pay in tribute, Quiculin offered to provide up to fifty pieces of low-grade silver and twenty of low-quality gold, "which he said before the principales of that pueblo, and he never gave it because of certain differences among them that existed that there always are, or they killed [one another] as they are wont to do and then they go to the mountains." Indeed, he claimed he never received anything from the caciques of Senticpac and that no deaths occurred there except that of Quiculin and one other man, the result of Quiculin's having been drunk "in the kind of revelry they are accustomed to making." He said that another cacique who was his relative killed him, further explaining that the two men belonged to rival factions and that the killer and other Indians subsequently left "because their custom in all this jurisdiction is that they kill one another where the Spaniards can't impede them."[90]

Guzmán also speculated that if the Indians of the pueblo rebelled, it was at the time that Cortés passed through the area and, further, that a cacique from the sierras, Coringa, had incited them to revolt.[91] Coringa was thought to have targeted peaceful pueblos that served the Spaniards. Thus Guzmán implied that the disorder that followed the cacique's death resulted not from internal disagreement over tribute demands for gold and silver but rather from external threats and pressures. Equally confusing, Guzmán, after denying that he had received anything at all from Senticpac and stating that the Indians possessed virtually nothing in the way of gold or silver, admitted that if Quiculin gave him something "it was during the time that he was captain for His Majesty and not later when he was governor."[92]

Although a couple of Guzmán's witnesses testified about disturbances caused by Coringa in the area between San Miguel and Compostela, none but Guzmán himself actually contradicted Simón's version of the events that led to the death of Quiculin and his family. The episode not only reflects Guzmán's continued determination to wrest treasure from the native peoples under his authority, which characterized his actions in central Mexico and Michoacan as well, but also sheds light on indigenous sociopolitical organization, at least in Senticpac. The other leaders' angry denial, reported by Simón, of the cacique's right to impose a levy on them could be further proof that no regular tribute system existed before the Spaniards' arrival, or perhaps they simply were unaccustomed to handing over gold. At the least the incident underscores the limits on the authority of the men whom the Spaniards recognized as native leaders. The testimony in this case strengthens the conclusion that sociopolitical organization in much of New Galicia did not support a tribute system comparable to that of central Mexico. Spaniards obtained much of what they did from the inhabitants of the region through intimidation and force. The encomienda in early New Galicia, as in other recently conquered areas, essentially licensed Spaniards to appropriate whatever they could extort from the people ostensibly under their authority.

Along with the encomiendas, the mines in the region generated income for some Spaniards and brought them into contact with Indians. The mines also promised a more regular basis for accruing wealth and establishing a tenable Spanish society in the West than did Guzmán's tactics of extortion, although he was heavily involved in mining enterprises as well. Spaniards mainly used indigenous labor in the mines. Africans were present as well, although the limited yields of the early mines probably did not support the use of many African slaves. Indigenous mine workers at least nominally fell into several categories—slaves, naborías, and possibly free people—but Spaniards themselves seem to have been hard put to distinguish one group from the other, especially as it is likely that in the earliest years slaves were not always branded.[93]

Nuño de Guzmán and his associates obtained slaves from local caciques. How the indigenous leaders acquired them is not entirely clear, but most likely they were the spoils of local conflicts and warfare. Melchor Alvarez, a vecino of Purificación in the 1530s, explained that "many of the Indians that the natives provide, they give them as slaves, and those that they do not provide as slaves are very poor, orphans who agree to serve someone who will give them what they need. . . . This witness [Alvarez] has questioned a cacique and he has told him that many of them are slaves taken in war because that is their custom."[94] The Spaniards' demands for slaves also might have encouraged some Indians to capture, enslave, and sell other Indians. In a letter of 1545 the oidor Licenciado Tejada wrote that "the principales and Indian merchants steal free Indians and sell them" and described the severe measures he had taken to put an end to the practice. He made this observation after the Mixton War, and possibly the practice expanded as a result of the dislocation and consequent social breakdown that the war left in its wake, but most likely the capture of Indians for sale as slaves already was taking place during the 1530s, given the Spaniards' demands for slave labor.[95]

The status of the Indians working in the mines was, therefore, ambiguous. When Francisco Vázquez de Coronado arrived in New Galicia he did not doubt that both slaves and free people had been put to work in the mines. In his letter of December 1538 to the king he wrote that "in the gold mines the pueblos give to their encomenderos Indians to extract gold, some of whom are those who among the Indians they sell and buy as slaves . . . and others who are free." He mentioned that although a large number of slaves had been taken in the region, they were sold elsewhere, and for this reason "the mines are worked with the slaves of Indians and free Indians."[96] Alonso López, who served as Guzmán's alcalde in the silver mines of Zacatlan (on the Ameca River, not far from the future site of Guachinango), testified in 1537 that he saw that many miners "have brought and at present bring indios naborías from the pueblos they hold, which are given by the caciques of the said pueblos and that the caciques . . . say that they are their slaves; they don't have a royal brand nor do they have any [other?] brand. And he sees that they make them work and they perform labor with them in these silver mines. . . . Juan de Mondragón, a vecino of Compostela . . . brings and works with . . . six or seven naborías that a cacique of a pueblo called Tepic, which belongs to Nuño de Guzmán, gave him."[97] Vázquez did write in 1538, however, that when he visited the mines at a site called Nuestra Señora de la Concepción he found the Indians well treated, with adequate food and clothing and seemingly among the very few in the region who received any instruction in Christianity. He decided, therefore, to await further orders from the Crown before making any changes in the situation.[98] Melchor Díaz also maintained that the slaves and naborías working in the mines are "happy and [suitably?] dressed and catechized in our holy Catholic faith" and claimed that the Spaniards treated them better than the caciques did.[99]

Indigenous slaves might not have constituted the majority of early workers in the mines of New Galicia. The involvement of encomenderos in mining meant that almost inevitably encomienda Indians would be used in mining operations even though the practice was illegal.[100] Martín de

Mondragón testified in the residencia that he worked with forty Indians, given to him by Guzmán's mayordomo, in the mines at Zacatlan. For the use of the Indians' labor he paid Guzmán three hundred pesos de minas a year, which covered their maintenance as well. Although the language is ambiguous, because he did not refer to naborías or slaves he probably was renting encomienda Indians. He said the Indians came from a "a place called Necuintle, which belonged to Nuño de Guzmán."[101] Charges brought against Francisco Vázquez during the residencia of his governorship alleged that well over one hundred men, women, and children from the pueblos he held in encomienda in partnership with Alvaro de Bracamonte worked in the mines of Tepehuacan, performing all manner of labor and living there continuously.[102]

The Xalisco account provides insight into the forcible recruitment of indigenous labor for Cristóbal de Oñate's mines, suggesting again the role that bargaining could play in the arrangements made between encomenderos and local leaders. Cristóbal de Oñate, with his mayordomo Domingo de Arteaga, demanded that the pueblo's señores provide eighty men and eighty women to work in the mines in Huichichila, although apparently people from Xalisco already were working in the mines in Culiacan. When the pueblo's lords refused to provide so many workers, Oñate demanded forty men and forty women. "He left very angry and then we discussed that we would provide twenty. We told him that is all we are going to give. . . . He said again that the total should be thirty men and the same number of women. So again we discussed [it] and we gave him sixty altogether."[103] The large number of women involved in this negotiation over workers for the mines is worth noting, although how the women were employed at the mines is not known.[104]

Although probably none of the early mining sites in the region were very large, they represented a significant focus of Spanish economic activity. Many of the same people who played a part in the early mining industry in New Galicia, such as Cristóbal de Oñate and Toribio de Bolaños, went on to become leading figures in the exploitation of larger mining sites such as Guachinango (opened in 1544–45) and Zacatecas (discovered late in 1546) to the north. In the early years, however, Nuño de Guzmán played a major role in local mining. Nearly all the other men that Alonso López mentioned in connection with the mines of Zacatlan—Francisco Villegas, Juan del Camino, Luis Salido—were Guzmán's close associates. Rodrigo Simón testified in 1537 that Guzmán had "two gangs of indios naborías from his pueblos who extracted gold from the gold mines that have been discovered on the Jalisco River . . . and that Luis Salido, who is a miner, is in charge of the gang."[105] Salido managed Guzmán's mines when the latter departed for Mexico City. To the frustration of other miners, Guzmán attempted to keep any new operations in abeyance until his return from the capital.[106] Guzmán also at least indirectly involved himself in efforts to establish mines near San Miguel; his appeal of the charges in the residencia claimed that to support the vecinos of San Miguel he sent a "gang of slaves to look for gold and silver mines and a forge along with a silver miner to whom he paid two hundred pesos a year and who was there two years and always had three or four paid workers, and four and five horses both to help the vecinos pacify the land and to look for the said mines and secure them as they were in enemy territory. . . . He gave them equipment to extract gold at no cost . . . and because the mines were in enemy territory they gave up extracting it."[107]

The earliest mining operations in New Galicia probably were successful enough to sustain the hopes of Spaniards in the region that precious metals might be found in abundance. Men who were active there in the 1530s and 1540s played a leading role in locating and developing the major mining site of Zacatecas in the late 1540s, and some prominent miners in Zacatecas continued to reside at least part of the time in Guadalajara. Thus the ties that the miners of New Galicia forged with what would become the first significant mining region in northern Mexico proved important and in some ways enduring.

No Middle Ground?

Details of the abuses associated with the imposition of Spanish rule and demands for tribute, labor, and precious metals suggest that relations between Spaniards and Indians in early New Galicia were starkly polarized. Indeed there are few if any signs that any workable ties not grounded in intimidation and force formed between the two groups. Indications of friendship, trust, or compassion are almost entirely absent. Most Spaniards viewed the local people as barbaric and unreasonable, prone to violence, human sacrifice, and cannibalism.[108] Given that the bulk of the documentation for the 1530s focuses on the abuses of Guzmán and his associates, however, situations in which Spaniards and Indians were not in conflict possibly received little comment. Intimate relations between Spanish men and indigenous women may be one area of contact that was not always exploitative, although given the violence associated with conquest, early settlement, and slaving expeditions, local women most certainly became victims of rape and other forms of abuse (recall the episode in which Francisco del Barco forced the wives of a cacique who died in the stocks to come to his house).

Some women might have entered voluntarily into relationships with the newcomers. Very few Spanish women settled in New Galicia in the 1530s, and most likely Spaniards lived with and married Indian women in some numbers. Fray Antonio Tello, for example, wrote that after Diego de Proaño left San Miguel and his successor Cristóbal de Tapia began to bring some stability to the area, many Spanish settlers (by then much reduced in numbers) married *"yndias* [sic] *de aquella tierra y mexicanas."*[109] Certainly there are known instances of marriage between Spaniards and local women. Other settlers, for example, credited Pedro de Bobadilla's alliance with an Indian woman for his, and his family's, narrow escape from death during the Mixton War. When Andrés de Villanueva executed a deposition in 1566 he was over fifty years old and a vecino and regidor of Guadalajara. He stated that he had been married to *"una muger soltera natural desta tierra"* (a single woman native of this country). In the petition he requested that his son by his indigenous wife, also named Andrés de Villanueva, be recognized as legitimate so that he could inherit his encomienda, estates, and other properties, casting some doubt as to whether he actually had been married to his son's mother.[110] While there must have been many such liaisons and marriages, they surface only infrequently in the existing records.[111]

Thus the bulk of the evidence suggests that friendly relations between Spaniards and Indians were not the norm. Nonetheless, Spanish households must have been staffed mainly by indigenous women, given the scarcity of white women and African slaves, and we catch occasional glimpses of a more mundane kind of interaction. Juan de Villarreal described seeing the daughters of Alonso López helping out in the kitchen of their house, "playing with some maize dough and making tortillas" under the instruction of some Indian women servants.[112] The evangelization efforts of the protector de naturales Pedraza, described earlier in this chapter, also might have fostered some peaceful contact. In particular he noted that many indigenous women responded favorably to his admonition that they bring their babies to be baptized "neither more nor less than do the women in Castile" and that they would tell him which of the saints' names they wanted for their children.[113] In general he reported success in attracting local people to hear Mass on Sundays, performing baptisms of men and women as well as children, and convincing men to take just one wife. As is true for other such claims on the part of the clergy in early Mexico, however, we must be cautious about accepting them as anything much beyond an indicator of what he aspired to do, especially given the brevity of his tenure in New Galicia. A curious discrepancy exists in the explanations offered for Pedraza's quick departure for Spain. Guzmán testified that Pedraza volunteered to go to court to give an account of the difficult state of affairs in New Galicia, while Pedraza himself stated that Guzmán asked him to report to the king in person. Could it be that, despite Guzmán's avowals of commitment to the spread of Christianity in the West, he was put off by Pedraza's enthusiasm and independence, possibly seeing his activities as undesired interference? There is no way to know the truth of the matter, but evidence that Guzmán tried to dominate all aspects of local society abounds. In this case we know for certain only that Pedraza's program of evangelization came to a halt with his departure, and that he never returned to New Galicia.[114]

By the end of the 1530s the Franciscan order had begun to establish itself in some of the larger indigenous communities in New Galicia. Guzmán, however, was no friend of the Franciscans and disparaged their efforts. He claimed that the friars wanted only to be in the "best places" and to exploit the Indians at the expense of their encomenderos. He also alleged that since they did not know the native languages they could understand the people only "through Indian interpreters they have in their houses, which are the sons of the most principal people, as much so that they [the lords' sons?] exercise authority in their land as to teach them, by which means they inform the Indians about things having to do with the faith and even permit them to go [around] without the friars accompanying them."[115] Following the widespread destruction that took place during the Mixton War, the Franciscans had to begin their efforts anew in the early 1540s.

On an individual basis some Spaniards did move around in the indigenous countryside unharmed, perhaps forging friendly contacts as traders or by allowing some latitude with Indians assigned to them in encomienda. An interesting example is that of Cristóbal Romero, a conquistador and longtime vecino of Guadalajara who survived the Mixton War and lived at

least until 1559, when he was about sixty years of age.[116] Romero was encomendero of Tequicistlan, Epatlan, and Tepaca, northwest of Guadalajara,
and purchased the encomienda of Yagualica northeast of Guadalajara
from Juan de Alaejos in the 1540s. He often served as an interpreter and
in the 1530s was an outspoken critic of some of Guzmán's associates. In
1550, during the course of his tour of inspection of the region, the oidor
Lic. Hernán Martínez de la Marcha charged Romero with having taken
Indians from the pueblo of Tequila to live on his encomienda on the understanding that if they did so, he would leave them alone to "live badly and
in accordance with their rites and customs."[117] Although the charge was
made much later than the period discussed here, no date was specified, and
Romero might well have made such arrangements with the Indians under
his authority all along. Significantly, after the Mixton War, he claimed
that at the time of its outbreak the people of his encomienda had warned
him to protect himself and his property.

Romero was not the only encomendero warned of the brewing hostilities, again suggesting that possibly the relations established between
individual encomenderos and the people of their encomiendas were not
always abusive and polarized. On the other hand, however, one can also
imagine the difficult position of local leaders who might have feared eventual punishment by their encomenderos if they failed to forewarn them.
But could there have existed some middle ground? The number of people
who already in the 1530s and early 1540s claimed knowledge of indigenous
languages and acted as official and unofficial interpreters at the very least
indicates a fairly high degree of interaction between some Spaniards and
Indians although, again, such contact need not have been friendly and
seemingly never was balanced. Very possibly many of the interpreters,
or *lenguas*, lived with or married indigenous women and learned native
languages in the intimacy of the household. There is much that we do not
know about life in this remote period. Yet even if it were true that some
Spaniards maintained friendly relations with some Indians, the almost
constant manifestations of disorder, flight, and conflict that characterized
New Galicia in the years after the conquest suggest that such relations
probably were not the norm. The next chapter explores the ongoing
disorder and conflict in the region in the years leading to the war.

CHAPTER 4

Disorder, Ambition, and Disillusion

With all the pueblos quiet and secure in those days, he [Nuño de Guzmán] sent at night people on foot and on horseback to attack them. . . . They took the ones they wanted; they made them slaves and with the iron, which they said belonged to the king, they ordered them branded. And in this way they made so many [slaves] as to be without number, men and women, children of all ages, leaving husbands without wives and wives without husbands, children without parents and parents without children.[1]

—Written in exile by Tenamaztle, a lord of Nochistlan, in 1555

✢ IN THE 1530S NEW GALICIA ATTRACTED THE INTEREST NOT ONLY of Nuño de Guzmán but of other powerful figures in the history of early Mexico as well. Remote, poor, and engulfed in turmoil, the West nonetheless figured significantly in the ambitions and schemes of several of New Spain's most prominent men. Hernando Cortés tried to lay claim to the region by sponsoring the expedition of his kinsman Francisco Cortés in the 1520s. In the 1530s, after his return from Spain, he both pursued those claims in his lawsuit with Guzmán and used the West as a base for new explorations and expeditions. Countering Cortés's ambitions on the Pacific coast—and with Nuño de Guzmán out of the picture after

1536—the viceroy don Antonio de Mendoza and his protégé Francisco Vázquez de Coronado, together with Cortés's former second-in-command Pedro de Alvarado, began to plan a major expedition up the coast and into the far north to the so-called Tierra Nueva (later known as New Mexico). If by the late 1520s rumors of wealthy societies in the North already were circulating and possibly accounted in part for Guzmán's move into the West, the sudden appearance in 1536 in northern New Galicia of a strange party led by Alvar Núñez Cabeza de Vaca signaled the beginning of much more intense interest in the North and its potential.[2] Thus, not only did internal conflict, both among indigenous groups and between Spaniards and Indians, beset the region during the 1530s, but external events and ambitions played a major role in fomenting change and unrest as well.

The middle years of the decade of the 1530s marked both the greatest period of activity of the short-lived Guzmán governorship and its abrupt end. In 1533 Guzmán sent Diego de Guzmán with a party of men as far north as the Yaqui River in an attempt to expand the territory under his jurisdiction, and around the same time he himself accomplished the difficult, if ultimately futile, trek from New Galicia to Pánuco and back.[3] Under his authority, major campaigns of pacification and slave taking once again brought the violence of conquest. In the midst of this activity, however, Guzmán left New Galicia—permanently, as it turned out. In 1536 he went to the capital to pay his respects to the viceroy, later explaining that he had not been able to do so previously. Viceroy Mendoza invited him to lodge in his house, where Guzmán stayed until Licenciado Pérez de la Torre—who was to replace Guzmán as governor of New Galicia and conduct the residencia of his term in office—arrived. Guzmán had barely recovered from a fever when the viceroy and judges of the audiencia met with Pérez de la Torre and then informed Guzmán of his imminent imprisonment.[4]

What was the impact of Guzmán's departure from New Galicia? He was probably one of the least sympathetic characters among the prominent Spaniards who arrived in New Spain to deceive, persuade, fight, and pillage their way to wealth and fame.[5] Unlike Cortés he never married and had no children, perhaps because his career came to such an abrupt end.[6] His megalomania, callousness, and lack of the rhetorical skills that Cortés employed to such useful effect would seem to have made him an isolated, intimidating figure. Nor did he share Pedro de Alvarado's reputation as a daring warrior or enjoy the sterling connections of first treasurer Alonso de Estrada or the viceroy's protégé Francisco Vázquez de Coronado. Yet Guzmán had his good friends, attentive clients, and loyal supporters, some of whom were shocked and dismayed by his sudden fall from power. One of these was Alvaro de Bracamonte, who participated in the conquest of New Galicia when he was around twenty years of age, receiving horses and money from Guzmán to equip him for the campaign. Bracamonte stayed in the region after the conquest, becoming a powerful man in his own right, although he owed much to his patron, under whom he served as regidor and then alcalde ordinario of Compostela. Guzmán also appointed him captain of a slaving entrada in Mascota (in the jurisdiction of Compostela) "to pacify and punish the said rebellious and disobedient Indians, and . . . enslave the Indians who don't want to come to the obedience of the church and His Majesty, as they should do, and to serve their masters."[7]

In 1537 Bracamonte wrote a letter from the mines of Zacatlan to Guzmán in jail in Mexico City, full of indignation on Guzmán's behalf. It reads in part:

> I received your lordship's letter. You know how little I wanted to see it or know what was said in it because such was the anger and disturbance we all felt that it would be impossible to describe it. . . . It must be a great effort to suffer patiently such hard lashings where you show on the one hand your pure intention and on the other the generosity of your soul. . . . Your lordship can believe that there is such grief among everyone that they say with one voice that if they do this, the country will depopulate, and that they are ready to lose their heads if necessary for anything that might affect you. And they speak of nothing but Peru . . . and this is what is discussed at all times and hours of the day. And this not one but all in one voice say, that they want nothing more than that he who has been the companion and witness of their labors and with whom they have lived in need should live in prosperity. . . . You should be pleased that now that His Majesty has wanted to do this and take away your governorship, he cannot take away the great love that your sons and servants have for you.[8]

As seen in the previous chapter, some of Guzmán's closest associates indeed left New Galicia around the time that he did—in particular those who must have anticipated prosecution as a result of the residencia—but many others remained, apparently coming to terms with their outrage at Guzmán's removal from power. Among the latter group was Bracamonte himself, who subsequently formed a useful alliance with Francisco Vázquez de Coronado, with whom he shared encomiendas and mining interests. He became a substantial miner in Guachinango, where in 1550 he maintained "two mills, one for smelting and the other for grinding and washing [ore], . . . a large house in which he lives covered with straw plus thirteen houses in which he has his slaves and equipment and metals."9

What changed with Guzmán's departure? His elimination from the scene brought an end to some of the factionalism that fomented disorder and speeded the departure of would-be settlers in the first years after the conquest. Licenciado Pérez de la Torre felt confident that the end of Guzmán's governorship signaled the beginning of a new era of stability. When he wrote to the king from Guadalajara in late November 1537, he painted a cautiously hopeful picture of affairs in New Galicia, where he had arrived with his wife and six children six months previously. He reported that the turmoil occasioned by Guzmán's slaving campaigns was at an end, writing that "those pueblos that were depopulated in this province by the war and through having been made slaves are once again being populated, and their vecinos who had gone in revolt in the mountains come to them, although they come timidly and agitated, fearing that they will be made slaves." He also reported recent discoveries of rich gold and silver mines and an increasing number of Spaniards married to Castilian women—"the number of Spanish vecinos married to women from Castile has reached twenty, which is a good beginning and security for this country."10 He did recognize, however, how little progress in evangelization had occurred.

Barely a year later Licenciado Pérez de la Torre died of injuries incurred in a campaign to suppress one of the region's incessant conflicts with the local Indians. Although de la Torre had recommended appointing Cristóbal de Oñate to succeed him as governor, Viceroy Mendoza chose his own young retainer, Francisco Vázquez, a man with no prior experience in the West, for the position. In his late twenties at the time, Vázquez was close to Mendoza and traveled with him from Spain to Mexico in 1535. His father had been the *corregidor* (governor) of Granada in Spain, the city with which Mendoza's family was associated.11 Once in New Spain, Francisco Vázquez further strengthened his ties to some of its most influential families by marrying doña Beatriz de Estrada, the daughter of the former royal treasurer Alonso de Estrada.12

The first letter that Vázquez wrote to the king, in mid-December 1538, differed considerably in its assessment of the state of affairs in the West from the optimistic report that his predecessor penned just slightly over a year earlier.[13] Having reached Guadalajara, he planned to move on to Compostela. Before doing so, however, he met with the representative (*procurador*) of the town of San Miguel (in Culiacan), who told him that the town's vecinos "were coming [here] and leaving it unpopulated and that the entire province was at the point of being lost." He begged the new governor to travel north to resolve the situation, arguing that if he did not do so within forty days, all the vecinos would leave because of their poverty and the harm that a nearby Indian leader was inflicting upon them. Vázquez wrote of the situation in New Galicia more generally that "most of the Indians are at war, some of whom had not been conquered," as well as others who had been conquered but subsequently revolted. The settlers "do little to instruct the Indians in matters of the faith but much to benefit from them more than they should."[14] He wrote that he planned to travel to Culiacan to bring the rebellion to an end by demonstrating fairness and good treatment, reinforced by the presence of the clergy to be sent for the purpose by the viceroy. In July 1539 he reported to the Crown his success in restoring peace to Culiacan, although he admitted that some pueblos had not yet rendered obedience.

The causes of unrest and violence in the region were multiple: campaigns of slave raiding on a large scale under Guzmán's authority, Indians who targeted vulnerable Spanish settlers or fled to escape demands for service and tribute, the continuation of what probably were long-standing conflicts among indigenous communities, the ambitions of powerful men like Cortés and Mendoza, and finally the departure of the new governor for the Tierra Nueva. This chapter examines the conflicts and confrontations of the 1530s.

Conquest and Enslavement

The enslavement of the indigenous inhabitants of Spanish America followed an erratic course. From the time of Columbus's first voyages and the earliest years of Spanish activity in the Caribbean, the Crown repeatedly modified or reversed its position regarding whether and under what circumstances the practice would be permitted.[15] During his governorship, Guzmán justified slave taking in Pánuco as a means of developing an

otherwise resource-poor region, promoting the export of slaves to the
Caribbean Islands in exchange for the livestock that the latter could supply.
Although the slaves exported from Pánuco numbered in the thousands and
this activity contributed to Guzmán's negative reputation, his involvement
in slave taking probably did not differ much from that of many other men
active in the early Caribbean and Mexico. At least technically, Guzmán
operated within the bounds of the fluctuating legal framework.[16]

In February 1534 the Crown rescinded a decree of 1530 prohibiting
the capture and enslavement of Indians, and Guzmán took advantage of
this reversal. Thus when he initiated slaving campaigns in New Galicia in
the mid-1530s, Guzmán acted according to the law at the time, although
questions arose during the residencia regarding the specifics of how the
campaigns were conducted and who was enslaved.[17] Certainly in authoriz-
ing the campaigns Guzmán responded to many settlers' demands. A letter
of February 19, 1533, from the town council of Compostela explained the
difficulties posed by the prohibition on taking slaves, since the settlers
were all very much in debt. With slaves "we could improve ourselves and
look for mines of gold and silver. . . . There are in these lands many Indians who are like animals . . . who have no other business than to steal and
kill the Indians who serve [us] and take them away to sacrifice and eat, and
if there exists a way to separate them from that and bring them to know
God . . . there is no other way than to make them slaves"—an interesting
take on evangelization.[18] A number of men insisted that enslaving and
exporting Indians who refused to render obedience to their new masters
was the only effective way of convincing others to serve.[19] As early as June
1532 Guzmán himself wrote to the Crown, pleading for authorization to
take slaves, arguing that the settlers lacked the wherewithal to acquire the
barest necessities.[20]

The slave-taking campaigns began in 1535 and focused in particular
on the valley of Banderas and the area north of Guadalajara.[21] Significantly, both areas would become centers of hostilities during the Mixton
War—indeed the latter area would be the cradle of the rebellion. Francisco
Cortés and his men passed through the valley of Banderas, close to the
Pacific coast, when they returned to Colima, and although Guzmán went
through the area in the early 1530s, several years later it remained largely
unconquered.[22] Reports of violent deaths of Spaniards there provided
the pretext for launching a campaign of pacification and slave taking in
which a number of prominent Spaniards, Guzmán not least among them,

took part.[23] Miguel de Ibarra testified in Guzmán's residencia that around Guadalajara they targeted Indian communities that ostensibly fought with and killed Spaniards and that they took five or six hundred slaves, including women and children under the age of fourteen. The campaigns lasted until early 1537; they had ended by the time Licenciado Pérez de la Torre arrived in New Galicia.[24]

Retaliation and pacification provided justification for the campaigns, but the expectation of profits furnished much of the motivation. Francisco Barrón explained that they took many slaves in New Galicia "because they [i.e., the Indians] didn't want to serve and killed some Spaniards. . . . Nuño de Guzmán ordered that slaves be taken and gave permission for it because the Spaniards who were in the said jurisdiction wanted to leave and because they had nothing to eat and were very much in debt. He [Barrón] knows that because he saw many [Indians] branded."[25] Indeed, according to Juan de Sosa, many people already had left the province: "The entire town of Chiametla mutinied together and half the vecinos left Culiacan with their banners flying, and this witness asked some of them why they had come and mutinied and they told him that [it was] because they were poor and in debt in His Majesty's service and for seven years there had been no progress." Sosa affirmed that only by taking slaves would "the country be certain of not depopulating."[26]

The entradas began in the valley of Banderas where, according to his own testimony, Guzmán participated personally. The residencia of his term as governor includes two accounts of the slaves captured. The first lists dates, numbers of slaves, where they were taken, and usually the name of the leader of a particular campaign. Prominent among the raiding parties' captains were Alvaro de Bracamonte, Alonso de Castañeda, Luis Salido, Juan de Villalba, Miguel de Ibarra, and Francisco de Godoy, most of them Guzmán's friends and captains. The second list appears in the residencia's audit of tax payments to the royal treasury, which includes information on the sale of slaves that were set aside to pay the *quinto*, or royal tax of one-fifth. This list also usually indicates who purchased the slaves at auction.[27] The two lists, then, reflect the official accounting of slaves that were registered and branded and for which the standard royal tax was paid.

The second list, prepared for the treasury, appears to be the more complete of the two and yields a total of 4,667 slaves taken in less than two years.[28] The largest numbers of slaves came from the valley of

Banderas (over 1,000), the Valle de Mascota (over 700), and the area north of Guadalajara (nearly 1,600). In July 1536 in the northern province of Culiacan, 845 slaves were taken. In addition Spaniards took slaves near Compostela in places like Chacala and Zacualpa. Spaniards captured the largest numbers of slaves during the first round of campaigns in the spring and summer of 1535. After setting aside slaves for the royal fifth, Spaniards who participated in the entradas divided the proceeds among themselves according to rank. Several witnesses testified that Guzmán claimed one-seventh of the captives, whether he participated in a raid in person or not. Usually the captains received twice the share of the other horsemen and the latter twice the share of the men on foot, the standard pattern for the distribution of profits gained in Spanish entradas.

Quite possibly the total number of slaves calculated from the treasury list is low. In the previous chapter we saw that Diego Segler testified that Juan de Oñate forced him to hand over the official branding iron so that Oñate could conduct unauthorized slaving raids. In New Galicia's more remote locales some slave-hunting activity could have taken place without official authority or notification. Illegal slave taking, however, probably involved only small numbers; it would have been difficult to conceal the organization of large raiding parties and the relocation or sale of significant numbers of unbranded captives.

Of the experience of the captives we know little. Given the nature of the campaigns and their profit orientation, it seems unlikely that the people captured actually were responsible for the reported deaths of Spaniards that ostensibly justified the raids. Testimony from many witnesses in the Guzmán residencia makes it clear that captives included men, women, and children of all ages; the words *"chicos y grandes"* (young and old) often appear in conjunction with *"esclavos"* (slaves). In one case 61 slaves intended for sale to pay the quinto on a group of 305 slaves captured in a raid led by Miguel de Ibarra were described as "men and women, children and adults, all of them sick. . . . They fell sick of a certain illness on the way coming from La Barranca and Tepeque where they were taken."[29] Presumably the entire group of more than 300 slaves was ill, not just those sold on behalf of the treasury. Not surprisingly those slaves sold for a very low price, less than two pesos each. Prices for slaves sold at auction in any case at this time all were low, normally falling somewhere between four and five and a half pesos each. There is no way to tell from this source if prices differed for men, women, and children.

We do not know where most slaves ended up or how they were trans-ported (probably on foot and in chains) and sold. Certainly there were slaves from "Jalisco"—in this context meaning the West in general—in central Mexico before the Mixton War, so probably the Mexico City area was the destination of at least some.[30] A number of the purchasers of slaves sold for the benefit of the royal treasury were men who were involved in mining, such as Melchor Díaz, Juan de Mondragón, and Luis Salido.[31] Although those purchasing slaves at auction could have resold them outside New Galicia, probably Spaniards kept at least some of these slaves to work in the mines, alongside the slaves and naborías that Spaniards obtained from the local rulers under their authority, as discussed in the previous chapter. Although it might seem impractical to allow potentially rebellious slaves to remain in the region, the ethnic diversity of New Galicia meant that captives who were forced into slavery could find themselves living in the lands of their enemies and therefore tied to their masters, even though they remained geographically fairly close to their home communities.

Rebellion and Reprisal

Guzmán's campaigns of enslavement in part represented a much-demanded response to attacks on the persons and property of Spanish settlers. Juan de Zaldívar claimed that soon after he arrived in New Galicia in 1533 the "Indians of Mescala killed their master who held them in encomienda and another Spaniard and did other damage for which reason captain Juan de Oñate [his uncle] . . . left this city [Guadalajara] taking with him the said Juan de Zaldívar and other soldiers to punish the guilty and to pacify the pueblos of Juchipila and Apozol and Mezquituta that were in revolt."[32] Punishment and pacification were the hallmarks of Spanish policy toward people who would not acquiesce to the new regime and whom they viewed as savages capable of the most reprehensible behavior. A state-ment included in Guzmán's appeal against the charges in the residencia exemplifies how many Spaniards felt about the people among whom they lived: "All the Indians in the jurisdiction of the city of Compostela and Purificación and the town of Espiritu Santo with all the rest are people without reason and they eat one another and sacrifice; they are great thieves and maintain neither faith nor friendship with one another, and their glory is to kill each other and take the heads away in triumph to their houses."[33] Juan Gallego, veteran of the conquest of Tenochtitlan and New

Galicia and later of the Vázquez de Coronado entrada, stated that "this witness has a pueblo that is in constant war with others, and those whom they can eat, they eat and kill [*sic*]."[34]

In late January 1533 members of the town council of Compostela convened to take testimony regarding recent attacks on Spaniards and Indians and to present a petition that they be allowed to take slaves to punish those who were responsible. The council's petition reads in part:

> We say that . . . many pueblos . . . have risen up and rebelled, having given obedience to His Majesty, and in one pueblo . . . they have killed eight Spaniards, and in another three, and near Aldeanueva they killed sixteen. And now a few days ago two leagues from here they killed another, and also many natives who serve the Spaniards, for no other reason than that they serve the Christians, and every day they kill naborías and Indians who serve. . . . And we expect that one day they will come to an agreement with those who serve and place us at much risk . . . by which the vecinos of this jurisdiction face much danger . . . the natives seeing that we don't punish or enslave them, which is the thing that they most fear.[35]

They went on to say that Indians called Chichimecs who lived close to the city came at night to assault the residents of Tepic, and "they go out to attack the Indians who go for firewood and fodder and other things necessary for the vecinos" and attack the farms where pigs are kept.[36] Pedro de Ulloa testified that while in his lodgings (presumably in Compostela) he heard "Chichimecas" attacking the residents of Tepic. He got on his horse to go help but could not overtake the attackers "because the land is so rough and he saw them fleeing with their shields. . . . And he knows that they have their homes in caves and in a place where they cannot be found."[37] Two of the indigenous witnesses from Tepic testified in the deposition regarding attacks but offered little detail.

The charges and testimony reflected the Spaniards' uncertainty regarding the causes of the violence. Were the dead men victims of rebellious pueblos, Chichimecs, or both? Were the Indians of the pueblos as much victims as the Spaniards were, or were they in collusion with the perpetrators? One episode probably hinged at least in part on long-standing patterns of local raiding, killing, and taking captives. Francisco de Villegas sent his African slave (or servant) Pedro to cut firewood in Zapocingo and asked Juan Navarro if he could provide a couple of Indians to help. Navarro testified that he sent a naguatato named Jacobo who was a señor (local lord) and some other people with Pedro. The men arrived in Zapocingo, where they spent the night. Navarro later heard that at four o'clock in the morning "the Chichimecs attacked them [Pedro and his party] at the pueblo of Zapocingo and killed them and took some of them alive to sacrifice . . . and to make them slaves." When he heard of this, Navarro took his horse and with Alvaro de Ribera rode to the pueblo, where a scene of carnage greeted them. Navarro stated that "he heard from the wife of the señor that they [the Chichimecs] killed the black man and the señor himself. They had found them dead and they asked permission from this witness to bury her husband." Alvaro de Ribera said that an Indian woman who suffered injuries from blows during the attack said to him, "'Look, señor, what the Chichimecs do to us because we serve the Christians,' and she told him that she had no father or mother or husband or siblings because the Chichimecs had killed all of them."[38]

In a separate incident three Spaniards were traveling through Xalacingo on their way from Compostela to Aldeanueva, the settlement where they lived, when the Indians of the pueblo suddenly attacked and killed them, "shooting arrows and they did cruel things to them and ate them and took their things." Pedro de Ulloa said that when he went to the pueblo he saw the bones of Spaniards and "found two heads broken into pieces . . . and later he saw another on top of a tree and this witness helped to bury them and he heard an Indian say . . . that the naguatato of the pueblo had put the head on top of the tree."[39]

Encomenderos commonly reported that the Indians of the pueblos under their authority complained of attacks. Iñigo Ortiz de Zúñiga said that many people came to him while he was serving as a magistrate in Purificación, begging for help because the "indios de guerra" stole from them and took their women and children to be sacrificed. He and another Spaniard captured thirty-two warriors thought to be responsible for the assaults and recovered the captive women and children, along with some clothing. He apparently executed the perpetrators.[40] Without knowing what prior circumstances led to the attacks or what relationship existed between the so-called Chichimecs and the residents of the pueblos, these incidents are difficult to interpret. While the Spaniards' presence in a particular place probably could trigger an attack, it is impossible to know if the residents' association with Spaniards constituted a principal reason for the violence or exacerbated longer-term enmities and hostility.[41] Although the Spanish presence in New Galicia clearly changed patterns of indigenous conflict and violence—whether in kind, scale, or frequency is difficult to say—there is little question that conflict between different ethnic groups and communities predated the conquest and continued long after it. The Spaniards might have added another layer of complexity to these conflicts, but events that took place well after the Mixton War suggest that indigenous objectives and enmities continued to lie at the core of at least some of the clashes.

An episode around 1537 involving the leaders of Xalisco and the "Chichimecs" of Acuitlapilco—a community east of Tepic and south of the Rio Grande that at some point was assigned in encomienda to Cristóbal de Oñate's mayordomo Domingo de Arteaga—suggests the complexity of relationships both among indigenous groups and between them and the Spaniards. Arteaga ordered the cacique don Cristóbal and Xalisco's other nobles to summon twenty people from Acuitlapilco in order to punish them for ostensible attacks. The men of Xalisco tried to refuse, arguing that the residents of Acuitlapilco were not necessarily their enemies. They were, indeed, Tecuales like the people of Xalisco, although they lived in the mountains north of the valley of Xalisco. Arteaga angrily brushed aside the protests of the lords and forced them to send some gold jewelry and salt to Acuitlapilco to convince the people of their friendly intentions. When eighteen men from Acuitlapilco finally arrived, Oñate had them seized and bound. Having done so the Spaniards told don Cristóbal "that they were going to pay me, that they would give me mantas and gold and they were going to give me a horse." The Spaniards imprisoned the Chichimecs, and some died of hunger. Then they ordered the pueblo to make ropes to hang the others.[42] Thus, the Spaniards directly involved and implicated the pueblo's lords, especially don Cristóbal, in an act of treachery against a community with whom they apparently had no real enmity and, indeed, probably maintained friendly ties. In the end, don Cristóbal did not receive the payoff he had been promised, nor did the rulers of Xalisco recover the items they were forced to provide to lure the people from Acuitlapilco. The possible existence of mining sites in this area might have motivated this act of reprisal against Acuitlapilco, which clearly was meant to intimidate the people and allow the Spaniards to extend their control over that area.[43]

This episode probably was identical to one that Licenciado Pérez de la Torre reported; many of the details and the timing coincide. The trial he described involved "*indios chichimecas*" accused of assaulting people on the royal road between Guadalajara and Compostela. He alleged that the seventeen prisoners "on different days had killed many Indians on the said road, shooting them with arrows and cutting off their heads . . . and many other cruelties." The judge condemned eleven to be taken from Compostela to the scene of their ostensible crime, where they would be hanged and shot with arrows. As they were standing by the gallows, the parish priest of Compostela spoke to them through interpreters regarding the Christian faith and asked if they wanted to become Christians. They responded that they did. The priest baptized them "with a jar of water and gave them Christian names with their godparents [present] and then at that very moment they were hanged." The judge then ordered that they be shot posthumously with arrows "to instill more fear in the others."[44] Two other prisoners died in the stocks in Compostela, and another four were judged to be minors under the age of eighteen and therefore not subject to capital punishment. Staging the executions on the royal road and the dual method by which they were carried out attest to the Spanish penchant for exemplary punishment; were the baptisms intended to demonstrate Christian mercy?[45] Given the disorder that prevailed through the late 1530s, neither campaigns of enslavement nor exemplary punishment appear to have accomplished their intended goals of intimidation and pacification.

The ambitions of Spaniards who employed brute force to impose their will over a mostly lawless countryside could wreak havoc and involve members of different indigenous communities. Antonio de Aguayo, a vecino of Purificación, was responsible for one of the most flagrant examples of the kind of unrestrained violence such men employed. A description of a series of episodes involving Aguayo that spanned a number of years appears in the visita (inspection) conducted by an oidor of the audiencia of New Galicia, established in 1548. The oidor, Lic. Lorenzo Lebrón de Quiñones, initiated his tour of inspection in 1551 and concluded it in early 1554. An earlier letter of 1544, however, also referred to violent acts by Antonio de Aguayo and Benito de Herrera, who were charged with burning a pueblo "two or three times," beating a corregidor (district administrator) with his staff of office, and illegally bestowing "*varas de justicia*" (staffs of justice) on some of "his" (Aguayo's) Indians who carried out the burning of the pueblo.[46]

Although the exact dates are uncertain, the events that Lebrón described clearly took place over a period of some years, most likely going back to the late 1530s.

The oidor Lebrón attempted to implement a judgment removing from Antonio de Aguayo's control a settlement that he had appropriated illegally by robbing and mistreating the Indians and forcing them off their lands. Aguayo treated the people who stayed like slaves. Lebrón made an arduous journey on foot to find the people who had fled their homes. "Ascertaining that the cruelties with which the said Aguayo had used them at the least merited the death penalty and loss of all his goods," he instructed the people to go back to the lands where they had lived "until perhaps fourteen years before," when Aguayo forced them out.[47]

Having returned with their few belongings, the residents began to rebuild their pueblo at the oidor's orders. Soon Aguayo arrived, "with little fear of God and of royal justice" but with an entourage of "Indians armed with bows and arrows and some mestizos and friends of his." He burned the pueblo and church, beating the principales and alguaciles (constables) whom Lebrón had left in charge. When they complained to Lebrón, he gave them a writ of protection and told them to rebuild again. Aguayo returned, beat the unfortunate alguacil who had obtained the order of protection so brutally that he died within three days, and again burned the pueblo, threatening to burn alive anyone who returned there.[48]

Informed of these events, Lebrón sent the corregidor of the nearest pueblo that had one, Autlan, with a notary and interpreter to take a deposition and arrest the guilty parties. An armed and enraged Aguayo, however, confronted the corregidor and took his staff of justice, breaking it into pieces and "saying very ugly words against me and against the corregidor." The latter, seeing that Aguayo probably would kill him if he tried to arrest him, left for Autlan but subsequently returned to the pueblo. There he found that the Indians once more had begun to build a church of straw as well as some houses. When the corregidor again attempted to take the deposition, Aguayo arrived with "three or four horsemen with their lances in their hands and many Indians with bows and arrows and others with staffs of alcaldes and alguaciles that Aguayo had given them." Once again he seized the corregidor's staff and beat him with it, then set fire to the church and other buildings and to all the straw and wood that had been collected for rebuilding and beat the local residents. Lebrón again initiated proceedings to arrest Aguayo and his partners in crime, whom he charged with other deaths as well, including that of at least one Spaniard. Having sentenced him to hang and forfeit all his goods, however, Lebrón to his dismay found that Aguayo had made a successful appeal to the audiencia. The result was that not only did Aguayo possibly go unpunished but he also boasted publicly that he was free and clear (*"libre y quito"*) of any charges. The discouraged oidor ended his report by saying that he had spent two and a half years conducting the visita and wished only to return home to rest.[49]

The name and exact location of the settlement that Aguayo repeatedly tried to take by force do not appear in the oidor's report. Aguayo was a conquistador and longtime vecino of Purificación, most likely a participant in the slaving campaigns of the mid-1530s. The lands that he appropriated were presumably not far from Autlan, which was south of Senticpac near the Río Grande. Clearly, he recognized no authority but the effective exercise of force—or that of the audiencia, if it acted in accord with his own objectives. In this episode, as in the one involving the "Chichimecs" of Acuitlapilco, Spaniards fomented violence and destruction in the countryside, embroiling Indians under their authority in acts of intimidation and revenge. In both cases their goal was to bolster their ability to impose their will over resources and people through the use of force. Although Lebrón's report makes it difficult to pinpoint dates, he probably was referring to events that occurred both before and after, or even during, the Mixton War.

These episodes suggest not only that Spaniards participated directly in the perpetuation or even instigation of violence that pitted members of one indigenous community against those of another but that their interests primarily were individual and private, focused mainly on their own enterprises and encomiendas. Larger issues of law, order, or justice mattered little to men such as Aguayo or even Cristóbal de Oñate, unless these abstractions coincided with their own objectives. Although Aguayo served on the town council of Purificación, and Oñate held office continuously from the time of the conquest, when it came to pursuing their own interests they readily flouted the law and ignored (or even defied) its representatives. If nearly every able-bodied man in the region would join in suppressing the widespread uprising of the early 1540s, their participation probably owed much less to a sense of collective responsibility than to the common recognition of the serious threat to their lives and livelihood the war posed. Spaniards in New Galicia, in other words, concerned themselves with indigenous violence and conflict when it threatened them or their property and could not be turned to their favor.

After assuming the governorship of New Galicia, Francisco Vázquez waged his first campaign in Culiacan—significantly, the area that he subsequently used as the staging ground for his entrada into the Tierra Nueva. In a letter of July 1539, by which time he had returned to Compostela, he wrote that most of the people of Culiacan rose in rebellion in concert with a cacique named Ayapin, whom they took for "their leader [*caudillo*] and captain of the uprising." He went to Culiacan at the urgent request of the vecinos of San Miguel, who were ready to abandon the town because of the danger that Ayapin posed and their inability to get the Indians to work for them. Supported by funds from the viceregal treasury, the governor was able to root out the rebellion, and "seeing that their revolt had been more from ignorance and mistreatment than malice, in the name of Your Majesty I promised them pardon from what had passed if they would come to the service" of the Crown. He claimed that there were no reprisals and that most of the people submitted peacefully. Ayapin retreated into the mountains, but the governor pursued, arrested, tried, and executed him. He explained that the rebels had been in the mountains but that they had begun to return to their old homes and lands, "although many of the warlike people that province used to have are missing because of the warriors and butcheries that there have been there."[50]

Vázquez did not elaborate on the kind or degree of force he brought to bear in the campaign, but the last statement suggests that he put the rebels down with a heavy hand. The constant turmoil in Culiacan in the 1530s should have settled the question about the efficacy of slave raiding in suppressing indigenous unrest; extensive slave raiding in the area had only exacerbated an already untenable situation. In this campaign, however, much more was at stake than salvaging a settlement that was in trouble from its inception. Both the urgency of Vázquez's response and the viceregal backing he received demonstrated that the governor and Mendoza were thinking in terms of the expedition they planned to the North, in which a pacified Culiacan and San Miguel would play a vital role.

News of the North: The Cabeza de Vaca Party

The travels and sojourn along the Gulf coast and in the interior of Texas of Alvar Núñez Cabeza de Vaca, his companions Andrés Dorantes and

Alonso del Castillo, and the African slave Estebanico constitute a fascinating tale of survival and adaptation, told most famously by Cabeza de Vaca himself in his account of their experiences with the varied indigenous groups among whom they lived.[51] Although the story merits the attention it has received, both in the narrator's own time and since, it is of interest here chiefly for two reasons. First, when Cabeza de Vaca and his companions, accompanied by a fluctuating entourage of Indians, made their way west and ultimately south into New Galicia, the first Spaniards they encountered after an eight-year absence from Spanish-occupied lands were the settlers and slavers of Culiacan. Second, the reports of Cabeza de Vaca and his companions stimulated the interest of Viceroy Mendoza and others in what were thought—or hoped—to be wealthy societies far to the north.

The final phase of the journey of Cabeza de Vaca and his companions took them into present-day Chihuahua and Sonora and then down through the mountain ranges and river valleys to the coast and the Río Petatlan in modern Sinaloa, into territory claimed by Spaniards as part of New Galicia.[52] This route brought them to densely settled lands on the western side of the Sierra Madre, where people lived in permanent settlements in houses built of adobe or reeds; produced abundant crops of maize, squash, and beans; and wore cotton clothing.[53] There Cabeza de Vaca and his companions found ample evidence of long-distance trade networks that connected Sinaloa with Sonora and the Pueblo country to the north as well as with the coast and areas south and east. Their reports of trade with the North fueled hopes of finding wealthy peoples in that direction. Cabeza de Vaca saw the cluster of settlements on the plain that they called Corazones as the "gateway to the northern provinces of the South Sea."[54] There was extensive game in the area, and many people lived on the floodplains of the rivers, especially in the lower reaches where the tidal surge from the sea allowed them to take advantage of ample resources for fishing.

As the survivors of Pánfilo de Narváez's expedition to Florida continued their journey south and west, they began to hear reports that other Europeans had been in the area. They saw objects of European manufacture that possibly originated with the expedition of Diego Hurtado de Mendoza to the Gulf of California in 1532, although they could just as well have been left behind by Diego de Guzmán's expedition of 1533 that reached the Yaqui River.[55] The travelers also began to hear

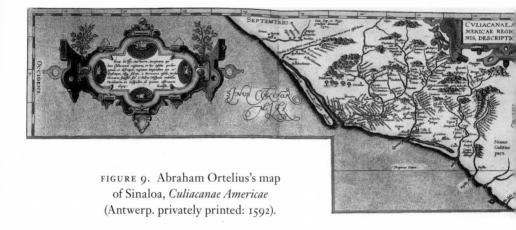

FIGURE 9. Abraham Ortelius's map
of Sinaloa, *Culiacanae Americae*
(Antwerp. privately printed: 1592).

stories of Spaniards who burned settlements and captured men, women, and children. In Cabeza de Vaca's words,

> We traveled through much land and we found all of it deserted, because the inhabitants of it went fleeing through the sierras without daring to keep houses or work the land for fear of the Christians. It was a thing that gave us great sorrow, seeing the land very fertile and very beautiful and very full of waterways and rivers, and seeing the places deserted and burned and the people so emaciated and sick, all of them having fled and in hiding.[56]

By the time they reached the area of the Río Petatlan and encountered Spanish slavers in the spring of 1536, they had passed through more fertile and well-watered agricultural lands but nonetheless suffered from lack of food because the former inhabitants fled in fear of the Spaniards. Guides led Cabeza de Vaca and his companions to a retreat in the highlands where the people had stored surpluses of maize. From there they received word of Spanish slavers who were moving Indians in chains.[57]

Accompanied by Estebanico, Cabeza de Vaca set out to find the Spaniards and finally encountered a party of men who took him to Diego de Alcaraz, who, ironically, asked Cabeza de Vaca for help in finding food and slaves. Cabeza de Vaca sent Estebanico and some Indians to bring their other companions to join them. They arrived accompanied by some six hundred people, presumably part of Cabeza de Vaca's growing entourage, many of whom had taken refuge in the highlands where the survivors found stores of maize. Some of these people came from as far north as Corazones. Others arrived thereafter, bringing maize. In return for this generosity, according to Cabeza de Vaca, Alcaraz pressured him unsuccessfully to allow them to take the Indians who were now gathered there as slaves.[58] This encounter, then, dramatically pitted Spaniards who had learned to live among a range of peoples and who advocated a peaceful approach to conversion and the incorporation of indigenous groups into Spanish society against other Spaniards who made their living exploiting and capturing Indians, causing them to flee their homes in fear for their safety and their lives.

Finally having reached the abundant valley of Culiacan, with its substantial markets, fruit trees, and great fisheries, Cabeza de Vaca and his companions were taken to meet Melchor Díaz, the alcalde mayor of Culiacan, near the main Spanish town of the region, San Miguel, located some distance south of the Culiacan Valley on the Río Cihuatlan (today the San Lorenzo). According to Cabeza de Vaca, when they met Melchor Díaz,

> He wept a great deal with us, praising God our Lord for having shown so much mercy to us. And he spoke to us and treated us very well. And on behalf of the governor, Nuño de Guzmán, as well as his own, he offered us everything that he had and could. And he showed much sorrow at the bad reception and treatment we had received from Alcaraz and the others.[59]

The settlement where they met Melchor Díaz lay in a populated valley. Before going on to the town of San Miguel itself, however, Cabeza de Vaca and his companions helped to resettle some of the uprooted people who had fled. Eventually several Indian lords came from the highlands and agreed to resettle peacefully, and Díaz vowed to put an end to all slave raiding in the province.[60] According to Cabeza de Vaca the repopulation of the area was well under way by the time they left. The campaign that Francisco Vázquez de Coronado waged there three years later, however, suggests that the reconciliation between Spanish settlers and the people of Culiacan did not last long.

Cabeza de Vaca and his party stayed a fortnight in San Miguel, leaving in mid-May to travel south to Compostela through territory that was in a virtual state of war. They began the dangerous journey accompanied first by an armed escort of twenty horsemen and later by a group of six Spaniards who were moving five hundred Indian slaves. Some time in early June, Nuño de Guzmán received them hospitably in Compostela, where they remained another ten or twelve days before departing for Mexico City to meet with the viceroy. Mendoza was impressed by the stories that the survivors told and interested in pursuing further discoveries, but he had to contend with another rival who had his own claims to explore and conquer the North. This was none other than the famous conqueror of Mexico himself, Hernando Cortés.

Cortés and the South Sea

Hernando Cortés's victory at Tenochtitlan, which signaled the fall of the largest indigenous state in Mesoamerica, made him the most powerful man in the newly established kingdom of New Spain. In recognition of his daring achievement in bringing the Aztec Empire under the authority of the Spanish Crown, the emperor Charles V granted him a noble title and huge estates and encomiendas in central and southern Mexico. Not surprisingly Cortés soon faced challenges both to his command of resources and to his political authority. In the latter respect especially he experienced a series of frustrations and disappointments, as little by little the Spanish Crown expanded its presence and interest in New Spain by first sending treasury officials, then establishing the first audiencia with Nuño de Guzmán as president, and finally appointing don Antonio de Mendoza as viceroy, an office to which Cortés himself aspired.

Neither Cortés's mixed fortunes nor the Crown's response to the conquest of Mexico and its aftermath were exceptional in early Spanish America. The deadly conflicts among Spaniards that followed the conquest of Peru resulted in the death of Francisco Pizarro in 1541, less than a decade after the execution of Inca emperor Atahualpa. Pizarro's half-brother Gonzalo led an ultimately futile rebellion against the Crown that ended with his own execution several years later. In contrast to the Pizarros in Peru, however, Cortés remained a powerful force in New Spain for nearly two decades after the conquest. The resilience and tenacity that had helped to ensure his success in central Mexico did not abandon him, even in the face of multiple challenges from new contenders for power and authority. While Guzmán and then Mendoza and Vázquez were pursuing their ambitions in western and northwestern New Spain, Cortés continued to press and expand his claims to New Spain's Pacific coast and points north and west at considerable cost in resources and people.

Cortés's interest in Colima and the area north of it—which Guzmán would dispute—formed the basis for his plans to explore the South Sea. In the early 1520s Cortés began to establish shipyards on the Pacific coast at Zacatula and Tehuantepec. In 1526 Charles V ordered Cortés to send ships to the Molucca Islands in the Pacific.[61] Having gone to Spain in 1528, late in 1529 Cortés—almost simultaneously with the inception of Guzmán's campaign in the West—obtained from the Crown the *capitulaciones* (agreement, contract) for the discovery and exploration of the South Sea. He returned to Mexico in mid-1530 and had new ships built in Tehuantepec for an expedition up the Pacific coast. They left Acapulco at the end of June 1532 under the command of Diego Hurtado de Mendoza, whose ship apparently was lost somewhere near Sinaloa. The other ship, under the command of Juan de Mazuela, turned back and landed at the Bahía de Banderas, where all the men were thought to have perished at the hands of the local Indians.[62]

Although Guzmán complained that Cortés was trespassing in his jurisdiction in New Galicia, Cortés went to Tehuantepec (where he held encomiendas) in late 1532 and spent a year there supervising the construction of new ships. At the end of October 1533 a second expedition departed, this time from Santiago in Colima. Hernando de Grijalva commanded a ship that sailed west to find a group of islands off the modern state of Colima. Diego Becerra sailed north where the men mutinied under the leadership of the pilot, Fortún Jiménez, who killed Becerra. The ship apparently reached the southern tip of the peninsula later known as Baja California. When the ship returned to New Galicia, Guzmán had it confiscated and imprisoned the survivors. The following year the Crown directed Guzmán to return Cortés's ship and men to him and reminded him that he had no authorization to explore the South Sea.

Cortés himself participated in a third expedition, lasting from April 1535 to April of the following year. The people he recruited crossed New Galicia to meet the three ships he had built and provisioned at Chiametla on the coast (recall that Cristóbal de Oñate ordered the people of Xalisco to provide them with supplies). Guzmán attempted to stop the expeditionary force at Ixtlan but then desisted. A month after departing Chiametla they reached the Bay of Santa Cruz at La Paz (Baja California), where Cortés took possession of the land. He then sent two of the ships

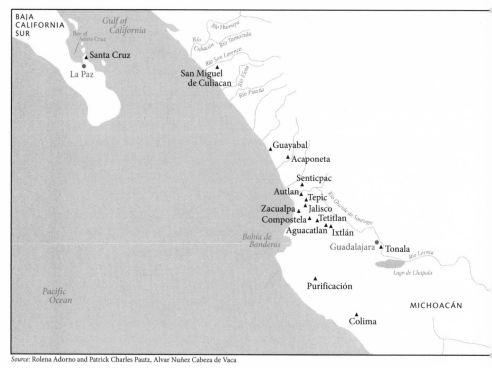

Source: Rolena Adorno and Patrick Charles Pautz, Alvar Nuñez Cabeza de Vaca

MAP 4. New Galicia and Baja California

back to New Galicia to pick up the remaining members of the expedition. One ship went aground on the coast and from there the settlers who had been aboard made their way back to Mexico City. Another ship went to Guayabal in Sinaloa, while Cortés himself returned in the third to San Miguel and then from there went back to the Bay of Santa Cruz. The enterprise attracted several hundred people, including women and numerous African slaves, but short supplies and hostile Indians meant that by November 1535 some seventy of the settlers had died. Cortés left Francisco de Ulloa in charge of a much-reduced colony and returned to the mainland, promising to return with supplies. At Mendoza's insistence the colony subsequently was abandoned.[63]

In 1539 Cortés mounted his last marine expedition to the north, sending Francisco de Ulloa with three ships that sailed up the west coast of New Galicia. They succeeded in mapping both sides of the Gulf of

California (today also called the Sea of Cortés) and in demonstrating that Baja California was a peninsula, not an island. By this time, however, Mendoza was determined to block further explorations under Cortés's sponsorship, forbidding anyone to sail from the ports on the Pacific without his permission. Although Cortés finally obtained a judgment from the Council of the Indies, ordering Mendoza not to interfere with his right to explore the northern coast, his return to Spain at the beginning of 1540 put an end to his South Sea ventures. With Guzmán also in exile in Spain by this time, Mendoza by default had won the contest to explore the northern lands. Sailing under his authority in June 1542, Juan Rodríguez Cabrillo reached the bay of San Diego in upper California and then Santa Catalina Island, where Cabrillo died of an infection from an injury. His chief pilot, Bartolomé Ferrer, sailed as far north as the modern boundary between California and Oregon before returning to Puerto de la Navidad in April 1543.[64] Already by the end of the 1530s, then, with both Guzmán and Cortés in Spain and his protégé Vázquez installed as governor of New Galicia, Mendoza had established himself as not only the ultimate arbiter of affairs in the West but by far the most powerful political figure in New Spain. This situation, of course, was precisely what the Spanish Crown hoped to accomplish in creating the office of the viceroy to supersede and mediate the claims of all other contenders to authority.

Meanwhile the ever-restless Pedro de Alvarado, Cortés's close associate in the conquest of central Mexico who went on to become conqueror of Guatemala and an extremely wealthy man, also became interested in Pacific explorations. He built a fleet in Guatemala, hoping like Cortés to reach the Spice Islands in the Pacific; but hearing of the vast wealth of the Inca Empire he decided to sail south to Peru in 1534. He failed to get past Quito and suffered extensive losses, then sold his fleet and returned to Guatemala, where he built another one and obtained authorization to explore the South Sea. At the end of November 1540 he effected an agreement of partnership with Viceroy Mendoza to pursue further explorations in the north and to help supply the expedition to Cibola. Alvarado then made his way north from Guatemala with a dozen ships and a thousand people. Thus it came about that he and his ships arrived at the Puerto de la Navidad on Christmas Day of 1540, when war was raging in New Galicia. Alvarado heeded the viceroy's order to leave the ships and go to the aid of New Galicia's settlers, with fateful consequences for himself.[65] Indeed, if we also take into account the failure of Vázquez de Coronado's expedition to the Tierra Nueva, it would be fair to say that, in the end, northern and western Mexico rewarded none of these ambitious men with anything other than heartache, exacting a huge cost in money, people, and livestock. Eventually the North yielded its riches—but too late for any of them. The stakes for which Guzmán, Cortés, Alvarado, Vázquez, and Mendoza played turned out to be illusory and elusive.

From New Galicia to the New Land

Both contemporaries and historians have debated the effects that Vázquez de Coronado's expedition and conditions in New Galicia had on the origins of the Mixton War. Charges brought against don Antonio de Mendoza as part of the residencia of his term as viceroy (conducted in 1546–47) specifically dealt with the impact of the expedition on indigenous communities in Colima and New Galicia. Critics of Mendoza—who was, after all, one of the expedition's major sponsors—alleged not only that the movement of the expeditionary force and its need for supplies negatively affected indigenous groups along the expedition's route but that recruitment of local residents for the entrada heightened the region's vulnerability by removing many of its leading settlers and potential defenders. Equally disruptive, according to Mendoza's critics, was the use of large numbers of indigenous workers to construct the ships for the exploration of the South Sea and to move supplies and building materials, even though the people who furnished the labor did not live in the communities that rose in rebellion in 1540.[66]

The argument that the expedition destabilized the situation in New Galicia and therefore helped to precipitate the widespread uprising of the early 1540s rested on the double assumption that, first, the region had been relatively quiet and secure up to that point and that, second, substantial numbers of New Galicia's vecinos departed for the far north. The viceroy also was criticized for focusing on the expedition to the north and delegating the new governor to organize it and for ignoring and downplaying concerns about the already troubled region. There can be little doubt about the truth of this contention. Leaving aside any possible consequences of Vázquez's relative neglect of affairs in New Galicia, the departure of the governor and at least some of New Galicia's leading vecinos certainly could have appeared to offer an opening and opportunity for the native residents of the region to assert themselves. Although the existence of a perceived vacuum of authority is impossible to document, it probably was a factor in the outbreak of the rebellion in late 1540. Nonetheless, Cristóbal de Oñate's acceptance of the position of acting governor in Vázquez's absence hardly would have signaled a weakening of Spanish authority. Oñate was a longtime, forceful presence in the region, a veteran of the conquest and of slaving and pacification campaigns, as well as the harsh and uncompromising encomendero of Xalisco and other communities. He was far more experienced in local affairs than was the new governor and highly regarded by other Spaniards.[67]

The situation in New Galicia in the 1530s, as discussed in this chapter and the previous one, was not necessarily deteriorating markedly during the months leading to the beginning of the war in the fall of 1540. Disorder, violence, flight, and rebellion were endemic in much of the region—indeed, the near-constant opposition to Spanish rule began even before the conquest was over.[68] The slave-taking campaigns of the middle of the decade might have exacerbated hostilities, but those effectively ended by early 1537. In a general sense, then, conditions overall neither improved nor sharply worsened toward the end of the decade. Nonetheless, Vázquez's initial reports when he reached New Galicia once again called official attention to significant problems and conflicts in the region. Did the viceroy recognize that appointing a new governor who shortly would depart on a major entrada might not be the best guarantee of order in the region? On this issue we can only speculate. No doubt Mendoza had confidence in Cristóbal de Oñate's abilities and long years of experience; but the viceroy, who actually was in New Galicia at the time the war began, entirely failed to anticipate the complexities of suppressing a widespread, as opposed to a localized, revolt. Yet in that respect he had much in common with local officials such as Oñate himself, who thought that they could contain the uprising as they had other violent episodes. In failing initially to grasp the magnitude of the threat they were as much at fault as Mendoza.

The question of whether large numbers of New Galicia's Spanish settlers participated in Vázquez's expedition to Tierra Nueva is less complex. Some scholars have affirmed that almost no one from the region departed with the expedition, while others assert that nearly the entire population of settlers emptied out, leaving New Galicia dangerously exposed to potential rebellion.[69] The truth lies between these views. Probably a dozen or so Spanish residents of New Galicia participated in

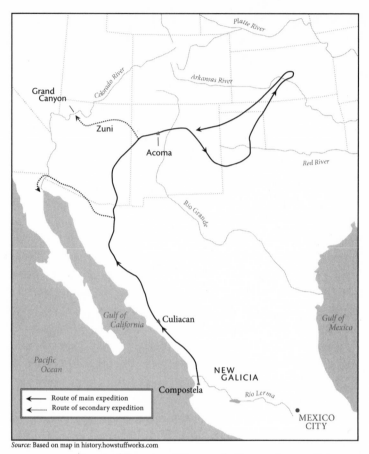

Source: Based on map in history.howstuffworks.com

MAP 5. Route of Francisco Vázquez de Coronado expedition

some phase of the expedition.[70] Some of them played prominent roles or were present during key events; others, like Juan de Zaldívar, would be important in the future development of the Mexican North. The fame (or notoriety) of some of these men could account for the impression that their numbers were larger than they actually were.[71] Cristóbal de Oñate himself stated that no one from Compostela left on the expedition but that "two residents of Guadalajara are going, one married to an Indian woman, the other a single man."[72] Natives of New Galicia accompanied the entrada, some of whom apparently stayed behind in Pueblo territory when the Spaniards returned south.[73]

The full account of the expedition to Tierra Nueva, like the story of Cabeza de Vaca and his companions, is interesting and of obvious importance to the history of the Spanish presence in the modern southwestern United States and of indigenous-Spanish relations there. Here we are concerned principally with aspects of the expedition that were relevant to people and events in New Galicia.[74] Most fundamentally, New Galicia acted as the immediate staging ground for the entrada. As the then northernmost part of Spanish New Galicia, Culiacan played an especially important role in the expedition, and not surprisingly some residents of San Miguel early on became involved in its planning and organization. Plans got under way in 1539 with the journey of Fray Marcos de Niza, who had been with Pedro de Alvarado in Peru, to reconnoiter the territory to the north. He took Estebanico, the African slave who returned to Mexico with Cabeza de Vaca and his companions, as his guide. Estebanico died, apparently when he went ahead on his own, reached the Zuni pueblo, and clashed with the people there; but Fray Marcos returned to Mexico, where he delivered a report to the viceroy, which Carl Sauer characterizes as "a strange tissue of hearsay, fantasy, fact and fraud."[75]

The viceroy then instructed Melchor Díaz, the alcalde of San Miguel who welcomed the Cabeza de Vaca party, to explore the route to the north. Díaz left Culiacan in mid-November with a small contingent of horsemen, among them Cristóbal de Oñate's nephew Juan de Zaldívar. The Díaz party moved north into the Sonora Valley, accompanied by Indian auxiliaries, many of whom were from Culiacan and knew a good deal about areas farther to the north. To the south in Compostela, preparations for the entrada already were being made. The expeditionary force was impressive, with more than three hundred Spaniards, one thousand Indian allies, six Franciscans, and around fifteen hundred horses and pack animals.[76] Leaving Compostela in late February 1540, in March Vázquez and his party met Díaz in Chiametla. Díaz brought the news that Lope de Samaniego, a veteran of the conquest of New Galicia whom the viceroy had appointed the expedition's *maestre de campo* (field marshal), had been killed near Chiametla in a skirmish with Indians from whom he had demanded supplies. He was the first of the New Galicia men to die in the effort to reach the Tierra Nueva. In retaliation for his death, Spaniards executed eight men and women from Chiametla. Thus began the violence that would characterize the expedition throughout its course.[77]

Both leading vecinos of San Miguel who met the Cabeza de Vaca party—Melchor Díaz and Diego de Alcaraz—also died as a result of their participation in the expedition. Vázquez established a settlement named San Gerónimo in northern Sonora in 1540 that subsequently relocated twice due to trouble with the local people. Melchor Díaz, left in charge as alcalde mayor, at Vázquez's order traveled to the coast with twenty-five men to look for supply ships that the viceroy sent north under command of Hernando de Alarcón. Díaz rode west to the Colorado River and crossed to the California side. He died from an accidental injury in late 1540 or early 1541.[78] In his absence trouble broke out between the settlers of San Gerónimo and local Indians, who in late 1541 or early 1542 destroyed the town and killed several Spaniards, among them the veteran slaver from Culiacan, Diego de Alcaraz. Another expedition member, Juan Troyano, later testified that the "cause of that uprising was the outrages and brutal acts committed by a [man named] Alcaraz. . . . [who] took wives and daughters from Indians in order to have sexual relations with them. And he took the provisions that they had." Some of the survivors returned to Culiacan, while others trekked north to rejoin the expedition.[79] In the summer of 1542 another veteran of the conquest of New Galicia, Juan Gallego, took revenge on some of the local people at San Gerónimo by burning villages and hanging some men.[80] Gallego, whose experience in campaigning in New Spain went back to the conquest of Tenochtitlan, had been one of the first to enlist for the expedition, bringing with him seven horses. He survived the expedition and in the 1540s was a vecino and encomendero in Purificación.[81]

Juan de Zaldívar's participation in the expedition is well documented.[82] He accompanied Melchor Díaz when he reconnoitered the route north. After they met Francisco Vázquez in Chiametla, he continued south to Colima to inform the viceroy about the state of affairs in the north. He then returned north by ship to pass along the viceroy's order that only a small party should proceed ahead toward Cibola, but by the time he arrived the main expedition had left. Zaldívar became captain of a company of horsemen and participated in the remainder of the expedition, during which he received a serious head wound. He was among the group that traveled with Vázquez to Quivira in present-day central Kansas, a journey that took them into the Great Plains, home to peoples who hunted buffalo and Caddoan tribes who farmed and hunted. Zaldívar returned with the main party to New Galicia in the spring of 1542. He subsequently claimed that the entrada left him five or six thousand pesos in debt, but he lived on for many years to become one of the wealthiest men in New Galicia.[83]

Several participants who lived in New Galicia before or after the expedition to the Tierra Nueva had close ties with Mendoza or Vázquez. Pedro de Tovar, a nephew of Mendoza, apparently participated in Guzmán's entrada at a very young age and became a vecino of Guadalajara. Following the expedition to New Mexico he settled in Culiacan, where he became an encomendero. Melchor Pérez, the son of Lic. Diego Pérez de la Torre, who had died in 1537 within two years of taking office as the governor of New Galicia, stayed on in the region and was the encomendero of Cuyupuztlan, just west of Guadalajara. He served in the company of Juan de Zaldívar during the entrada to the Tierra Nueva and as alguacil mayor and billeting officer for the entire expeditionary force.[84] He also might have served previously with Vázquez when the latter suppressed the rebellion in Culiacan in 1539.[85] Pérez brought with him Pedro de Ledesma, who subsequently married Pérez's daughter Catalina Mejía and in turn became encomendero of Cuyupuztlan, which his wife received in dowry from her father. Ledesma was from Vázquez's hometown near Salamanca in Castile. He served in his household and went with him to New Galicia and then to the Tierra Nueva.[86] Ledesma might have lived in Pérez's house for a time after they returned from the expedition and before he married Pérez's daughter. After leaving Guadalajara, Melchor Pérez lived for some years in Compostela and later in Mexico City, but he was a vecino of Colima in 1566 when he testified in Juan de Zaldívar's *información* (deposition) at the age of fifty-three.[87]

Although the results ultimately would be disappointing, the planning and realization of the expedition to New Mexico signaled a major shift in power and authority in New Spain, from Cortés to Mendoza and his retainers and relatives. The arduous and often brutally violent expedition to the Tierra Nueva and the fabled Cibola yielded little to its participants beyond a return home for those who survived and increased indebtedness for those who invested in horses, arms, and livestock. The entrada's participants did, of course, miss the turmoil of the Mixton War, which took place in their absence; but, as will be seen, this did not mean that they returned to a peaceful New Galicia. Given the complaints of settlers in New Galicia during the 1530s about their poverty, difficulties in controlling the Indians who were supposed to serve them, and dangers to which they were constantly exposed, perhaps it is surprising that so few of them joined the expedition in the hope of finding something better. They might have thought that circumstances in New Galicia were improving, or perhaps they feared sacrificing whatever gains they had made by joining what might be a lengthy enterprise. Those who stayed behind, however, soon faced a threat greater than any they had encountered to that point. Whether the causes of the uprising hinged on increasing demands for labor and goods, ineffective government, a perceived lack of authority, or the millenarian expectations spread by independent Indians from the mountains, the Spaniards who remained in New Galicia soon discovered that their decade-long effort to impose a secure and workable colonial order accomplished little beyond fomenting further disorder, resentment, and defiance.

CHAPTER 5

The Indians' War

I have been sent to these kingdoms of Castile by the viceroy of
New Spain, don Luis de Velasco, prisoner and exile; alone, dispos-
sessed of my estate and lordship and of my wife and children, with
all poverty, thirst and hunger and extreme need, by sea and by
land. . . . Because it has not been enough that the Spaniards have
done to me . . . irreparable harm, waging cruel and unjust wars,
killing my subjects and people and relatives . . . forcing me to flee
in exile from my home and country and wife and children in the
mountains for many years . . . And I, the said don Francisco, and
my people and many other caciques and lords were placed in the
harsh captivity and servitude that the Spaniards call encomiendas,
distributing to each Spaniard the pueblos and their people, as if
we were animals in the countryside. . . . And I and mine suffered patiently the said captivity. . . . And later the friars of San
Francisco came here [and] told us that the reason they had come
was to teach us so that we should know the one and true God.[1]
—Written in exile by don Francisco Tenamaztle, 1555

✢ MORE THAN A DECADE AFTER THE END OF THE MIXTON WAR,
Tenamaztle, once a lord of Nochistlan, produced his deposition while

living in exile in Valladolid in north central Castile. During the years he lived in that dour city on the Pisuerga River, he had much to recall. He had survived—and lost—everything. He witnessed the arrival of the Christians with Nuño de Guzmán, accompanied by their hosts of Nahua and Purépecha warriors. He lived with and accommodated the Spaniards; he was among the first to be baptized by the Franciscans, who established themselves in his community of Nochistlan. With his people he endured the alien and harsh work regimen and cruel punishments, "increasing day by day the injuries and irreparable harm, the calamities, the harsh captivity, deaths and losses of population that we suffered." As the damage, injuries, offenses, and deaths multiplied, "being free people, as we are . . . they [we] decided to flee to the mountains and create strongholds there, to defend their own lives and those of their women and children."[2] Tenamaztle rebelled, was taken prisoner, escaped, and fled to the mountains, where he continued fighting. Finally he attempted to come to terms with the Spaniards by seeking the Franciscans' protection. The authorities sent him into exile in Spain.

While in Valladolid, where he may have been confined to a Dominican monastery rather than a jail, Tenamaztle apparently met Bartolomé de las Casas, venerable defender of the rights of the indigenous peoples of the Americas, who possibly assisted him in preparing his deposition.[3] Las Casas very likely influenced the phrasing of Tenamaztle's explanation for the uprising in New Galicia, pictured unequivocally as being rooted in the unjust and cruel treatment that Tenamaztle and others experienced at the hands of Guzmán and his captains and followers. Whatever other factors of timing and opportunity might have contributed to the outbreak of large-scale insurrection, at the core of the revolt lay the unendurable strains and losses experienced by subjugated groups during the decade of Spanish rule in the West. Interestingly, Tenamaztle's statement accords with the explanation of the war's causes offered by Jerónimo López, an encomendero and regidor of Mexico City, who years before accompanied Francisco Cortés on his entrada. In a letter to Charles V in 1542, López wrote straightforwardly that the revolt began because the Indians in New Galicia did not want to pay tribute to their encomenderos.[4] There is a striking coincidence in these two explanations of the causes for the war, set down more than a decade and thousands of miles apart, from a Cazcan rebel leader, on the one hand, and a Spanish conquistador on the other.

Did other factors come into play in the rebellion? Spaniards insisted that the millenarian expectations instilled by messengers from the Zacatecas—Indians who lived in the mountains to the north and remained independent and thus were cast in the classic role of "outside agitators"—culminated in the Indians' violent defiance of Spanish rule and Christianity.[5] In the aftermath of the war many Spaniards testified about wild dances and "diabolical" rites that they witnessed and the Indians' desecration and mockery of Christian symbols and practices. Some indigenous survivors, including many who admitted to having participated in the rebellion, also testified that the teachings of certain native religious figures and their millenarian promises and the influence of messengers from Chichimec groups to the north, rather than bad treatment at the hands of the Spaniards, accounted for the uprising. Given what is known of Spanish-indigenous relations in the 1530s, we must weigh the testimony of the survivors against the likelihood that Spaniards intimidated the witnesses who accepted baptism and amnesty in exchange for their lives and loyalty.[6] Certainly this explanation of events appealed to the viceroy and other Spaniards, as it rendered them blameless in the disaster and further justified harsh suppression of the revolt in the guise of defending the holy faith.

Evidence for the presence of the Zacateca Indians and the significance of religious and millenarian motives, even if biased and compromised, nonetheless is substantial. Most of the documentation on the war comes from official Spanish sources. Tenamaztle's deposition was a rare exception in that it appears to have been made voluntarily, rather than under pressure. Nonetheless it almost certainly was mediated by a Spanish translator, scribe, or collaborator, as it is highly unlikely that he learned to write Castilian during his years in exile, although he might have learned to speak it.[7] We can consider only the evidence we have, both of testimony and action. The violence directed toward Spaniards and their institutions assumed an undeniably anti-Christian form, as rebels destroyed churches and artifacts and attacked and killed members of the clergy. The presence and participation of people from groups not under Spanish control also is well documented. It is very possible, however, that the anti-Christian and millenarian aspects of the movement were more important in spreading than in instigating the rebellion, offering a rallying point around which the perhaps uneasily allied multiethnic communities of New Galicia could unite, rather than constituting a root cause for revolt.[8] The arrival of religious messengers from the north might have acted as a catalyst for a conflagration awaiting a spark, at least in some communities.[9] In ethnically diverse New Galicia, contact among people from different groups was commonplace. Some Cazcan communities were located very close to areas inhabited by the independent Zacatecas, and their languages were likely mutually intelligible.

The sources offer a fairly complete narrative of the major events of the conflict, although pinpointing the timing of particular episodes is difficult. Spanish testimony and accounts often are more elliptical than linear. Witnesses usually were more concerned with describing particular incidents than establishing a sequential time line of events. Not only did they not always offer a strictly chronological account, they also frequently failed to note how much time elapsed during and between the events they reported. Thus, it is often difficult to know if a specific episode took place in a day or over the course of a week or longer, or how much time passed between different incidents and in what order they occurred.

The overall narrative can be summarized as follows. Scattered (and perhaps increasingly audacious) attacks on Spaniards and their slaves, servants, and property in the countryside and pueblos north of Guadalajara took place around mid-1540. Around the same time officials and other local residents made the unsettling discovery that substantial numbers of Indians, probably mainly Cazcanes, had been fortifying at least one stronghold, Tepetistaque, and amassing supplies to sustain themselves there, apparently with the aid or encouragement of independent (that is, unconquered) Zacatecas who lived in the area. Spaniards found several pueblos in the mainly Cazcan-speaking Juchipila Valley in central New Galicia abandoned or partly empty. The local residents, either at the same time or soon after, were fortifying other mountain strongholds, or *peñoles*, as well. Spaniards tried to persuade these people to return to their homes and approached rebel strongholds to initiate negotiations or to demand surrender, actions prefaced by reading the requerimiento, sometimes repeatedly, that urged the people to submit to God and king. These approaches generally met with mocking and defiant responses.

Early engagements were either indecisive or disastrous for the Spanish, especially as they discovered that they could not always trust their indigenous allies—the indios amigos—whom they recruited locally. In its initial phase the rebellion mainly was a Cazcan phenomenon, but connections between Cazcanes and other groups such as the Tecuexes made it very difficult for Spaniards to know whom they could trust. The viceroy was visiting New Galicia in late 1540 and so learned about the rebellion fairly soon after it began. Local officials, however, underestimated the scale of the revolt and felt confident they could suppress it without additional aid, notwithstanding their relatively small numbers. Although the viceroy returned to Mexico City, he sent reinforcements to help suppress the uprising. The rebels nearly destroyed Guadalajara, but the Spanish defenders of the town finally won a decisive victory in September 1541. Soon after that the viceroy himself arrived leading an army of several hundred Spanish horsemen and footmen, together with thousands of Indians from central Mexico. Viceregal intervention determined the outcome of the war, as one by one the rebel strongholds surrendered or fell. Thousands of native residents died in battle, committed suicide, fled, or faced execution or enslavement. The conclusion in early 1542 of what has come to be known as the Mixton War did not bring violence and disorder in New Galicia to an end, but never again would the core of the region witness widespread insurrection that at least temporarily united so many communities. This chapter and the one that follows examine these events and the people who participated in them.

The War Begins

How did the war begin? Many believe that the murder of an encomendero, Juan de Arce, by the Indians of his encomienda in Nayarit in 1540 signaled the beginning of the revolt. Juan de Arce had been assigned the Guaynamateco people, a Cora-speaking group, in encomienda.[10] The story is that he complained to the Indians in his service that they no longer brought him food and supplies. They responded that they had ceased to do so for fear of his dogs (notoriously associated with Spanish attacks on Indians), which they actually had been starving rather than feeding, turning them savage as a result. Arce agreed to destroy the animals and, having done so, was left without protection.[11] Fray Antonio Tello included this episode in his famous history, which has served as a source for others who have written about the war. It is a dramatic story that underscores indigenous skillful planning. There is only one problem: Arce survived the war and later executed a deposition detailing his services. He eventually did die at the hands of the people of his encomienda, but not until the end of the 1540s.[12]

It is unfortunate that the apocryphal story of Arce's death has entered into the historical record of the war, especially as the narrative is dramatic enough without such embellishment. The persistence of the tale underscores how murky some aspects of the war and its implications have remained. Issues such as the numbers of combatants on both sides, mortality among all groups, numbers of Indian slaves the Spaniards took and the slaves' ultimate fate, the extent of depopulation and relocation, and, as noted earlier, even precise chronology and timing all can be elusive. In addition to these uncertainties, reliance on Tello's seventeenth-century history has fostered misunderstandings. While Tello almost certainly had access to records that no longer exist, he generally failed to identify them (although sometimes, as in the case of town council proceedings, the source is obvious), and he often confused or conflated events and chronology.[13]

Spanish reaction to a series of attacks led to the discovery of the first of the fortified strongholds in the mountains and then to major confrontations. Again, it must be emphasized that it is sometimes impossible to establish the exact sequence in which these incidents occurred; probably several of them were more or less simultaneous. Bearing this in mind, precise timing probably mattered much less than the reality of the growing threat to Spanish control and security in the countryside, reflecting increasingly effective indigenous organization and communication.

The viceroy's report—which for the first year of the war largely drew on information he gathered from others on the scene—mentions several of these incidents. One of the first took place in the Cazcan community of Xalpa, where "the natives ran off Diego de Proaño to whom they were commended and Bartolomé de Mendoza [and] the whole pueblo [then] went to the mountains."[14] Hernando Martel recounted how the ruler Petacatl and another principal of Xalpa named Maya had gone "to the house where the Spaniard of the said pueblo lived and ran him off and said they would kill him." This man (probably Bartolomé de Mendoza) found Martel and Diego de Proaño and told them what had happened, adding that the following day all of Xalpa rebelled and forced the remaining Spaniards out. Martel said that another cacique of Xalpa, Aboaquinte (his Christian name was don Diego), and "other naguatatos of the said pueblo many times told him that the Zacatecas came from far away and said, 'what are you doing and why don't you all rise up, or is it true that you want to live in servitude?'" The cacique told him that he had laughed at their words. Later, however, Martel noticed that Aboaquinte would be absent from Xalpa for three or four days at a time; when he asked to speak with him he was told that he was sick or tending his fields.[15]

Some naguatatos of the pueblo came to Martel and the Spaniard who was calpixque (tribute collector) and told them that the cacique had gone many times to *mitotes* (dances) in the valley of Tlaltenango that were held well outside the pueblo so their master and the calpixque would not find out about them.[16] The dances lasted three or four days, sometimes taking place in Juchipila and attended by a large number of Zacatecas, and in nearby Mecatabasco, which was subject to Xalpa. Martel's informants said that the mitotes were intended to rouse the people to rebel "and kill all the Spaniards and take their women as their concubines."[17] According to them, these activities had been going on for more than two years. From Martel's testimony it is difficult to judge whether this conversation with the naguatatos of Xalpa and the events they described took place before the incident in which the Spaniards were forced out of the pueblo. It could have taken place then, but that would mean that Martel and others had received specific warning regarding clandestine activities involving the independent Zacatecas that had been going on for quite some time, and had done nothing. Either the warning came after they learned about the fortification of Tepetistaque, or the Spaniards discounted the threat.

Mendoza's report stated that after the incident at Xalpa some of the lords and commoners of Tlaltenango stoned Gonzalo Varela, injuring him seriously.[18] Another serious episode also took place in Tlaltenango. A Spaniard named Gonzalo Garijo barely escaped from a hail of stones and arrows by riding off on a mare. He probably was in Tlaltenango working for Toribio de Bolaños, who at the time was the alcalde of Guadalajara and the encomendero of the pueblo.[19] Indians apparently robbed Bolaños's house, drove off his pigs, and burned the church and its cross. Taking with him a man named Alonso Pérez, Bolaños went to the pueblo to apprehend Teuquitate, the lord of a part of Tlaltenango, who he thought was responsible for the attacks. He planned to take him to Miguel de Ibarra, the captain for the district who was with Fray Antonio de Segovia in Juchipila trying to reestablish order there. Two hours before dawn, as Bolaños and Pérez slept in the countryside, the "principales y maceguales" (lords and commoners) of Tlaltenango attacked, freeing Teuquitate and robbing the Spaniards. Miguel de Ibarra later testified that when he found Bolaños, seriously injured and on foot, the latter did not know where Pérez was. Three days later Ibarra and his men found Pérez's body hidden among some rocks.[20]

In these instances the encomendero himself or his agents, servants, or slaves—as well as his property—became targets of attack. At the nearby community of Juchipila the principales refused to appear when summoned by their encomendero, Hernán Flores. "Xiutleque was the lord of this pueblo, whom everyone in the country respected. . . . He persuaded them not to serve the Spaniards, and when he knew of some who did serve, he would call them sodomites and other insults . . . for which reason all of them . . . ceased to serve. And at this time they stoned a Spaniard named Alonso López and another named Francisco Íñiguez and a black who was in the said pueblo of Juchipila."[21]

The attacks on the encomenderos and their establishments lend support to Tenamaztle's claim that fierce resentment of the encomienda regime was the root cause of the rebellion. It also should be noted that the people of the larger communities, like Juchipila and Nochistlan, seldom acted as a single unit, as indeed they were not. References to men who were rulers of "part" of a pueblo and to more than one cacique remind us not only that the region as a whole was diverse but that individual native communities were as well. Each community could be a complex entity that encompassed more than one sociopolitical unit (which sometimes comprised distinct ethnic groups).[22] This fragmentation and diversity probably accounts at least in part for some of the inscrutable behavior and complex movement of people described in the reports, where some leaders would leave their pueblos, accompanying their people, while others stayed behind and continued to deal with the Spaniards, or at least appeared to be willing to do so. Tensions within and between communities doubtless shaped individual and collective choices and actions.

The War Escalates

All sources agree that Tepetistaque was the first of the fortified peñoles, or at least the first one that the Spaniards discovered.[23] Its location north of the Juchipila Valley, in territory where the Zacatecas lived, certainly suggests the collaboration of the Zacatecas in the uprising. Miguel de Ibarra, a man of long experience in New Spain and New Galicia, and Hernando Martel, who at the time of the war probably shared the encomienda of the

Spanish Towns
Indian Communities
peñol

MAP 6. Main sites of the Mixton war

Río de Tepeque with Diego de Proaño, provided detailed accounts of the
Spaniards' discovery of the peñol and how they responded to the threat.[24]
The events described took place late in 1540.

Martel testified that while he was in Guadalajara, messengers arrived
for Miguel de Ibarra, a captain and the encomendero of Nochistlan,
informing him that Tenamaztle, who was the brother of the ruler of
Nochistlan, had gathered a certain number of the residents of the pueblo
and others from some outlying settlements and left. Tenamaztle's defec-
tion must have been especially bitter for Ibarra. He later testified that
Tenamaztle, who had been baptized don Francisco, served the Franciscan
church and monastery in Nochistlan. "Trusting him, believing he was

a good Christian, this witness, who at the time was alcalde mayor and because the said priests begged him, conferred the office and staff of justice on the said Tenamaztle so he could administer and govern the said pueblo." Tenamaztle's conversion to Christianity might have convinced Ibarra, at the insistence of the Franciscans, to place authority in his hands, even though his brother was the recognized ruler.[25]

The cacique of Nochistlan, don Juan, who had not joined the rebels, sent a message to Ibarra stating that he did not know where his people had gone but that he "understood they went to the Zacatecas." Ibarra and Martel together went to Nochistlan, where they spoke with the cacique, questioning him about who had left. Don Juan took them through the pueblo, pointing out the neighborhoods and houses that stood empty. Once aware of the situation, Miguel de Ibarra wrote to the town council in Guadalajara, telling them to send reinforcements to Juchipila, where he would meet them. In Juchipila, which is west of Nochistlan, the cacique and naguatatos told the Spaniards that some people from that community also had gone to join the Zacatecas. Heading north to Apozol, Ibarra and his men discovered the same situation there. Continuing northward they reached Xalpa, where the "cacique and principales" told them that some of their people had left with Petacatl, who was ruler of part of the pueblo. They also informed Ibarra that Acachoa, the señor of Mecatabasco (today Tabasco, north of Xalpa), with all his people and some of the principales of Xalpa "had made very large supplies of provisions and they had all of them together gone to fortify themselves in the peñol de Tepetistaque ten leagues from the said pueblo of Xalpa and that along with them Tenamaztle and his people and the people of Juchipila . . . had rebelled and risen up and Teuquitate and the naguatatos and principales and all the people of Tlaltenango. And . . . with them it is said there are more than three or four thousand Zacatecas."[26]

According to Martel, certain Indians informed Miguel de Ibarra that some of the people of Xalpa, Juchipila, Apozol, Mezquitute, and Cuzpatlan who appeared to be peaceful actually were responsible for some Spanish deaths. Ibarra convened the caciques of those pueblos and, in the presence of two Franciscans and a notary, read the requerimiento "four or five times." He told them that he knew of their "evil and treachery" and admonished them to change their ways. The caciques and principales assured him that all those intent on killing and destruction had departed already. Ibarra then took Martel and four other Spaniards who were also in Xalpa, together with the caciques and principales of Xalpa, Juchipila, and Apozol, and left for the peñol of Tepetistaque to judge the situation there for himself "because he still thought that the Indians lied." When they got close enough to the site they saw a host of three or four thousand men, many of whom descended a slope of the mountain to approach them. Ibarra realized that with only six Spaniards he could not hope to fight against such numbers. Retreating to Juchipila, he again wrote to the town council in Guadalajara, urging them to send ten horsemen and friendly Indians from Tonala as soon as possible.[27]

In response to this plea, sixteen or seventeen more Spaniards arrived along with fifteen hundred indios amigos from Tonala and more than three thousand Cazcanes. Many of the Cazcanes were from the immediate area; Ibarra referred to them as "many other allies from Juchipila and Xalpa and other pueblos of Cazcanes."[28] Ibarra asked the two Franciscans who lived in the monastery in Juchipila, Fray Martín de Chia and Fray Pedro de la Concepción, to assist him in warning the rulers of the towns who were with them against joining the rebels. With the reinforcements, Ibarra departed again for Tepetistaque and spent the night in the now-empty pueblo of Mecatabasco. Before they reached the peñol, however, the Indians from Juchipila and other Cazcanes who accompanied them began to create a disturbance among the indios amigos from Tonala, threatening to kill the Spaniards' Tecuexe allies. The terrified men from Tonala began to desert, leaving only some of their principales.

The next day Ibarra sent Toribio de Bolaños and four other Spaniards ahead. After this group had traveled about half a day they saw "two Indians, Tecuexes of the language of Tonala," approaching them. The two men did not resist when Bolaños detained them. When Ibarra caught up with the advance party he questioned the two men separately and discovered that the people at the peñol and the Cazcanes accompanying him were acting in concert. The men informed him that they had come from the peñol, where they had been sent by the caciques of their pueblos. They admitted that people from all the Tecuexe pueblos in the area were at the peñol, more than four thousand in all, but that the defenders of Tepetistaque were mainly counting on the men who accompanied Ibarra to betray and kill the Spaniards. Martel testified that the two detainees told him that from the moment he arrived in Xalpa, messengers had traveled daily to the peñol to inform the people there "what was happening and what the Spaniards were saying and how many people they had."[29]

Ibarra certainly understood the immediacy of the threat. He was able to extract—presumably by force or intimidation—details of the plot from the two captives. The people at the peñol anticipated that Ibarra's party would make their camp along a river that ran close to Tepetistaque where there was a wooded gully and that the Spaniards would pronounce the customary requirement urging them to submit peacefully. The rebels planned to approach them with peace offerings—deer and rabbits and quail; once inside the camp they would turn on them. They expected that the Cazcanes who accompanied the Spaniards as their allies would be nearest to them, with those from Tonala behind. The men at the peñol also expected to be joined by five or six thousand more men who would arrive at the Spaniards' rear. The Cazcanes "who appeared to be friends who accompanied the captain and Spaniards" had agreed to kill the horses, while those who descended from the peñol would kill Ibarra and his men.[30]

Hearing this, Ibarra sent a warning to Bolaños not to enter the gully. Bolaños started to break up the camp, at which point the Cazcanes began assembling on the heights. Ibarra found one of the caciques from Juchipila and ordered him and the other caciques to instruct their people to come down. Ibarra pretended to trust them but took four horsemen with him to reconnoiter the area near their camp. When it seemed secure he returned and ordered the Spaniards to saddle their horses and be on the alert. Next, he ordered the leaders of his Cazcan allies to gather so he could talk to them, but then he quickly had them seized and put in chains. He reminded them that he had warned them many times not to rebel or plot against the Spaniards. He released a naguatato, promising to spare his life if he would tell the truth. The man confirmed everything the messengers had said. Asked how he knew so much, he explained that "he was an interpreter and a messenger who traveled from one pueblo to another" and that for more than two years the rebels had been engaged in these pacts. He also confirmed that when the people came down from the peñol to occupy the heights it was to effect "*la matanza*" (massacre) that night. Ibarra then extracted confessions from some of the others as well.[31]

Ibarra conferred with the other Spaniards, who responded that they already understood what was afoot before they left Xalpa. They urged the captain to execute the Cazcan leaders, given that they were so greatly outnumbered. Apparently more cautious than his companions, Ibarra favored waiting another day to see what would happen. His men, however, threatened to desert and return to Guadalajara if he did so, forcing Ibarra to carry out the executions immediately.[32] Ibarra later stated that he executed "ten or twelve of the principales and captains who were most guilty in the episode."[33] As they started to hang the condemned men, some of them began to call out to their people to attack the Spaniards. The Spaniards were armed and on horseback, however, and, at least according to Martel, still accompanied by Indians from Tonala. Furthermore, it was "good land for the horses"—that is, the kind of terrain in which the cavalry functioned best.[34] In these circumstances the Cazcanes did not dare attack. Ibarra's hasty execution of the caciques took a toll on the native leadership at an early stage of the rebellion. The dead men included Xiutleque (Xiutecutli), the lord of Juchipila; don Diego, a lord of Xalpa; don Martin, the lord of Apozol; and others.[35]

Perhaps thinking that with the execution of the native leaders he had reestablished control, Ibarra dispersed the Cazcanes who had been with him, and the Spaniards spent that night in their camp with only the remaining allies from Tonala, waiting to see if an attack would materialize. The next day they approached the peñol, where the rebels again refused to submit. A battle ensued. After four hours of fighting, with several Spaniards as well as some of the horses wounded, Ibarra, himself wounded, ordered a retreat. They spent a miserable night near the peñol. The next morning Ibarra, after conferring with the Franciscans and the other Spaniards, decided that they could not prevail, given the strength of the forces at the peñol. Returning to Xalpa, Ibarra found the pueblo almost empty. He summoned the "*señora natural*" (native female ruler), mother of one of the executed caciques, and explained that her son's execution had been necessary. She responded that "it was true that her son had made that pact and that he was part of the agreement but that they [the other leaders?] had deceived him as [one would] a youth [*le habían engañado como a mozo*]." From there the Spaniards returned to Guadalajara, where the two Franciscans explained to him everything that had happened in Juchipila, saying that they were afraid to be there. Ibarra returned with them to the pueblo, where he executed some of the guilty parties. When he departed, the pueblo apparently was peaceful, although that situation did not last long.

The Spanish received news of other attacks and disturbances in the countryside around this time. When Ibarra reached Juchipila, a messenger arrived from Tepechitlan, in the valley of Tlaltenango, with news that his encomendero, Pedro de Bobadilla, had been threatened. Juan de Zubia testified that "he saw at that time Pedro de Bobadilla come fleeing and ill-treated, complaining and lamenting the loss of his property and a black [slave] and a son whom he left among the said Indians, who later appeared." Bobadilla was married to an Indian woman, so his son might have been with relatives on his mother's side. Zubia believed that the marriage accounted for the survival of Bobadilla's family. Zubia testified that he had told all of this to Miguel de Ibarra, who was unable to warn Bobadilla. Ibarra himself stated that when he returned from Tepetistaque to Juchipila, "he was advised by the Indians of Teul that Bobadilla was in great danger and difficulty because his Indians wanted to kill him." Ibarra later found an extremely distressed Bobadilla and his family in a settlement near Teul, where they apparently took refuge.[36]

Another episode that took place in Juchipila perhaps indicated an escalation and broadening of the targets of violence. Once again, it is difficult to say exactly when this incident occurred in relation to the confrontation at Tepetistique; almost certainly it took place later, but just how long afterward is not clear. According to Ibarra, he was in Nochistlan—the pueblo he held in encomienda—when he received letters from Fray Antonio de Segovia, the guardian of the monastery (presumably of Juchipila, although he referred only to "*aquel* [that] *pueblo*") pleading with him "for the love of God to go to help them because they were in danger." Ibarra took some people to the pueblo, where they engaged in a series of skirmishes with the Indians, who that night burned one of the encomendero's buildings. Ibarra remained there for twenty days or more amid constant "skirmishes and clamor."[37]

Hernando Martel actually arrived in Juchipila before Ibarra did. He had been in Xalpa, where the people told him that the Indians of Apozol had gone to a peñol called Mixton, the place that ultimately gave its name to the war. He found Apozol empty and then proceeded to Juchipila, where he found three Spaniards and two Franciscans, who said that the Indians had threatened to kill them. They had spent two sleepless nights keeping watch and asked Martel to send for the alcalde of Guadalajara until Miguel de Ibarra arrived. They begged Martel to stay, which he did for the three days it took Ibarra to arrive with five horsemen. Ibarra summoned the principales and warned them not to be fooled by "the devil" and that if any messengers arrived "from the pueblos in revolt," to apprehend them and bring them to him.[38]

According to Martel, Ibarra posted "guards and sentinels" and told him to be on alert. As he and Ibarra stood guard they saw two Indians approach, one of them an "alguacil principal" and the other a naguatato, carrying eight arrows and banners of feathers. When questioned, they told Ibarra that the cacique wished to inform him of the arrival of messengers from Tlaltenango who were urging their community to revolt. The cacique's messengers said that he detained the men from Tlaltenango and seized the banners and arrows that belonged to them. Ibarra then ordered all the Spaniards to saddle their horses and went with three of the horsemen to the cacique's house, leaving the others behind. At that point Ibarra discovered it was a trick; the entire pueblo was deserted.

Ibarra left the messengers behind and returned to where his men were camped. Accompanied by four horsemen, he rode to Apozol, on the way detaining some Indians who were carrying supplies to Mixton. When he inquired as to where the caciques and principales of Juchipila were, they answered that everyone had gone to Mixton. He ordered them to tell the lords of Juchipila and Apozol to meet him the following day in Apozol, but when he arrived there he found it empty. The church and cross were burned, and the stores of maize that he had seen the previous day were gone. The rulers of the two pueblos failed to appear. That night while they were in Juchipila some corrals and several hundred pigs burned; the next night, close to the monastery, a building where more than two thousand fanegas of maize were stored also went up in flames. After another attack the following night, Ibarra and the Franciscans decided to abandon the monastery. They had barely left the pueblo when the Indians set the monastery itself on fire.[39]

According to Martel, four days after they abandoned Juchipila, Andrés de Salinas and two other Spaniards went to Cuzpatlan, a pueblo south of Juchipila and near Mezquituta, which Salinas held in encomienda. They planned to collect some of the cattle that Salinas kept there. Possibly the Indians sent for Salinas, luring him into a trap. Salinas apparently suspected something was afoot, yet he failed to protect himself adequately.[40] When the three men arrived, the pueblo appeared to be peaceful, but before dawn the Indians overpowered and killed Salinas and the two others.[41] Pedro Cuadrado, a vecino of Guadalajara, testified that he was in Nochistlan with Miguel de Ibarra when a man from Mezquituta came to report the murders. Cuadrado then went with Ibarra to Mezquituta "which was at peace" to find out what had happened. They learned that

Cuzpatlan was full of *"muchos indios de guerra"* (many warriors), as was the entire countryside. Ibarra rode with some men to the pueblo, where they found "the church and houses burned and the Christians dead from arrow shots and other wounds and scorched and thrown in the church plaza." Here too he learned that many of the local residents had gone to Mixton. He decided that with so few Spaniards they should return to Nochistlan, leaving instructions with the people of Mezquituta to retrieve the bodies of the dead Spaniards for burial. The Indians there said they had already buried them, and a few days later Ibarra and Cuadrado were able to enter Cuzpatlan and saw the graves.[42]

Spaniards by now had lost control of the countryside north of Guadalajara and become aware of the existence of more than one rebel stronghold, including what would be the largest of the peñoles, Mixton. At this point the violence still was mainly confined to that region. The pattern of attacks on Spaniards and their property revealed, however, a substantial degree of organization; the indigenous rebellion was by no means spontaneous. Spaniards' conversations with local people suggested that planning had been underway for months and very possibly years.[43] The Indians who remained in the affected pueblos were well aware of the plans and knew who was involved. For their part the Spaniards could do nothing but respond to threats and attacks. Having only partial knowledge of insurgent intentions and organization, they failed to take preemptive action; by the time they tried to do so, enemy forces were far too large and well situated and supplied. The rebels were solidly entrenched in their strongholds and maintained networks of contacts in the surrounding pueblos to inform them of Spanish movements and plans. As the Spaniards soon discovered, the Indians also could use those contacts to tap into a large pool of willing supporters. The Spaniard who played the most important leadership role in the first phase of the war, Miguel de Ibarra, had years of military and other experience in the region.[44] The Spaniards were, however, outnumbered, outmaneuvered, and handicapped by their notions of what the local people could and would do. During the 1530s, most of the disorder in the region was fairly localized; the Spaniards were able, through the exercise of superior force, intimidation, and brutal punishment, to bring people into line. Now the rebels turned the tables on them: they had numerical and strategic superiority and used them to daunting advantage.

At Christmas 1540 Viceroy Mendoza arrived at the Puerto de la Navidad, initially paying little heed to the rebellion to the north, most likely discounting its importance. Mendoza was in Purificación near the coast when Miguel de Ibarra arrived with the news that Mixton was attracting growing numbers of rebels.[45] The viceroy sent him with a number of horsemen to Juchipila with Fray Martín de la Coruña (or de Jesús) and Juan de León, notary of the audiencia in Mexico, to make one last peaceful overture to the Indians.[46] On March 4, 1541, they reached Juchipila, where they found the church, monastery, and other buildings burned and two partially charred crosses lying on the ground. In Apozol, houses were reduced to charred rubble. The next day Ibarra and his company went to the peñol (presumably Mixton, although it could have been Juchipila), climbing to a place where they would be safe from harm but could communicate with the defenders. Some men who appeared to be in command approached the Spaniards. "We showed them the writ of requerimiento . . . and told them in loud voices so that they could hear that we wanted to speak to them in the name of the viceroy." They communicated through a series of interpreters—local Spaniards Cristóbal Romero and Juan Delgado, who spoke Nahuatl, and two men from Apozol and Amatitlan who spoke Cazcan. The Indians' response was hardly encouraging; the men at the peñol jeered at the Spaniards, calling out "that we should come up, that they were men and had heart and they weren't women and they would defend themselves." The Spaniards went to Mezquituta and then back to Guadalajara.[47]

In Guadalajara the viceroy convened a high-level council to deliberate on the best course of action. In addition to Ibarra and Cristóbal de Oñate, who was acting governor in Francisco Vázquez's absence, there were other officials "and prominent persons." Fray Martín de la Coruña; Pedro de Alvarado, who had arrived with his fleet; and Bishop Marroquín of Guatemala were in attendance.[48] This group, which met in the house of Juan del Camino where the viceroy was lodging, unanimously concluded that Mendoza himself should not confront the rebels, given his weighty responsibilities in the capital and as viceroy; instead, they entrusted the military command to Cristóbal de Oñate.[49] Once Mendoza received word from Oñate that his forces reached Mixton and "had them surrounded so they couldn't escape," he returned to Mexico City.[50]

Later, defending himself against charges brought against him in the residencia of his term of office that he responded inadequately to the threat in New Galicia, Mendoza stated that Cristóbal de Oñate left Guadalajara with a force of fifty Spaniards, most on horseback, including

FIGURE 10. Photo of what is thought to be El Mixton, today known as Mesa La Manga Larga and located in the modern township of Apozol. Courtesy of Thomas Hillerkuss.

both vecinos of New Galicia and men from the fleet and the household of the viceroy himself, along with an unspecified number of native allies, "the largest group of people that had been gathered since the said province was conquered and as such appeared to everyone to be sufficient."[51] If these numbers hardly seem impressive, they reflected the region's sparse Spanish population. Juan Hernández de Híjar, the longtime alcalde of Purificación, estimated that at the time there were fourteen vecinos in his town, about thirty in Guadalajara, and twenty-five or thirty in Compostela.[52] In any event, in good conditions and on open, level ground, even a relatively small force of horsemen could prevail against much larger numbers of native warriors. It surely was no coincidence that, after nearly a decade of struggling against the Spanish presence in New Galicia, the Indians had learned the advantages of taking to the high ground in strongholds that were inaccessible on horseback.

Judging that it would be impossible to storm the stronghold, Oñate resolved to surround and starve the defenders. The siege of Mixton lasted several weeks.[53] The Spaniards again misjudged not only the strength and organization of their adversaries but the effectiveness with which they could communicate with their allies who were located elsewhere. After days of minor skirmishes, a group of Indians from the peñol of Teul attacked the Spanish camp. About a dozen Spaniards rode out with Oñate, pursuing the attackers for half a league before they were able to overcome them. This sudden assault that drew off a number of the Spaniards' best fighting men very likely was planned in concert with the defenders of Mixton. When the Spaniards returned to the peñol, a major battle took place.[54] The rebels "brought together all the rest of the Indians that they could from the whole country, both enemies and friends, together with those who one day left the peñol, in one part, and the Indians from nearby pueblos in another two parts." The furious combat went on for four hours. In the end the rebels burned and robbed the Spanish camp, killing up to thirteen Spaniards, six blacks, and more than three hundred Indian allies. The beleaguered Spanish forces made a dangerous retreat to Guadalajara.[55]

The rebels' solid victory at Mixton in early April 1541 triggered a new round of revolts in communities such as Nochistlan, which earlier was a haven for people from Juchipila who had refused to participate. Martín, a principal and naguatato of Juchipila, testified that with Oñate's defeat the communities of Contla, Ocotique, Acatique, and Matlatlan also all rebelled—significantly, all Tecuexe pueblos, confirming that the rebellion had spread beyond Cazcan territory. Oñate was forced to send an urgent request for aid to Mendoza in Mexico City. The viceroy instructed don Luis de Castilla and Pedro de Alvarado, who had returned to the fleet and were waiting in the Pueblos de Avalos (today part of Colima) to embark on their voyage of discovery to the South Sea, to go to the immediate aid of the Spaniards of New Galicia, even if it meant sacrificing the equipment and supplies they had amassed for their voyage. Oñate asked directly for their help as well. They responded promptly, probably arriving in Guadalajara in mid-June 1541.[56] They also sent companies of men to various locales: Diego López de Zúñiga to Etzatlan with thirty men on horse and foot, Miguel de Ibarra to Tonala with forty horsemen, Hernán Nieto with twelve to Ameca, Juan del Camino with twelve to Cuiseo, Martín Monje with ten to Tenamaztlan, Francisco de Godoy with thirty to Compostela, and Hernando de Alarcón with thirty Spanish footmen to Autlan.[57] Mendoza also sent Íñigo López de Anuncibay from

Mexico City with an additional company of one hundred horsemen and told Juan de Alvarado to take thirty horsemen and six thousand Indian allies from Michoacan to New Galicia. Juan Hernández de Híjar, alcalde of Purificación, sent notice to don Luis de Castilla "that all the Indians are overtaking the town." Around the same time Oñate also requested that the viceroy declare *"justa la guerra,"* allow slaves to be taken, and send the official branding iron.[58]

The War of the Pueblos

What today we know as the Mixton War was a large-scale indigenous movement for liberation from Spanish rule, characterized by widespread (but far from unanimous) native participation, interethnic collaboration and friction, conflicting loyalties, and repeated betrayals. Before considering the key events that marked the end of the first phase of the war—the Spanish defeat at the peñol of Nochistlan, followed by the successful defense of Guadalajara—we must try to understand what was going on in the indigenous countryside. Clandestine communication among pueblos, the formation of new alliances, cooperation and participation that at times was willing and other times reluctant, and the expression of long-standing resentments as well as new hopes reflected and expressed the varied and complex response of Indian communities to the rebellion. The Spaniards' motivations for fighting, by contrast, were simple. They intended to suppress the rebellion and force the Indians to serve them, either through the encomienda or as slaves, and to pacify the region so they could continue to search for sources of precious metals.[59] It was not, however, the Spaniards' war. Their position was defensive and reactive. Our understanding of the indigenous insurrection is, of course, limited by the sources. Although the residencia of the viceroy's conduct of the war includes testimony from many indigenous witnesses, these men either had accepted amnesty for their role in the uprising or claimed that they remained loyal to the Spaniards throughout the upheaval. These biases notwithstanding, the postwar testimony of Spaniards and reconciled Indians affords the best key we have to the indigenous perspective and must be examined for what it reveals.

The testimony coalesces around several interrelated issues. One concerns the part that "outsider" religious figures played in the revolt. They were reported to have instigated rebellion by promising the coming of a radical new order once Indians freed themselves from Spanish rule and all trappings of Christianity. A related series of questions involves organization. How did committed rebels persuade or coerce communities, or parts of them, to participate? How did the conspirators communicate? Why did some people rebel, while others did not? Why were some pueblos (or parts of them) loyal to their Spanish masters? Some Spaniards and Indian survivors claimed that Indians warned encomenderos of coming attacks and protected them or their property. Did they do so out of fear of retribution? Or were they retaliating against longtime enemies by informing the Spaniards of their movements and intentions? Certainly motivations could have been mixed and decisions colored by ambivalence.

The events discussed up to this point have pointed to the crucial interaction between the Zacateca people of the mountains and the Cazcanes. Occupying areas that were in proximity, these groups had long experience of contact. Their languages, both closely related to the Nahuatl widely spoken in central Mexico, probably were mutually intelligible.[60] The contacts between them need not always have been friendly, but possibly as Cazcanes increasingly chafed under Spanish rule and as they began relocating either temporarily or permanently to less accessible mountainous areas to the north to escape Spanish demands, the ties between these groups might have strengthened. The Zacatecas surely understood that they too might face the threat (and consequences) of the expanding colonial order—as indeed they later did. Making common cause with the Cazcanes, then, could have made a good deal of sense from their point of view.

Spaniards testified at length regarding the Zacateca (or Chichimec) "messengers of the devil," as they called them, and their promises, which at their simplest guaranteed the restoration of all that was lost: "they would end up with the land because it was theirs."[61] Mendoza, whose report reflects the views of most Spaniards, detailed how the rebels anticipated and preached a millenarian order in which their ancestors would revive. With them would come "many riches and jewels of gold and turquoise and feathers and mirrors and bows and arrows that never break" and ornaments for the women. No one would die; the old would become young again. The fields would flourish without cultivation, firewood would appear in houses without having been cut, fish would jump out of the water to be caught, and food would be prepared without cooking. The "devil" would provide superior arms and battle regalia, even assuring that the warriors' face painting would become indelible. Men could have as many women as they wanted, contrary to the friars' insistence "that they should be content with one until the day they die." Wild beasts, however, would attack and eat any man or woman who persisted in believing in the Christian god.[62]

Juan Hernández de Híjar, always expansive in his testimony, provided further details that he had heard from Antón and Alonso, respectively a lord and brother of the cacique of Etzatlan. They and other "indios principales" told him that it was the Cazcanes and Zacatecas and especially the people of Atengoychan who had tried to persuade them to rebel, saying that the devil "would kill the Christians of this New Spain and those who came by sea and those from Castile with three arrows. And that it was no longer necessary to cultivate maize because by planting in the morning, by midday it would be green (*elote*) and by night ready to harvest."[63] He also heard of "abominations," including a diabolical ritual of "throwing water on their shameful parts, saying that was baptism." He also discovered that Indians were buying "hundreds of devils" (idols?) in or from Atengoychan and that around Purificación "the Indians reverted to their temples and rituals and diabolical ceremonies that they had before."[64]

Many Spaniards and Indians said that the messengers were mainly Zacatecas, but people from the Cazcan pueblos also began to act as emissaries. A man named Alonso, who after the war was a principal of Apozol, explained that a principal from Mecatabasco had traveled along with the Zacateca messengers, sent by his lord "who had been converted. . . . And to give them more credibility he sent with the principal the said messengers from whom they understood the chant and speech of the devil and they believed it all."[65] The main vehicle by which the message of liberation (and death for the Christians) spread was a *tlatol* (from Nahuatl *tlatolli*, meaning a statement, although in New Galicia the Spaniards seem to suggest that it was a song or chant). The messengers also carried arrows wrapped or tied in deerskin and gourds that they used as drums to summon people.

These media of communication carried special powers—and not solely from the indigenous perspective. The acting governor of New Galicia, Cristóbal de Oñate, made the remarkable statement that once the rebels brought the tlatol to the pueblos, "they could not fail to rise." Francisco Delgadillo, the encomendero of Apozol, said that in Tlaltenango the messengers gathered people from many other Cazcan pueblos and "gave them to understand that all those who heard the chant and the gourd-drum would revive their parents and grandparents and would join together and kill all the Christians and all the Indians who did not come to hear the gourd." Francisco, a man from the Tecuexe community of Tequila, explained that the arrows wrapped in leather signified war and stated that people from his pueblo—himself included—rebelled with the Zacatecas.[66] Another man from Tequila confessed that he since had realized that everything the messengers said was "a joke and a lie," but at the time he believed it, and because of it he suffered greatly. He was hardly alone in believing the message and its promises. Alonso, a principal of Suchipil in the valley of Aguacatlan, testified that he saw the Indians arrive with the tlatol and that "all the people of his province rebelled and he with them, believing . . . that it was true about the coming of their ancestors and the death of Christians and for that reason the Indians of this province planted few fields."[67]

Communication also took the normal form of word of mouth. Given the relatively small size and dispersed situation of many of the pueblos in New Galicia, people commonly moved around and between them. Martín, a naguatato of Juchipila, explained that in the early stages of the rebellion the various communities kept one another informed and up-to-date on events. In those uneasy days the customary volume of movement along the roads may well have increased but perhaps did not appear to be outside the norm, contributing to the Spaniards' ignorance of or confusion about what was going on. Given that the Indians often were away from their pueblos, such absences might long go unnoticed or, if noted, were more likely to cause anger or frustration than alarm.

The anti-Christian message of the Zacatecas and their allies seemingly resonated strongly in many communities. Spaniards and Indians reported what appeared to be systematic burning and destruction of monasteries, churches, and sacred objects, including the desecration of the latter by rubbing them against their private parts.[68] Rebels ridiculed and reviled key rituals of Roman Catholicism, raising tortillas in mockery of the sacrament of the Eucharist and washing their heads in a black dye to remove all vestiges of Christian baptism.[69] Not only did the symbols of Christianity become targets for retaliation, however; the clergy did as well. Rebels forced the friars out of their establishment in Juchipila and killed Fray Juan de Esperanza and Fray Antonio de Cuellar, who lived in the monastery of Etzatlan. Antonio, who after the war was a principal and brother of the lord of Etzatlan, said that he was accompanying Fray

Antonio de Cuellar from Ameca to Etzatlan when "some Indians from among the rebels came out in the road and shot the said friar with arrows ... and with a macana [wooden sword edged with obsidian] broke his mouth and teeth, saying now he would not say to them the words of God and Saint Mary." Diego Hurtado testified that Antonio came to Ameca to tell him that Fray Antonio de Cuellar had been attacked. Hurtado and some other men found him still alive but grievously wounded; within two days he died. Cuellar was reputed to be one of the best interpreters in the region and ostensibly regarded by the Indians (although evidently not by all) "as a father."[70]

Given the evidence that some communities, or parts of communities, resisted the rebels' message of liberation to Indians and death to Christians, to what extent did these differences reflect indigenous enmities or factionalism as opposed to fear of Spanish retribution? Juan, a naguatato and alguacil of Cuzpatlan, where the encomendero Andrés de Salinas was killed, testified that he was aware that many people warned their masters of the coming violence. Juan stated that he wanted to do the same but that Malachan, the son of Xiuteque, the lord of Juchipila, together with a lord of another part of Juchipila and a number of rebels, would not allow him (or presumably others) to do so; "rather they threatened them" that if they failed to rebel "they would eat them as they did the Christians, and from this fear they rebelled with the others."[71] We cannot know, of course, to what extent this testimony was self-serving. Yet some people did put themselves in harm's way to help the Spaniards. Don Pedro, the señor and gobernador of Agualulco after the war, testified that he "always was a friend of the Christians and a good subject of the king [and] refused to accept the tlatol." He actually turned two of the messengers over to Diego López de Zúñiga, the captain of the garrison stationed at Etzatlan, who hanged them. Don Pedro's own pueblo joined the rebellion, and he fled to Etzatlan to put himself under the protection of the Spaniards there. Don Juan, lord of Suchipil, testified that he warned Alonso Delgado and actually fled with Delgado "so they would not kill him as well because he had told them he would not rebel."[72]

Another don Pedro, lord of Tetitlan, said that don Juan, lord of Etzatlan, and Cazcan Indians told him that "if they didn't rebel the devil's fire would come and encompass all of them," and so he and his people rebelled out of fear. He also testified that in his pueblo he witnessed the sacrifice of "an Indian from Xalisco and an Indian from Juchipila who had been raised among them."[73] This act probably was meant to intimidate the people of Xalisco, who tried to remain neutral in the upheaval. The long-suffering cacique of Xalisco, don Cristóbal, explained at length his experience of the war. He became aware of the message of rebellion and the tlatol that the Zacatecas and Cazcanes were spreading in the area. Concerned about the consequences, he "sent his Indians to other pueblos that they thought of as friends so that they would know and understand that everything the Cazcanes and Zacatecas were saying . . . was lies and he did this two or three times. And the messengers . . . told him how those friendly pueblos, which are Tetitlan and Etzatlan, did not want to do what he advised." Don Cristóbal then sent another messenger, a principal of his pueblo, to Tetitlan, where he was killed (probably the man mentioned by don Pedro, the lord of Tetitlan, as having been sacrificed). Alonso, a "naguatato principal of Xalisco," testified that they were all "terrified and had great fear of the rebels" and looked to the Spaniards for help.[74]

Alonso Rodríguez, a vecino of Compostela after the war, testified that he heard from many people, especially don Cristóbal and the lords of Tepic and Suchipil, that many times they were pressured to rebel with the pueblos of Juchipila and Tlaltenango and other Cazcan communities. Another vecino of Compostela, Juan Durán, said that he witnessed don Cristóbal come "to beg help in this city because the rebel Indians were coming to make war and do other harm and [to ask] that the authorities of this city favor him so they could defend themselves from them."[75] The community of Xalisco clearly found itself in a very difficult position. As discussed in chapter 3, they were Tecuales and therefore perhaps somewhat isolated ethnically in the area. The people of Tetitlan also might have been Tecual but apparently had a Cazcan ruler, probably accounting for their participation in the rebellion.[76] Xalisco belonged to the powerful acting governor of New Galicia, Cristóbal de Oñate, who, as seen, exploited his encomienda of Xalisco with a strong hand. Given their subjection to Oñate, the community's rulers must have felt they had no choice but to try to sit the war out.

Very likely other communities also weighed their fears of their Spanish masters and the protection the latter could afford against the threats and blandishments of the messengers and rebels. A surprising number of witnesses, both Spanish and Indian, even including those who affirmed that they participated in the rebellion, mentioned warnings that they received or made regarding the imminent threat to persons or property. The people of Hernando de Acebedo's encomienda of Zapotlan warned not only him but also Juan Gallego, Ortiz de Zúñiga, Antonio de Aguayo, and other vecinos of Purificación. Those who received warnings (such as Antonio de Aguayo) included Spaniards who were notorious for their mistreatment of the Indians, such as Cristóbal de Oñate's harsh mayordomo, Domingo de Arteaga. Even in the Cazcanes' stronghold, men such as Juan de Zubia (encomendero of Mezquituta) and Francisco Delgadillo (encomendero of Apozol) received warnings and were able to salvage some of their property or move their livestock out of harm's way.[77] These warnings suggest that perhaps some Indians were more interested in making common cause with their neighbors than in taking revenge on Spaniards by harming them or their property.

The information from Spanish and indigenous witnesses who survived the war affords only a partial, if suggestive, picture of complicated individual and collective decision making based on a range of considerations—ethnicity, geographic location, factionalism and rivalry, and fear of Spanish reprisals weighed against the intimidation and inducements offered by rebels. Tenamaztle's deposition, which at present is the only known source other than the testimony presented in the residencia that reflects the perspective of local Indians on events, has to be considered political or polemical in nature; he mentions none of these factors that surely played a crucial role in determining who rebelled, why, and when.

Certain conclusions do seem likely. The main rebellion probably originated with an alliance between Zacatecas and Cazcanes. The former participated not just as outside agitators carrying an anti-Spanish message of millenarian revival but were present in substantial numbers at least in the first of the peñoles, Tepetistaque, which was virtually within their territory. Within specific communities, even Cazcan ones, existing splits, rivalries, and complex forms of sociopolitical organization meant that some people responded positively to the call to rise up, while others tried to remain neutral. Individuals and communities that failed to join the insurrection often found themselves at the mercy of rebels—who might have been their longtime enemies in any case. Hoping for protection or to gain favor, or fearing retribution, some who eschewed the rebellion turned to Spanish officials and encomenderos. Others yielded to rebel intimidation, or had a change of heart as the rebels' victories accumulated and they appeared to have the upper hand. In the next stage of the war, many more communities would join the war against the Spaniards.

The End of the Beginning

Once Pedro de Alvarado arrived in Guadalajara with a force from the now-abandoned South Sea fleet (in which he invested, along with the viceroy and don Luis de Castilla), he quickly became impatient with the pace of deliberations on the next course of action. He was ready once again to exercise the fighting ardor that yielded victories in the past (but that also led to disaster during Cortés's absence from Tenochtitlan, when Alvarado brought on open revolt among the Mexica with his bloody massacre of the nobles). Unlike Guzmán, who used combat and violence as a means to gain his ends, Alvarado was a true warrior and devotee of battle. He failed to grasp, however, that Spaniards in New Galicia had been forced into a defensive position in which a daring offensive, insufficiently prepared and confronting far more formidable warriors than the ones he faced in central Mexico, could bring disaster. Cristóbal de Oñate and others urged caution, perhaps not least because the rainy season had created difficult conditions for fighting, but the headstrong Alvarado insisted on departing immediately for the peñol of Nochistlan.[78]

He arrived there in late June with a large force of one hundred Spanish horsemen and another hundred Spaniards on foot, together with several thousand indigenous allies recruited in Michoacan. In contrast to Oñate's decision to besiege Mixton for several weeks, Alvarado had little patience with attempts at negotiation and instead made a direct assault, precipitating a counterattack by a dauntingly large number of rebels. The overwhelmed Spaniards began to panic and flee along with their allies. Alvarado was forced to dismount to lead his horse through muddy terrain. As the routed forces retreated down a slope, another man's mount slipped and fell on Alvarado, throwing him into a ravine where his own horse fell on top of him. Oñate had followed Alvarado to the area of the peñol and, observing the disaster, helped the survivors to escape. They carried the mortally injured Alvarado back to Guadalajara, where he died a few days later, in early July, at the home of Juan del Camino, the former criado of Nuño de Guzmán.[79]

The pointless death of the seemingly invincible Alvarado carried more than just symbolic significance. For Spaniards, perhaps those in central Mexico more than in New Galicia, where the implications of the war were by then all too well understood, the shocking news of Alvarado's death underscored the seriousness of the revolt and what they perceived as

PETRUS ALVARADUS MISSUS AB ANTONIO   22
de Mendozza in Sibollæ provinciam, cum plerifque è fuis
à Xalifcanis occiditur.

A NTONIUS de Mendozza Novæ Hifpaniæ Prorex, Petrum Alvaradum in Sibol-
lam Provinciam (quam prædivitem effe intellexerat) cum feptingentis militibus
mittit. Ille comparatis equis & multis aliis rebus ad profectionem neceffariis, in
itinere audit Indos Xalifco incolas rebellionem molites adverfus Hifpanos: in quorum
auxilium cum maxima exercitus parte proficifcitur. Invenit in via Petrum de Zuinga valde
triftem ob multorum Hifpanorum ab Indis cæforum mortem: eum ad fe receptum adverfus Xalifcanos ducit, atque collem, in quem confugerant & fefe munierant, cingunt. Cæfas
enim integras arbores fimul colligarant, infertis inter eas magnis faxis, poft quas latebant
tanquam in propugnaculo Indi, atque alia ingentia faxa fimiliter congefferant. Poftquam
eò pervenerunt Hifpani, ftatim concitatis equis in collem adverfum contendunt. Indi fub-
lato magno & horrendo clamore, vincula, quibus arbores cæfæ ligatæ, fecant, atque ipfas
arbores cum faxis, magno impetu in fubeuntes collem Hifpanos provolvunt, atque infu-
per ingentia illa faxa. Illa cum arboribus in hunc modum provoluta, quotquot obvios ha-
buerunt Hifpanos profternunt & proterunt. Ipfe Alvaradus ab equo cum reliquis deturba-
to dejectus, fimiliter in præceps ruit, & altero poft die moritur. Interrogatus ubi dolorem
fentiret, Extremum, inquit, in anima.

F 3

FIGURE 11. This engraving from Theodor de Bry is an imaginary portrayal
of the battle of Nochistlan, in which Pedro de Alvarado was injured. The
caption in the de Bry volume refers to Xalisco but not to Nochistlan. At the
lower left the mortally injured Alvarado is being helped from the battlefield.
There is no indication that the Spaniards at the time were in full retreat, and
the native warriors shown at the summit of the peñol are depicted as club-
swinging primitives. *Americae pars quinta* (Frankfurt: privately printed, 1595),
courtesy of Florida State University Libraries Special Collections.

FIGURE 12. Codex Telleriano-Remensis (plate 46r). The Spanish gloss for the complex representation on the left reads, "This year of Ten Houses and of 1541 the Indians of Jalisco rose up, whom don Antonio de Mendoza suppressed. Retreating from the Indians, don Pedro de Alvarado, whom the Indians called Tonatiuh, which means the sun, died." Alvarado is represented on the upper left with eyes closed (symbolizing his death), with the sun sign attached. To his right is a member of a religious order baptizing an Indian. He probably is not a Franciscan, in contrast to the figure shown under the year 1543, wearing the typical robe of the Franciscan order. Below Alvarado is the peñol of Nochistlan (note the flowering nopal cactus representing its place name), surrounded by stone barricades and a stream of water. A naked Indian defends it with a bow and arrow. The Spaniard fighting him may be don Antonio de Mendoza (the two icons attached to him, the maguey plant [*metl*] and gopher [*tozan*] combined may be *metozan*, or Mendoza; see Quiñones Keber, *Codex Telleriano-Remensis*, 237). Reproduced by permission of the Bibliothèque Nationale de France.

a potential threat to all of New Spain were it not thoroughly suppressed. The message that the Indians received—probably more from the resounding success of their defense of the peñol than from the death of Alvarado as such—was quite different: they could vanquish the mightiest of their foes and oppressors. In the aftermath of this victory, the rebellion spread rapidly; according to the viceroy's report, it was at this time that Fray Antonio de Cuellar was killed in or near Etzatlan in the incident described earlier. The swelling momentum of revolt reached communities and areas that heretofore were relatively unaffected: "part of Tonala, part of Cuiseo and Oconabal, the peñoles of La Laguna de Etzatlan and Tenamaztlan, part of the valley of Milpa, Tequila, Abaluco [Agualulco?], Aguacatlan, Xala, the valley of Guaxacatlan, Ixtlan, Aguatlan, Xalacingo, Amatlan, Xistique, and many other pueblos in the jurisdiction of Compostela."[80] These communities included ethnic groups and pueblos located well outside Cazcan territory. Tonala was Tecuexe (and once considered reliably loyal); Cuiseo (Cuitzeo) was a community of Coca speakers southeast of Guadalajara (in what is today the state of Michoacan); the Guaxacatlan Valley, also to the southeast, was home to Coanos.

Because the revolt had spread to Coyna and other areas close to Michoacan, the viceroy sent Lic. Alonso Maldonado, one of the oidores of the audiencia in Mexico City, with some horsemen to the Pueblos de Avalos. After he arrived, Maldonado as well as Oñate and Castilla all wrote to Mendoza insisting that only the viceroy's presence could bring the rebellion to an end. The viceroy resolved to go himself to "extinguish the fire," taking with him "the leading Indians of this country in order to leave it secure."[81] When he arrived in Michoacan he found letters from Oñate informing him that the rebels had surrounded Guadalajara, where the residents had fortified two houses belonging to Juan del Camino and taken refuge there. According to Melchor Alvarez, who was there, the houses were in the part of the town called "*el río de la barranca*," near the pueblo of Tlacotlan.[82] The Indians burned the church and a number of houses and began to knock down the buildings where the residents were sheltering.[83]

One of the settlers who remained in Guadalajara was Andrés de Villanueva, who had lived in New Galicia since arriving there with Guzmán. In 1554, when he was alcalde ordinario in Guadalajara, he prepared a deposition detailing his services during the war. He explained that all the married men in the town made and signed an agreement that they would evacuate the women and children "outside this kingdom." Villanueva refused to sign. Instead "he swore by God and the cross that neither he nor his wife would leave that city until all the country was quiet and pacified, so that all the infidels would come to the knowledge of God, our lord, and the dominion of the king." The defenders tore up the agreement, and their families remained in Guadalajara. Villanueva's wife was an indigenous woman; perhaps her ties to both communities strengthened her, and her husband's, resolve to see the conflict through to the end.[84]

Repeated alarms and calls to arms sounded as the townspeople awaited reinforcements, apparently receiving some foodstuffs from Indians to the south who remained friendly.[85] By late September a force of fifteen thousand native warriors surrounded the city.[86] Jerónimo López, who was not in Guadalajara but presumably talked to people who were, described how the warriors approached the town "in rows of seven by seven. They were naked and each squadron of three rows came with different colors—yellow, black, and blue—and feathers, with their bows and arrows."[87] Andrés de Villanueva was among a company of thirty-seven horsemen—perhaps half the Spanish men in the city—who mounted a series of successful forays and finally broke the siege and dispelled the attackers. Among the Spanish participants was the captain whom the viceroy had sent from Mexico City, Iñigo López de Anuncibay. Although the numbers seem extremely uneven, the Spanish horsemen targeted a squadron of elite warriors; for once the Spanish horsemen were fighting on the kind of open ground where their cavalry could dominate and disperse the enemy. When the horsemen finally routed the elite warriors, the rest of the forces surrounding the town fled. Perhaps one thousand of the attackers died. Some Spaniards ostensibly credited the victory to the warrior saint, Santiago, who was said to have appeared reliably during other campaigns, although neither Villanueva nor any of his witnesses mentioned this "miraculous intervention."[88] By whatever means, and with the viceroy's reinforcements yet to arrive, Guadalajara and its residents survived, although the semidestroyed town soon moved for the fourth and last time. With the siege broken, the war entered a new phase.

CHAPTER 6

The Viceroy's War

Because in this New Spain many Indian pueblos have risen up and
rebelled against His Majesty, it serves His Majesty that I should
go in person well armed to pacify those pueblos and Indians
and punish and warn them and bring them to submission to the
authority of His Majesty and rectify the trouble and damage that
could occur in all of New Spain.
    —Testimony of Viceroy don Antonio de Mendoza, May 1544[1]

✝ THE FIRST STAGE OF THE WAR LASTED ABOUT A YEAR AND ENDED
when the Spanish defenders broke the siege of Guadalajara in September
1541. The next began with the arrival of the viceroy, who brought massive
reinforcements to the beleaguered Spaniards in the region. Although the
focus in the previous chapter on key episodes at Tepetistaque, Mixton,
Nochistlan, and finally Guadalajara might suggest that the struggle was
discontinuous, that impression is misleading. All of central and southern
New Galicia was on a war footing. If major engagements were intermit-
tent, at no point was there a real hiatus in the conflict that might have
afforded an opportunity for reconciliation or compromise; indeed, there
is no evidence that either side wanted to pursue those options. Probably
many minor skirmishes and even some fairly substantial episodes of combat went unreported or were only minimally noted and thus do not figure

in the better-known narrative defined by the main battles. For much of this time, especially after the Spanish defeat at Mixton, the rebels so dominated the countryside in central and southern New Galicia that Spaniards had trouble maintaining contact with one another and moving from place to place.

Whether the war also embroiled the northern province of Culiacan, which was in turmoil through most of the 1530s, is not clear. Throughout this period the men involved in the expedition to New Mexico were sporadically present in Culiacan, possibly discouraging widespread revolt there. The linguistic and other dissimilarities between the indigenous groups of Sinaloa and those of central and southern New Galicia also could have impeded their making common cause.

The various companies of Spanish horsemen and foot soldiers dispatched to what were considered strategic or vulnerable outposts after Alvarado and Castilla mobilized the men from the South Sea fleet very likely met with opposition from the rebels. These companies entered hostile territory and struggled to create or maintain garrisons and reestablish Spanish authority. Andrés de Villanueva, for example, detailed his participation in what was a substantial engagement that otherwise seems to have gone unreported; possibly it preceded the defeat at Mixton. According to Villanueva, Oñate, the acting governor, led a company into Guaxacatlan. For three days "the Indian natives did not cease waging war [on us] night and day. . . . At the end of three days the captain wished to cross the country where there was a military camp located near Cacaluta. For one entire day, from before dawn until nightfall, the natives did not desist waging war, without allowing the said Andrés de Villanueva or the captain or other Spaniards of the said company to eat or drink." The Indians had cut them off from the only source of water. Villanueva and Alonso de Castañeda were in the rearguard with ten others, but the fighting so exhausted most of the men that toward the end of the day only those two fought on, trying to defend the others. Pursued by their enemies down a steep slope on which they could not use their horses, Castañeda placed his harquebus on Villanueva's shoulder to fire at the Indian "captain," whom he killed.[2] The leader's death ended the Indians' attack, and the Spaniards regained access to the crucial source of water.

A deposition executed on behalf of Juan Michel in Compostela in 1548 detailed another series of engagements during the first phase of the war. Michel had fought with Oñate at Mixton, where he received wounds that were nearly fatal. According to Diego Vázquez, after the defeat at Mixton, "within a few days the whole country rose up, [so] that from Michoacan to here there wasn't a single pueblo at peace except those where the Spaniards had garrisons." Although not fully recovered from his wounds, Michel joined the company of horsemen led by treasurer Francisco de Godoy that Oñate sent to defend Compostela. Vázquez recalled that on reaching the city, Godoy essentially turned all responsibility over to captain Juan de Villalba, who named Juan Michel "caudillo of the horsemen." Michel and Villalba then headed to the valley of Aguacatlan to set up camp where they learned that the rebels had established a stronghold at Xala. The two led their horsemen to attack the peñol. Because Villalba and his men were pinned down under a hail of stones, out of the company of twenty horsemen only Michel and three other men were able to ascend. They were wounded and forced to make a dangerous descent and retreat.[3]

A few days later, while Juan de Villalba remained with a garrison at Aguacatlan, Michel took nine horsemen to the sierra of Iztlan, a pueblo that belonged to encomendero Alonso López.[4] Ascending the mountain, they overcame a squadron of Indian defenders, but on the descent they encountered an even larger force. With their horses exhausted and overheated, the Spaniards argued that they should retreat, but Michel did not trust their ostensible Indian allies, who he thought might turn on them. He pointed out that if they descended, "some Indians that they had with them, who in fear had hidden underneath the horses, would kill them" and that "the Spaniards would receive more harm in descending than in breaking those Indians." They succeeded in breaking the Indians' ranks, but Michel again found himself in jeopardy, his horse having fallen twice amid the enemy. The Spaniards returned to the camp to find Villalba in a state of high anxiety, as by then days had passed with no news or messengers. Although he desperately needed information about the situation elsewhere, Villalba quailed at the notion of sending the still bleeding and exhausted Michel to try to penetrate the mountain pass, but Michel insisted that "he wanted to go to find out what was going on in the world."[5] Like most men who later recounted their military services in hopes of gaining recognition and concessions from the Crown or its officials, Michel might have exaggerated the extremity of both the dangers he faced and his own accomplishments. Even so, events most likely played out in much the way he described.[6]

Despite the fears of Villalba and his companions, Michel with some companions headed for Etzatlan, where a garrison of thirty horsemen in a state of constant alert expressed their astonishment that Michel had managed to cross the pass with only a few horsemen.[7] Learning that Pedro de Alvarado had died and that Guadalajara was surrounded, Michel took all the food he could gather and returned to Villalba and the others, who "received them in tears because they feared he had died and to see that the said Juan Michel had returned from Etzatlan without going to Guadalajara to see his home, mother, and siblings."[8] Michel's mother, Elvira Ordoñez, was said to be the first married Spanish woman who settled in New Galicia with her family. By the late 1540s Michel's wife Catalina de Mena had died, although apparently not during the war itself.

Prior to the arrival of Mendoza from Mexico City, this succession of skirmishes and attacks in the countryside probably accounted for much of the fighting and casualties during the first year of the war. Few of these engagements ended in the Spaniards' favor. By this time virtually all able-bodied Spaniards had become embroiled in the conflict in one way or another, either defending the main towns or attempting, as in this case, to establish or defend outposts in rebel territory. In addition to the region's settlers, the mobilization of the personnel from the South Sea fleet introduced outsiders into the struggle, including the men who traveled from Guatemala with Pedro de Alvarado. His relative Juan de Alvarado also arrived with a large force of Spaniards and Indians from Michoacan at the viceroy's orders.[9] When Mendoza arrived in the late fall of 1541, he brought yet another group of Spaniards and thousands of indigenous allies from central Mexico to New Galicia. This very substantial influx of outsiders not only marked a shift in the balance of military power from the rebels to the Spaniards for the first time since the war began but also led to significant demographic change after the war's conclusion. The diverse individuals and groups who participated in suppressing the rebellion during the second phase of the war played a vital part in the final conquest of New Galicia.

Spanish Defenders of New Galicia

The settlers of New Galicia were playing for very high stakes. They were defending their lands, livelihood, families, and control over Indian communities. Their participation in the campaign to suppress the rebellion hardly requires an explanation. What, then, were the motivations of the men who participated in the war but lacked a comparable investment in local society?

It is generally assumed that, as Spaniards conquered and occupied one part of Mexico after another, many of the men who participated in these entradas were relative newcomers to the Indies who had not yet established themselves. Often they were men who failed to receive encomiendas or other grants, or who arrived too late—or lacked the connections—to be contenders for these rewards. The war in western Mexico, however, took place twenty years—essentially a generation—after the conquest of Tenochtitlan and the Aztec Empire, by which time socioeconomic and political conditions in central Mexico had begun to stabilize and consolidate.[10] This was an era of expanding economic opportunities, as Spaniards established an array of enterprises using indigenous labor, relying also on the African slaves they brought with them.[11] Newly arrived immigrants, therefore, should have found suitable niches pretty readily, especially if they could turn to already established family members or acquaintances.

The rapidly changing direction of society in New Spain—from the militarism of the conquest to the more peaceful and less heady pursuit of economic gain—might have left some of the old-timers stranded. While some newcomers responded to the viceroy's call for men to join in the pacification or "reconquest" of New Galicia, a surprising number of participants in the campaign already had spent years in the Indies and accrued a good deal of fighting experience before entering the fray in the West. Although the question of prior experience is impossible to quantify because the data on participants is incomplete, a look at some of the men known to have fought in New Galicia makes it clear that not only did many of them have ample prior experience campaigning in the Indies but some fought in Europe as well. One of these was don Luis de Castilla, who (probably with his father) fought on the royal side to suppress the comuneros' revolt in Castile, as well as in Navarra, before emigrating to New Spain.[12] Castilla, a member of the Order of Santiago, had impeccable royal and noble connections in Spain, as well as ties with some of New Spain's most influential figures. Antonio de Agudelo also fought against the comuneros in Castile as well as in Melilla in North Africa before emigrating to Mexico, while Clemente de Mederos fought in Italy, France, and Tunisia before arriving in Mexico and going to fight in the Mixton War, where he lost a hand.[13]

Another participant in the war, Juan Juárez, claimed that he accompanied Fray Nicolás de Ovando to Hispaniola and then spent many years in Cuba before departing with Cortés for Mexico in 1519.[14] He subsequently participated in the campaigns in Pánuco and Michoacan but apparently did not receive an encomienda. Juan de Avila participated in Pánfilo de Narváez's 1528 expedition to Florida, from which he (fortuitously) returned to Cuba; went to Hispaniola, where he joined the campaign against longtime rebel Enriquillo; and then moved on to New Spain.[15] He received a small encomienda in the area of Pánuco and later accompanied Nuño de Guzmán on his entrada into the West.[16] Antonio de Aller accompanied Licenciado Ayllón to Florida in 1526 and later spent a year and a half in Venezuela before going to Mexico and fighting in the war in New Galicia, where he received serious wounds in the face and elsewhere and claimed to have spent more than three thousand pesos. In 1542 he was a vecino of Mexico City.[17] Both Antonio Busto and Juan de Moscoso were in Santa Marta and Cartagena before they went to New Spain. The latter left Cuba for Mexico with Mendoza and took six horses and eight retainers to the war in New Galicia.[18] Some of these men had long experience just in New Spain. Juan de Cuevas fought in the conquests of Michoacan and Colima. Francisco Santos de la Rosa participated in the conquest of Mexico with Cortés, then went on to the conquest of Colima and the expedition of Francisco Cortés into New Galicia, returning to the region fifteen years later with Viceroy Mendoza to suppress the indigenous rebellion.[19]

For other Spaniards the Mixton War might have marked the beginning of careers that would take them elsewhere as well. A number of veterans of this conflict later went on to Peru. Francisco Mejía de Loaysa fought against Gonzalo Pizarro in Peru in the mid-1540s and stayed on to become a vecino (and probably encomendero) of La Paz.[20] Don Hernando de Cárdenas was a vecino of Arequipa in 1549 when he made a deposition stating that he went with Viceroy Mendoza to New Galicia. He subsequently accompanied the ill-fated viceroy Blasco Núñez Vela to Peru, where he was captured.[21] Gonzalo Pizarro would have executed him if friends had not interceded on Cárdenas's behalf.[22] Perhaps the most extraordinary odyssey (complete with its Penelope) of a Spanish veteran of the Mixton War was that of Juan de Ribas, who fought in New Galicia with the viceroy and then went on to Yucatan. He married there but, leaving his wife with her parents, departed for Peru. There he fought against Gonzalo Pizarro and was wounded, losing two fingers on one hand. From Peru

he went on to Chile with Pedro de Valdivia. After twenty-four years'
absence he returned to Mérida in Yucatan to resume his long-interrupted
marriage.[23]

Although in recent years scholars have downplayed, with good reason, the notion that most participants in early conquests and campaigns
in the Indies were soldiers in the professional sense, the careers of these
men nonetheless suggest a degree of military experience that cannot be
discounted altogether.[24] Military campaigning was one of their vocations,
and they responded to the call to arms with alacrity, although had they
gained the security and prestige conferred by a good encomienda they
most likely would have put campaigning behind them. Antonio de Nava
fought in New Galicia, where he claimed that many of the Africans he
brought with him were killed. In Spain he had been the *alcaide* (warden)
of Mérida, and he later held *corregimientos* (administrative districts) in
New Spain.[25] Regardless of prior military background, however, many
participants in the war surely had failed to find adequate means of sup-
porting themselves and therefore responded to the opportunity that the
campaign presented, hoping their services might bring some reward from
the viceroy.

Although the men who arrived in New Galicia on the fleet of Pedro
de Alvarado had not intended to fight in the war, not surprisingly some
of them had careers similar to the men who accompanied Mendoza from
central Mexico; before the war intervened, they already had signed on
for an expedition of exploration and possible conquest. Alvaro de Paz was
the *proveedor general* (general purveyor) of Alvarado's fleet. Following the
Mixton War he went to Peru to fight Gonzalo Pizarro. He also participated in the conquest of Honduras, where he served as royal treasurer
in San Pedro, and was governor of Nicaragua. He eventually became a
vecino of Santiago de Guatemala.[26] Cristóbal de Zuleta also returned to
Guatemala after the war, where he was a vecino of Santiago in 1570. In
1556, however, he was a vecino and regidor of the town of Trinidad, which
he claimed he helped to establish.[27]

The Viceroy's Inner Circle

An important group of participants in the campaign were the men who
constituted Mendoza's inner circle of close associates, business partners,
officials, and interpreters. Don Luis de Castilla was a key figure during
Mendoza's tenure as viceroy. His father, don Pedro de Castilla, was a close

friend of Alonso de Estrada, the first royal treasurer in Mexico. While still in Spain, Estrada was appointed corregidor of the city of Cáceres in Extremadura in 1521. The local elite, however, apparently sympathized with the comuneros and refused to allow him to take up his duties.[28] At the time, don Pedro de Castilla was stationed in the nearby royal city of Trujillo. He took advantage of his ties of friendship with Cáceres's noble families to influence them to accept Estrada's appointment and, more persuasively, promised them he would use the forces at his disposal to lay waste to the city and countryside, burning and destroying every house in the city's jurisdiction and carrying off all the livestock to Trujillo, if they did not obey. The aristocrats of Cáceres backed down and accepted Estrada, who served his term and was replaced by Castilla. In 1523 Estrada went to Mexico as the first treasurer.[29]

Probably born in 1501 or 1502, don Luis de Castilla traveled to Mexico in 1529 in the entourage of his relative doña Juana de Zúñiga, Cortés's high-born second wife.[30] Soon after he arrived, the second audiencia sent him to establish a settlement near Tonala, an effort that Guzmán foiled, as seen in chapter 2. In the 1530s Castilla acquired the substantial encomiendas of Tuctepec and Nopala in Oaxaca. He was a regidor in Mexico City and made a fortune in silver mining in Taxco, where after the Mixton War Mendoza appointed him alcalde mayor. He also served as the corregidor of the important towns of Texcoco, Mexicalcingo, and Teozapotlan.[31] From the time that Mendoza ordered the abandonment of the fleet in Navidad so that the men could go to the aid of the settlers in New Galicia, Castilla took an active role in the Mixton War. When some of the indigenous allies who had accompanied Mendoza began to desert, Castilla personally went to the Pueblos de Avalos and nearby areas, where he recruited and accompanied four or five thousand warriors as reinforcements.[32] Castilla lived into the 1580s.

Castilla was a friend and associate of another key figure in the viceroy's campaign, the oidor Lic. Alonso Maldonado, who also had business ties with the viceroy's protégé Francisco Vázquez de Coronado, with whom he invested in mining interests in Taxco.[33] Maldonado was an important military commander during the war. Hernán Pérez de Bocanegra, a veteran of Guzmán's campaign in New Galicia and Mendoza's captain general during the war, as well as the viceroy's business partner, also had close ties with this group. Himself a kinsman of don Luis de Castilla, his grandson eventually obtained a dispensation to marry Castilla's granddaughter, and three of his sons married three daughters of Francisco Vázquez de Coronado.[34]

Another Mendoza protégé and relative (through his mother) who participated in the war was don Luis de Quesada, who accompanied the viceroy to Mexico in 1535 when he was seventeen. In 1541, shortly before joining the viceroy's entourage to fight in New Galicia, he married doña María Jaramillo, the daughter of Juan Jaramillo and his first wife, Cortés's famous interpreter, doña Marina. Although Jaramillo opposed the marriage, apparently he soon became sufficiently reconciled that he helped to outfit his son-in-law for the campaign.[35] Following the war, Quesada and his wife became embroiled in a bitter dispute with her stepmother (Jaramillo's second wife) over their inheritance from Jaramillo.

Thus the viceroy's personal and business associations once again brought the intricate politics of kinship and high political office to New Galicia, as members of his inner circle committed themselves to the campaign. Another member of the viceroy's entourage who, although lacking the noble status of men like Castilla or Quesada, nonetheless played a crucial role in the campaign was Agustín Guerrero, his mayordomo. Guerrero was captain of the viceroy's guard, in which capacity he worked with don Luis de Castilla. He also held the position of chancellor of the audiencia, responsible for the official seal that attested to the legality of any documents produced.[36] Unofficially Guerrero did a great deal more, such as auditing the treasury records, a time-consuming and important responsibility that he shared with the oidor Francisco Ceynos. Indeed, Guerrero probably was the single most important figure in Mendoza's administration, as the viceroy relied on him in nearly every aspect of his private and public affairs.[37] In 1540 Mendoza sent Guerrero, together with don Luis de Castilla, to conduct the negotiations with Pedro de Alvarado over the rights to the exploration of the South Sea; they met at the home of Pedro's relative Juan de Alvarado in Tiripitío in Michoacan at the end of November.[38] It is hardly surprising, then, that Guerrero also played a key role in the New Galicia campaign. He served as Mendoza's lieutenant general, although clearly his talents were in the financial rather than the military sphere. He was responsible for coordinating supplies and provisions for the viceroy's massive forces, disbursing payments and salaries. Probably before and certainly after the war, Guerrero also proved indispensable in the conduct of Mendoza's business affairs.[39] He might have been older than Mendoza; according to Jerónimo López, the Indian allies from central Mexico called Guerrero the *"Ytachi* of the viceroy, which in their language means father."[40]

The future first bishop of New Galicia, Bachiller Pedro Gómez de Maraver, who was from Granada and had connections with Mendoza's family there, also participated in the campaign. Arriving in New Spain in 1538, he was appointed ecclesiastical inspector for the Mixteca region. He was there when he heard that Mendoza was gathering his forces for the war in New Galicia. Gómez de Maraver returned to Mexico City to accompany Mendoza as his adviser on the conduct of "just war." Still only in his late twenties at the conclusion of the war, the future bishop later strongly defended the rigor with which the viceroy prosecuted the campaign against the rebels in the West. After accompanying Mendoza back to Mexico City, he returned to Oaxaca, where he served as dean of the cathedral and again as inspector of the diocese, receiving his appointment as bishop of New Galicia in 1546.[41] In the few years he served in the position before his death in 1551, he is thought to have shown the same general lack of interest in the welfare of indigenous residents in his diocese that he earlier demonstrated in Oaxaca.[42]

Maestro Juan Infante de Barrios, another prominent member of the clergy, possibly a Franciscan (or former Franciscan), already was present in New Galicia at the outbreak of the war. He accompanied Mendoza to New Galicia in 1540, probably in conjunction with the preparations for the expedition to the Tierra Nueva and with the authorization of Fray don Juan de Zumárraga, the bishop of Mexico. Mendoza appointed Barrios protector of the Indians, a post that had been vacant since the departure of Licenciado Pedraza in 1537, describing him in a letter to the king as a "man of learning and good life." Apart from witnessing and participating in many readings of the requerimiento that preceded the second battle of Nochistlan and other engagements during the last part of the war, it is not known what Barrios's position as the Indians "protector" actually entailed.[43]

Interpreters

A number of established settlers served as interpreters during the war, attempting to facilitate negotiations with the rebels or translating the requerimiento before hostilities commenced. Given the importance of the indios amigos from central Mexico, the viceroy also relied heavily on Antonio Ortiz and Hernando de Tapia, two interpreters who could communicate in Nahuatl with his Indian allies. Although of very different backgrounds and reputations, both served as interpreters for the audiencia in Mexico City.

Antonio Ortiz belonged to a closely connected group of official interpreters who were—or were thought to be—Moriscos (descendants of Iberian Muslims) and possibly slaves or former slaves. These men became notorious in Mexico for scandalous behavior, extortion, and accepting bribes. Perhaps the key problem with the early interpreters used by the audiencia was that, like Cortés's (and later Guzmán's) interpreter García del Pilar, they wielded considerable power, exercising leverage over both Indians and Spaniards, but failed entirely to meet the social standards associated with prominent officeholders. As was true for Columbus, who during his first voyage to the Caribbean sent Luis de Torres (who knew Hebrew, Chaldean, and some Arabic) as emissary to the Tainos of Cuba, Spaniards in early New Spain might have assumed that people who already were bi- or multilingual would learn indigenous languages quickly—as might well have been the case. The early audiencia interpreters who were thought to be Moriscos indeed might have been bilingual before they arrived in New Spain. With their sudden elevation in wealth and power, these men, Ortiz prominent among them, proved difficult to control.

Lic. Lorenzo de Tejada, one of the oidores of the second audiencia, in the 1540s bitterly denounced Antonio de Ortiz, whom he accused of being "a great drunk, gambler, blasphemer, very deceitful and of little truth, and [he is] a man who . . . cares little for honor." Tejada alleged that, although married to an indigenous woman, Ortiz publicly carried on affairs with both Indian and mestiza women. Tejada claimed that during the sixty days that Antonio de Ortiz was in Toluca, which because of its location on the main road to Michoacan and New Galicia the viceroy designated as a supply base for his campaign in the Mixton War, he had extorted large amounts of maize from the local governor and principales for his own purposes for little or no payment. He had shaken them down for other items as well, including a carved and painted wooden bed. The residencia included many other charges of accepting bribes, extorting funds, and deliberately misconstruing the words of the viceroy and oidores.[44] In the past Tejada had worked closely with Ortiz, and at some point he allowed Ortiz the use of lands, belonging to the Indians of Tlatelolco, that bordered on Chapultepec.[45] Obviously by the time of the residencia the two men had become seriously estranged. Ortiz for his part testified against

Tejada, while Tejada declared that Ortiz was his avowed enemy because the viceroy had ordered him to conduct a residencia of the "briberies and thefts and crimes and excesses" that Ortiz had committed as an interpreter for the audiencia. As a result Ortiz lost his position, and criminal proceedings were brought against him.

Despite Ortiz's likely character flaws, during the war the viceroy relied on his services, both to help operate the supply system and as an interpreter and intermediary in dealing with the leaders of the indios amigos from central Mexico. Don Francisco de Sandoval Acacitli, the native ruler from Chalco who accompanied Mendoza, frequently mentioned Ortiz in his account of the campaign in New Galicia. Mendoza's dependence on Ortiz, who surely had exhibited some of the unacceptable behavior that Tejada described well before the Mixton War, suggests that even twenty years after the conquest of Tenochtitlan, interpreters of Nahuatl were still far from numerous in New Spain and thus retained considerable leverage with both Spanish officials and their indigenous subjects.

Hernando de Tapia, who also played an important role in the campaign, enjoyed a quite different reputation, although he too associated closely with Tejada (the difference being, perhaps, that unlike Ortiz, he never ran afoul of the oidor). A witness in the residencia of the viceroy and second audiencia in the 1540s, for example, referred to Tapia as "a friend of Spaniards with whom he deals and converses a lot."[46] Hernando de Tapia was the son of don Andrés de Tapia Motelchiuhtzin, an interim ruler (*quauhtlatoani*) of Tenochtitlan who fought with Cuauhtemoc, was captured by Cortés, and later participated in campaigns with both Cortés and Guzmán.[47] Unlike many other indigenous nobles, Hernando's name never appeared with the title "don," probably because his father belonged to a group of men who were elevated to, rather than being born into, noble rank.

In the 1530s Hernando de Tapia was in Spain, apparently having accompanied or joined indigenous nobles don Martín, don Juan, don Francisco, and don Pedro—probably the sons of Aztec emperor Moctezoma—whom Cortés took to the royal court when he went to Spain in 1528. Don Juan died in Spain and don Martín on the return trip while traveling from Veracruz to Mexico City. There is no subsequent mention of don Francisco, so only don Pedro is known to have survived. While at court, Hernando de Tapia married a Spanish woman, but she died before he left Spain. Tapia probably returned to Mexico in 1537.[48] He married again in Mexico, this time to a mestiza woman (her father was said to be a Spaniard).[49] While in Spain he tried to recover pueblos or lands that he claimed had belonged to his father, and in 1535 he received a coat of arms and was made a knight of the Golden Spur by Pope Paul III. Although Spaniards fairly consistently referred to Hernando de Tapia as "indio," through his work, marriages, and associations, he made his place in the Spanish world. Unlike his father, he did not hold a position of authority in indigenous society. Having cast his lot with the new Spanish rulers of the land—he was described as dressing in the Spanish fashion and he received permission to carry a sword—in his will of 1555 he stipulated that his daughters should marry Spaniards.[50]

No doubt returning from Castile proficient in Spanish, Tapia became an interpreter for the audiencia, eventually working closely with the oidor Tejada and helping settlers to negotiate purchases of Indian lands.[51] Apart from the suit over his father's possessions (the resolution of which is unknown), he acquired some property of his own near Mexico City, probably as a result of his alliance with Tejada. In 1543 he also received from the viceroy the grant of a lot to build a house in the city on the "street that goes from the monastery of la Madre de Dios to San Pablo."[52] During the campaign in New Galicia, Hernando de Tapia probably served in a quasi-military capacity; don Francisco de Sandoval Acacitli, the native ruler of Tlalmanalco who kept an account of his experiences during the viceroy's campaign, referred to him as one of the "'caudillos' of the Mexicans."[53] Officially, Tapia received an allotment of eleven slaves after the defeat of the peñol of Coyna, although, as discussed later, there are reasons to doubt the trustworthiness of the official account of the numbers of slaves distributed there and elsewhere.[54] As interpreter for the audiencia, he earned a modest annual salary of eighty pesos, although, like other interpreters, he doubtless had additional opportunities for remuneration.

The Spaniards' Indigenous Allies

As in Nuño de Guzmán's campaign ten years before, large indigenous forces recruited in central Mexico, Michoacan, and Colima (Pueblos de Avalos) played a crucial role in the final months of the Mixton War. These Indian allies performed the heaviest and most dangerous work, clearing roads and passes through the mountains, building pontoons or earthen bridges across rivers, seeing to the livestock, and hauling heavy and cumbersome artillery. They also often provided the "shock" troops first sent into combat. Their sheer numbers meant that for the first time since the war began, the Spaniards were able to redress the rebels' numerical superiority. Together with the Spaniards' artillery and the psychological impact of the arrival of the viceroy himself leading large forces into battle, the presence of the indios amigos tipped the balance of military power in favor of the Spaniards.

It is difficult to estimate of the total number of indigenous troops. Juan de Alvarado brought some six thousand Indians from Michoacan, and don Luis de Castilla stated that he recruited about an equal number from the Pueblos de Avalos; altogether, then, around ten to twelve thousand recruits from Michoacan and Colima went to New Galicia. Estimating the size of the forces from central Mexico is more problematic. Viceroy Mendoza stated that he brought five thousand Indian allies; Cortés and Jerónimo López claimed the number was forty or fifty thousand. Both the low and high numbers are questionable. The timing of the war, which took place just a few years before major epidemics devastated indigenous populations in New Spain in the mid- to late 1540s, was fortuitous in terms of recruitment; the Spaniards still could readily summon very large numbers of indigenous men to fight with them.[55] Having been criticized for aspects of his conduct of the war, including the disruptive impact on recruits and the possibility that he was leaving central Mexico undefended, Mendoza might have had reason to downplay the size of the forces that he mobilized. On the other hand, Cortés and López were among the viceroy's most assiduous critics and could have exaggerated the extent of recruitment to make it look as if Mendoza had placed New Spain in jeopardy.

Assuming that the numbers of troops from central Mexico about equaled those from Michoacan and Colima, an estimate of around thirty thousand indios amigos who participated in the campaign seems plausible. Although lower than the figures offered by Cortés and López, these numbers still would have created enormous logistical problems. Moving and supplying an army of this size was a vast undertaking. Not surprisingly, despite a fairly efficient provisioning system, many of the native troops abandoned the campaign and returned home before the war's conclusion. Thus, it is unlikely that the total number of native allies ever was in the field simultaneously (recall that Castilla stated that he recruited several thousand men in the Pueblos de Avalos as replacements for troops from Michoacan who had deserted), but at any given time during the campaign the viceroy probably had fifteen to twenty thousand native troops at his disposal, in addition to several hundred Spanish cavalry and infantry.

Indigenous leaders who exercised sociopolitical power in their own communities played a crucial role in Mendoza's recruitment and organization of Indian allies. From the account of don Francisco de Sandoval Acacitli, the ruler of Tlalmanalco in Chalco, and from other sources, it is clear that the viceroy's system of military command depended on the leadership of local rulers whose companies of warriors remained distinct and recognizable.[56] The viceroy did not attempt to amalgamate them into a single army, and probably it did not occur to him to try to do so. Indeed, such a drastic reorganization most likely would not have been workable, so strong were the existing ethnic and local divisions and consequent identities and allegiances in the various indigenous states and provinces of central Mexico at that time.

Although we know little about don Francisco de Sandoval Acacitli's life apart from his participation in the war in New Galicia, the account of the campaign set down at his behest not only is an invaluable source of information on his experiences but also is the most detailed account we have of the activities of any single participant. Although the man who served as don Francisco's scribe, Gabriel de Castañeda, wrote the account in Nahuatl, in 1641 an interpreter for the audiencia translated it into Spanish; this is the only version that survives.[57] From it we know that don Francisco offered his services, and those of his men, to the viceroy "for the war in the land of the Chichimecas of Xuchipila." He brought with him two of his sons, strikingly named don Bernardino del Castillo and don Pedro de Alvarado, whom he equipped with arms, although don Francisco does not mention their participation in the battles in which he fought.[58] Also among the high-born participants from Tlalmanalco were three principales, don Fernando de Guzmán, his younger brother don Diego Quataxochitl, and their eldest brother Martín Quaxolocatl; the last two probably died during the campaign. Don Francisco himself, however, returned home to receive a triumphal welcome at the war's conclusion.[59] Presumably his sons returned with him.

The account covers the full six months of Mendoza's campaign in the West, as don Francisco stayed until the viceroy officially disbanded his troops and then accompanied Mendoza back to Mexico City. Although don Francisco's perspective is limited to his personal observations and experiences, nonetheless the account reveals a great deal about the role of the indigenous allies in the campaign. Don Francisco was fairly close to Mendoza, as suggested by his description of an episode in which they spent the night in Misquititlan.[60] There the viceroy personally reconnoitered the area, taking with him only the Spaniards in his company and three of the Indian lords: don Francisco of Tlalmanalco, don Juan of Coyoacan, and don Mateo of Cuitlahuac.[61] Don Francisco and his men often functioned under the command of the oidor Maldonado, who played a very active role in the campaign. The relationship between don Francisco and the oidor was uneasy, and when it was time to return to Mexico City, don Francisco accompanied Maldonado only reluctantly. Don Francisco had good reason not to trust Maldonado. At one point in the campaign he abruptly ordered don Francisco to go with him to Xalpa without allowing him time to prepare adequately. Don Francisco complied with the order but, according to the account, "there the lord [don Francisco] suffered greatly, because he had nothing to eat except toasted maize, and without clothing, because he only carried his arms and a thin blanket . . . and he slept armed with his quilted armor on, and all the rest of [his] people suffered greatly because they were all without clothes or food." At Xalpa they saw the church the rebels had destroyed. They captured some of the "Chichimecas" there, cutting off the hands of two men and the breasts of two women and then burning the houses. Whether don Francisco and his men participated in these acts, or did so at Maldonado's orders, is not clear.[62]

In contrast to the Spaniards, who usually referred to the indios amigos in general terms, don Francisco was well aware of the identities of the indigenous participants and their leaders, the roles they played, and contributions they made. He described the formation for one battle as follows: "The artillery was put in the middle, and on one side of the road went the Tlaxcaltecas, Huexotzincas, Quauquechultecas, followed by the Mexicanos and Xilotepecas, and then the Aculhuas; on the other those [men] of Mechoacan, Mestitlan, and the Chalcos." As they advanced they encountered first a wooden fence or barricade and then a stone one erected by the rebels. Don Francisco, wearing his "device of Quetzalpatzactli of green feathers," participated in the attack "with which they reached the fence, and broke it, and burned the huts, and began to fight with them [i.e., the rebels]."[63]

Certainly don Francisco's experiences of the campaign differed from those of the viceroy and other Spaniards, not only because the Indian allies performed the most dangerous work and often formed the vanguard that led the attack on the enemy but also because his perceptions and priorities were unlike those of the Spaniards. He recorded the actions of other indigenous leaders and their followers and was interested in the people and places in the West that he saw for the first time. They must have seemed both strange and oddly familiar. He described a temple and pueblo (probably Teul) in the sierra de Juchipila as follows:

> We saw the summit of the Sierra de Xuchipiltepetl, where the very large temple of the devil was. . . . The room was fifteen *brazas* [one braza is around six feet] long and three wide, and the walls made of stone something like adobe, of very ancient construction, and it is not known who built it. . . . The inhabitants that are there, all their houses were very pretty, [built of] flagstones and . . . the stones in the form of bricks, adobes, and the stairs of the same rock. This rock is like what they quarry in Senoc.[64]

He also discussed the celebrations that took place at Christmas and the friendship he forged with don Pedro, a native lord of Xalpa who apparently had fled to the sierras during the fighting. While the Spaniards and their allies made preparations for the holiday festivities, don Pedro arrived to meet with the viceroy. They apparently came to terms, and don Pedro offered to send for some of the other local rulers. He returned the next day with his elderly mother and another woman. After this, the indigenous allies celebrated the nativity of Jesus in a field that offered open ground because all the houses had been burned. Maldonado provided fish and quail. On Sunday (Christmas Day) the people of Amecamecan danced, and on the third day don Francisco himself danced "and they sang the Chichimeca song; there were flowers and incense sticks, food and cacao, which was given to the lords, and all the nations of the different provinces danced with their arms, shields, and macanas; everyone without exception danced."[65] Don Pedro, the local ruler, went to visit don Francisco "and gave him one of his shirts, and don Pedro took away fish, and they became great friends."[66]

Don Francisco's account provides unequaled insight into his experiences, but other prominent indigenous leaders appear in the records and literature as well. Their survival and return home stands in considerable contrast to the fate of the Indian rulers who had accompanied Nuño de Guzmán more than a decade earlier, virtually all of whom perished during that entrada.[67] Don Francisco mentioned another prominent ruler, don Juan de Guzmán Itztlollinqui, the *tlatoani* (indigenous ruler) of Coyoacan who had been installed in his position by Cortés (the latter located his headquarters in Coyoacan while Tenochtitlan was rebuilt) and who ruled until 1569. Apparently don Juan spoke some Spanish and was quite successful in pursuing claims to property and privileges from the Crown and the viceroy. He married a cacica of Texcoco, and the couple owned extensive properties in lands and houses near Coyoacan, Xochimilco, and elsewhere; don Juan also continued to receive tributes and services from his many retainers.[68] Don Francisco, the son of the Cazonci of Michoacan, was another close ally of Mendoza. He had been educated at the Franciscan monastery in Michoacan but had joined the viceregal court as a page, adopted the Spanish manner of dress, and married a Spanish woman. He accompanied Mendoza throughout the campaign in New Galicia.[69] Another prominent noble from Michoacan, don Pedro, who served as governor there during the war, also participated in the campaign but soon afterward faced accusations that he had usurped and sold lands that should not have been alienated.[70]

Like don Francisco de Sandoval Acacitli, many of the indigenous leaders probably viewed their participation in Mendoza's campaign as a voluntary alliance with the viceroy. It seems likely that they viewed the conquest of the peñoles of New Galicia as an indigenous war waged alongside New Spain's most powerful leader. As was true during Guzmán's entrada, native warriors maintained their own traditions of conquest, burning houses and destroying fields. In Apozol "all day they pulled up the magueys and cut the mesquites," and, at Juchipila, don Francisco de Sandoval Acacitli noted that "as soon as we arrived, the Tlaxcaltecas and Mexicanos began to pull up the magueys."[71] Indeed some witnesses testified that the rebels ensconced at the peñol of Nochistlan offered to negotiate a truce with the Spaniards to keep their tunales (nopal cacti) from being destroyed.[72]

In the history he wrote in Nahuatl in the early seventeenth century, the Nahua chronicler Chimalpahin assigned the leading role in the campaign in New Galicia to the people of Tenochtitlan: "And when things began in Xuchipila, the son of the ruler who governed, Tezcatlipopocatzin, resident of the barrio of San Pablo Teopan, in Tenochtitlan, went there at his [father's?] orders. And don Antonio de Mendoza, the viceroy, also got underway."[73] As don Francisco's account makes quite clear, however, the indigenous leaders who fought with the viceroy and his captains had no illusions about who was in charge. Nonetheless, they might have thought—as did Spaniards who went to fight—that they had reasonable expectations of reward for their contributions. The native rulers probably anticipated and usually received favorable treatment in return for their services after the war was over. This hope for reward might have motivated don Francisco to document his experiences in writing. His account included this encomium from the viceroy, delivered when the leader from Tlalmanalco took his leave of Mendoza after they returned to Mexico City. Antonio Ortiz acted as interpreter in their congratulatory exchange.

> I am deeply grateful to don Francisco, and very satisfied with the good that the Chalcas have done with the Marqués [Cortés] when he came for the conquest and pacification of this kingdom, and that they helped in all the wars that the Marqués fought. Go with congratulations to your house and pueblo of Tlalmanalco to rest, and in each and any thing that arises I will do what you ask me and favor you.[74]

The Fall of the Peñoles

Don Antonio de Mendoza and his forces finally arrived in New Galicia in the autumn of 1541, perhaps a month after the successful Spanish defense of Guadalajara. According to don Francisco's account, they left Mexico City on September 29 and took about a month to get there.[75] The viceroy and his host passed through Toluca, which became an important entrepot for the supply system that he and his mayordomo Agustin Guerrero devised, and then moved through Michoacan to the area of their first major engagement, the peñol of Coyna (Tototlan), north of Lake Chapala. At the Tazazalca River, a day's journey from Coyna, the viceroy met Juan del Camino, the encomendero of Coyna, and Captain Miguel de Ibarra, who had been sent by Cristóbal de Oñate to greet the viceroy, inform him of the state of affairs, and guide him along the route.[76] They told him they had warned the rebels at Coyna of the viceroy's approach but to no avail.

Mendoza spent the night a league and a half from the peñol.[77] Fearing that the Indians might escape and that it would be difficult to pursue and round them up, he sent Pedro Almíndez Cherinos, Licenciado Maldonado, and Agustín Guerrero "to bring the vanguard and Captain Urdaneta with

tototlan.

FIGURE 13. This image from the Lienzo de Tlaxcala shows the Battle of Tototlan (Coyna) (plate 54). In this scene the Tlaxcalan warriors on the left wield Spanish steel, rather than indigenous wood and obsidian, swords. The drawing shows the barricades constructed to defend the peñol. Chavero, *Lienzo de Tlaxcala*.

the *arcabuceros* [musketeers] to go in advance to surround them with the Tarascan Indians he brought but not to attack until I arrived with all the people."[78] When Mendoza arrived with the horsemen, he found that the advance party already had gained two of the barricades; he then reconnoitered the surrounding area, leaving small companies of horsemen at strategic positions. Maldonado and Guerrero told him that they had seen smoke signals from another hill, which they took to indicate that the rebels were calling for aid. According to Ibarra the local native lords left the peñol to go on horseback to Juchipila for help.[79] Mendoza delayed fighting, in part because he was waiting for the artillery, which had gotten stuck en route in a craggy pass. Finally they attacked and fought the rebels to exhaustion.

The viceroy claimed that there were around fifteen hundred men in the peñol. He thought that altogether no more than twenty escaped "because those who fled the peñol were stopped by the horsemen that I had left on the plain." Clearly women and children were present as well, since he stated that he tried to minimize any harm to them (but admitted that under the circumstances he did not always succeed).[80]

In addition to enemy casualties the viceroy's army took an unknown number of captives to be enslaved. On May 31, 1541, the audiencia in Mexico City authorized the conduct of war "of fire and blood" in New Galicia in which all captives could be made "perpetual slaves," with the exception of children under the age of fourteen and women of any age or status.[81] The manner in which Mendoza distributed the captives from Coyna later would become highly controversial. The residencia of the mid-1540s includes a list of slaves who had been officially branded and registered and then handed over to Spanish officials and participants, including Agustín Guerrero, who received seventeen, "Ortiz naguatato," who received five, and "Tapia naguatato," who received eleven. Juan del Camino, who had played a key role in the battle, received eighteen slaves. The viceroy gave the surgeon, Maestre Diego, one slave and an additional twenty-five who were seriously wounded for him to treat. Most other participants received very small numbers of between one and five slaves.[82]

These numbers are suspiciously low. The viceroy himself affirmed that he turned the majority of captives over to his Indian allies without registering them "to encourage them for the war and because it was the first thing that they had taken by force of arms." He explained that by doing this he had hoped to prevent the allies from killing all the potential captives, as they would have done had they expected that they would all be handed over to the Spaniards.[83] He also contended that Cristóbal de Oñate, who held the official branding iron, was not present at Coyna and therefore the enslaved rebels could be branded only when they met up with Oñate at Nochistlan, by which time ostensibly many of the captives had run off. He also claimed that the numbers of slaves taken at Coyna were very small.[84]

The controversy did not end there, however, as witnesses hostile to the viceroy later contended that at his orders Agustín Guerrero subsequently persuaded or forced the Indian allies to sell him their captives at extremely low prices, acquiring over one thousand slaves in this manner.

Jerónimo López claimed that, sitting in his tent one day, the viceroy "told the Spaniards that were there, I have given the Indians from this peñol to the peaceful Indians who have come to help, and any of you who want to trade for them" should do so. Iñigo López de Anuncibay, who had a very public and damaging falling out with the viceroy during the war, testified that Guerrero and "certain naguatatos and other persons" made these purchases for the absurdly low price of one and a half pesos per slave, and that furthermore, the leaders of the indios amigos resisted selling the captives, claiming that they could not because "they are for the Gran Tatian," which is what he said they called the viceroy. Anuncibay himself attempted (unsuccessfully) to purchase some of the slaves in partnership with Tomás de Rijoles, another interpreter with long experience in central Mexico. He also claimed that one of the caciques of the indios amigos traded thirty or forty slaves taken at Coyna to Agustín Guerrero for a horse.[85] These reports strongly suggest that some Spaniards, Guerrero in particular, intimidated the indigenous allies into giving up their newly acquired slaves at prices well below the current ones.

Although probably no other single episode of slave taking during the war was as controversial as the aftermath of the battle for Coyna, the uncertainties and mutual accusations that surround this entire aspect of the war make it nearly impossible to estimate how many were enslaved. The viceroy's forces probably returned to central Mexico at the war's conclusion with several thousand slaves.[86] It also is likely that in the immediate aftermath of the war, local men in New Galicia took advantage of the turmoil to scour the countryside and recently pacified areas for more rebels. Iñigo López de Anuncibay testified that, after Mendoza returned to Mexico City, certain Spaniards went to Purificación with a branding iron and the viceroy gave a branding iron to Miguel de Ibarra in Guadalajara "so that he could brand the warriors who were found in Juchipila and Apozol and Tlaltenango." He went on to say that he heard from vecinos in Guadalajara that they were searching for Indians who were natives of the pueblos that rebelled. While in Guadalajara he saw vecinos and "some soldiers" bring slaves to Ibarra to be branded, as many as "ten and twelve and twenty and thirty and forty slaves, and there was not a single vecino for whom Miguel de Ibarra did not use his brand." Finally the viceroy sent orders to have the iron taken away from Ibarra.[87]

The fall of Coyna and the punishments that its defenders suffered doubtless helped the viceroy and Oñate to persuade two or three other strongholds to surrender. Alonso de Santa Cruz, who understood *"la lengua mexicana,"* explained the role that he played in the surrender of Acatique:

> One night when Diego and this witness were on guard and being at the peñol . . . around midnight they began to speak to the Indians of the said peñol of Acatique and they made many requerimientos and warnings. . . . And they were speaking with them all night until dawn, both saying that if they did not agree to peace, they and their wives and children and estates would be dead and destroyed and captives, and that in agreeing to peace, no evil or harm would be done to them. Now that the sun was rising the Indians said that they wanted and would be happy to agree to peace. . . . And this witness at the orders of Diego Pardo, who was in command of thirteen or twelve [*sic*] horsemen, went to the viceroy and told him how the Indians of the peñol of Acatique were at peace, at which the viceroy was very pleased.[88]

The next major engagement took place at the peñol of Nochistlan, where previously the Indians repelled the Spaniards and Alvarado was mortally injured in the retreat. This episode also proved controversial. Mendoza sent Miguel de Ibarra, who was the encomendero of the pueblo of Nochistlan, to persuade the defenders of the peñol to desist and accept the viceroy's pardon, as occurred at Acatique and other places. Subsequently, he sent the Franciscan Fray Antonio de Segovia and the Augustinian guardian, Fray Juan de San Román, and finally Maestro Juan Infante de Barrios, the cleric he had appointed as protector of the Indians, to plead with the rebels. With reinforcements from the now unthreatened town of Guadalajara, the viceroy prepared to initiate a siege, cutting off the rebels' water supply. These actions occupied about two weeks. According to Mendoza the negotiations came to a halt because his Indian allies were on the brink of mutiny, threatening to return home if they were not allowed to fight. As a consequence he gave the order to attack. The bitter fighting began at sunrise and ended at sunset with the fall of the peñol.[89] The number of captives taken after the battle for the peñol of Nochistlan is not known. According to one story, Miguel de Ibarra connived at the escape of many defenders because he did not want the people he hoped would return to his service to be enslaved.[90]

Decades later Francisco Torres discussed the battle for Nochistlan. He maintained that it was the most heavily fortified and important of the rebel strongholds and that its defeat meant securing New Galicia for the Spaniards. Mixton is usually thought to have been the largest of the strongholds. Very likely refugees from Nochistlan and other peñoles that had surrendered or been defeated fled there, strengthening its defenses for what would be nearly the last confrontation. So it may be true that, until its defeat, Nochistlan was the key rebel stronghold rather than Mixton. Torres claimed that, along with Cristóbal de Oñate and one other man, he managed to fight his way to the top of the peñol of Nochistlan. The three Spaniards scaled four or five barricades as they made the ascent, although Oñate received a head wound in the battle.[91] Finally Mendoza himself reached the barricades and rallied the others to follow. According to Andrés de Villanueva, six hundred Spaniards and fifteen to twenty thousand Indian allies participated in the battle "and there were many deaths of Spaniards," although the viceroy claimed the casualties on his side were minimal.[92]

Among the charges subsequently brought against the viceroy in the residencia of his conduct in office was the allegation that the defenders of Nochistlan sued for peace but Mendoza attacked them nonetheless.[93] The viceroy claimed that the reason some of the rebels descended from the stronghold was to try to protect their tunales from destruction and that in any case the conditions that they proposed for surrender were entirely unacceptable—namely, that they should be allowed to remain fortified at Nochistlan while the viceroy and his army passed on to Mixton.[94] Alonso de Olivares and others understood this as an attempt to trap the viceroy's forces between the two peñoles, thus cutting them off from supplies and reinforcements.[95] Others, however, argued that the people at Nochistlan tried to continue negotiations. Rodrigo de Castañeda said that two or three Indians came down from the peñol to talk to Licenciado Maldonado regarding surrender. After the rebels left, Castañeda asked some men who had been with Maldonado what happened and was told that the Indians tried to discuss terms of surrender but Licenciado Maldonado refused to negotiate with them. Iñigo López de Anuncibay went further, saying that the Indians offered to surrender if they would be pardoned, but Maldonado replied that they "would grant them their lives but they all would be slaves, and seeing this the Indians agreed that they would die before they gave up." Diego de Orozco, however, thought that after the attempt to convince the Indians at Nochistlan to surrender, the delay in attacking strengthened the defenders' belief that the Spaniards were afraid to fight. He said that once the battle began, the Indians fought extremely hard and very courageously. In his opinion it was far better that they took the stronghold by force rather than by peaceful means "in order to break their wings," so they would not fortify themselves elsewhere, and because the "Indians said and proclaimed that the Spaniards were only brave on horseback and on flat ground, and that for the peñoles they were worthless, and with this they attracted many to their side."[96]

From Nochistlan the viceroy moved on to Juchipila, where Mendoza claimed that Indians from Mixton raided the camp, burning huts and injuring some of their Indian allies. When Mendoza sent Licenciado Maldonado with his company in pursuit, the people at Mixton nearly killed them, stole some pieces of silver, and captured some of the Indian allies who accompanied them.[97] It probably was after this incident that some eight hundred men from the peñol attacked the viceroy's camp in Juchipila at mid-day, "singing the song of the devil" and capturing some of the Indian allies. Mendoza then decided to send Miguel de Ibarra "as a person who had credibility with them" to try to persuade the rebels to desist. The Indians demanded to speak to Tenamaztle, evidently taken captive after the defeat of Nochistlan, as a sign of good faith. The viceroy thought it was a ruse but nevertheless sent Ibarra with a company of one hundred horsemen and Tenamaztle. When they arrived at Mixton, a party of warriors attacked and freed the native leader, wounding Ibarra and several other Spaniards.[98] The successful liberation of Tenamaztle probably took place following an initial parley; it is hard to imagine that the rebels could have prevailed against that number of cavalry without mounting a major attack.

Clearly the majority of rebels remained undaunted by the Spaniards' successes to that point; indeed, the freeing of Tenamaztle underscores how resilient the rebel forces still were. From their stronghold of Mixton, they could strike at the viceroy's army with relative impunity while the main body of the defenders and their families remained out of reach. The attack on Ibarra, reminiscent of the assault on Toribio de Bolaños early in the war when he was transporting the cacique Teuquitate, demonstrates that the rebels' networks of intelligence and communication continued to function effectively. Very likely by the time of the final confrontation refugees from other peñoles had swollen considerably the numbers

FIGURE 14. This image from the Lienzo de Tlaxcala shows the Battle of Juchipila (plate 58). This drawing also depicts barricades constructed by the defenders of the peñol, who aim their arrows downward at the Spanish and central Mexican attackers. At the top the warriors at Juchipila are drawn with the eye band but those below them are not; perhaps this distinction was meant to suggest that warriors from more than one ethnic group fought at the peñol. Chavero, *Lienzo de Tlaxcala.*

gathered at Mixton. Mendoza said that at the news of his approach to the area, the people who had been at Juchipila left to join the defenders of Mixton "because they held it to be impregnable because with it they had defended themselves from and defeated Cristóbal de Oñate." Tello's figure of a hundred thousand people at Mixton seems improbable, a logistical impossibility, but as in most aspects of the conflict, numbers are elusive. Given its location, many of the people at Mixton could have been Zacateca Indians, and they and others (like Tenamaztle) later would manage to flee north into the mountains.

Mendoza's forces massed at Juchipila, about three leagues from Mixton. After the attacks on Maldonado and Ibarra, it was clear that the Spaniards could not expect an easy surrender. The viceroy was able to move his forces closer to gain better access to the stronghold, and skirmishes took place intermittently over a period of three weeks with exchanges of artillery fire and arrows. By this point in the war, the viceroy and his captains and forces seem to have worked out a fairly reliable approach to taking the strongholds: surround them with large numbers of warriors; cut off access to water and, if possible, other supplies; bombard the fortifications with artillery; and attempt to gain access to the summit from more than one direction. The desertion of a substantial body of warriors from the peñol might have helped to ensure ultimate Spanish victory at Mixton. These men apparently revealed the existence of a pass that led to the top of the mountain—whether willingly or under coercion is not known. Finally able to attack the stronghold from both sides, the Spaniards overwhelmed the defenders, and the fighting came to an end.[99] Mendoza said that he prevented his horsemen from pursuing the Indians who fled so they [the Spaniards] would not kill them, which meant there were few captives to be enslaved.[100] Mendoza did keep about two hundred slaves for himself. The other slaves went to "the soldiers who were the first to enter Mixton as had been promised to them and to compensate for horses that had been killed in the war and expenses for medications, doctors, and surgeons who were in the war to treat the wounds as is customary, and this was done by the said Licenciado Maldonado and Cristóbal de Oñate."[101]

Although it did not mean the end of the campaign, the fall of Mixton in mid-December 1541 signaled the end of large-scale resistance on the part of the rebels.[102] The viceroy's forces marched north to Teul, Tlaltenango, Xalpa, and Apozol, the very communities where the revolt originated. While the Spaniards were there, some of the defenders of Mixton and the other strongholds began to return home, which the viceroy allowed them to do.[103] Mendoza then proceeded south to the area of Tequila and Etzatlan, where he disbanded his troops, probably in the late winter or early spring of 1542. The indigenous revolt collapsed in face of the successes of the viceroy and the still very substantial forces that he could field. Captain Juan de Villalba finally captured Aguacatlan, the base for the rebels in the area around the Spanish capital of Compostela.[104] Francisco Vázquez de Coronado, his foray deep into North America at an end, by this time was moving south, pacifying a few pockets of revolt along the way. Officially the war was over.

The Conduct of the War

As seen earlier in the residencia of the governorship of Nuño de Guzmán, the Spanish practice of conducting detailed inquiries into the term in office of its highest officials produced a wealth of information useful to historians. Some of this material is conflicting, especially with regard to practices and actions that might have been illegal or resulted in the abuse or exploitation of Indians who were not involved in the revolt.[105] With regard to the viceroy's conduct of the war, controversy centered on the enslavement of captives. Questions also arose over his manner of executing prisoners. Mendoza's decision to allow many rebels to escape or to accept amnesty, the experience of the indios amigos, and the effectiveness of the supply system also all were examined.

The viceroy faced allegations that, in the aftermath of the battle of Mixton, he condoned a "new genre" of execution that was especially cruel and deviated from acceptable judicial practice. These methods included blowing up captives with cannons, setting dogs on them, and turning them over to African slaves who attacked them with knives. Neither the viceroy nor anyone else denied that after the battle prisoners were killed in those ways, but the viceroy argued that he was blameless, having entrusted responsibility for the prisoners to Cristóbal de Oñate and Licenciado Maldonado. He said that in any case there were very few such executions, "and even if there were more, to me it would not seem bad bearing in mind the . . . enormous crimes the Indian rebels had committed against God and his Majesty." He claimed that it was not possible to control the blacks and Indians who, without permission, "assaulted them [the prisoners] as is done in Spain with heretics and infidels, that people stab and kill [them] in the road without having judicial office. The setting of dogs on some of the most guilty Indians and using cannon fire were necessary as a warning and to put fear in the Indians."[106]

In rather contradictory fashion Mendoza also maintained that in Granada (in southern Spain) it was customary for magistrates to authorize setting dogs on Moors who were renegades from Christianity. Should he not be justified, therefore, in using such methods, "being viceroy and general commander and being at war and they being the head of the entire revolt and having killed at that peñol [Mixton] many Christians [Spaniards] and Indians who were with Cristóbal de Oñate"?[107] A number of witnesses suggested that such extreme forms of punishment and execution were necessary because the Indians did not take death by hanging seriously. Juan Durán, for example, testified that "he had seen many times that taking the Indians to be hanged . . . [they would] go singing and laughing and invoking the devil and they would hang themselves and kill themselves with their own hands." Alonso Alvarez said he had seen how little regard the Indians had for "ordinary deaths. . . . They go singing as if it were a thing of pleasure."[108]

At the other end of the spectrum in terms of the treatment of the rebels was the issue of amnesty. Although slave taking clearly was not insignificant, at a certain point Mendoza seems to have decided—perhaps at least partly in response to the desires of local settlers who had fought in the war and hoped to reclaim their encomiendas—that amnesty rather than large-scale reprisals and enslavement offered the only viable means of repopulating the province with Indians who would serve the Spaniards. Thus, as seen, when Mendoza took his forces back to the Juchipila Valley, he allowed refugees from Mixton to return unharmed to their pueblos (at least initially; later some were relocated). Nearly all the indigenous witnesses who testified in the residencia in the mid-1540s had been baptized and received Christian names, surely part of the trade-off for receiving pardons. A number of them stated that they participated in the rebellion. Thus don Juan, "lord and governor of Iztlan," stated that he was baptized and "one of those who rebelled." Don Francisco, lord of Aguacatlan, also a baptized Christian, said he "was present in the said uprising, and this witness along with the rest of his maceguales rose up and rebelled." Don Diego, señor of Mezpan, participated in the rebellion for "many days." There were many other indigenous leaders who after the war clearly came to terms with the Spaniards.[109]

Did the supply system function adequately and not take unfair advantage of the people who helped to furnish provisions for the army? Alonso de Santa Cruz declared that he left Mexico City with the viceroy and that, as they passed through Michoacan, they not only paid for everything they obtained from the people there but that the prices were very high, "much more than they used to be." He said that on the entire route there was no lack of supplies for either Spaniards or Indians and that in many pueblos the viceroy stationed a Spaniard to collect provisions, "which they then gave both to Spaniards and to Indians without their having to pay anything, all at the expense of the viceroy."[110] Alonso de Olivares, who was the alguacil of don Luis de Castilla, said that he saw "wherever the people went at the time of the uprising of New Galicia [there was] a Spaniard with many provisions of food, sheep, and poultry to give to the people to eat who went there, to Spaniards and to Indians so that they would not take anything from the Indians or mistreat them in any way and what they did take they paid everything that they asked for, much to their content, for all of which this witness was present."[111]

Probably the system did not always operate so smoothly. Some individuals and communities waited quite a while to be reimbursed for the supplies they provided. In late 1542 and during the following year, the viceroy still was trying to settle debts for provisions used during the war. In late December 1542, for example, he ordered the contador (accountant) of New Galicia, Juan de Ojeda, to pay what was owed to the people of Xacona in northwestern Michoacan for the thousand fanegas of maize they had provided Cristóbal de Oñate for the defenders of Guadalajara.[112] There is no way to know, however, if everyone who furnished supplies actually received compensation in some form. Beyond the system that the viceroy tried to maintain, the kind of profiteering that often surfaces during times of war made an appearance in New Galicia as well. Witnesses testified that captain Iñigo López de Anuncibay "sold wine, oil, vinegar, and other things in his house" during the campaign.[113]

The supply system certainly broke down at times and probably increasingly often as the campaign wore on. Don Francisco de Sandoval Acacitli, the ruler of Tlalmanalco, recorded a number of occasions on which he barely had anything to eat or was forced to depend on the generosity of other allies for food. Not long after the Christmas festivities at the end of 1541, everyone, even the viceroy, subsisted on hearts of palm for at least two days. The situation did not improve thereafter, and on some days don Francisco had virtually nothing to eat and little to feed his horse; in some places water was in short supply as well. At Texistlan he stated, "the hunger began," and some people started selling their clothes, presumably in exchange for food.[114] Large-scale desertions began around this time. Notably the viceroy, although he reproved the Tlaxcaltecas for abandoning the campaign prematurely, took no action to punish them or others as deserters, probably recognizing that it was no longer feasible to keep the troops adequately provisioned.

Mendoza was moderate in his dealings with the various groups and individuals who campaigned with him in New Galicia, and to a great degree he retained their loyalty. When don Francisco de Sandoval Acacitli fell ill, Mendoza urged him to go to Etzatlan, where he could rest and receive treatment; but don Francisco insisted on staying with the viceroy even though he remained sick off and on for the next two weeks.[115] Mendoza understood the importance of his indigenous allies. During the period when supplies were running short, some of the allies held a dance. The viceroy gave them a young bull, which they roasted together with fleshy leaves from maguey plants "which the Spaniards also ate, as by then there was nothing else with which to feed themselves."[116] Mendoza was careful to express proper gratitude toward the allies who stayed with him until the end, addressing the troops in Etzatlan when he disbanded them: "Sons, natives that you are of various provinces, go with congratulations, now that the war has finished and come to an end. . . . You who have gone in my company following me, I hold you as sons, and I will favor you in everything possible." Once again he contrasted their steadfastness with the perfidy of the troops that deserted and returned home early.[117]

His relations with other Spaniards generally appear to have been successful as well. The major exception was his notorious falling out with Captain Anuncibay, who was in charge of moving some artillery from Juchipila to Mixton but left it behind when they got close to the peñol. The viceroy, incensed because the artillery had been left unguarded where it could have been stolen, publicly excoriated Anuncibay about his dereliction of duty and sent Cristóbal de Oñate to see to the retrieval of the equipment. Witnesses sympathetic to the viceroy suggested that Anuncibay neglected the artillery because he was more interested in pursuing his illegal trade in oil and wine or possibly because he resented an earlier slight. The viceroy had all but gutted Anuncibay's cavalry company when he discovered that many of its so-called horsemen were inexperienced and could have proved an impediment to the experienced cavalry. Anuncibay subsequently spoke frequently against the viceroy, and he was the leading witness against Mendoza in the residencia.[118]

On the whole, then, the viceroy conducted a successful campaign, in six months breaking the back of large-scale revolt in New Galicia without incurring huge losses among his own troops. There are no figures for casualties among the indios amigos. Although certainly they were much higher than for Spaniards, the debacle that had occurred among the Indian allies during Guzmán's entrada ten years before did not recur during the viceroy's campaign. Spanish casualties also are difficult to calculate, but probably no more than one hundred Spaniards in all died in the course of the war.

For the Spaniards the end of the war marked the beginning of a new era of opportunity, while the Indians of New Galicia, whether they had rebelled or remained neutral, found themselves facing new realities that indeed might have been worse than the circumstances that fostered the revolt. Those who were enslaved, if they survived, ended up far from home and family, performing harsh labor in unfamiliar settings. The war displaced thousands of people, some of whom took refuge in the mountains, often having lost or been separated from their families and communities. Others were relocated by Spanish authorities, probably with an eye to dispersing groups like the Cazcanes, who were at the core of the rebellion. Indigenous violence in the region by no means came to an end with the conclusion of the viceroy's campaign, but the rebels' hope of expunging all traces of the hated Spaniards and their demanding religion had been shattered. Never again would they challenge Spanish rule so extensively and directly.

CHAPTER 7

The Transformation of New Galicia

It [New Galicia] is one of the good provinces of this New Spain, but with little Christianity and less justice, for lack of clergy to teach the catechism and, second, because of the failings of the governor who was in it. Much of it is in rebellion and at war, not because of mistreatment by the Spaniards but rather because the land is rough and the natives disorderly and rebellious. . . . I sent to require them to come to peace and promised in the king's name to pardon past excesses and that they would be well treated. . . . And not only did they not want to but they tried to kill the messengers. Since I left the province . . . the rebellious pueblos have waged regular war and [caused] great deaths and damages to those who were at peace because they serve and have made them rise up and rebel with them.

—Letter from the oidor Lic. Lorenzo de Tejada
to the king, March 1545[1]

✣ HAD THE VISITOR FROM THE AUDIENCIA IN MEXICO CITY WRITTEN these words in 1540 they would come as no surprise, but Tejada wrote this letter on March 11, 1545, several years after the conclusion of the viceroy's war against the rebels of New Galicia. Spaniards might now be the undisputed rulers of the West, but peace and prosperity continued to be elusive. Even as they consolidated their victory and used their recently gained advantage to impose a more effective regimen of political and economic control over the remaining inhabitants of the region, Spaniards continued to face indigenous resistance. Tejada pointed out that it would be wise to avoid resorting to war again; the spoils would be very disappointing "because the Indians are so poor that all their property is a blanket to cover themselves and a stone on which to cook their food."[2]

Despite the ongoing violence, Spanish rule was becoming increasingly well established in the West and beginning to extend more effectively into the countryside. In the late 1540s the creation of another audiencia for New Galicia that was quasi-independent of the audiencia in Mexico City—together with a more concerted and organized effort on the part of the church, especially the Franciscan order, to establish itself in the region—signaled and reflected growing institutionalization.[3] Pedro Gómez de Maraver arrived as bishop in 1546, and the Crown appointed the first audiencia in New Galicia in 1548. In the same letter quoted earlier, Tejada wrote that he had ordered the pueblos near the main Spanish towns to build town halls that the justices could use when they visited and where "women, children, and old people with their possessions" could stay in times of necessity. He also ordered construction of a "house of adobes" in the valley of Banderas, once the scene of Guzmán's relentless slaving campaigns, "where they are beginning to establish rich plantations of cacao with which they will improve the land, and for the natives it is little work." These actions suggest the growth and strengthening of Spanish economic activity in and political control over the countryside.

Settlers new and old found land for grazing cattle, especially as some areas had experienced significant losses of population, and flocked to recently opened silver mines. Economic growth, along with construction that took place in the towns and at the behest of the friars, put more pressure on the reduced indigenous population to provide labor and goods as well as personal service and transportation of goods and tribute. At the same time, the expanded presence of clerical and civil authorities might have led to some tempering of Spanish demands on the native population, since some officials tried to revise tribute assessments and curtail the most abusive labor practices. Tejada went to New Galicia with the mission, among other things, of introducing the New Laws of 1542, which were intended to curb some of the worst abuses to which the Indians were subject. After he left the kingdom, however, most authorities ignored these provisions.[4]

Indigenous resistance became increasingly localized and no longer challenged Spanish dominion as directly as it did in the 1530s and during the rebellion of the early 1540s. Indeed, resistance that continued after the suppression of the uprising more likely took the form of avoiding Spanish authority and demands rather than violent confrontation. However, the presence of growing numbers of new arrivals in the region such as African slaves, who also chafed under Spanish rule, and the migration and relocation of individuals and groups added new elements to indigenous defiance of authority. Older patterns of indigenous conflict persisted as well, although these patterns continued to reflect a response to the Spanish presence. Hostilities between indigenous groups seem to have pitted Indians who maintained at least de facto independence from Spanish rule against communities they considered to be Christianized and under Spanish control and therefore fair targets for attack. Even as the numbers of Spanish residents in New Galicia grew, the Hispanic sector became more ethnically mixed. White women remained scarce and, as one friar pointed out, all the Spaniards lived with Indian women, regardless of whether they were married to them or had wives in Spain.[5] An increasingly mestizo population that to some extent was bilingual would have been the result.

This chapter examines some of the developments that characterized the period following the suppression of the uprising, looking both at continuities from the earlier years of Spanish settlement and Spanish-indigenous interaction and at changes that promised to carry New Galicia into its next stage of development. To end the story of the prolonged conquest of the West, we should consider how quickly following the war New Galicia began to be transformed from a turbulent and marginal outpost of Spanish settlement into a region with a thriving economy based on mining, agriculture, and stock raising and the impact of that transformation on New Galicia's remaining indigenous inhabitants.

The Aftermath of War

For the Indians of New Galicia, the immediate consequences of the war were disarray and loss. Commenting on the deplorable state of the indigenous communities in the early 1550s, Licenciado Lebrón de Quiñones wrote that "many pueblos that fifteen or twenty years ago had ten thousand Indians and more now have forty or fifty."[6] In May 1550 Fray Rodrigo de la Cruz, a Franciscan at the monastery of Aguacatlan, wrote that the town of Tetitlan, which sixteen years earlier had 440 Indians (he probably meant tributaries or adult men), now had less than half that number. The once-populous valley of Banderas, scene of bloody slaving campaigns in the mid-1530s, was nearly empty; a pueblo that once had 600 adult men now had 70. Hardly anyone was left in the valley of Mascotlan beyond a single pueblo with fewer than 300 adult men.[7] Not only had thousands of native residents died or fled during and after the conflict, many others were refugees stranded away from home. Yet others experienced forcible relocation at the hands of Spanish authorities or encomenderos.

Some who joined the rebellion or fled to escape it found it impossible to return home once the war was over. In June 1542, for example, the viceroy responded to a petition from the principales of the pueblo of Tepetitango in Colima, who declared that to escape demands for service and labor relating to the war, some of the commoners of the pueblo left. "And now that the said war has ended, although they want to return to their pueblo and homes, they are not allowed and are detained"—presumably by Spaniards who continued to exploit their labor. Mendoza instructed local officials in the area to find out if there were Indians from Tepetitango living in their pueblos and, if so, to send them back to their homes.[8] One man who complained was veteran Juan de Almesto, a vecino of Colima who once was Nuño de Guzmán's constable and held an encomienda near Purificación. He noted that because the area was "heavily traveled on the way to the South Sea and the province of Jalisco . . . the natives of the pueblo, to be relieved from work [demanded by] those who pass through and from furnishing supplies . . . have left and absented themselves." In August 1542 the viceroy authorized him to bring the missing residents back.[9]

A number of such petitions were directed to the viceroy's attention. Juan del Camino, once Guzmán's retainer and close associate, complained that the people of his encomienda of Coyna had left because of the war. In this case as well, Mendoza instructed local officials to try to identify anyone in the area who was from Coyna and to find out if they left the pueblo because of the war. Those who had should be told to return to their homes; those who left for other reasons "should be placed in complete liberty so that if they want they can return to their pueblo." Juan del Camino also sought and obtained the viceroy's permission to pursue slaves who escaped.[10]

Mendoza attempted to settle debts owed for services or supplies that had not been compensated during the war, and he rewarded at least some of the participants with land grants and offices, especially corregimientos (administrative districts in the countryside). He also took some minor steps toward compensating communities that were especially burdened during the war. In February 1543 he instructed that the tributes paid by the pueblos of Etzatlan, Agualulco, and Ameca be reduced by half for a period of two years "because of their great services in it [the war] to His Majesty and the expenses that they incurred with the people who were in those pueblos and for other just causes." Because of the labor and effort that the residents at present were devoting to the construction of a monastery (presumably at Etzatlan), their tributes would also be reduced for a third year by one-third.[11] Mendoza disbanded his forces at Etzatlan at the end of the war, and the temporary concentration of the still numerous host must have imposed an enormous burden on the resources of the people of that area.

The viceroy was well aware that the war's conclusion did not mean an end to violence in New Galicia. In January 1543 he noted that some "some pueblos are at war and they don't . . . want to come in peace, for which reason the governor and people . . . could run great risk and danger." He ordered that "all the corregidores and their lieutenants of the towns and provinces around the said jurisdiction of New Galicia and the persons who have Indians in encomienda and the vecinos and residents of the town of Colima" be prepared to go to the aid of the people of New Galicia should they need help, instructing that they should respond with all due haste "without any excuse or delay, and it should be according to and in the manner that it is asked and demanded under pain of a fine of 500 pesos of gold . . . and loss of their offices and privation of the Indians they have in encomienda." A few months later he acknowledged that some Indians from the area of Purificación had robbed another pueblo. He instructed Andrés de Urdaneta, the corregidor of the Pueblos de Avalos, that if these depredations persisted he should provide assistance if necessary, for which purpose he could call on "any and all Spaniards who are in all of that region and the governors, caciques, principales, and natives of its pueblos, both those that belong to the king and those that are in encomienda."[12]

The combined effects of casualties in the war, epidemics that ravaged the area in the mid-1540s, and the opening of new mining sites affected both centers of Spanish settlement and the indigenous population. A report of 1548 by Licenciado Lebrón de Quiñones, the first of the oidores of the newly constituted audiencia of New Galicia to arrive in the region, stated that Compostela had perhaps twenty-five Spanish vecinos, Guadalajara thirty-five, and Purificación fifteen.[13] Lebrón de Quiñones revised his population figures after completing the first part of his tour of inspection in 1552. According to this later report, Guadalajara had eighty vecinos, Compostela thirty-five or forty, Culiacan eighty, Purificación twenty to twenty-five. The booming mining town of Zacatecas by then had some three hundred vecinos as well as "more than one thousand other traders," while the mines of Guachinango had between eighty and one hundred residents and those of Guaxacatlan and Culiacan a comparable number.[14]

With the end of the war, complaints about the unsuitability of Compostela as the kingdom's administrative capital mounted, especially with the rapid development of the Zacatecas silver mines after 1548. In late January 1549 royal accountant Juan de Ojeda wrote that Compostela "is a pueblo where there aren't twenty vecinos and these [being] very poor men who because of not having anything to eat for most of the year don't live in their houses but work on their estates. . . . And this pueblo lacks all the necessary things, both supplies and everything else, because as there are few people, nothing is brought to sell nor can one find anything to buy." Miners in Zacatecas were forced to travel eighty leagues to pay the tax on their silver at Compostela but were unable to purchase what they needed there and would have to travel even farther to Mexico City for supplies. Ojeda, like others, advocated moving the audiencia and the treasury to Guadalajara, which he called the "most principal pueblo that His Majesty has in this province," pointing out that the greatest concentration of remaining indigenous population was now in the vicinity of Guadalajara.[15] The town council of Compostela explained the situation there:

When this city was founded it had an abundance of Spaniards and at its beginning seemed to have a [populous] district with the pueblos of Xalisco, Tepic, Senticpac, Aguacatlan, and the valleys of Zacualpa and Banderas. But as the natives were weak people of the hot country and sunken in vice, for their and our sins God has punished them with plague and pestilence to such a degree that for fifteen leagues around this city there aren't four thousand workers under the authority of the king and encomenderos, for which reason this pueblo is greatly diminished and the Spaniards have gone to Peru and other places. Only we married and poor men remain here, although certainly [we are] the most loyal and desirous of serving Your Majesty.

The council members proposed a solution that, under the circumstances, seems pure fantasy: send six thousand men with their wives from New Spain to settle the fertile and irrigated but now mostly depopulated lands around Compostela, with the guarantee that they would remain free of any obligations to furnish labor or tribute. They also requested that two thousand black slaves be provided "at moderate prices, which would be divided among the conquistadors and settlers."[16]

The council bemoaned the difficulty of undertaking the construction needed to accommodate the new audiencia and build a cathedral, pointing out that the present church and *ayuntamiento* (town hall) were made of poles and straw "for lack of pine wood and [other] materials that can't be found in fourteen or fifteen leagues. . . . It has been necessary to make do with these wretched and sad houses and if now, with the arrival of the audiencia and bishop it were necessary to build a cathedral and house for the royal audiencia and the rest of the houses and buildings, it would (be to) end up killing and destroying these sad natives." In February 1552 the dean of the church in Guadalajara wrote to the Council of the Indies that the church in Compostela was so poor "that in the least pueblo of Indians there is a better one."[17] Despite these gloomy observations, the seat of the audiencia remained in Compostela until 1560, although Guadalajara was the effective seat of the bishopric from the outset.

The establishment of the audiencia generated another set of problems and controversies—hardly surprising, given that the oidores were newcomers to the region who arrived with a rather vaguely defined charge. The Crown intended that the new audiencia would be subordinate and report to the audiencia in Mexico City, which also would hear appeals. The new officials' title of "oidores alcaldes mayores" itself suggests their status differed in some regard from that of the oidores in Mexico City.[18] Given the difficulties the first justices experienced just in reaching New Galicia, the institution got off to a ragged start. Of the four justices appointed in 1548, only Lic. Lorenzo Lebrón de Quiñones actually arrived in New Galicia late that year. Lic. Hernando Martínez de la Marcha literally missed the boat on which his colleagues traveled from Spain to New Spain, arriving several months later. Miguel Ladrón de Contreras y Guevara became ill on the voyage and spent several months in Mexico City recuperating before he traveled to Compostela. A fourth appointee died in Santo Domingo en route to Mexico and was not immediately replaced.[19]

At the end of 1549 the vecinos of Compostela wrote to the king complaining about the lack of experience of the oidores alcaldes mayores. Indians traveling along the royal road from Guadalajara suffered attacks to which the justices failed to respond; the vecinos argued that they needed officials who understood the conditions of the region. The lengthy visitas, or tours of inspection, conducted first by de la Marcha and then by Lebrón meant at the very least that the oidores soon gained considerable familiarity with the region. J. H. Parry suggests that they erred in strictly following their charge to establish the audiencia in isolated and minimally populated Compostela. In a letter of December 1550, the bishop Pedro Gómez de Maraver—who opted to remain in Guadalajara—was scathing in his appraisal of the audiencia's situation:

> They hold audiencia in a straw hut, and lodge in the houses of the neighbours, for they have there neither the material nor the labour necessary for constructing new buildings. There are no attorneys or advocates, only the oidores, who have no one upon whom to exercise their jurisdiction. . . . The whole kingdom has begged the oidores to move to Guadalajara where they are needed. . . . For these reasons no benefit whatever has been derived from the establishment of the audiencia; on the contrary, the whole kingdom is divided by disorders . . . and will soon become depopulated, through the work of partial and inexperienced judges.[20]

Gómez de Maraver, who died a year after penning this critique, did not do a great deal to improve the situation of the Indians. He spent much of his relatively short time in New Galicia contending with the bishop of Michoacan over the boundaries between the two bishoprics.[21] The people of Apozol, however, apparently credited de Maraver with restoring them to their pueblo. They claimed that after the war (during which they rebelled) they were dispersed until the bishop talked with their encomendero and managed to bring them back in 1549, convincing the principal don Hernando and one hundred of his followers to renounce war and resettle the pueblo.[22]

When he first became bishop in 1547, Gómez de Maraver asked the Crown to send more Franciscans to convert the Indians, as at the time there were only twelve friars and three Franciscan monasteries in all of New Galicia.[23] In view of the linguistic diversity of the region, the bishop, like the first protector of Indians, Cristóbal de Pedraza, recommended instructing the Indians in Castilian. Fray Rodrigo de la Cruz argued for using Nahuatl as the language of evangelization, pointing out that many people already understood it and that those who did not learned it easily. Furthermore *"la lengua mexicana"* was *"elegantísima"* (the Mexican language was very elegant), and by this time there were grammars and vocabularies available, as well as texts translated into Nahuatl, and friars who could speak the language.[24] The bishop's proposal prevailed, however, with the cabildo *eclesiástico* (ecclesiastical council) ordering the establishment of schools to teach Spanish to the Indians in Guadalajara, Juchipila, Aguacatlan, and Atoyac, although they do not appear to have functioned for very long.[25]

Certainly there is nothing new or surprising in the bickering and mutual criticisms and accusations exchanged among clergy, royal officials, and settlers in the aftermath of the war in New Galicia; such disagreements were par for the course in early Spanish America. All groups in Spanish society ultimately sought the same general objective—to resettle and pacify the country and secure the labor of the remaining indigenous population to achieve economic growth and stability. Both officials and settlers saw the clergy as playing a crucial role in this effort, as only Indians brought within the fold of Christianity could be expected to be compliant and peaceful. From the lay Spaniards' point of view, however, the clergy could fall short of expectations. A letter of September 1550 from prominent vecinos of Guadalajara commented on the lack of clergy in the region.[26] The ecclesiastical establishment itself certainly did not function as a unified entity. The Franciscans criticized the diocesan clergy.[27] Other religious orders began to join the Franciscans in the region. Officials, settlers, and clergy at one time or another all accused the others of being negligent in conversion efforts and of exploiting indigenous labor.

Settlers and officials complained that friars made excessive and idiosyncratic demands on the Indians whose labor they used to build their monasteries and churches. The audiencia oidor Martínez de la Marcha wrote to the king in March 1552, bitterly criticizing the friars' building efforts and detailing at considerable length the waste and harm that resulted from them. According to Martínez, there was a decent church and residence for the Franciscans in Guadalajara with more than enough room for the customary two friars and a covered area for occasions when the Indians gathered in large numbers. Not content with this, however, the Franciscan guardian decided to demolish the existing complex and build a "*grandísima*" (huge) new church and much larger residence in a different location. He attempted to do so in such haste and pressured the "innumerable" Indians to work so fast that parts of the new building began to fall down. When the Franciscan order's general commissioner arrived, he ordered most of the new structure demolished. Nonetheless the order began yet again to rebuild the church and residence, with the result that in a little over a year there were "two churches made and two unmade. The ill treatment and toil of the Indian men and women was enormous," as they were forced to carry stones on their backs and to make adobe, "and others to build ovens for lime and [make] lime, and others to cut wood . . . and others to make clay and set the adobe and stones, and others to build ovens for bricks and [make] bricks," all of it without receiving any kind of pay. In the pueblo of Poncitlan the friars ordered that a decent church be torn down, allegedly because of its inconvenient location, and then built another larger church and residence "all of stone." In Aguacatlan also the friars insisted on knocking down the church and "with excessive labor of the natives built another very large and curious church and residence," to which they subsequently added a chapel and a number of further embellishments. The disapproving oidor commented, "I don't believe that there is or could be any purpose for the church other than for those who pass through to look at it."[28] In a letter of May 1552, however, several Franciscans countered with a description of their modest establishment at Guadalajara and argued that their monasteries in New Galicia were in keeping with the humility of their order.[29]

For his part Fray Rodrigo de la Cruz criticized the oidores for doing nothing to help the Indians or to protect them from the demands of the settlers, alleging that most of the oidores were "against the Indians and very passionate" (meaning intemperate and strongly opinionated). On one occasion when Fray Rodrigo tried to speak to two of the oidores, "they wanted to eat me alive and shout me down." He alleged that "if a poor friar speaks, they say it's because he wants to be governor, which is the common term of the Spaniards."[30] The friar criticized the Spanish settlers for forcing the Indians to transport tributes over excessive distances and the audiencia for failing to free any of the slaves who petitioned them, including many people who technically were not slaves but naborías. It is somewhat ironic that he identified the oidores with the interests of the encomenderos and miners, given that the settlers also were often critical of the audiencia. Fray Rodrigo had positive things to say only about the oidor Licenciado Lebrón de Quiñones, who "did many good things regarding the Indians. . . . He does what he can for them."[31] In 1557 several Franciscans described Lebrón as a "lily among thorns" in a letter to the king and pleaded that he be named governor of New Galicia, "because the audiencia isn't necessary."[32] During the visita (tour of inspection) that commenced in October 1551 and lasted almost two and a half years, Lebrón visited more than two hundred pueblos and encountered "many offenses and tyrannies that the natives . . . have received both from priests and from lay people." He identified many instances in which individuals took possession of pueblos to which they had no legal title.[33] Not surprisingly, Lebrón often was at odds with the settlers and with the other oidores.[34]

In the years following the war, then, Spaniards in New Galicia were contentious and uncertain as they tried to forge a secure life and future for themselves. Indigenous society was in far greater disarray, devastated by huge losses of population from war, disease, and migration. The Indians who rebelled had gained nothing in terms of mitigating Spanish demands that they adopt Christianity and forfeit part—often a very large share—of their labor and productivity. Encomiendas still functioned, and the numbers of slaves had soared. Conflict among indigenous groups and resistance to Spanish rule meant that violence continued to plague the region. In addition, the accelerated pace of development of the mining economy brought yet more change to the region.

The Mining Economy

The opening of new and larger mines in New Galicia or nearby constituted the most noteworthy change in the kingdom in the years following the war. This development heralded an era of economic growth that affected not only the struggling western province but central Mexico as well, as

FIGURE 15. Map of New Galicia in 1550. This interesting map was
prepared in conjunction with the visit of inspection of oidor Lic.
Hernando Martínez de la Marcha. The Pacific coast is at the bottom;
Tepic, Xalisco, and Compostela appear near the lower left-hand corner.
With a grid pattern of four blocks, Guadalajara, in the center right, is
shown as a more substantial city than Compostela. In the upper left
corner various groups of warriors are depicted with scenes of sacrifice
or cannibalism. Reproduced by permission of the Spanish Ministry of
Culture, Archivo General de Indias, Mapas y Planos, Mexico 560.

over time efforts to supply the northern mines and maintain the production of silver became increasingly important to the Mexican economy. As
the mines brought more people and wealth to the region, other economic
enterprises also took hold or expanded. Stock raising increased, and some
Spaniards attempted to use their landholdings and access to Indian labor
to cultivate cacao. The establishment or improvement of roads that connected mining zones to the towns of New Galicia and central Mexico
brought increased traffic into and through the region.

The most spectacular of the silver mining strikes, made in Zacatecas in late 1546, directly involved several of New Galicia's most prominent settlers and tied the fortunes of some of the region's leading families, such as the Oñate-Zaldívar clan, to what would become the premier mining region of sixteenth-century New Spain. Although stories of the discovery of silver at Zacatecas, some 150 miles northeast of Guadalajara, differ in detail, in all of them the principal figures involved were Basque mining entrepreneurs, some of whom, like Cristóbal de Oñate and Miguel de Ibarra, were conquistadores with many years of experience in New Galicia.[35] Juan (or Juanes) de Tolosa usually receives credit for having discovered the mines. He claimed to have participated in the pacification of New Galicia during the Mixton War and probably arrived in the region with the viceroy, as there is no indication of his presence earlier. The other consistent element in different versions of the story is the importance of the area north of Guadalajara—the very core of the Cazcan uprising and Mixton War—for both the discovery and initial development of the mines. Although problems of supply and the hostility of the Indians in the area plagued the early mining camp at Zacatecas, within a few years the mines became productive, a town took root, and men like Oñate and Diego de Ibarra made fortunes.

In 1550 Juan de Tolosa executed a deposition in Zacatecas. In it Pedro de Torres, a vecino of Zacatecas, stated that a few years earlier he had been in the pueblo of Tlaltenango, where he and others had found (or most likely were given) a piece of ore, which they showed to Juan de Tolosa and Miguel de Ibarra.[36] Don Francisco, who in 1550 was the cacique and governor of the nearby pueblo of Nochistlan, testified that Tolosa and Miguel de Ibarra (who died by 1550) had used Nochistlan, which still belonged to Ibarra in encomienda, as a base to explore for mines. Don Francisco said that about four years previously he had been with Tolosa when some Indians informed them that there were mines to the north.[37] A man from another nearby pueblo, called Tenanco, told them about mines located more than a week's journey away and agreed to guide them there.[38] Accompanied by don Francisco, as well as nearly thirty Indian slaves who belonged to Miguel de Ibarra and some other Indians, Tolosa reached Zacatecas, where they took samples of the ore and transported them back to Nochistlan. Miguel de Ibarra and Diego de Ibarra smelted the ore, extracting lead and silver.[39] This first visit to the site probably took place in the fall of 1546.

Although four men—Tolosa, Cristóbal de Oñate, Diego de Ibarra, and Baltasar Temiño de Banuelos, who traveled to New Spain as the criado of don Antonio de Mendoza—emerged as the dominant figures in early Zacatecas, they were not all equally successful. As Peter Bakewell has pointed out, the mines were a private commercial venture from the outset, meaning that the early entrepreneurs bore the entire financial burden of sponsoring their development, purchasing equipment, and securing labor.[40] Thus Tolosa, despite a marriage that brought him connections to one of the most illustrious families of early New Spain—his wife was doña Leonor Cortés, the daughter of Hernando Cortés and doña Isabel Moctezuma, daughter of the last Aztec emperor—as a relative newcomer to New Spain probably he had not been there long enough to amass a large fortune that could underwrite the substantial investments that mining required. He also seems to have reinvested much of his early profits in exploring for additional sites. Cristóbal de Oñate, long established in the region, a landowner and holder of encomiendas in central Mexico, Michoacan, and New Galicia, who for some years had been involved in mining in the West, most likely commanded much greater resources.[41] Diego de Ibarra could probably afford early expenses as well; he was the nephew of Miguel de Ibarra and possibly his heir.[42] Although Tolosa is credited as the founder of the Zacatecas mines, their success depended largely on the efforts of Oñate and Ibarra, who had the connections and influence to recruit miners and workers and support them during the initial lean times.[43]

The first years at the mining site were indeed difficult ones, particularly in terms of supply and transportation; Zacatecas lay well to the north of any existing Spanish settlement. The first route by which people and supplies reached the mines went from Guadalajara through Juchipila and Nochistlan to Zacatecas; a second route went northeast from Guadalajara through Teocaltiche and the site of the future town of Aguascalientes. Thus, although initially the area that had been the Cazcan heartland prior to the war played a crucial role in providing supplies and labor for the mines, the close ties between the core of New Galicia and Zacatecas did not endure. Increasingly the road from Mexico City to Zacatecas via Querétaro superseded the original route that connected Guadalajara to the new mining zone.[44]

Lack of food, fears of Indian hostilities, and difficulties of transportation drove away some early arrivals at the mines and discouraged

others from trying their luck there. By the end of the decade, however,
Zacatecas already was attracting significant numbers of would-be miners.
In 1550 Diego de Ibarra maintained a casa poblada (large household establishment) that welcomed travelers and newcomers, and he had African
slaves and other workers, mule trains, wagons, and mills.[45] A report of
April 1550 stated that "Cristóbal de Oñate and his partners [compañía] have
thirteen mills for grinding and refining and one hundred and one houses
for slaves and his residence with a church where everyone at the mines
goes to hear mass."[46] According to the report, there were thirty-four mining companies (or partnerships) and more than 150 veins in operation and
nearly 350 "houses of slaves."[47]

A notable number of conquistadors, vecinos, and veterans of the
Mixton War found their way to the new mines, although not all remained
there. The veteran Juan de Amusco accompanied Miguel de Ibarra to
the mines, as did Diego Romero. In 1550 encomendero and interpreter
Cristóbal Romero still was a vecino of Guadalajara, but he too had spent
time in Zacatecas.[48] Hernando Martel, who shared the encomienda of
the Río de Tepeque with Diego de Proaño after the war and probably
was involved in mining there, in 1550 owned, with his partner Baltasar de
Gallegos, "a smelting mill and residence and twelve houses for slaves and
a church that had begun to be built." Alonso de Santa Cruz, who played
a crucial role in helping to convince the rebels at the peñol of Acatique to
surrender, had a refinery at Zacatecas and "four houses for himself and his
people." Although he fought in the war, he apparently gained some mining
experience in Taxco in the mid-1540s before moving on to Zacatecas.[49]

Juan Delgado said that he was in the area of Zacatecas even before the
mines were discovered and that he and Juan de Torres had a partnership
with Andrés de Villanueva "who had discovered the richest mines there."
Villanueva was the staunch defender of Guadalajara who urged the other
vecinos not to evacuate their families from the city. Juan Valiente, who
had known Villanueva for twenty years, reported that he heard that one
of the latter's slaves had been responsible for the discovery of the very
rich mines that belonged to Villanueva, although he was vague about the
source of this information. Bartolomé García testified that he was present
in the mines at the beginning "and he saw that in the house of the said
Andrés de Villanueva most of the Spaniards that were in the said mines
went to eat as well as in the house of Diego de Ibarra because there was
nowhere else to go."[50]

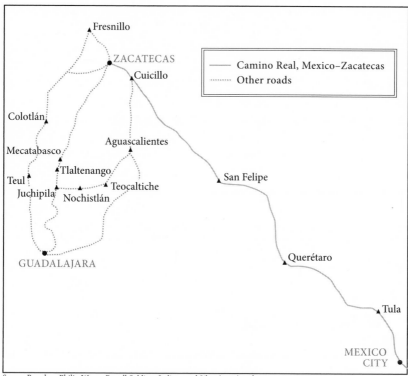

Source: Based on Philip Wayne Powell *Soldiers, Indians and Silver* (p. 20) and
P. J. Bakewell, *Silver Mining and Society in Colonial Zacateca, 1546-1700*

MAP 7. Routes to Zacatecas

Another man who did well in Zacatecas was Diego Hernández de Proaño, Guzmán's captain and the notorious first alcalde mayor of Culiacan. In February 1569 in Zacatecas, his widow, doña Ana de Corral, presented a deposition in the name of her two sons. In it she stated that in 1550 Proaño owned a residence, refining mill, another grinding mill that was being built, and sixteen houses for slaves at the mines.[51] As did many of the other early mining entrepreneurs of Zacatecas, Proaño continued to search for new mines. In the 1550s he found a hill with silver ore about eight leagues northwest of Zacatecas, near a spring that became known as the "cerro de [hill of] Proaño." Although the ores initially did not seem to be of high quality, the site later became the mines of El Fresnillo, and the Cerro de Proaño ultimately proved to be quite rich.[52]

One of the most successful of the Zacatecas mining entrepreneurs was Cristóbal de Oñate's nephew Juan de Zaldívar, who arrived in New Galicia soon after the conquest and took over the encomiendas that his uncle Juan de Oñate held. Zaldívar threw himself into the constant campaigning that embroiled the region during the 1530s and early 1540s, participating in slaving entradas and accompanying Licenciado Pérez de la Torre when he went to suppress an uprising in Xocotlan (where the governor received the injury that caused his death in 1537). He subsequently served as a captain of cavalry with Vázquez de Coronado's expedition to New Mexico and, soon after his return to New Galicia, participated in the campaign against the Tecoxquines led by his uncle Cristóbal.[53] Although the wealth he accumulated during his career in New Galicia may have derived as much from his encomiendas and investments in estates and stock raising as from mining, he and his family established a lasting connection with Zacatecas. His brother, Vicente de Zaldívar, also a miner in Zacatecas, served as lieutenant captain general of New Galicia under the viceroy don Martín Enríquez in the 1570s.[54]

The growing wealth and influence of these men whose families forged multiple ties through marriage, partnership, and common interest brought them into the forefront of political and military power in northern New Spain in the second half of the sixteenth century. Vicente de Zaldívar married the daughter of his uncle Cristóbal de Oñate's wife, doña Catalina de Salazar, by her first marriage. Their son Cristóbal de Zaldívar y Mendoza would marry the daughter of Juan de Tolosa and doña Leonor Cortés. Cristóbal de Oñate and doña Catalina de Salazar's son married another daughter of Tolosa and his wife doña Leonor.[55] This son, don Juan de Oñate, would become the *adelantado* and conqueror of New Mexico in the 1590s. The families maintained their tradition of intermarriage into succeeding generations; don Juan de Oñate's daughter doña María de Oñate, for example, married her distant cousin, Vicente de Zaldívar, son of the military captain and miner Vicente de Zaldívar and doña Magdalena de Mendoza y Salazar.[56]

Although he maintained a residence near Zacatecas and probably traveled there with some frequency, Cristóbal de Oñate spent much of his remaining life in Mexico City. His nephew Juan de Zaldívar, by contrast, maintained his ties with Guadalajara. He participated in the fourth, and final, founding of the city in the valley of Atemajac in February 1542, building an impressive house on the main plaza, and there he served in various municipal offices. His brother Vicente de Zaldívar also lived and held offices in Guadalajara through the early 1560s, but he became increasingly involved in the family's mining interests. He acquired a majority interest in the Pánuco mines, which his uncle Cristóbal de Oñate, who died in 1567, had owned, and eventually moved permanently to Zacatecas, where he held office during the 1570s and 1580s.[57]

In February 1566 Juan de Zaldívar presented a deposition before the audiencia detailing his many services to the Crown.[58] He stated that he maintained in Guadalajara "one of the leading houses of this entire kingdom and in it he has many arms and horses and servants as the hidalgo that I am." The extent of his wealth can be judged from the ambitious offer he made to the Crown to undertake the settlement and conversion of one (or more) of the recently conquered Philippine Islands. Zaldívar stated that within two and a half years he could provide the ships, horses, arms, and supplies necessary to equip five hundred men, whom he would either accompany personally or send to the Pacific Islands under someone else's command. In compensation he asked for the title of adelantado; a grant of fifty leagues of land that would belong to him and his heirs in perpetuity; the title of admiral, which would include jurisdiction over the seas surrounding the island, extending twelve leagues, also in perpetuity; governorship of the island; and authority to name its officials and assign encomiendas.[59]

The witnesses who provided testimony on Zaldívar's behalf for the most part were longtime residents and officeholders, reflecting the stability that increasingly characterized Guadalajara after the turbulent early years. Pedro de Plasencia, a conquistador of New Galicia, was a regidor in Guadalajara in 1566 and Zaldívar's compadre and godfather of his children. Pedro de Ledesma, who had gone with Zaldívar to the Tierra Nueva, also was a regidor.[60] Other old-timers in the region who testified were Francisco Delgadillo, an alcalde ordinario; Andrés de Villanueva, a regidor; Diego Vázquez, once Guzmán's captain and mayordomo; and Francisco Rojo, interpreter for the audiencia of New Galicia, who with his father also had accompanied Zaldívar to the Tierra Nueva. There is no record of the king's response to Zaldívar's proposal to settle and evangelize one of the islands of the Philippines. Clearly Zaldívar was not ready to retire to the life of a wealthy man of leisure, despite his years of campaigning, in which, according to Pedro de Ledesma, he was always first to offer his services, "spending his wealth . . . accompanying governors and going to punish the Zacatecas Indians. . . . And for his sake many have gone to the war . . . because with him they had assistance and favor and for this reason he has been greatly loved by the governors and other vecinos of this realm."[61]

The importance of the Zacatecas mines has overshadowed other sites in New Galicia. While none of them rivaled Zacatecas in size and wealth, the mines of Guachinango developed rapidly and generated a good deal of interest, although their heyday did not last long.[62] Juan Hernández de Híjar, the founder and longtime alcalde mayor of Purificación, discovered the first veins of ore there in 1544 or 1545. The Guachinango mines brought a rush of newcomers to the region and attracted the interest of long-time residents. The mines' reputation was such that two oidores of the audiencia in Mexico City invested in them. One of them, Lic. Hernando Gómez Santillán, maintained two mills, one for smelting and the other for grinding and washing; a house for his mayordomo; and seven other buildings for slaves and equipment, while his colleague Lic. Lorenzo de Tejada had a "house in which his miner lives," along with four houses for slaves and equipment.[63]

In addition, a number of men who had been active in the region for some time invested in the mines. Both Alvaro de Bracamonte and Francisco de Estrada held encomiendas nearby. Bracamonte, the conquistador who was once the protégé of Nuño de Guzmán and an active participant in the slaving campaigns of the mid-1530s, built one of the largest establishments at Guachinango, with two mills, a refinery, a large residence with a straw roof in which he lived, and thirteen houses for his slaves, servants, and equipment. Francisco de Cifontes (or Cifuentes), who participated in the conquest of Mexico and later Colima and held encomiendas in New Galicia and Colima, also had a very large house surrounded by a palisade, as well as a hand smelter, refinery, and "fourteen houses of slaves and kitchens and storerooms and stables and metals." Other longtime residents of New Galicia who maintained a presence at the mines included Juan López, Alonso Rodríguez, Francisco Rojo *"el viejo"* (the elder), and the corregidor Andrés de Urdaneta. Many of the miners, however, appear to have been newcomers to the region. The report of 1550 lists scores of veins that had opened in just five years. The influx of miners with their slaves and other workers was such that in 1549 the audiencia named an alcalde mayor for the mines of Guachinango.[64] Within just a few years of the war's conclusion, then, Spanish society in New Galicia had grown rapidly in size and complexity.

Ongoing Conflict

Although it is often assumed that following the Mixton War, conflict in the region mainly shifted northeast toward the newly established mining zone of Zacatecas and beyond, leaving the core of New Galicia relatively quiet, violence continued to be endemic throughout the kingdom.[65] Indeed, the persistence of conflict reflected the continued tenuousness of the Spanish presence in the region. No sooner had Francisco Vázquez de Coronado returned from the expedition to the Tierra Nueva than he delegated Cristóbal de Oñate to put down a rebellion of the Tecoxquines, who mostly lived in the mountains of the western part of the modern state of Jalisco. Veteran captain Miguel de Ibarra participated, together with Oñate's nephew Juan de Zaldívar, who returned from New Mexico with Vázquez de Coronado. After they suppressed the rebels, the Spaniards settled some of the people in villages near Compostela; other survivors retreated into the mountains.[66]

In Culiacan in the north, security and stability continued to elude Spaniards. Licenciado Martínez de la Marcha reported in March 1552 that the town of San Miguel had moved to a much better site ten leagues away because of flooding from the river. The people of the relocated town, however, were surrounded by a "multitude of barbarous Chichimeca enemies" and in constant danger of attack. Lacking sufficient funds in the treasury, the oidor was uncertain whether he could offer assistance. Although he wrote that he would have liked to see the new town, his advancing age would not allow him to travel so far.[67]

Episodes of conflict and violence recorded during the period suggest that, despite the enormous changes that had taken place since Guzmán's conquest and as a result of the traumatic upheaval of the Mixton War, both Spaniards and the Indians involved in hostilities were mainly concerned with local circumstances, enmities, and objectives. Martínez de la Marcha's letter about the threat of attack on San Miguel could have been written at almost any time in the previous twenty years. Recall from chapter 3 that the oidor Lebrón de Quiñones reported a series of violent attacks on one pueblo, orchestrated by the vecino of Purificación, Antonio de Aguayo, during a period of some fifteen years—before, during, and after the Mixton War. That long-standing conflict, in other words, was the product of Aguayo's particular ambitions and the resources he commanded and had little to do with broader issues or events. Despite this kind of endemic violence, however, there were no major confrontations that came anywhere close to matching the scale of the war of 1540–41.[68]

During Martínez de la Marcha's visita of 1549–50, he reported complaints about "Chichimec" leaders such as Chapuli and Coringa, who were mentioned by witnesses as early as the time of Guzmán's residencia in 1537.[69] The oidor took testimony in October 1549 at the mines of Tepeque from several residents of the pueblo of Pochotitlan who alleged that Chapuli or his people had attacked the pueblo, burning the church and some houses before carrying off four women and killing two or three men. The residents of Pochotitlan fortunately received advance warning from a man from another pueblo, which allowed most of them to gather their families and cross the river to safety.[70] The witnesses testified in Cazcan, which a man named Diego, a native of Tlaltenango, translated into "lengua mexicana," which Spaniard Juan de Covarrubias in turn translated into Spanish. The witnesses all referred to "the people of Chapuli," not to the leader himself, as being responsible for the attacks. Martínez de la Marcha actually entered into negotiations with Chapuli and apparently met with him more than once, but ultimately nothing came of this initiative. Chapuli was reported dead in early 1551.[71]

In late November 1549 Martínez de la Marcha reported a series of attacks on the pueblos of Tequila and Teul, carried out by caciques of Tezol over a number of years.[72] The first witness in the inquiry that the oidor conducted, a twenty-five-year-old woman named Amoche who was born in Tequila, testified that she had been taken from Tequila to Talistacan, where she married a man named Picachan; he was one of the prisoners being held by authorities in connection with the attacks. Perhaps she had been a captive, but she did not elaborate on the circumstances in which she left her native community. Although Tequila was a Tecuexe pueblo, she testified through a man named "Juan, Indian interpreter and naguatato, who understands the Chichimeca language. . . . The said Juan declared what he understood from the said Indian woman in the language of Mexico, and Francisco the black understood," presumably providing the Spanish translation.[73] Apparently she spoke the language of her husband's people.

Amoche testified that the pueblo of Talistacan was at war with other pueblos; she did not know for how long "because she does not know how to count time." She had seen the cacique, Elote, and other men who were now prisoners of the Spaniards, form a war party to attack Tequila and another pueblo that belonged to encomendero Juan Delgado, which would have been Teul. The warriors returned with nine captives taken in Teul and another eight captives taken from a third settlement subject to Tequila. The captives—men, women, and children—were taken to the "house of the devil," where they were sacrificed and eaten by the whole community. The victims' hearts were cut out and their blood and guts offered to the devil that sat on the shoulders of a well-dressed man, presumably a religious leader, who carried him "like a tameme [porter]." Several days of dancing and festivity followed the sacrifices. On another occasion, the warriors of Talistacan captured five Christianized Indians in Tequila and sacrificed them as well.[74]

Like everyone else in the pueblo, Amoche was unbaptized. She stated that "they aren't Christians because in the pueblo there aren't churches except that of the devil, whom they worship." She also said that friars came to Talistican to try to convince them to convert, but neither the cacique Elote nor his macehuales (commoners) were willing to do so. Apparently Spaniards did not desist altogether from their efforts to convert the pueblo. Amoche mentioned that just the day before, the Day of All Saints, the oidor had sent an interpreter, Juan, to summon them. In response, all the people in the pueblo fled to the river and refused to come, the men declaring that "if the Spaniards wanted something from them they should go there."[75]

The cacique Elote himself testified in Compostela a few days later. He affirmed that the pueblo of Tezol (unlike the first two witnesses, his testimony referred to Tezol rather than Talistacan) waged war on others and that about five years previously they killed many people in Teul and brought others back to be sacrificed. Their attack on Tequila, in which they killed three people and took fifteen captive for sacrifice, took place eight years before under the leadership of a previous cacique, Tatle. If his reckoning was accurate, that attack would have occurred in the midst of the Mixton War. The more recent attack on Tequila, during which a man named Coyacal shot another man in the ear with an arrow, had taken place only two months before. The friars came to the pueblo about three and a half years previously, but the pueblo did not respond to them "nor to the summons of any person."[76]

The chronology of events varied from one witness to another; Amoche apparently was not the only one who did not know how to keep track of time with any precision. Notably, a man named Cuychaniña thought he might be one hundred years old, but the Spanish scribe noted that he looked to be around forty. One witness reported that the attacks on Teul and Tequila respectively had taken place nine rather than five years and three rather than eight years previously and the most recent raid on Tequila about four months before. The details of the attacks and capture of sacrificial victims are fairly consistent, however, although any testimony on such practices rendered before Spanish authorities and mediated through two interpreters must be weighed cautiously. We may well question the details regarding sacrifices and cannibalism, although there is no direct evidence that the testimony of the witnesses, including one recorded as saying that he "had eaten their flesh and it's very good," was coerced. Yet some of the witnesses were being held prisoner by the Spaniards and others were the wives or other relatives of prisoners. As in other situations where Spaniards solicited testimony from indigenous witnesses, the latter —assisted by interpreters—certainly could have been or felt pressured to supply the responses the Spaniards wanted.[77]

Don Gonzalo, a cacique of Tequila, brought the complaint against "the Tezoles who oppress them [and] who are at war" before the audiencia, which sent Martínez de la Marcha to the mines of Tepeque to conduct an investigation. He summoned the cacique Elote, who brought with him eight principales, all of whom were then arrested "for never having come in peace and for being at war." According to de la Marcha "the main reason for this inquiry is in order that it be seen how these people spend their lives and how they are so close by and how the people at peace with whom they border are in fear." While the Tezoles' ostensible practice of taking captives to sacrifice and communally cannibalize probably long predated the arrival of the Spaniards, their continued adamant rejection of Christianity in face of other pueblos' acceptance of the alien religion provided them with additional justification "to make war on the Christian Indians."[78]

The opening or rapid development of new mining sites in the core of New Galicia strengthened the Spanish presence in places where it previously was weak or nonexistent, placing increasing demands and pressures on nearby communities. Thus, much of the conflict in these years took place near the mining sites that attracted growing interest in the 1540s. As Spanish society spread into areas that once were relatively remote and inaccessible, it encroached on groups that up to that point had managed to remain virtually independent.[79]

In one episode Spanish authorities decided to eliminate a settlement at the peñol of Zacatlan that had become a haven for both Indians and African slaves. The refugees were mostly indigenous fugitives from encomiendas in the area—especially those of Alvaro de Bracamonte and Francisco de Estrada, who both had mines at Guachinango—and African and Indian slaves who escaped from the mines. The refugees appear to have been culpable mainly of trying to escape Spanish demands for labor. Reminiscent of the period leading to the Mixton War, people at the peñol had established the rudiments of a community: witnesses mentioned houses, including a building large enough for substantial gatherings, as well as extensive cultivated fields. Very possibly there were people living at the peñol for several years before the oidor Ladrón de Contreras y Guevara decided to dislodge them in the autumn of 1550. There is little evidence that the settlement at the peñol was responsible for attacks or raids on the Spaniards and their property, nor had the people living there sought to create a network of potential allies in the nearby countryside.[80] Spanish authorities seem to have become concerned only when miners at Guachinango complained that their African slaves were fleeing the mines to take refuge there.[81]

Contreras made the customary overtures to the people at the peñol, sending a naguatato named Alonso, who belonged to one of Estrada's encomiendas, along with another Indian, to negotiate with the fugitives. The latter rebuffed the demands that they render obedience, offering instead to meet the Spaniards with bows and arrows and boasting that one of their number easily could take on four Christians. The Indians and Africans gathered at the peñol quite reasonably pointed out that there they were free, but if they capitulated, they would become slaves of the Christians. The interpreter Alonso spent the night in a house at the peñol and narrowly escaped death at the hands of the Africans only through the intervention of the Indians' leader.[82]

When this initial effort at negotiation failed, Contreras sent encomenderos Alonso Alvarez and Francisco de Estrada, who took a position on a rocky point above the peñol. From there they sent don Juan, the cacique of Acatitlan, to parley with the fugitives. The cacique claimed to have visited the peñol many times because a number of the people there were from his pueblo, which belonged to Estrada in encomienda. In the meantime Alvarez and Estrada, both of whom apparently understood and spoke Nahuatl, talked to a man named Fernando, a naguatato who together with a woman named Isabel, called *nahuatlata*, acted as spokespersons for the group at the peñol.[83] Fernando persuaded don Juan and two Indian men with him to enter the peñol, assuring them they would not be harmed, while Alvarez and Estrada departed. Soon thereafter, however, some of don Juan's men who decided to wait for him on the rocky crag caught up with the Spaniards, declaring that don Juan and his companion Pedro had been killed.

Why the Indians reported the deaths of don Juan and Pedro is not clear. Apparently after the naguatato Fernando persuaded them to remain at the peñol, disagreements over what was to be done with them arose almost immediately. The women at the peñol especially distrusted the hostages, convinced that they must be spies.[84] Later Contreras found out that don Juan and his companion Pedro did not die at the peñol, although they were beaten and threatened and restrained until the following morning, when some Indian merchants released them. Pedro testified that they took his clothing and tore up an order from the oidor that he was carrying, saying that it was not the two Indians whom they wanted but the Christians.[85] Some of the testimony about this episode offered by the Spaniards was contradictory. Alvaro de Bracamonte stated that Fernando and Isabel, the naguatatos for the peñol, were Christians who belonged to his encomienda and that the leaders at the peñol also were from one of his pueblos. The origins of many of the people at the peñol, however, are not clear. Bracamonte also claimed that the fugitives at the peñol were responsible for an attack on his mines at Tepeguacan, where they killed slaves and a Spaniard, but the evidence connecting the people at the peñol with the episode is thin; none of the witnesses stated when it took place, and most did not mention it at all.

After sending Fray Francisco Lorenzo to make one last plea that the fugitives at the peñol submit, Contreras ordered an attack, although no details of the actual battle appear in the record. At some point the Spaniards captured a man named Tenuiz, who told them that there were twenty warriors and around seventy people at the peñol. He said that the cacique was a man named Francisco, who did not want to surrender or give up the Africans, who belonged to Bracamonte and were armed with "swords from Castile."[86] Contreras ordered Tenuiz flogged and hanged from a tree above the peñol; he agreed to be baptized by the cleric Andrés de las Heras before he died.[87] The Spaniards' forces either overwhelmed the peñol or the defenders surrendered.

Compared to the battles fought during the Mixton War, the episode at Zacatlan was far more circumscribed. It involved fairly small numbers and unfolded in the short space of a month, but the confrontation reflected both the changes and continuities in the conflicts of the time. The people living at the peñol insisted on the inherent opposition between themselves and the Christians, questioning the Spaniards' Indian emissaries as to why they would make common cause with the Christians. Although they distrusted Indians who had converted, they apparently felt these new Christians still could be persuaded of the error of their ways. The influential role exercised by the women is of interest, as is the willingness of local Indians to make common cause with fugitive African and Indian slaves. The presence of the two Indian merchants (who secured the release of don Juan and his companion Pedro), together with reports of cultivated fields, suggests that the main objective of the varied individuals that established themselves at the peñol was not to pit themselves against the despised Christians but rather to recreate a semblance of normal life well away from Spanish authority and economic activity, growing their crops and participating in a traditional system of trade. The oidor's decision to eliminate the settlement, despite scant evidence that it posed a threat other than to the miners' property in slaves, reflects a new determination to tolerate no resistance to Spanish rule, particularly in the form of fortified strongholds so reminiscent of the recent war.

The Indians under Spanish Rule

For the majority of Indians in New Galicia, the hope of resuming or reconstituting an existence free of external demands, abuse, and punishment was no more likely to be fulfilled following the Mixton War and the proclamation of the New Laws than it was before. When Martínez de la Marcha visited the mines of Zacatecas and Guachinango, he reported that he heard the cases of people who were unjustly enslaved, forced into unpaid labor, or rented by their encomenderos for work in the mines—all abuses that were reported in the 1530s at the earlier mining sites and that now were banned, clearly ineffectually, by the New Laws. His colleague

Lebrón de Quiñones later alleged that de la Marcha in fact did not consider the cases of slaves at the mines and that, rather than banning personal service, in some instances he expanded these obligations, as in the town of Purificación. Diego Ramírez, who participated in the effort to settle the border dispute between the bishoprics of New Galicia and Michoacan, wrote to the king that Martínez de la Marcha did nothing to free any of the enslaved Indians but instead treated those who solicited a hearing harshly. Nor had the oidor acted to alleviate the high tributes many were forced to pay. Ramírez also accused de la Marcha of refusing to publicize the royal ordinance prohibiting the use of tamemes and of continuing to use them during his travels, in which he sometimes was carried on a litter.[88]

The account produced by the rulers of the pueblo of Xalisco makes it very clear that if authorities lacked the will or capacity to enforce the mitigating provisions of the New Laws, communities were unlikely to experience any improvement in their situation. Although the visita of the oidor Lorenzo de Tejada in the mid-1540s resulted in a reassessment and reduction of tribute payments and the elimination of most of the personal labor service and household maintenance that encomendero Cristóbal de Oñate and his mayordomo exacted, they resumed their former practices almost as soon as the inspector was gone, leaving the people of Xalisco once again defenseless against the threats and punishments of their Spanish masters.[89] The mayordomo Arteaga, whom Tejada banned from the pueblo, returned and again demanded that village women resume work in his house and that the ten or eleven "muchachos" who took care of the irrigation system also return to work. Arteaga intimidated and mistreated the men in charge into compliance, taunting them about their impotence to seek redress, and he and other Spaniards once again began commandeering food and other supplies. If anything, the demands on the pueblo may have increased as the enterprises that Oñate operated in conjunction with his encomienda grew in size and complexity. The community had to see to the care and maintenance of horses, sheep, and slaves. Contrary to Tejada's optimistic comment that working on cacao plantations required only light work from the Indians, labor on Oñate's cacao estate in Tecomatlan took a large toll, according to the rulers of Xalisco. They reported that "some died on the road; some died in the woods; some came to their homes to die. . . . Altogether 123 of our sons . . . all died."[90]

If slaves, naborías, and Indians in encomiendas experienced no relief at the hands of authorities ostensibly empowered to implement laws meant to protect them, others faced relocation far from their homes and lands. In December 1547 accountant Juan de Ojeda and other vecinos of Compostela wrote to the king that "the Indians who live in the sierras around this city are wild people who don't wish to know God Our Lord nor Your Majesty but rather understand only sacrifices and drunken revels and cruel wars among themselves." They asked that the king authorize their removal and relocation elsewhere.[91] Whether any action was taken in this case is not known, but other relocations certainly took place in the 1540s. Martínez de la Marcha reported the burning of houses in the area of Etzatlan where the viceroy "transported" Cazcanes from Tepetichan, Apozol, Juchipila, and Teul, "where it is said the past uprising had its beginning."[92] Although groups relocated in alien territory might have become targets of resentment and violence, this was not always the case. In 1557 Cazcanes from Juchipila who in 1542 were resettled in Suchipil, a barrio of Aguacatlan, testified that they were living and working the land there peacefully.[93] In addition to the relocation of former rebels, Indians from central Mexico established themselves in New Galicia, either staying on in the area following the war's conclusion or arriving some time later, encouraged by authorities who hoped to repopulate decimated areas and perhaps provide a buffer between Spanish residents and groups with whom they remained in conflict. At the end of the war, for example, the viceroy settled a number of his central Mexican allies at Mexicalcingo, near the newly relocated future capital, Guadalajara.[94]

The expansion of Spanish society and economy circumscribed the Indians' post-war world in New Galicia while at the same time many local residents were forced to adapt to new circumstances as they moved (or were moved), permanently or temporarily, to new lands or to mines and towns. By the end of the 1540s, economic progress, the establishment of new institutions of church and state, the drastic depopulation of much of the territory, and the Spaniards' growing intolerance of any form of resistance that might be an obstacle to the pursuit of their economic goals, especially the expansion of silver mining, fostered an increasingly restricted environment for all indigenous groups, whether subject to encomenderos, working in mines, or struggling to maintain refuges in the mountains. It is in this light that we should consider the decision of Cazcan veteran and survivor Tenamaztle, who as late as 1549 still was thought to be fighting in alliance with Chapuli, to turn himself over to the Franciscans.[95] He might have hoped for some sort of reconciliation. Spanish authorities, however, saw his "surrender" as an opportunity both to make an example and to rid themselves of one of the most tenacious rebels against their regime, a man who once was baptized and attempted to accommodate the aggressive newcomers to his homeland. He lived out his days in exile.[96]

Shortly before Tenamaztle departed for Spain, don Antonio de Mendoza set sail in mid-1552 from Puerto de la Navidad for Peru, where he again was to assume the high office of viceroy. Exhausted, in poor health, and disappointed that the Crown failed to appoint his son don Francisco de Mendoza to succeed him as New Spain's viceroy, Mendoza nonetheless complied with the royal directive to assume the viceregal office in Peru. He left behind a very different New Spain than he had found on his arrival a decade and a half previously. He had made himself by far the greatest power in the viceroyalty and an effective proxy for the Crown. During his term in office, which proved to be the longest served by any viceroy of New Spain, circumstances, policy, and Mendoza's own ambitions spelled the end of the aspirations and rivalries of the strong men who shaped and disturbed post-conquest Mexico—Hernando Cortés, Nuño de Guzmán, Pedro de Alvarado. Institutions such as the viceregal court, the audiencia, and the episcopal dioceses replaced individual leaders as the focal points of authority and dispensers of justice and patronage. Mendoza could count among his successes the definitive pacification of the West, followed by the opening of major silver mines. Under his rule Spanish society achieved economic progress and a new social stability.

The Indians benefited not at all; Spaniards won the West at massive cost to native society. Indigenous communities still existed, but population loss, migration, and relocation eroded their viability, and the demands of encomenderos and Spanish authorities undermined their autonomy. The influx of Spanish and indigenous settlers from central Mexico helped to spread Nahuatl as something of a lingua franca in the region, leaving an indelible mark on local cultures and probably accelerating the demise of some indigenous languages as well as, in many cases, ethnic distinctions and allegiances.

The history of the people of Xalisco exemplifies much of the experience of indigenous people in New Galicia. The pueblo fought and then apparently came to terms with Spaniards when they first arrived with

FIGURE 16. Don Antonio de Mendoza as viceroy of Peru in the early seventeenth-century chronicle of Guaman Poma de Ayala. Rolena Adorno and Ivan Boserup, *New Studies of the Autograph Manuscript of Felipe Guaman Poma de Ayala's Nueva corónica y buen gobierno* (Copenhagen. Museum Tusculanum Press, 2003).

Francisco Cortés; resisted Nuño de Guzmán and his captains at the price of violent punishment, destruction, and enslavement; attempted to comply with endless and excessive demands, exploitation, and mistreatment from Cristóbal de Oñate and his henchmen; and remained neutral during the Mixton War. The promises of relief offered by the oidor Licenciado Tejada in the mid-1540s and the New Laws came to naught in face of the brutal determination of the Spaniards to continue to exploit the pueblo's labor and resources for their own benefit. By 1545, the year of Tejada's visit and twenty years after the first appearance of the Spaniards in their midst, Xalisco's population probably had fallen by half, from somewhere around 3,000 to around 1,500. At the end of the sixteenth century, perhaps 250 people still lived there, the lonely survivors of exploitation, epidemics, and migration.[97] A small and poor settlement was all that remained of the once fiercely independent community that to Spaniards so epitomized the West that they used its name for the region and later for one of the states of modern Mexico. Xalisco's decline from flourishing autonomous pueblo to insignificant backwater indeed made it emblematic of the fate of many of New Galicia's indigenous peoples.

Reflections on a Violent History

✳

✤ THE EVENTS RECOUNTED HERE TOOK PLACE IN THE LARGER context of the establishment of Spanish dominion over extensive territories in the Americas, stretching from what now are often called the Spanish borderlands of the present-day southern United States to the far south of South America. The nature of both initial and subsequent contacts and confrontations between Europeans and indigenous Americans varied considerably, depending on the numbers of people present in a specific place and their degree and form of organization, timing, and the expectations and objectives of the groups involved. Where Europeans were few in number and Indian communities were autonomous, accustomed to defending themselves, and relatively mobile, the newcomers from across the Atlantic often found themselves at a disadvantage, as was the case in early North America, the Río de la Plata region, and much of Chile. Where indigenous societies were more settled and organized and waging war was the responsibility of specialists, Spaniards often were able to take advantage of these more structured situations by forging key alliances and targeting indigenous leadership. In Hispaniola, central Mexico, and the Andean region, Spaniards prevailed not solely by virtue of their superior technology but also because the structure of indigenous societies facilitated their intrusion and eventual usurpation of political and military power.

All situations in which Spaniards and Indians contended possessed particular characteristics that complicated or facilitated the establishment of Spanish control and the extent to which that control could be maintained without serious challenge. While the audacious capture in 1532 of the Inca emperor Atahualpa under the leadership of Francisco Pizarro is often seen as epitomizing the superiority of Spanish weaponry and organization, the determined attacks on Lima and Cuzco that followed within a few years and the survival of a remnant of the Inca state in the highlands for another four decades are noted far less frequently. Situations of confrontation and conquest nearly always reveal particular circumstances that complicate the accustomed picture of straightforward Spanish victory and establishment of dominion.

The prolonged conquest of New Galicia, which arguably extended through the upheaval of the Mixton War, entailed elements that were present in many other situations that Spaniards encountered. What made it—as every other situation of conquest—distinctive were the ways in which those elements combined. Nuño de Guzmán had little experience in campaigning prior to undertaking his campaign in western Mexico. He understood, however, that he needed a strong base from which to move forward and a great deal of indigenous support. He initiated his entrada by securing Michoacan; detaining and then executing the native ruler, the Cazonci; and recruiting and conscripting thousands of Indian "allies." During the campaign the Spaniards on foot and on horseback, together with the thousands of native warriors who accompanied them, overwhelmed the far less numerous warriors whom they confronted in the West, perhaps as much by virtue of their greater numbers as by any critical military superiority of arms or tactics.

Yet this conquest, as Guzmán and the other Spaniards called it, was not definitive. Guzmán failed to perceive that the techniques that had allowed Spaniards to prevail in other situations would not necessarily produce the same outcome in the West. The accounts of the conquest are full of references to Guzmán having seized and taken hostage or killed local native rulers, but these aggressive acts did not yield the dividends that followed the destruction of much of the Taino leadership in Hispaniola or Cortés's making Moctezoma his prisoner in Tenochtitlan. In New Galicia the native communities were far less centralized and hierarchical than those of central Mexico or even Hispaniola and often had more than one ruler. There is no indication that the capture or death of a local ruler in the West ever resulted in a community's capitulation to the invaders. Rather than acknowledging Spanish dominion, the peoples of the West—while suffering the devastating impact of the destruction of homes and fields and the death and dislocation of relatives and neighbors—more than likely understood the tenuousness of the conquest and the vulnerability of the new Spanish regime. They took advantage of whatever opportunities they could find to defy and undermine it.

This ongoing opposition and the degree to which it frustrated Spanish attempts to mobilize native labor and productivity might have been substantial enough to convince them that the undertaking did not justify the continued commitment of men and resources. Indeed, many of the conquistadors (and potential settlers) left New Galicia in the 1530s. That a Spanish society took shape at all in the early years owed a great deal to Guzmán's determination that his entrada should be a success—hence he founded towns, appointed officials, and distributed encomiendas—and to indications that the region might yield sources of precious metals.

The indigenous uprising of 1540 began with the at least temporary alliance of the ostensibly pacified Cazcanes and the independent Zacatecas and spread to other groups, offering substantial evidence that much of the indigenous population of New Galicia had not accepted Spanish rule. Far from being a spontaneous rebellion of fairly primitive peoples, as it often is portrayed, the uprising entailed long-term planning, the formation of interethnic alliances that most likely involved some delicate negotiations, and constant (and very effective) communication among various communities and groups—none of which the Spaniards recognized or understood, at least until it was too late. Having survived Guzmán's invasion, the skilled fighters of the West within just a few years grasped—and turned to their advantage—the importance of their numbers and of preventing the Spaniards from engaging in the kind of combat (on horseback, in open areas) that usually ensured them victory. Employing considerable subterfuge, the Indians of New Galicia fortified and supplied their peñoles, continuing to live in their communities and labor for the Spaniards until they were ready to take a stand and repudiate Spanish rule. They went to their strongholds and waited for the Spaniards to come to them. The Spaniards suffered one defeat after another.

Viceroy don Antonio de Mendoza in a sense was the true conqueror of New Galicia. The mostly local defenders of Guadalajara saved the town from complete destruction before Mendoza arrived from Mexico City, but that hardly was a definitive victory. Significant Spanish military progress began only with the arrival of the viceroy with his Spanish cavalry and troops and thousands of Indian allies. Mendoza's defeat of one after another of the peñoles marked the beginning of the lasting subjugation of much of New Galicia's remaining native population. The combination of casualties of war, flight of refugees into the still-independent mountainous regions to the north, epidemic disease, relocation of some groups, and arrival of others in the region finally succeeded in eliminating serious challenges to Spanish rule in the region. Guzmán might have laid the basis for Spanish dominion in New Galicia, but Mendoza ensured its survival and opened the way for much more extensive settlement and the serious pursuit of mining opportunities.

The millenarian aspects of the great uprising often have been assumed rather than examined. The anti-Christian tenor of the uprising suggests that the rebels associated the Spaniards' attempts to impose their religion with their excessive and unbearable demands for labor and tribute. Rather than seeing Christianity and its clergy as possibly mitigating the extremes of Spanish rule, many of the Indians of the West must have considered the new religion as being intrinsic to the exploitative new regime. The rebels were not indifferent to Christianity; they mocked its rituals, killed its priests, and destroyed its churches and monasteries. As seen in the last chapter, a decade after the war's conclusion some native communities still drew sharp distinctions between themselves and the Christians— both Spanish and indigenous—and continued to repudiate the church and its clergy.

The millenarian promises conveyed and spread in part by the Zacateca messengers doubtless struck a responsive chord among people who were not only skeptical of, but bitterly opposed to, Christianity. The readiness with which many Indians embraced those promises might have reflected the existence of religious cults and practices that were shared by many communities, as well as their desperation to find a way out of their miserable circumstances. In a region where ethnically diverse communities often were located fairly close to one another, people of different ethnicities sometimes lived in the same pueblos, and many groups lived in very similar fashion despite ethnic distinctions, the existence of widely shared beliefs and rites would not be surprising. Such common religious points of reference and experience, if they existed, could serve as vehicles for communication, for unifying against a common enemy, and for rallying larger numbers to a common cause. In this respect, the indigenous uprising in New Galicia might have resembled other, later, indigenous movements characterized by millenarian promises and expectations; what is notable is how early such millenarian and specifically anti-Christian sentiments emerged in western Mexico and how apparently widespread they were.[1]

In telling the story of the experiences of the native peoples of western Mexico from the time that Spaniards arrived in their lands to the end of the great uprising and its immediate denouement, I have tried to underscore the diversity of the indigenous communities and how their circumstances might have fostered varying responses to Spanish rule. The reverse was true as well, of course; Spaniards readily understood and responded to the differences between relatively large, prosperous, and organized communities like Xalisco or Tepic and the pueblos of the sierras or the valley of Banderas that would scarcely—if at all—provide labor or tribute. Thus, as they did everywhere, Spaniards focused their efforts and attention on the most substantial communities, which bore the brunt of their demands. Assigned in encomienda to the powerful Cristóbal de Oñate, Xalisco suffered disproportionately from the weight of Spanish exploitation because of its location, prosperity, and degree of organization. Nuño de Guzmán focused much of his early activity on the comparably prosperous community of Tepic and nearby pueblos, establishing his capital of Compostela in the vicinity. Within a decade or two the settlers in Compostela were complaining that hardly anyone remained of the area's once substantial population.

The Cazcan communities, some of which likewise were good-sized and prosperous, also were assigned to encomenderos and seemingly brought under Spanish control. In contrast to Tepic and Xalisco, which were south of the Río Grande and thus closer to Michoacan and Colima (both of which were firmly under Spanish rule), the Cazcan pueblos were located close to the mountainous frontier to the north that was the stronghold of the independent Zacateca Indians. The advantages of this location in retrospect are obvious. Not only were the Cazcanes in direct contact with the Zacatecas, they could reach with relative ease the mountainous zones of refuge that were all but inaccessible to Spaniards.

The conquest of New Galicia unfolded in the context of the complex politics and rivalries of early Spanish society in Mexico. Powerful figures such as Nuño de Guzmán, Hernando Cortés, Pedro de Alvarado, Francisco Vázquez de Coronado, and even the viceroy, don Antonio de Mendoza, contended for domination and opportunities for enrichment in New Galicia, the Pacific, and the region to the north. For the indigenous communities, their struggle with the newcomers was much less complex but far more desperate: they fought for survival and to maintain their independence in their own lands. The eventual outcome of that struggle ensured Spanish control of the land, even though none of the leading Spanish contenders for power remained or survived long enough to reap the benefits of the substantial silver mines that were opened beginning in the late 1540s. The real beneficiaries of the pacification of New Galicia were men like the Oñates, Zaldívars, and Ibarras, who acquired wealth and influence mainly in the West rather than in central Mexico. Their rise to power reflected New Galicia's emergence as a distinctive and quasi-independent region of New Spain, not only politically (as reflected in the establishment of the new audiencia) but socioeconomically as well.

Dramatic, irreversible changes overtook the indigenous peoples of western Mexico within twenty years of their first contacts with Spaniards. As discussed, the possibilities for Spanish activity and imposition of rule depended above all on the nature of indigenous societies and the resources found in a particular area. Although probably the majority of the Indians who lived in the West were agriculturalists, unlike the Nahua of central Mexico or the Purépecha of Michoacan, the Cazcanes, Tecuexes, Cocas, and other western groups were not organized into large political entities. Probably most groups were unaccustomed to handing over tribute to their leaders or performing collective labor on a regular basis. The basic unit of sociopolitical organization was the community, together with possibly a small number of outlying settlements. Local conflict and the proximity of the sierras with their resources of game meant that most men were skilled in the use of weapons. The natives of the West were more mobile than most of the people who lived in central Mexico, moving around a good deal in the normal course of their lives, although not necessarily over long distances. In many ways, then, the Indians of New Galicia differed considerably from the Indians of central Mexico, limiting how effectively Spaniards could impose their demands for labor and tribute.

The distinctive characteristics of the western groups determined what Spaniards could do when they tried to appropriate New Galicia for themselves. The Indians' skills in fighting, their mobility, and their frequent refusal to acquiesce to the imposition of Spanish institutions—whether the encomienda or the church—all presented considerable obstacles to the establishment of Spanish control. Spaniards, however, did not want to eliminate the Indians. They needed the native population, however intractable. As seen, at the conclusion of the Mixton War, Mendoza deliberately avoided mass enslavement of rebels in hopes that resettled populations would begin to provide labor and form the basis for a stable and productive society.[2] Problematic as relations with the local Indians were in the 1530s, given the distance from central Mexico and impossibility of supplying so poor and remote a region from there, early Spanish settlement in New Galicia could survive only by relying on the local residents, even if the Indians served them or handed over their staples of production under duress. Mining too depended on the Indians in a dual sense: for labor and for knowledge of potential mining sites. Very likely in most cases local Indians were responsible for Spanish "discoveries" of valuable ores.

The Indians of New Galicia did not disappear at the end of the Mixton War, but their numbers were greatly reduced and in many cases their communities emerged from the conflict and its aftermath barely viable. If Guzmán's conquest first brought large numbers of outsiders—both European and indigenous—into the region, it was only after the uprising and the end of the war that dislocations, relocations, and epidemic disease had the greatest demographic impact. Indians from central Mexico stayed on or arrived to settle after the war; the owners of newly opened mines brought growing numbers of African slaves into the region; and the numbers of Spanish settlers, mestizos, officials, and clergy all increased as the indigenous population plummeted. The result was the long-term transformation of the demographic and ethnic composition of the region. People still live today at the sites of the once proudly independent native communities of the West. Places such as Nochistlan, Juchipila, Tonala, Xalisco, and Etzatlan continue to exist nearly five hundred years after Europeans first saw them. The indigenous groups that once inhabited them, however, survive only in memory.

Timeline for the History
of Early New Galicia

1524 Francisco Cortés leads *entrada* (expedition) north from Colima

1525 *Visitación* (inspection) conducted of communities contacted by Cortés

1527 Nuño de Guzmán arrives in New Spain as governor of Pánuco

1528 Nuño de Guzmán is appointed president of the first audiencia of Mexico

May 1529 Audiencia authorizes Guzmán's expedition to the West

Dec. 1529 Guzmán departs Mexico City for Michoacan and the entrada to the West

Feb. 1530 Expedition departs Michoacan; Cazonci of Michoacan is executed

Mid-1530 Hernando Cortés returns to Mexico from Spain

July 1530 Guzmán writes letter to the king from Omitlan on the Pacific coast

Sept. 1530 Hurricane and flood cause huge mortality and damage at Aztatlan

Jan. 1531	Guzmán's expedition departs Chiametla for the North
Apr. 1531	Expedition reaches Culiacan
1531	San Miguel de Culicacan, Compostela, and Guadalajara are founded
1533–34	Guzmán travels from New Galicia to Pánuco and back
	Expedition of Diego de Guzmán heads north to the Yaqui River
1535–36	Guzmán authorizes and carries out slaving campaigns in New Galicia
Apr. 1535	Don Antonio de Mendoza is appointed first viceroy of New Spain
	Cortés launches third expedition to establish a colony in Baja California
Mar. 1536	Licenciado Diego Pérez de la Torre arrives in New Spain, appointed as new governor of New Galicia
Spring 1536	Cabeza de Vaca party reaches Culiacan
June 1536	Cabeza de Vaca party arrives in Compostela and is received by Guzmán
Late 1536	Guzmán travels to Mexico City to greet the viceroy
Jan. 1537	Guzmán is arrested and jailed in Mexico City
Apr. 1537	Licenciado Pérez de la Torre arrives in New Galicia to initiate residencia
Late 1538	Guzmán goes into exile in Spain
	Francisco Vázquez de Coronado arrives in New Galicia as new governor
Early 1540	Hernando Cortés returns permanently to Spain
Feb. 1540	Francisco Vázquez de Coronado departs from Compostela with expedition to the Tierra Nueva
Mid-1540	Indigenous rebellion begins in New Galicia
Dec. 1540	Pedro de Alvarado meets with Mendoza in Michoacan and agrees to become a partner in the exploration of the South Sea

Mar. 1541	Miguel de Ibarra and Franciscans go to Juchipila and try unsuccessfully to persuade the Indians to submit; Mendoza meets with local officials, Franciscans, and others to deliberate on a course of action
Apr. 1541	Cristóbal de Oñate and his forces are defeated after besieging Mixton
June 1541	Reinforcements from the South Sea fleet arrive in Guadalajara and other places; Juan de Alvarado brings Spanish and indigenous troops from Michoacan
Late June 1541	Pedro de Alvarado attacks Nochistlan and in early July dies of injuries received during the retreat
Summer 1541	Indigenous rebellion spreads
Sept. 1541	Siege of Guadalajara is broken
Oct. 1541	Mendoza arrives at Coyna leading a large Spanish and indigenous army
Dec. 1541	The *peñol* of Mixton falls
Feb./Mar. 1542	Mixton War ends
1542–43	Under the sponsorship of Viceroy Mendoza, Juan Rodríguez Cabrillo expedition reconnoiters the California coast
1544–45	Guachinango mines are discovered
Late 1546	Zacatecas mines are discovered
1547	Pedro Gómez de Maraver is appointed the first bishop of New Galicia
1548	First audiencia of New Galicia is established in the capital, Compostela
1552	Viceroy Mendoza leaves New Spain for Peru
	Tenamaztle, former lord of Nochistlan, Christian convert, and rebel leader, is sent into exile in Spain

Notes

PREFACE

1. Peter Gerhard, *The North Frontier of New Spain*, rev. ed. (Norman: University of Oklahoma Press, 1993), 39.

2. Cynthia Radding, *Wandering Peoples: Colonialism, Ethnic Spaces and Ecological Frontiers in Northwestern Mexico, 1700–1850* (Durham, NC: Duke University Press, 1997); Susan M. Deeds, *Defiance and Deference in Mexico's Colonial North: Indians under Spanish Rule in Nueva Vizcaya* (Austin: University of Texas Press, 2003).

CHAPTER I

1. "Nuño de Guzmán contra Hernán Cortés, sobre los descubrimientos y conquistas en Jalisco y Tepic, 1531," *Boletín del Archivo General de la Nación* 8 (1937), 552; hereafter referred to as *BAGN* 8. The lawsuit that includes a copy of the 1525 visitación is in the Archivo General de la Nación (hereafter AGN), ramo Hospital de Jesús, legajo 409, expediente 7. The France V. Scholes Collection of the Latin American Library of Tulane University has a photocopy of the 1525 visitación, which dates to 1531. The text of the visitación in the Hospital de Jesús records was copied from the 1525 original, which apparently has never been found. As the 1937 transcription in the *BAGN* is accurate and is generally cited by (and accessible to) scholars, all references here will be to it rather than to the documents in the Hospital de Jesús records. All translations from Spanish documents and texts in this book are my own except where noted.

2. Scholars also refer to the Aztec Empire as the Triple Alliance, a reference to the three allied provinces that dominated a large number of other provinces in central Mexico.

3. Carl O. Sauer, *Colima of New Spain in the Sixteenth Century* (Berkeley: University of California Press, 1948), 6. This move followed a period of several months during which small numbers of Spaniards entered the area.

4. For the recruitment and use of large numbers of indigenous allies and auxiliaries in some of the expeditions that followed the conquest of central Mexico, see Laura E. Matthew and Michel R. Oudjik, eds., *Indian Conquistadors: Indigenous Allies in the Conquest of Mesoamerica* (Norman: University of Oklahoma Press, 2007), especially the chapters by Laura E. Matthew, "Whose Conquest? Nahua, Zapoteca, and Mixteca Allies in the Conquest of Central America," and John F. Chuchiak IV, "Forgotten Allies: The Origins and Roles of Native Mesoamerican Auxiliaries and Indios Conquistadores in the Conquest of Yucatan, 1526–1550." Chuchiak argues that the failure of Montejo's first expedition convinced him of the necessity of using indigenous warriors and auxiliaries.

5. Sauer, *Colima*, 3–4, 9–11. Sauer bases his description of events on Cortés's fourth letter, written in October 1524. Cortés claimed to have assigned encomiendas to the 25 horsemen and 120 footmen who elected to settle in Colima. These grants were made at the end of 1523. Sauer concludes that the conquest of Colima probably was initiated by Juan Rodríguez de Villafuerte but that Gonzalo de Sandoval was responsible for its general pacification (16–17).

6. Since the time of Columbus and his mistaken assumption that his voyage across the Atlantic had taken him to Asia, the term Indians (*indios*, in Spanish) has been used to refer to all the native peoples of the Americas. These peoples, of course, did not think of themselves as belonging to a single category but rather identified with their particular group, each with its own name and traditions. In the region the Spaniards called New Galicia there were many such groups—Cazcanes, Tecuexes, Coras, Cocas, Tecuales, and Guaynamotas, to name but a few. Although the term Indian is imprecise, nonetheless it remains useful in referring to peoples who understood themselves to be separate and distinct but whom Spaniards saw as constituting a single racial and legal category.

7. See Chuchiak, "Forgotten Allies," and Matthew Restall, *Maya Conquistador* (Boston: Beacon, 1998).

8. The quest to find the legendary but elusive Amazons figured in early explorations of the interior of Colombia as well; see J. Michael Francis, *Invading Colombia: Spanish Accounts of the Gonzalo Jiménez de Quesada Expedition of Conquest* (University Park: Pennsylvania State University Press, 2007), 90–91n16. Cortés included reports of the province of Cihuatlan and an island supposed to be entirely inhabited by women off the Pacific coast in his fourth letter to the king in 1524. For a detailed discussion of the origins and influence of the Amazon legend (although with some factual errors regarding

actual events), see Irving A. Leonard, *Books of the Brave: Being an Account of Books and of Men in the Spanish Conquest and Settlement of the Sixteenth-Century New World* (Berkeley: University of California Press, 1992), chs. 4, 5.

9. The classic account of the conquest of the "near north," which included the mining region of Zacatecas, by the end of the sixteenth century is Philip Wayne Powell, *Soldiers, Indians and Silver: North America's First Frontier War* (Tempe: Center for Latin American Studies, Arizona State University, 1975).

10. Until fairly recently, archaeological work in western Mexico lagged far behind comparable work in Yucatan or central Mexico. See Phil C. Weigand and Acelia García de Weigand, *Tenamaxtli y Guaxicar: Las raíces profundas de la Rebelión de Nueva Galicia* (Zamora: El Colegio de Michoacán/Guadalajara: Secretaría de Cultural de Jalisco, 1996), 10–11. The authors offer a useful synthesis and overview of archaeological work in the region, both by themselves and others, and its implications for understanding western cultures. Another valuable discussion of research to date is Helen Perlstein Pollard's article, "Recent Research in West Mexican Archaeology," *Journal of Archaeological Research* 4 (1997): 345–82, which includes an extensive bibliography. She points out that despite increasing scholarly interest in the West over the last twenty years or so, "there remains a large backlog of data never analyzed or published" (353). Even so, she suggests that the "regional research is no longer driven primarily by the need to understand *central* Mexican prehistory, but by the challenge of understanding the dynamics of cultural change in *west* Mexico itself" (370; her emphasis). A recent article by Peter F. Jiménez Betts and J. Andrew Darling also summarizes, clarifies, and updates some of the conclusions of Weigand and others. "Archaeology of Southern Zacatecas: The Malpaso, Juchipila, and Valparaiso-Bolaños Valleys," in *Greater Mesoamerica: The Archaeology of West and Northwest Mexico*, ed. Michael S. Foster and Shirley Gorenstein (Salt Lake City: University of Utah Press, 2000).

11. Sources relating to New Galicia that were generated in later years inevitably reflected and incorporated changes that already had taken place among the native societies following the arrival of the Spaniards and thus are difficult to use for purposes of reconstructing contact-era conditions and societies. Despite the limitations even of contemporary records, Donald D. Brand, in his influential article "Ethnohistoric Synthesis of Western Mexico," states that "of the utmost importance are the evaluation and critical selection of the written sources that are available. No use is made of archaeological data" in his survey. *Archaeology of Northern Mesoamerica*, pt. 2, vol. 11, ed. Gorden F. Ekholm and Ignacio Bernal, *Handbook of Middle American Indians* (Austin: University of Texas Press, 1971), 633. There also are problems in defining the "West" as a geographic unit; Pollard comments that "in western

Mexico, where there is no evidence of linguistic, political, economic, social or ecological unity at any time in the past, boundaries are completely arbitrary" ("Recent Research," 348).

12. Francisco is variously called Hernando's cousin and nephew, and sometimes "de San Buenaventura" is added to his name. José Miguel Romero de Solís's fairly short but careful study, *El conquistador Francisco Cortés: Reivindicación de un cobarde*, points out that we have virtually no biographical data for him (Colima: Archivo Histórico del Municipio de Colima, 1994), 6. No *probanza de méritos* (deposition detailing services), will, or similar document that might provide information on his origins and background has yet come to light.

13. Cortés described this expedition in his fifth letter to the Crown. For an English translation, see Anthony Pagden, trans. and ed., *Hernán Cortés: Letters from Mexico* (New Haven: Yale University Press, 1986), 339–431.

14. Romero de Solís, *El conquistador Francisco Cortés*, 7. On the shipyards and construction of ships, and the advantages of Acapulco over Zacatula as a port, see pages 10–12. On Hernando Cortés's South Sea explorations and ambitions, see chapter 4 of the present study. On the origins of his claims to the "discovery" of the South Sea, see Sauer, *Colima*, 2–3.

15. Romero de Solís, *El conquistador Francisco Cortés*, 26. Nuño de Guzmán discussed the possibility of finding a society of Amazons as well.

16. None of the testimony relating to the Francisco Cortés expedition or to the visitación conducted afterward mentions interpreters or language problems, suggesting that communication might not have been a problem if the Spaniards relied on people from Colima. In a letter of November 1549, some leading vecinos of Compostela commented on the similarity of languages spoken in Colima and in New Galicia south of the Rio Grande: "la villa de Colima esta de la ciudad de Guadalajara veinte leguas y treynta de Compostela. Los naturales son como los desta provincia y la misma lengua con los demas que confinan hasta Guadalajara, porque esta provincia pueblos de Avalos y Colima es lengua distinta y gente apartada de la de Michoacán"; in Archivo General de Indias (hereafter AGI), Guadalajara, legajo 51.

17. Romero de Solís, *Conquistador Francisco Cortés*, 26–29.

18. The appearance of languages classified as Uto-Aztecan (Tecuexe, Coca, Totorame, Cora, Huichol, and Tecual) suggests the northern origins of the people who settled in the region; see Weigand and García de Weigand, *Tenamaxtli y Guaxicar*, 30–31. Although they point out how little is known about these languages and their relationships, they argue that Tecuexe and Coca were closely related and that the other four "clearly form a group, probably with some degree of mutual intelligibility," and that they all are different from Cazcan, which is much more closely related to the Nahuatl of central Mexico (31).

19. The Cazcanes might have emerged in the wake of the so-far unexplained collapse in the ninth or tenth century of another important economic and cultural complex, the mining tradition of Chalchihuites that began in Zacatecas, perhaps around 200 CE; see Weigand and García de Weigand, *Tenamaxtli y Guaxicar*, 86–87 and ch. 5. The decline or collapse of this complex and economy possibly set in motion the southward movement of the Cazcanes. Their expansion might have hinged on conquests realized by a relatively small contingent that moved into an area inhabited by groups with whom they shared cultural and ethnic ties and similarities, rather than a large-scale migration of a distinct people (105). The apparently close linguistic affinity between the Cazcan language and the Nahuatl widely spoken in central Mexico suggests a possible common origin for groups that perhaps diverged geographically in the thirteenth century. As either conquerors or migrants, the Cazcanes took over such important communities as Juchipila, Tlaltenango, Teocaltiche, and Nochistlan.

20. According to Pollard, metallurgy is "believed to have been brought to west Mexico after A.D. 600 from Ecuador in the form of a specific technology, a set of tool types, and a range of artifact styles. . . . A second wave of metal technologies, including alloying, is similarly documented after A.D. 1000. Once adopted by west Mexican populations, innovations extended and changed the metallurgy to a distinctively Mesoamerican craft" ("Recent Research," 349). Arguments have been made for other kinds of exchanges and influence between western Mexico and coastal Ecuador (textile technology, shaft tombs, and certain ceramic styles entering west Mexico from Ecuador, hairless west Mexican dogs depicted in Andean art as early as A.D. 750). Pollard concludes that the evidence of these Pacific coast contacts relating to metallurgy is most persuasive, but she notes "the limited research conducted along the west Mexican coast . . . and the difficulty of archaeologically monitoring long-distance exchange" (351). On the introduction of new metallurgic techniques and alloys around 1200 CE, see page 366. For more on the debate about South American influence on western Mexican textiles, which centers on the work of Patricia Anawalt, see "Ancient Cultural Contacts between Ecuador, West Mexico, and the American Southwest: Clothing Similarities," *Latin American Antiquity* 3, no. 2 (1992): 114–29; on indigenous textiles and clothing, see Rodrigo Martínez Baracs, *Convivencia y utopía: El gobierno indio y español de la "ciudad de Mechuacan" 1521–1580* (Mexico City: Instituto Nacional de Antropología e Historia / Fondo de Cultura Económica, 2005), 93–94.

21. Of the precious stones and metals most prized by Mesoamericans, only jade and turquoise were lacking in the area, and these stones moved to and through the West via trade networks that had operated for many hundreds

of years; see Weigand and García de Weigand, *Tenamaxtli y Guaxicar*, 14, 16. They suggest that these trade networks for jade and turquoise might go back to the so-called Formative period, which for Mesoamerica generally is dated to around 1500 BCE. Referring to what they call the "trans-Tarascan zone," they write that "esta zona, junto con Nayarit, produjo más metal que cualquier otra area de la Antigua Mesoamérica" (16). The products that they list as circulating in the trade networks include "cacao, plumas, sal, cobre, oro, plata, malaquita, azurita, criscacola, estaño, concha, algodón, hermatita, cinabrio, pirita, plomo, hierro especular, ópalo, cuarzo, calcedonia, pedernal, obsidiana (roja, anaranjada, negra, gris, moteada, verde, azul, leonada, amarillo), y riolita" (16).

22. Notwithstanding the cultural affinities of the West with central Mexico, monumental construction there produced a distinctive style of circular, stepped pyramids, known as the Teuchitlan tradition, in the area around the volcano of Tequila. These symmetrical and well-proportioned buildings (*guachimontones*), dating to the period 400–700 CE, could include ball courts as well as administrative complexes, workshops, elite residences, and shaft tombs. In design and execution they are unique to western Mexico. The largest of the centers exhibiting this form of construction included ceremonial precincts, ball courts, residences for elites and commoners, and obsidian workshops, as well as terraces and *chinampas*, plots of land built up along the shores of lakes. Possibly they were home to populations in the tens of thousands. Huge quarries in the area around the Volcán de Tequila produced obsidian. Although these monumental sites probably exercised some influence over a larger area, archaeologists believe that neither their political power nor the architectural style that characterized them extended very far.

23. In 1550 Fray Rodrigo de la Cruz described the evidence of terracing and irrigation works as follows: "In all the land there were many, many people, and evidence of this is in the sierras that they cultivated for bread, that in the very sterile and dry lands they built stone walls and leveled the ground in order to collect there the water [needed] to make their corn fields." See Mariano Cuevas, comp., *Documentos inéditos del siglo XVI para la historia de México* (Mexico City: Museo Nacional de Arqueología, Historia y Etnología, 1914), 156. His observation reminds us that the topography—and hence the conditions for agriculture—in the region varied considerably, especially between the temperate and sometimes dry uplands and the wetter lowlands. According to Gerhard, "by far the densest population was found in the rich alluvial coast plain where annual flooding resulted in a congested if temporary settlement pattern on mounds and terraces" (*North Frontier*, 42).

24. Phil C. Weigand emphasizes the varied environment and resource base: "The region is characterized by closely-spaced, accessible and dramatically different ecological zones. . . . The foothills, mountains, and barrancas [rocky canyons] all had their own special resource configurations and niches. . . . The range of biotic resources is impressive. . . . The packing of different niches within each major ecological zone, and the concomitant proximity of the zones per se facilitated the exploitation of a very wide range of plants, animals, and minerals." "Evidence for Complex Societies during the Western Mesoamerican Classic Period," in *The Archaeology of West and Northwest Mesoamerica*, ed. Michael S. Foster and Phil C. Weigand (Boulder: Westview, 1985), 60.

25. A study of two of the major groups of the region, based mainly on the early Spanish accounts and the codices, suggests that both peaceful and hostile interactions characterized their relations; see Carolyn Baus de Czitrom, *Tecuexes y cocas: Dos grupos de la región Jalisco en el siglo XVI*. Serie Etnohistoria, Colección Científica 112 (Mexico City: Instituto Nacional de Antropología e Historia, 1982).

26. On the origins and use of the terms Tarascan and Purépecha in the colonial period, see the discussion in Martínez Baracs, *Convivencia y utopía*, 63–84. The Spaniards used the term Tarascan very early; possibly they adopted it from Nahuatl. Purépecha seems likely to have originated as the term used for commoners in pre-Hispanic Michoacan and possibly for their language, which might have differed from that of the ruling group. It seems to have come into more general use for the people of Michoacan in the nineteenth century.

27. Sauer, *Colima*, 20. Romero de Solís points out that the founder of the town of Purificación, Juan Hernández de Híjar, later would claim to have discovered the bay (*Conquistador Francisco Cortés*, 30).

28. *BAGN* 8:567.

29. Ibid., 8:568. There is no indication in the report of what, if any, relationship existed between the two rulers. This is one of the few cases in which the number of "hombres" was not simply double the number of "casas." Use of the word *hombres* is taken to refer only to adult men, not to the population in general.

30. Spaniards used the term "principales" for men of the upper or ruling classes of Mesoamerican communities. Given the youth of the cacique, they might have been the elders of the pueblo who acted as his advisers.

31. *BAGN* 8:569.

32. Ibid., 8:557.

33. Ibid., 8:558. The Spanish used the term *cabecera* to designate a main settlement that had other settlements subject to or dependent on it, having in

mind the Castilian system of municipal government in which a main city or town often controlled smaller communities within its designated jurisdiction. In this context an *estancia* was a subordinate community.

34. Brand poses the question, "how did the insignificant village of Jalisco become converted into a presumably great lordship, and how did its name become attached to such a large area?" but offers no explanation ("Ethnohistoric Synthesis," 635). The usage emerged very early. In Guzmán's defense against Cortés's suit one of the questions put to witnesses refers to his arrival "in the province of Xalisco, and . . . its *cabecera*, which is called Tepic." Witness Juan Hernández Infante referred to "las provincias de Xalisco." See *BAGN* 8:371, 382. Very clearly Tepic and Xalisco did not belong to the same "province." Xalisco hardly was an insignificant village as Brand suggests, however; as Cristóbal de Oñate's encomienda, it played a significant role in the development of his agricultural and mining enterprises.

35. *BAGN* 8:563. Juan Bautista, who was called on to testify on Guzmán's behalf in the suit, participated in the entrada and reported that they found Xalisco at war and fought with the people there. He also testified that when Pablos de Luzón, the vecino of Colima who received Xalisco in encomienda, later returned there, he was forced to flee; "the Indians wanted to kill him and had come in war"; see *BAGN* 8:388. Alonso Díaz offered similar testimony regarding Luzón's experience. Jerónimo López implied that there were initial hostilities, testifying that "after the said skirmishes the lords of Xalisco, and those of Tepic, came in peace . . . and all gave their obedience to His Majesty, and thus they were received by the said Francisco Cortés in His Majesty's name" (*BAGN* 8:553). Although the visitors did not record any communities that were subject to Tepic, testimony of the 1530s after Guzmán's conquest suggests that it did exercise control over other settlements; see chapter 3.

36. Thomas Calvo and others, *Xalisco: La voz de un pueblo en el siglo XVI* (Mexico City: Centro de Investigaciones y Estudios Superiores en Antropología Social / Centro de Estudios Mexicanos y Centroamericanos, 1993), quote on 80, 106n15. This document, written in Nahuatl and transcribed and translated into Spanish by Calvo and his colleagues, is discussed at some length in chapter 3.

37. *BAGN* 8:378.

38. The arrival of first Pedro Almíndez Cherinos and then Guzmán is discussed in chapter 2. As suggested in note 73 of that chapter, the first party of Spaniards led by Cherinos apparently arrived in Xalisco from a different direction than was customary, which itself might have been interpreted by the people of the pueblo as indicating hostile intentions.

39. Sauer, *Colima*, 21.

40. Romero de Solís, *Conquistador Francisco Cortés*, 35.

41. See *BAGN* 8:552. Jerónimo López was a longtime vecino and *regidor* of Mexico City who over the years wrote a number of detailed reports to the king about affairs in New Spain. Perhaps because of his experience with Francisco Cortés, he took a particular interest in New Galicia, although he never lived there. It is possible that Hernando Cortés himself never saw López's report. If he had a copy, perhaps he would have used or referred to it in his suit with Guzmán over claims to New Galicia.

42. Romero de Solís estimates that it lasted five rather than nine months. The discrepancy underscores how little is known about the entrada (*Conquistador Francisco Cortés*, 36).

43. According to Sauer, no encomiendas were assigned along the coast, but the grants handed out by Francisco Cortés included the Etzatlan lake basin. The *provincia* or Pueblos de Avalos, on the western end of Lake Chapala and north of Tamazula, which Hernando Cortés held in encomienda, was not part of the territory that Cortés assigned in encomienda to vecinos of Colima but rather belonged to what Sauer terms "the remaining fringe of what was formerly Tarascan-dominated territory" (*Colima*, 26; see also 23–25). This area was first held by Alonso de Avalos (26–32). It never was considered part of New Galicia, although Alonso de Avalos apparently participated in the Francisco Cortés entrada. He married a daughter of the first treasurer of New Spain, Alonso de Estrada. Francisco Cortés testified that he granted Xalisco to Pablos de Luzon; Tepic to Marcos de Aguilar and Manrique; Tetitlan to Hernando Moreno, vecino of Colima "and they gave him slaves"; Zacualpa to Luis Sánchez; Aguacatlan to Alonso del Río and Alonso López; Etzatlan to Escarcena and Pedro de Villofrío; Tenamaztlan to Pedro Gómez and Martín Monje; the valley of Espuchimilco to Pedro de Simancas; Autlan to Mexía, Hernán Gómez, and Hernando de la Peña (*BAGN* 8:556).

44. For a brief but useful discussion of the account, see María de los Dolores Soto de Arechavaleta, "El primer censo neogallego: *Treslado de una vesitación . . . de 1525*," in *Contribuciones a la arqueología y etnohistoria del Occidente de México,* ed. Eduardo Williams, 341–53 (Zamora: El Colegio de Michoacán, 1994).

45. Calpixque in Nahuatl means "one who keeps or guards the house" and often is translated as tribute or tax collector or receptor.

46. Soto de Arechavaleta writes that there were joint rulers in seven, or 8.83 percent, of the pueblos surveyed ("Primer censo neogallego," 346).

47. The quotation regarding Ixtlan is from *BAGN* 8, 562. For Aguacatlan and Xalpa, see 560 and 561, respectively.

48. Lockhart's explanation (pers. comm.).

49. Many of the place names the inspectors recorded appear to be closely related to Nahuatl. This could have been the result of the Spaniards' reliance on their interpreters, who, as James Lockhart suggests, might have translated

place names into Nahuatl equivalents (pers. comm.). As a result, as with many other questions relating to this region before Spanish contact, there is no way to know whether the place names are original or date to the period of Spanish contact and beyond. Brand, for example, criticizes the "assumption that the numerous and widespread Nahuatlan place names are native, and that most of the Indians of western Mexico (with the exception of the Tarascans and a few Otomi and Chichimec) spoke either Mexicano (Nahuatl) or a related language that was scarcely more than a regional dialect" ("Ethnohistoric Synthesis," 634).

50. *BAGN* 8, 572.

51. Juan de Sámano, in Joaquín García Icazbalceta, *Colección de documentos para la historia de Mexico.* 1858–66 (Mexico City: Porrúa, 1971), 2:269.

52. Gerhard, *North Frontier*, 138. He writes of the three native states that existed in that area at contact that "in all of them the people were divided into two groups described in the 1525 visita as Naguatatos and Otomies. It seems that the first was the ruling class while the Otomies were commoners, and implication is that one group had conquered the other and that they spoke different languages" (60). As suggested, however, the presence of corulers could imply a more complex relationship than that of ruling and commoner groups, in some cases at least.

53. Soto de Arechavaleta, "Primer censo neogallego," 346–49.

54. "Son otomíes y aun dicen que son teules chichimecas, que son como bestias. . . . Es gente muy pobre" (*BAGN* 8:561). The world *teul* (in Nahuatl *teotl*) usually is translated as "god" but more broadly could imply a powerful or strong person. The Chichimecs were known for their prowess as warriors.

55. Certainly there is evidence of complex indigenous households in central Mexico. See Susan Kellogg's discussion of household structure and size in "Households in Late Prehispanic and Early Colonial Mexico City: Their Structure and Its Implications for the Study of Historical Demography," based on data from eighty-eight households, in which two-thirds were consanguineal or complex. *The Americas* 44, no. 4 (1988): 483–94, 489, table 1. See also Sarah Cline's "The Spiritual Conquest Reexamined: Baptism and Christian Marriage in Early Sixteenth Century Mexico" for additional evidence of complex households in central Mexico in the 1530s. *Hispanic American Historical Review* 73, no. 3 (1993): 453–80, 467, esp. table 7. Although we cannot assume that the same held true for western societies, they could well have shared a broad Mesoamerican pattern of complex, consanguineal, and multigenerational households. The inspectors of 1525 might have assumed that they did.

56. Soto de Arechavaleta comments that these numbers at the least provide us with "a minimal calculation, that is, very conservative, of population

density." She refers to the work of archaeologist Isabel Kelly, who, according to Soto de Arechavaleta, concludes that "the total population could not have been less than three times the total number of men" ("Primer censo neogallego," 345). The work in question is Isabel Kelly, *The Archaeology of the Autlán-Tuxcacueso Area of Jalisco*, part 1: *The Autlán Zone*, Iberoamericana 26 (Berkeley: University of California Press, 1945). Gerhard writes of Tetitlan (near Aguacatlan) that "the head count of Tetitlan (304 family heads) made in 1525 can hardly be trusted. The population of that community was said to have declined by more than half between 1534 and 1550, and the *Suma de Visitas* (ca. 1548) shows 636 families there. The total for the area in the *Suma* was 1,216 tributaries, say 4,000 people. Thus there would have been at least 8,000 Indians here in 1534, and 12,000 is perhaps too conservative an estimate for 1524" (*North Frontier*, 145).

57. See chapter 7 for cases of ostensible cannibalism. Allegations of cannibalism generally were lodged not against the main indigenous groups that the Spaniards dealt with in New Galicia but rather those that were more peripheral and independent and resisted evangelization.

58. On the Pueblos de Avalos, see Sauer, *Colima*, 26–32.

59. See Weigand and García de Weigand, *Tenamaxtli y Guaxicar*, 16–18.

CHAPTER 2

1. In José Luis Razo Zaragoza, *Crónicas de la conquista del reino de Nueva Galicia* (Guadalajara: Instituto Jalisciense de Antropología e Historia, 1963), 25.

2. In the "Memoria" of his services (probably executed in 1539) Guzmán himself said that he arrived in Pánuco in 1526, but Chipman argues it was 1527; see Donald E. Chipman, *Nuño de Guzmán and the Province of Pánuco in New Spain, 1518–1533* (Glendale, CA: Clark, 1967), 143. By the standards of many prominent figures of the early period of Spanish American history, Guzmán was something of a late bloomer, as he probably was close to forty when he arrived in the Indies. For Guzmán's "Memoria," see *Cuatro crónicas de la conquista del reino de Nueva Galicia* (Guadalajara: Instituto Jalisciense de Antropología e Historia, 1960).

3. The most thorough study of Guzmán's life and his activities in Pánuco is the work of Chipman, especially his book *Nuño de Guzmán*. Also important are his articles on Guzmán, including "The Traffic in Indian Slaves in the Province of Pánuco, New Spain, 1523–1533," *The Americas* 23 (1966): 142–55, and "The Will of Nuño de Guzmán: President, Governor and Captain General of New Spain and the Province of Pánuco, 1558," *The Americas* 35 (1978): 238–48. Another useful source for Guzmán, which includes an excellent biography and a series of important documents that shed light

on Guzmán's career is Adrián Blázquez and Thomas Calvo, *Guadalajara y el nuevo mundo: Nuño Beltrán de Guzmán; Semblanza de un conquistador* (Guadalajara: Institución Provincial de Cultura, 1992).

4. J. H. Parry, *The Audiencia of New Galicia in the Sixteenth Century* (Cambridge: Cambridge University Press, 1948). Chipman notes that Guzmán "is almost universally regarded as the personification of the Black Legend"—a statement probably as true today as it was more than forty years ago when Chipman published his study (*Nuño de Guzmán*, 141). Inga Clendinnen makes a passing reference to "the gangster regime of Nuño de Guzmán" in "Disciplining the Indians: Franciscan Ideology and Missionary Violence in Sixteenth-Century Yucatán," *Past and Present* 94 (February 1982): 42.

5. Conducting an inquiry or investigation into the term of office of an official was normal procedure, although usually the residencia was conducted by an official's successor in office.

6. Chipman, *Nuño de Guzmán*, 231–33.

7. On this point, see Blázquez and Calvo, *Guadalajara*, 26–27. For a recent brief discussion of the Franciscans in early Mexico, see Francisco Morales, OFM, "The Native Encounter with Christianity: Franciscans and Nahuas in Sixteenth-Century Mexico," *The Americas* 65, no. 2 (October 2008): 137–59.

8. The accounts referenced here have been published in two edited volumes: García Icazbalceta, *Colección de documentos*, vol. 2, and Razo Zaragoza, *Crónicas de la conquista*. There is some redundancy in the two collections, and all the accounts in the second have been published elsewhere as well. García Icazbalceta's collection includes accounts by García del Pilar ("Relación de la entrada de Nuño de Guzmán"), Juan de Sámano ("Relación de la conquista de los teules chichimecas"), the "Primera relación anónima de la jornada que hizo Nuño de Guzmán," "Segunda relación anónima," "Tercera relación anónima," and "Cuarta relación anónima." In *Crónicas de la conquista*, Razo Zaragoza includes the letter that Nuño de Guzmán sent to the Crown in July 1530; the "Relación escrita por Gonzalo López"; the account of Pedro de Carranza; the account of Cristóbal Flores (which appears as the "Cuarta relación" in García Icazbalceta); the account of Francisco de Arceo (from Oviedo); the "Relación . . . escrita por Pedro de Guzmán" (which is the same as García Icazbalceta's second anonymous account); and the two other anonymous accounts that appear in García Icazbalceta. Rolena Adorno and Patrick Charles Pautz argue that Jorge Robledo, not Pedro de Guzmán, was author of the second anonymous account, which describes an expedition that Guzmán commissioned to reconnoiter Sinaloa up to the Yaqui River in 1533. *Álvar Núñez Cabeza de Vaca: His Account, His Life, and the Expedition of Pánfilo de Narváez*, 3 vols. (Lincoln: University of Nebraska Press, 1999), 3:330–31.

9. García Icazbalceta thought that Flores probably was the author of what appears in his collection as the fourth anonymous chronicle; the same account appears under Flores's name in Razo Zaragoza, *Crónicas de la conquista*.

10. García Icazbalceta suggests that because García del Pilar's abilities as an interpreter were not of great use to Guzmán during his entrada, he was able to distance himself from Guzmán's excesses. Like some other early interpreters in New Spain, Pilar had a shady reputation among his contemporaries (for more on interpreters, see the discussion in chapter 6). García Icazbalceta states that Pilar accompanied Cortés to Mexico (*Colección de documentos*, 2:xlii–xliv). Cortés subsequently ordered him to cease all dealings with the Indians. See also J. Benedict Warren, *The Conquest of Michoacán: The Spanish Domination of the Tarascan Kingdom in Western Mexico, 1521–1530* (Norman: University of Oklahoma Press, 1985), 143. He quotes from a letter from bishop-elect fray Juan de Zumárraga, describing Pilar in the most negative terms. Although Pilar was accused of using his position to extort bribes and gifts from the Indians whom he served as interpreter and intermediary, there can be no doubt of the close relationship that he established with the Indians, probably accounting for the sympathy for their plight expressed in his relación. Warren quotes Nuño de Guzmán on the subject of Pilar as follows: "a bad Christian, a perjurer, a man of ill-repute, drunken, slandering, living in public concubinage with an Indian woman . . . and the said Pilar used to dress like an Indian with a loincloth and blanket over his naked body and with his feathers and gold ornaments, and he performed dances with the said Cazonci and ate and drank with them and performed sacrifices so that they would give him gold" (144). According to García Icazbalceta, Pilar died soon after the end of the campaign, in January 1532, at the age of thirty-eight (*Colección de documentos*, 2:xliv). García del Pilar's account of the conquest has been translated into English and published in Patricia de Fuentes, ed. and trans., *The Conquistadors* (Norman: University of Oklahoma Press, 1993), 197–208. As far as I am aware, this is the only one of the accounts that has been published in English.

11. The "Primera relación anónima" is in García Icazbalceta, *Colección de documentos*, 2:288–95.

12. Arceo participated in the expedition as the ensign of captain Francisco Verdugo, one of Guzmán's close associates. This account appears in Razo Zaragoza, *Crónicas de la conquista*, 240–68.

13. Warren, *Conquest of Michoacán*, 149.

14. See Nuño de Guzmán, "Memoria," 180–81; I have used Warren's translation of this passage; see his *Conquest of Michoacán*, 213.

15. See testimony in AGI Justicia 116:1 (copy in box 41, Scholes Collection, Latin American Library of Tulane University). According to the case that Carranza

brought against Guzmán before the second audiencia in April 1532, Guzmán wanted him to go on the entrada but Carranza refused, as he had requested and received license to leave New Spain to travel to Castile to get his wife and children. Accompanied by two other constables, Diego Hernández de Proaño, the *alguacil mayor*, arrested Carranza and kept him in jail in the capital for some unspecified time. Then, on the evening of December 20, 1529, they carried Carranza to Guzmán's house outside the city, near Chapultepec, in shackles and on a hammock, to which all three constables also testified. When they got to Michoacan, Carranza was placed in the stocks while remaining shackled. Guzmán argued that he had treated Carranza well and given him the option of returning to Mexico City if he wished, a claim that Carranza denied. He said that Guzmán continued to threaten him, saying he would not release him unless he posted a bond of three thousand pesos as guarantee that he would remain with the expeditionary force. He further testified that Guzmán told him that if he failed to accompany the expedition from Michoacan, he would leave him behind hanging from a tree; according to Carranza, Guzmán was a man "who is used to putting his threats into action." The audiencia awarded Carranza six hundred pesos in damages. While witnesses referred to Guzmán's having confiscated horses and other items, in this lawsuit Carranza did not mention any other Spaniard who had been pressed into service as he was, although in his account of the expedition he did.

16. For testimony in Guzmán's residencia of 1529 regarding his coercive methods, see Warren, *Conquest of Michoacán*, 212, and Blázquez and Calvo, *Guadalajara*, 34–35. The records from the cabildo of July 7, 1531, include the council's wish that Guzmán be brought to Mexico City for his residencia: "quel dicho Nuño de Guzmán benga a hacer residencia personalmente porque en esta cibdad hizo muchos agravios a los bezinos dellas y les tomo los caballos y armas por fuerza y a otros llebo presos en amacas por fuerza"; see *Actas de cabildo de la ciudad de Mexico*, vol. 2, edición del Municipio Libre, 54 vols. (Mexico City: Bejarano, 1889). See also Adorno and Pautz, who write that Zumárraga declared the war unjust and "testified that he knew of no other reasons, apart from their idolatry and heathen rites, why the Indians should be subjected to war; [and] . . . if such a conquest expedition were to be carried out, it should be led by a captain with experience, not Nuño de Guzmán, who lacked it" (*Álvar Núñez*, 3:344).

17. Francisco de Arceo, in Razo Zaragoza, *Crónicas de la conquista*, 241–42. It was common, both in early entradas and politics, for leaders to fill their entourages with their friends, relatives, and people who shared a place of origin and to put such people in positions of trust and authority. José López-Portillo y Weber includes a list, compiled from various sources, of 267 participants in the conquest. The list does not include consistent information

about specific origins or how long participants had been in the Indies or New Spain. *La conquista de la Nueva Galicia* (Mexico City: Talleres Gráficos de la Nación, 1935), 120–28.

18. See *Actas de cabildo*, vol. 2, minutes of December 3, 1529.

19. See Warren, *Conquest of Michoacán*, 212, 214.

20. See Guzmán's letter, in Razo Zaragoza, *Crónicas de la conquista*, 25.

21. See *Harkness Collection in the Library of Congress: Manuscripts concerning Mexico* (Washington, DC: Library of Congress, 1974), 104, 109, 114, 117, 119. This volume includes portions of the lawsuit (transcribed and translated by J. Benedict Warren), as well as reproductions and explanations of the Codex Huejotzinco; see page 64 for painting 6, which contains the reference to the number of warriors. See also Warren, *Conquest of Michoacán*, 213–14. The discrepancies in numbers most likely reflected varying methods of counting or recording the men recruited; in accordance with normal practice of rotating duty in central Mexico, the different units or subunits of local society each would have been required to provide a certain number of men.

22. See *Harkness Collection*, 107, 109; see also page 117 for a description of how the gold and feathered banner was made.

23. Warren suggests that according to the *Relación de Michoacán*, around eight thousand men were recruited but many deserted before leaving Michoacan (*Conquest of Michoacán*, 228).

24. Ibid. It is highly unlikely that the Spaniards could have come up with the quantity of metal (and the necessary blacksmiths) to fashion the chains needed for so many people; more likely, as Flores stated, they kept the lords and nobles in chains as hostages for the rest.

25. Pedro de Carranza, in Razo Zaragoza, *Crónicas de la conquista*, 156.

26. "Cuarta relación anónima," in García Icazbalceta, *Colección de documentos*, 2:464.

27. Ibid., 2:462.

28. Francisco de Arceo, in Razo Zaragoza, *Crónicas de la conquista*, 243.

29. Pedro de Carranza, in Razo Zaragoza, *Crónicas de la conquista*, 171.

30. Ross Hassig, *Aztec Warfare: Imperial Expansion and Political Control* (Norman: University of Oklahoma Press, 1988), 63–64; Warren, *Conquest of Michoacán*, 67.

31. Francisco de Arceo, in Razo Zaragoza, *Crónicas de la conquista*, 242.

32. "Cuarta relación anónima," in García Icazbalceta, *Colección de documentos*, 2:467.

33. "Tercera relación anónima," in García Icazbalceta, *Colección de documentos*, 2:458.

34. See Guzmán's letter to the king of July 8, 1530, in Blázquez and Calvo, *Guadalajara*, 214. See also their introduction, in which they comment that,

compared to central Mexico, the societies of the West were "more egalitarian and seemed better prepared for war" (41).

35. The main exception seems to have been in Culiacan, where possibly larger coalitions of communities already existed; Spaniards reported facing twenty-five to thirty thousand warriors there. Spanish accounts noted that the lords of two of the main pueblos (Colombo and Culiacan) were brothers, which could indicate the existence of dynastic alliances based on kinship.

36. Gonzalo López, in Razo Zaragoza, *Crónicas de la conquista*, 84–85.

37. "Cuarta relación anónima," in García Icazbalceta, *Colección de documentos*, 2:467. The Tapia in question probably was don Andrés de Tapia Motelchiuhtzin, who had been interim ruler of Tenochtitlan and accompanied Guzmán. On don Andrés de Tapia Motelchiuhtzin's appearance in the Codex Telleriano, see Eloise Quiñones Keber, *Codex Telleriano-Remensis: Ritual, Divination, and History in a Pictorial Aztec Manuscript* (Austin: University of Texas Press, 1995), 233–34.

38. Pedro de Carranza, in Razo Zaragoza, *Crónicas de la conquista*, 175.

39. For example, according to Gonzalo López, after leaving Omitlan the expedition came to a pueblo where there was no maize but plenty of fish and dogs "de lo cual los amigos cargaron cuanto pudieron" (Razo Zaragoza, *Crónicas de la conquista*, 84).

40. Guzmán's letter of 1530, in Razo Zaragoza, *Crónicas de la conquista*, 27.

41. Ibid., 28–29.

42. See "Cuarta relación anónima," in García Icazbalceta, *Colección de documentos*, 2:469. The account states that after leaving Xalisco, they went to a pueblo one and a half leagues distant, where they spent a month. While they were there "vinieron los señores de Xalisco de paz y con comida, á los cuales les fué señalado que diesen cierta cantidad de tributo: muchos de nosotros creimos, no sé si es ansí, que por no lo poder cumplir se alzaron, y esto sabrá bien Rodrigo Ximon, lengua, criado de Nuño de Guzman, porque este trataba mucho con ellos y les mandaba lo que habian de hacer."

43. For a detailed examination of the conquest of Michoacan and Guzmán's dealings with the Cazonci, see Warren, *Conquest of Michoacán*.

44. Guzmán wrote that after they had eliminated the Cazonci, the people of Michoacan had begun to serve and the friars to build monasteries and convert the people, and subsequently gold and silver mines were discovered. In his "Memoria," he states that "everyone knows that I won the province of Michoacán and conveyed it to Your Majesty by virtue of the execution of the Cazonci" (*Cuatro crónicas*, 181–82).

45. Guzmán's letter of 1530, in Razo Zaragoza, *Crónicas de la conquista*, 25–26.

46. Ibid., 26.

47. The requerimiento, written in 1513 by Juan López de Palacio Rubios, explained Spain's legal and religious claims to the territories of the Indies and called on the Indians to acknowledge the authority of the church and Crown. Their failure to do so provided justification for the waging of "just war."

48. Apparently sympathizing with the plight of the Cazonci and his companions, Cristóbal Flores, always critical of Guzmán's actions, took advantage of the opportunity to send home a high-ranking Purépecha woman, a relative of the Cazonci, whom Guzmán's interpreter Juan Pascual had handed over to him to protect her and her entourage from mistreatment. See the "Cuarta relación anónima," in García Icazbalceta, *Colección de documentos*, 2:464.

49. Gonzalo López, in Razo Zaragoza, *Crónicas de la conquista*, 65.

50. Juan de Sámano, "Relación de la conquista de los teules chichimecas," in García Icazbalceta, *Colección de documentos*, 2:262.

51. Pedro de Carranza, in Razo Zaragoza, *Crónicas de la conquista*, 158–59.

52. "Cuarta relación anónima," in García Icazbalceta, *Colección de documentos*, 2:466.

53. Adorno and Pautz give the date of the Cazonci's execution as February 14, 1530 (*Álvar Núñez*, 3:341).

54. García del Pilar, in García Icazbalceta, *Colección de documentos*, 2:251. Carranza also records this episode (Razo Zaragoza, *Crónicas de la conquista*, 160), as does the fourth anonymous account, the last in words so similar to those of Pilar that he might have heard the story from him; see García Icazbalceta, *Colección de documentos*, 2:467. Gonzalo López reports the incident but says it took place in another pueblo near Lake Chapala (Razo Zaragoza, *Crónicas de la conquista*, 70).

55. Guzmán's letter from Omitlan, in Blázquez and Calvo, *Guadalajara*, 210–12; quotations are on 210 and 211, respectively. Europeans in the Americas noted the presence of transgendered people among indigenous groups. Known for their skills and powers, they often played special roles in native societies as healers, ritual leaders, or, as in this case, principal warriors.

56. Carranza, in *Crónicas de la conquista*, 159.

57. Arceo, in Razo Zaragoza, *Crónicas de la conquista*, 249.

58. Guzmán wrote that "la señora de aquella provincia, porque señor no lo ay . . . me estava esperando con buena voluntad para rresçibirme de paz y darme de lo que tuviese, aunque sus vezinos, los de la otra parte del rrio, estavan que heran tres provincias coyula, coyutla y cuynacaro heran locos y no querian paz" (letter from Omitlan, in Blázquez and Calvo, *Guadalajara*, 213).

59. García del Pilar, in García Icazbalceta, *Colección de documentos*, 2:252.

60. "Tercera relacion anónima," in García Icazbalceta, *Colección de documentos*, 2:441.

61. Guzmán's letter from Omitlan, in Blázquez and Calvo, *Guadalajara*, 214.
62. Carranza, in *Crónicas de la conquista*, 161.
63. Guzmán's letter from Omitlan, in Blázquez and Calvo, *Guadalajara*, 215.
64. Gonzalo López, in *Crônicas de la conquista*, 71.
65. García del Pilar, in García Icazbalceta, *Colección de documentos*, 2:252.
66. Guzmán's letter from Omitlan, in Blázquez and Calvo, *Guadalajara*, 216.
67. "Tercera relacion anónima," in García Icazbalceta, *Colección de documentos*, 2:442.
68. Guzmán's letter from Omitlan, in Blázquez and Calvo, *Guadalajara*, 217.
69. Ibid., 217–18.
70. Ibid., 218.
71. "Tercera relacion anónoma," in García Icazbalceta, *Colección de documentos*, 2:443.
72. Guzmán's letter from Omitlan, in Blázquez and Calvo, *Guadalajara*, 2:219.
73. Gregorio de Salamanca, who testified in the suit between Guzmán and Cortés over claims to settle New Galicia, was with Cherinos when he arrived in Xalisco and described a somewhat different scenario. He explained that because they came from a different direction than people normally arrived at Xalisco, they took them by surprise "because they were in the middle of a drunken revelry. And that they killed certain Indians who came out to make war, and the lord was in another house" (*BAGN* 8:395).
74. López, in Razo Zaragoza, *Crónicas de la conquista*, 75–77.
75. *BAGN* 8:563–64. Xalisco was described as having four hundred houses and eight hundred men, with dispersed settlement and many fruit trees and much maize. Tepic had two hundred houses and four hundred men. The people grew and traded cotton and maize and had a market, which Xalisco lacked.
76. This probably is the Ispan of the 1525 visitación and distinct from Izatlan (Etzatlan), both of which Francisco Cortés visited.
77. See the account of García del Pilar in Fuentes, *Conquistadors*, 202.
78. "Cuarta relación anónima," in García Icazbalceta, *Colección de documentos*, 2:468.
79. Carranza, in Razo Zaragoza, *Crónicas de la conquista*, 163. He noted that at Aguacatlan "they say the people greeted Francisco Cortés peacefully."
80. Guzmán's letter from Omitlan, Blázquez and Calvo, *Guadalajara*, 220.
81. Ibid.
82. "Cuarta relación anónima," in García Icazbalceta, *Colección de documentos*, 2:469. It may be that, in referring to the people of Xalisco being enslaved, Flores confused this episode with the later one in which Gonzalo López returned south and took people captive in Xalisco and other communities. Other accounts, however, do refer to this act of submission by Xalisco, which

forced them to go to Tepic to pledge obedience to the Spaniards who were ensconced there.

83. This version comes from Carranza, in Razo Zaragoza, *Crónicas de la conquista*, 164.

84. Guzmán's letter from Omitlan, in Blázquez and Calvo, *Guadalajara*; quotes appear on 222 and 221, respectively.

85. Ibid., 222. The veedor was the official responsible for collecting the *quinto*, the twenty percent tax owed to the king.

86. Ibid., 223.

87. Carranza, in Razo Zaragoza, *Crónicas de la conquista*, 165.

88. Guzmán's letter from Omitlan, in Blázquez and Calvo, *Guadalajara*, 224. The mention of gold and silver might have been a reference to a report that Cristóbal Barrios made. According to Juan de Sámano, Barrios crossed the river and clashed with some warriors who wore gold belts with mirrors and headdresses of silver (García Icazbalceta, *Colección de documentos*, 2:277).

89. Guzmán's letter from Omitlan, in Blázquez and Calvo, *Guadalajara*, 224.

90. Gonzalo López, in Razo Zaragoza, *Crónicas de la conquista*, 82, 83 (quote on 82).

91. See Gerhard, *North Frontier*, 57.

92. Blázquez and Calvo, *Guadalajara*, 225.

93. Gonzalo López, in Razo Zaragoza, *Crónicas de la conquista*, 87.

94. García del Pilar states that they reached Aztatlan in July and had been there approximately two months before the river flooded (García Icazbalceta, *Colección de documentos*, 2:254).

95. López, in Razo Zaragoza, *Crónicas de la conquista*, 88. It probably was a hurricane, although the accounts describe the initial event as a windstorm with very little rain. Sherry Johnson, who has done extensive research on weather patterns in the region, points out that beginning in 1530 and lasting until 1580, there were a number of severe storms and other weather events related to el Niño patterns (pers. comm.).

96. García del Pilar, in García Icazbalceta, *Colección de documentos*, 2:254, 255. He is the only one who suggested that a number of Indians already were ill before the flood.

97. López, in Razo Zaragoza, *Crónicas de la conquista*, 89; "Cuarta relación anónima," in García Icazbalceta, *Colección de documentos*, 2:471. Arceo thought that two-thirds of the twenty thousand indios amigos had died and noted that all the cattle and pigs died (Razo Zaragoza, *Crónicas de la conquista*, 261–62).

98. "Cuarta relación anónima," in García Icazbalceta, *Colección de documentos*, 2:471; García del Pilar, in García Icazbalceta, *Colección de documentos*, 2:255.

99. "Cuarta relación anónima," in García Icazbalceta, *Colección de documentos*, 2:471. Pedro de Carranza said the lords asked to be allowed to go to Tepic

with a guard of Spaniards who could ensure that they would not leave, pledging that when they were well they would return, but Guzmán refused to give them permission (Razo Zaragoza, *Crónicas de la conquista*, 167). The author of the "Tercera relación anónima" stated that "in the pueblo of Aztatlan, Tapiezuela and other principales, lords of Mexico and Tlatelolco, died" (García Icazbalceta, *Colección de documentos*, 2:447).

100. Carranza, in Razo Zaragoza, *Crónicas de la conquista*, 169.

101. Gonzalo López, in Razo Zaragoza, *Crónicas de la conquista*, 89–90.

102. Carranza, in Razo Zaragoza, *Crónicas de la conquista*, 169.

103. "Cuarta relación anónima," in García Icazbalceta, *Colección de documentos*, 2:472.

104. Carranza, in Razo Zaragoza, *Crónicas de la conquista*, 173. Interestingly, this is one of the very few episodes from the conquest that received mention in the residencia of Guzmán's governorship of New Galicia in 1537, probably because it caused so much dissent.

105. Gonzalo López, in Razo Zaragoza, *Crónicas de la conquista*, 101.

106. Both quotes in this paragraph appear in "Cuarta relación anónima," in García Icazbalceta, *Colección de documentos*, 2:472. According to García del Pilar, he and Samaniego asked Guzmán to be allowed to go to Chiametla (García Icazbalceta, *Colección de documentos*, 2:255). The third account suggests that being forced to carry the equipment caused the people of Chiametla to rebel but mentioned also that they fled to avoid having to continue to provision the newcomers ("Tercera relación anónima," in García Icazbalceta, *Colección de documentos*, 2:448).

107. Pilar, in García Icazbalceta, *Colección de documentos*, 2:256–57. Both quotes appear on 256.

108. The three pueblos mentioned—Aguacatlan, Zacualpa, and Xalisco—all lie between the Rio Grande and Ameca rivers. Zacualpa was closest to the Pacific coast.

109. Carranza, in Razo Zaragoza, *Crónicas de la conquista*, 168. Carranza appears to have gotten his information from Pilar but actually provides a fuller report of the episode than does Pilar, so he might have talked to others who were there as well.

110. Cuarta relación, in García Icazbalceta, *Colección de documentos*, 2:473–74.

111. See discussion in chapter 4. Although testimony about this episode varied, in February 1532 Gonzalo López himself testified that he took about one thousand slaves, including men, women, and children in Aguacatlan, Xalisco, and Zacualpa in late 1530 and that they had been sold for five pesos each, with one peso going toward the payment of the royal quinto (López, in Razo Zaragoza, *Crónicas de la conquista*, 111–12).

112. Although obviously Guzmán exploited the pueblos for labor and resources as he did Michoacan, he did not try to annex them to New Galicia.

113. Both quotes in this paragraph are from "Cuarta relación anónima," in García Icazbalceta, *Colección de documentos*, 2:474.

114. The "Tercera relación anónima" gives this date. He also stated that three horsemen and one of Proaño's foot soldiers died there from illness, not just two men (García Icazbalceta, *Colección de documentos*, 2:449).

115. Gonzalo López stated that Guzmán had been informed that many of the indios amigos had made an agreement to mutiny (Razo Zaragoza, *Crónicas de la conquista*, 92). Flores said that of those who left, "the enemies" killed all but one who escaped ("Cuarta relación anónima," in García Icazbalceta, *Colección de documentos*, 2:475).

116. "Primera relación anónima," in García Icazbalceta, *Colección de documentos*, 2:290.

117. "Tercera relación anónima," in García Icazbalceta, *Colección de documentos*, 2:450–51.

118. López, in Razo Zaragoza, *Crónicas de la conquista*, 93. The evidence that the burning of pueblos took place mainly at the initiative of the indios amigos is strong, although clearly, despite Guzmán's apparent disapproval of the practice, some of his captains readily adopted this tactic. According to Hassig, the successful defeat of a rival city often meant burning the main temple but not necessarily the town itself. He writes, however, that "the city might be burned if it did not surrender once its main temple had been fired" (*Aztec Warfare*, 105). It is not difficult to imagine that the Indian allies from central Mexico might have viewed the people of the western communities either as intractable or unlikely to hand over anything of value. In any case, as Hassig explains, "burning a town did not mean its complete and eternal obliteration; if a defeated town was burned, its inhabitants were expected to rebuild it" (106). Thus, most of the communities that were said to have been burned during the conquest (such as Nochistlan, Xalisco, and Teul) still existed in the 1530s and 1540s.

119. This certainly was the impression of Cristóbal Flores, who stated that if the men were absent "era porque se andaban acabdillando los varones para nos dar guerra" (Cuarta relación anónimo, in García Icazbalceta, *Colección de documentos*, 2:476)

120. "Tercera relación anónima," in García Icazbalceta, *Colección de documentos*, 2:451.

121. Pilar, in García Icazbalceta, *Colección de documentos*, 2:259; Flores said the same; see "Cuarta relación anónima," in García Icazbalceta, *Colección de documentos*, 2:476.

122. Both quotes are from "Cuarta relación anónima," in García Icazbalceta, *Colección de documentos*, 2:476.

123. Ibid., 2:477.

124. "Tercera relación anónima," in García Icazbalceta, *Colección de documentos*, 2:453. For a fairly detailed discussion of the second half of the entrada after the departure from Tepic, emphasizing the geography and ethnography of the area, see Adorno and Pautz, *Álvar Núñez*, 3:359–70.

125. Quotes are from "Primera relación anónima," in García Icazbalceta, *Colección de documentos*, 2:290 and 291, respectively.

126. "Cuarta relación anónima," in García Icazbalceta, *Colección de documentos*, 2:481.

127. "Tercera relación anónima," in García Icazbalceta, *Colección de documentos*, 2:453.

128. According to Adorno and Pautz, "Guzmán began a series of attempts to scale the mountain barrier to the east. . . . They could not go via the coast because of the dense vegetation. . . . The trek north revealed uninhabited areas and the lack of any potential passageway by which to traverse them. The explorations eastward led to some upland areas that were well populated and rich in foodstuffs, but the sierras were too rugged for the full army or even small reconnaissance parties to successfully penetrate" (*Álvar Núñez*, 3:365). For a summary of the efforts by Cristóbal de Oñate, Lope de Samaniego, Gonzalo López, and Guzmán himself to follow the rivers and penetrate the Sierra Madre Occidental, see 366–68.

129. One account actually deals with this expedition rather than the earlier one led by Guzmán: the relación de Pedro de Guzmán (see *Crónicas de la conquista*) or the "Segunda relación anónima" (García Icazbalceta, *Colección de documentos*, vol. 2), which Adorno and Pautz have concluded was written by Jorge Robledo (*Álvar Núñez*).

130. Carranza, in Razo Zaragoza, *Crónicas de la conquista*, 176.

131. "Cuarta relación anónima," in García Icazbalceta, *Colección de documentos*, 2:480–81.

132. See the articles in Matthew and Oudjik, *Indian Conquistadors*.

133. Carranza, in Razo Zaragoza, *Crónicas de la conquista*, 176.

134. Ibid., 177.

135. García del Pilar, in García Icazbalceta, *Colección de documentos*, 2:261.

136. "Cuarta relación anónima," in García Icazbalceta, *Colección de documentos*, 2:481.

137. See the letter to the Crown from the audiencia of Mexico in late April 1532 (Paso y Troncoso, *Epistolario*, 2:124). A letter from the audiencia of July 1532 in the same volume states that "a son of a nephew of Moctezoma and a son of a former governor of this city who died in the entrada of Nuño de

Guzmán are people to whom the Indians pay attention and are principales. They are very poor and offended to be such. They have been determined to go to petition Your Majesty to grant them favor." They asked that the king provide them some support "being as they are good Christians" (188). One of these men must have been the future interpreter of the audiencia, Hernando de Tapia, who accompanied the viceroy to fight in the Mixton War; see chapter 6.

138. Juan de Sámano, in García Icazbalceta, *Colección de documentos*, 2:269.

139. The "Primera relación anónima" states that after the flood "algunos de los indios que aquí quedaron vivos se fueron veinte, treinta leguas a la sierra a vivir y juntar con otros que en ella estaban." Unfortunately the statement is ambiguous; the term "indios" here might refer to amigos or to local people in the area (García Icazbalceta, *Colección de documentos*, 2:289).

140. Although most people (including some modern scholars) state that Cortés sent Castilla, the second audiencia authorized the expedition. See the letter from the audiencia to the empress of April 19, 1532, "giving notice of having sent don Luis de Castilla to settle Jalisco" (Paso y Troncoso, *Epistolario* 2:111–12). The letter clearly states that Castilla went under the orders of the audiencia on the basis of Cortés's prior claim. Given the evidence that no actual settlement had taken place and that Guzmán had the people needed to occupy the area effectively, however, the audiencia ordered Castilla to return to the capital.

141. Blázquez and Calvo write "La creación de una audiencia de Nueva Galicia en 1548 representaba algo así como una victoria casi póstuma de Nuño. . . . Alrededor de ella [la audiencia] y de Guadalajara, se constituyó una verdadera entidad regional que perdura hasta nuestros días y que, se quiera o no se quiera, deba algo a la megalomania del *'muy magnífico señor'* Don Nuño Beltrán de Guzmán" (*Guadalajara*, 32–33).

142. Three of Guzmán's brothers were members of the order of Santiago. His brother Gómez Suárez de Figueroa, who was the third oldest, had a distinguished career in the military and diplomatic service, serving as ambassador to Genoa for more than thirty years. On Guzmán's brothers, see Chipman, *Nuño de Guzmán*, 115–17.

143. See Bartolomé de Las Casas's account of Guzmán's activities in Pánuco, Michoacan, and New Galicia. *An Account, Much Abbreviated, of the Destruction of the Indies*, ed. Franklin Knight, trans. Andrew Hurley (Indianapolis: Hackett, 2003), 43–47. Although Las Casas exaggerated and conflated events, most of what he wrote is based on actual episodes. He states, for example, that Guzmán enslaved 4,500 men, women, and children, a figure very close to the numbers that appear in the residencia of 1537 (see chapter 4). Blázquez and Calvo argue that "más probablemente la Corona quiso hacer de él un chivo

expiatorio, sacrificar a Nuño sobre el altar de la alianza con la Iglesia, de la que Zumárraga y Las Casas eran los portavoces" (*Guadalajara*, 37).

144. As is true for a number of other documents, Guzmán's "Memoria" of his services has been published in several sources. For Guzmán's description of his imprisonment after he had gone to pay his respects to the viceroy, see *Cuatro crónicas*, 196–97.

CHAPTER 3

1. Calvo and others, *Xalisco*, 86.

2. See Adorno and Pautz, *Álvar Núñez*, 3:351. They suggest that complaints about the first audiencia already in 1529 had led the Crown to consider appointing a second audiencia to replace it, as well as possibly sending a viceroy to govern.

3. Guzmán was removed as president of the audiencia by a decree of April 11, 1530, and the new president took office in September of the following year; see Adorno and Pautz, *Álvar Núñez*, 3:352.

4. In March 1533 Pánuco once again came under the jurisdiction of the audiencia of New Spain; see Adorno and Pautz, *Álvar Núñez*, 3:354.

5. It was normal practice for the person appointed to succeed a high-ranking official to begin his term by conducting an investigation into his predecessor's term in office.

6. See Arthur Scott Aiton, *Antonio de Mendoza: First Viceroy of New Spain* (New York: Russell and Russell, 1927), 20, 26, 34–35.

7. On Guzmán's later years in Spain, see Chipman, "Will of Nuño de Guzmán," and Blázquez and Calvo, *Guadalajara*, intro.

8. In the early years, the terms "encomienda" and "repartimiento" were used interchangeably.

9. See Gerhard, *North Frontier*, 140. A short-lived settlement that Guzmán sent Cristóbal de Barrios to establish midway between Chiametla and San Miguel confusingly also was called Espíritu Santo.

10. Ibid., 79, 91. See also the discussion in the introduction to Blázquez and Calvo, *Guadalajara*, on the successive sites of Guadalajara. They point out that Nochistlan, although a pivotal community for the Cazcanes, was located on a dry meseta and "surrounded by hostile tribes" (33–34). In May 1533 Guzmán decided to relocate the town close to the river, in Tlacotlan, even though many vecinos preferred Tonala and some remained there; in 1535 he again insisted on the Tlacotlan site. In 1542, after the near destruction of the town during the war, it was relocated in the Atemajac Valley, close to Tonala and near the river.

11. Antonio Tello apparently copied the records of the cabildo of Guadalajara for 1532, which included assignments of *solares* (house lots) and *huertas* (orchards or gardens, usually irrigated) to vecinos and *moradores* (residents) as well as the appointment of officials. These records no longer exist. *Crónica miscelánea de la sancta provincia de Xalisco: Libro segundo*, vol. 1 (Guadalajara: Gobierno del Estado de Jalisco / Universidad de Guadalajara / Instituto Jalisciense de Antropología e Historia / Instituto Nacional de Antropología e Historia, 1968), ch. 58, pp. 225–37.

12. Tello, *Crónica miscelánea*, 1:213.

13. See the letter of July 1539 from Francisco Vázquez de Coronado to the king (AGI Guadalajara 5, ramo 1, no. 6).

14. See *BAGN* 8:371.

15. See question 91 in the interrogatorio for Guzmán's defense during his residencia (AGI Justicia 337).

16. In January 1536, when Pedraza made his deposition in Compostela, the church was nearly complete; see AGI Guadalajara 46, no. 3. Nuño de Guzmán, with his usual hubris, claimed that he actually worked with his own hands to build the church in San Miguel before leaving the new town to return south; see question 71 in his appeal against the charges in the residencia (AGI Justicia 337).

17. AGI Justicia 338.

18. AGI Justicia 337, question 95.

19. See letter of December 6, 1538, from Francisco Vázquez to the king (AGI Guadalajara 5, ramo 1, no. 5). It is transcribed with an introduction in Arthur Scott Aiton, "Coronado's First Report on the Government of New Galicia," *Hispanic American Historical Review* 19, no. 3 (1939): 306–13.

20. In his letter from Compostela of June 12, 1532, Guzmán complained of the very high prices for goods and livestock and the lack of such basic items as medicines and wine and flour for the host to celebrate mass (Blázquez and Calvo, *Guadalajara*, 245).

21. AGI Justicia 338.

22. See Guzmán's letter of June 12, 1532, to the empress, where he lists the men whom he appointed (Paso y Troncoso, *Epistolario*, 2:155, 171–72).

23. Juan de Oñate was the elder of the two brothers, born in 1501; Cristóbal de Oñate was born in 1504. On the Oñate-Zaldívar families, see Thomas Hillerkuss, "La familia Zaldívar y su red de parentesco durante los siglos XVI y XVII," *Revista del Seminario de Historia Americana* 6, no. 4 (Winter 2006): 7–38.

24. Angulo's testimony is in AGI Justicia 337.

25. All this testimony appears in the first half of Guzmán's residencia, in the charges against Guzmán (AGI Justicia 337). Diego Segler had been a

prominent participant in the entrada of conquest and the criado of Pedro Almíndez Cherinos, Guzmán's veedor. Several witnesses referred to Segler as *oficial de cordonería*, which could mean a maker of rope or lace but in this case probably the former. Segler, only twenty-six years old in 1537, died several years later in the Mixton War. His unusual name suggests a possible German or Flemish family origin.

26. See the *probanza* (deposition detailing services) presented in Zacatecas in February 1569 by Proaño's widow, Ana del Corral, on behalf of their two sons, which includes Proaño's información done in Guadalajara in 1545 (AGI Patronato 71, ramo 5). Himmerich y Valencia includes a biography of the Comendador Diego Hernández de Proaño but apparently confuses the two men (as have others); the Diego de Proaño who accompanied Guzmán and lived in San Miguel, Guadalajara, and Zacatecas never returned to live in Mexico City as Himmerich suggests; see *The Encomenderos of New Spain, 1521–1555* (Austin: University of Texas Press, 1991), 155. The testimony in Proaño's probanza makes it clear that they were two different men.

27. García Icazbalceta, *Colección de documentos*, 2:294. The second anonymous relación in the same collection provides a similar account of early events in San Miguel de Culiacan (303). According to Adorno and Pautz, the first anonymous account was not written by someone who participated in the conquest but rather arrived thereafter having been sent by Guzmán and therefore would be in a position to report on affairs in early San Miguel (*Álvar Núñez*, 3:331).

28. For specific incidents in which Caniego was involved, see Chipman, *Nuño de Guzmán*, 162.

29. Testimony of Juan Pascual, who was living in San Miguel at the time (AGI Justicia 337). In the various treasury accounts included in the residencia (see AGI Justicia 338), it was alleged that a number of vecinos of San Miguel departed without paying their debts; witnesses testified that it was impossible to detain them as they rode armed through Compostela.

30. AGI Justicia 337. At the time Melchor Díaz was alcalde mayor; Lázaro de Cebrero alcalde ordinario; and Juan de la Bastida, Francisco de Buzón, Cristóbal de Tapia, and Alvaro de Arroyo were regidores.

31. See AGI Justicia 338.

32. The 1550 visita of Licenciado Hernán Martínez de la Marcha that includes these details can be found in AGI Guadalajara 5, ramo 4, no. 10.

33. See Gerhard, *North Frontier*, 118–19, and Jesús Amaya, *Los conquistadores Fernández de Híjar y Bracamonte* (Guadalajara: Gráfica, 1952), 21. Amaya concludes that Purificación also shifted site at least once. Hernández de Híjar executed his probanza at the Guachinango mines in 1574 (39–42).

34. AGI Justicia 337.

35. See the following discussion of encomiendas and tribute.

36. All quotations appear in AGI Guadalajara 46, no. 3. On the failure of the early Franciscans in New Galicia to develop a campaign of evangelization similar to that of Pedraza in the 1530s, see José Francisco Román Gutiérrez, *Sociedad y evangelización en Nueva Galicia durante el siglo XVI* (Zapopan: El Colegio de Jalisco, Instituto Nacional de Antropología e Historia, Universidad Autónoma de Zacatecas, 1993), 151.

37. AGI Justicia 337, question 114, of Guzmán's appeal against the charges states that "viendo la pobreza de la dicha gobernacion y el poco remedio que la real audiencia daba para ello y dando los esclavos por libres, determino con el cabildo que el Licenciado Cristóbal de Pedraza, protector de la dicha gobernacion de la cual llevo poder, fuese a España a hacer relacion a su magestad de todo lo que pava [*sic* for pasaba?] y de la necesidad que todos habian padecido y padecen y para procurar su remedio. Y para su ida y para los negocios le dio mil y trescientos pesos de minas de los cuales busco prestado."

38. See the description of this survey of the coast in Hernández de Híjar's probanza, transcribed in Amaya, *Conquistadores*, 41–42.

39. Gerhard's *North Frontier* provides detailed information on the assignment and reassignment of encomiendas in New Galicia and is indispensable for the study of western and northwestern Mexico. Using the book as a reference tool at times can be frustrating—for example, he does not always reconcile different spellings of place names, making it difficult to understand whether they are distinct places or the same—and his material is stronger for the period after 1540. Nonetheless, it is unlikely that anyone will duplicate or supersede his research as a whole.

40. Sánchez's testimony is in AGI Justicia 337.

41. The testimony of Juan Sánchez, Martín de Castañeda, and Juan de Villalba appears in AGI Justicia 337. Obviously, they were testifying against Guzmán, not in his favor. Sánchez stated that he already had a wife and children in the jurisdiction, hence he should have been a good candidate for a repartimiento.

42. Chipman, *Nuño de Guzmán*, 197.

43. Testimony in AGI Justicia 337. Given the benefits that Oñate derived from his encomienda of Xalisco, which included not only tributes but labor for his gold mines and agricultural enterprises in Tecomatlan and elsewhere, it strains credulity that he would have volunteered to surrender it; see Calvo and others, *Xalisco*, intro. and ch. 2, "'Que sepan nuestro sufrimiento': Xalisco bajo el regimen de encomienda."

44. Juan de Sosa, who left New Galicia to live in Puebla by the mid-1530s, said that in the pueblo of Tepic, Guzmán every year had a field planted "from which they ate and he divided among the vecinos of the city who were in need and he also believes and knows that when the Indians were in need he

also gave to them from it because the said Nuño de Guzmán loves them very much" and that he gave them clothes and sandals and other things for that reason (AGI Justicia 338).

45. Hernández de Híjar testified in October 1537; see AGI Justicia 237.

46. See question 11 of the interrogatorio for Guzmán's defense in AGI Justicia 337.

47. See testimony in AGI Justicia 237.

48. Santiago de Aguirre was a vecino of Guadalajara. In the residencia he stated that he had lived there only, so it might be assumed that his assessment was based on his knowledge of the communities closest to Guadalajara; see AGI Justicia 237.

49. AGI Justicia 338.

50. AGI Justicia 337. Varela was a vecino of Purificación, an area with few indigenous farmers.

51. Maximiano de Angulo's testimony is in AGI Justicia 237. Witnesses said that Angulo received in encomienda the Cazcan community of Juchipila, which in the 1540s was held by Hernando Flores, so Angulo must have died or left the area following the residencia. See Gerhard, *North Frontier*, 101, and José Francisco Román Gutiérrez, "Los indígenas de Juchipila alrededor de 1540–1547," *Estudios Jaliscienses* 23 (February 1996): 21–29, neither of whom mentions Angulo. Guzmán countered Angulo's complaints about his repartimiento and other charges that he lodged by stating that he had given Angulo one of the best and most populous grants and that "they always served well until because of his mistreatment of the Indians and for having taken many Indian women and men to be sent to Mexico and other places and for selling and exchanging them for a horse and taking them away from their homes they rebelled and would no longer serve as they once had." See question 138 in Guzmán's appeal, AGI Justicia 337.

52. Gonzalo Varela's testimony is in AGI Justicia 337.

53. Calvo and others, *Xalisco*. The documents included in this collection might have been compiled at different times during the sixteenth century and are written in Nahuatl. Although they were found in poor condition, Calvo and his colleagues have transcribed the original language and translated the texts into Spanish. The introduction and notes are by Calvo, who speculates that the documents were directed to a Franciscan authority or authorities and perhaps were kept at the monastery of San Francisco in Guadalajara until the disamortization of the nineteenth century; in any case, they came to light in the public library of modern Jalisco. The people of Xalisco were Tecual speakers, so possibly a local resident who was bilingual in Tecual and Nahuatl wrote the reports, or someone attached to the monastery might have translated them into Nahuatl. The one of most relevance to

the present discussion appears in chapter 2. It describes, in both single and multiple voices—all of them of members of the pueblo's ruling group—the operation of Cristóbal de Oñate's encomienda in Xalisco and events that occurred there between 1524 and 1551 (see Calvo's comments on pages 49 and 52). References to specific events (the arrival of Francisco Cortés, then of Guzmán, then later of *visitador* Tejada in 1545) and to individual Spaniards known to have been active in the area during that period allow a fair degree of certainty regarding these dates, although the document itself does not mention any. It is more difficult to correlate particular local events with specific times, although in its present form, the report progresses chronologically; hence, for example, it probably can be assumed that events described after Tejada's visit occurred post-1545, or at least after the Mixton War. Interestingly, there is no mention of the war of the early 1540s, although the cacique don Cristóbal's testimony after the war (see discussion in chapter 5) makes it clear that he and his community were affected by the events of that time.

54. The cotton mantles probably were used to supply slaves and workers in mines and elsewhere or sold or exchanged in Mexico City.

55. Unless otherwise noted, all the testimony in this paragraph about tributes and the responses of Indians to Spanish demands and their treatment comes from the residencia proceedings in AGI Justicia 337. The pueblos named in item 10 of the charges were Tonala, Tetlan, Talpa, Ocotlan, Tlaquepaque, Tlatlan, Taxomulco, Cuiseo, Amapa, Centiquipaque (Senticpac), "y otros muchos pueblos." Guzmán also assigned himself repartimientos in Culiacan, for which his claim that he did not benefit in any way seems more plausible than in the case of the communities near Guadalajara and Compostela, given the conflict that reigned in Culiacan and Guzmán's absence from that area.

56. Vázquez's testimony is in AGI Justicia 337. According to the charges, Guzmán was the encomendero of Tlaxomulco; see also Gerhard, *North Frontier*, 151. Possibly the pueblo was assigned to Romero and a change or exchange made subsequently.

57. Oyequante and Quigua's testimony is in AGI Justicia 337. Gerhard does not list Francisco Barrón anywhere as an encomendero, and this testimony would appear to contradict the statement by don Pedro that Cuiseo belonged to Guzmán. Although the alternative spellings do not appear to have significance, it could be that the "*lugar*" (place) held by Barrón was a different, perhaps subject, community, or that Barrón—who by the time of the residencia definitely was in the anti-Guzmán party—initially shared Cuiseo with Guzmán. Gerhard uses "Cuiseo," "Cuitseo," and "Cuitzeo" interchangeably. The caciques stated that there were eighty houses in the pueblo.

58. See Guzmán's general response to the charges and questions 4, 10, 16, 17, and 29 (quotes appear on 17 and 4) in the interrogatorio in AGI Justicia 337. In question 29 he stated that Tonala and Tetlan never provided any "cloth or clothing in tribute," a statement contradicted in question 28, in which he maintained that "the cloth and maize that the pueblos of Tonala and Tetlan and others have given Nuño de Guzmán have been given as tribute to the person who conquered them . . . and because they belong to him in repartimiento and as captain."

59. See Gerhard, *North Frontier*, 140–41; Oñate had the rights to the encomienda assigned to his son Cristóbal de Oñate in 1541.

60. See Calvo and others, *Xalisco*, 12, 50.

61. See ibid., 90, for example. In discussing who delivered bolts of cloth to Arteaga the report mentions "tres que aun no son bautizados el llamado Uimac entregué una manta mía, y yo Cauan entregué una manta grande, y yo Ciuil entregué una manta grande."

62. Calvo and others, *Xalisco*, 85.

63. Ibid., 86–87.

64. Traditionally, indigenous women were responsible for weaving textiles. The lords' claim that they were forced to participate in weaving cloth likely did not mean that they personally worked producing cloth but rather that the women of their households did.

65. In the visitación of 1525, Tecomatlan was described as having 115 houses and 230 men and being a "land of much cotton and maize." See *BAGN* 8 (1937): 564.

66. Calvo and others, *Xalisco*, 91.

67. Ibid., 94–102. Around this time Spaniards introduced yet another commercial enterprise, attempting to establish cacao in the low-lying hotter country, again with the use of encomienda labor. There are no indications that Spaniards were trying to cultivate cacao in New Galicia before the Mixton War, so this development most likely belongs to the 1540s. The visita of the mid-1520s mentions that some cacao was grown in the area covered by the report but not in large amounts.

68. Ibid. They said that they bought the fish but this could mean that they obtained it through barter rather than purchase.

69. The figure in the relaciones is one thousand. The accounts in AGI Justicia 338 include an assessment for "los esclavos que el maestre de campo Gonzalo Lopez traxo a Chiametla de Aguacatlan y Jalisco y Zacualpa que fueron 532 esclavos grandes y chicos." Some of the people—according to witnesses, most certainly the children—could have died before reaching Chiametla. For Guzmán's explanation of what happened in Xalisco, see his letter of June 12, 1532, to the empress (Paso y Troncoso, *Epistolario*, 2:148, also printed in

Blázquez and Calvo, *Guadalajara*); the editors point out that Guzmán lied in this letter, alleging that when he had sent Francisco Verdugo to Mexico to recruit settlers, Verdugo left "part of his estate and slaves and naborías" behind in Tepic (243n118). According to Guzmán, in his absence people from Xalisco stole his property and "sacrificed all of his slaves and naborías and burned the houses of the natives and killed many of them" (243). Verdugo, however, did not go to Mexico City until January 1531, and López returned to Xalisco in the late fall of 1530 to punish the community. Thus, whether the attack on Verdugo's people and property occurred or not, it could not have been the cause for the punitive measures taken by Gonzalo López.

70. See Calvo and others, *Xalisco*, 16–18, for a brief summary of these events; see also Gerhard, *North Frontier*, 138–40. Calvo points out that Xalisco's vulnerability might have hinged on its geographic and ethnic isolation, as the Tecual community was located close to communities of predominantly Cora speakers.

71. According to Gerhard, Pascual himself held pueblos near Senticpac on both sides of the Río Grande de Santiago in both lowlands and mountains. At least some, probably the ones in the mountains, were Tecual communities (*North Frontier*, 125).

72. Aguayo's testimony is in AGI Justicia 337.

73. Castellón's testimony is in AGI Justicia 337.

74. Guzmán, the cacique of Tetlan, testified that Nuño de Guzmán burned the cacique of Cuiseo "because he said he was rebellious and every time the said governor Nuño de Guzmán went to Cuiseo he would hide, and because he went there once to [see] him and he did not receive him, he burned him" (see AGI Justicia 337, Guzmán's response to question 18). Pedro de Plasencia, vecino of Guadalajara, confirmed this statement.

75. Zacualpa was located west of Compostela and Chacala a little to the southwest of Zacualpa, near the Pacific coast (see Gerhard, *North Frontier*, 138–39). There was a community called Xalpa on the Juchipila River, but most likely Simón was referring to a different community with a similar name.

76. All of Simón's testimony quoted in this paragraph appears in AGI Justicia 338.

77. Melchor Díaz offered the vague statement that Barco was "a well-intentioned man of good conscience" (AGI Justicia 338).

78. In question 87 of AGI Justicia 338, Guzmán stated that "siempre estuvieron los indios de la costa levantados y que no servian sino solo la cabezeta de Zacualpa y que todo lo sujeto estaban levantados y amenazaban los indios de la cabezeta y al español que alli estaba que los habian de venir a matar porque servian a los cristianos." There also is uncertainty about Barco's status. All the witnesses referred to him as Guzmán's mayordomo, and Miguel Sánchez

stated categorically that Barco was not a *justicia* (magistrate, judicial official). Guzmán himself, however, in the questions prepared for his defense in the residencia, maintained that he "puso por justicia en los dichos pueblos de Zacualpa y Centiquipaque por tener justicia y razon y en todo para los indios de los dichos pueblos y para conservarlos de los que por alli pasaban porque eran lugares pasajeros y que no les llevasen tamemes a un Francisco del Barco por hombre de buena conciencia en todo y le dio instruccion como habia de tratar los dichos indios con mucho amor."

79. Martín Benítez's testimony is in AGI Justicia 337. He sometimes served as an interpreter.

80. In his letter to the king in December 1538, Vázquez noted that because the tribute situation had not been regularized, the normal practice was to use Indians for personal service ("hay mucha necesidad que los indios se tasen porque aunque dan poco tributo, como no estan tasados sirvense dellos en servicios personales como quieren"); see AGI Guadalajara 5, ramo 1, no. 5. He also noted that only Guzmán really received anything in tribute and even that was not much. Some years later, however, in the 1544–45 residencia that Licenciado Lorenzo de Tejada conducted of Vázquez's term in office, he also was charged with sending married men from Aguacatlan and Xala, which he held in encomienda with Alvaro de Bracamonte, to Mexico City; see George P. Hammond and Agapito Rey, eds., *Narratives of the Coronado Expedition, 1540–1542* (Glendale, CA: Clark, 1940), 374, charge 9, which went on to state that the Indians had "returned to this city of Compostela bearing burdens and some of them died on the way or in the hospital at Patzcuaro." Vázquez responded that "when he went from Compostela to Mexico he took some Indians from the said pueblos to carry his belongings. He believes that this must have happened two or three times, and that each time he took some twenty or thirty Indians, that they came with their loads to this city, and that he sent them back from here and ordered them paid for their work" (374).

81. See the testimony of Alonso Quintero and Juan Bautista, *BAGN* 8:377, 387.

82. The word *tejuelo* is often used in reference to gold and silver handed over to the Spaniards and translated as ingot, but it is not associated with a specific weight, shape, or size.

83. Juan Pascual's testimony about this episode is in AGI Justicia 337.

84. See AGI Guadalajara 5, ramo 1, no. 4, for the charges and findings; by May 1537 Guzmán was in prison in Mexico City.

85. Francisco de Godoy, who received an encomienda in Tepic, close to Senticpac, testified only that he accompanied the cacique to see Guzmán and that the quantity of gold he brought was worth no more than around fifty pesos.

86. Simón's testimony and all quotations in this paragraph are in AGI Justicia 337.

87. All quotations in this paragraph are in AGI Justicia 337. Juan Pascual confirmed Simón's version of events. Although it is not clear whether he was referring to the same episode, Martín Benítez testified that he heard Tomás Gil, who served as the *calpixque* (administrator, tribute receptor) of Senticpac, say that when Guzmán conquered it, he took some caciques prisoner and demanded that they send for gold and silver before they would be released. He also testified that Alonso Díaz, who died before 1537 but also had been calpixque in Senticpac, brought "certain naguatatos and caciques" from Senticpac to Guzmán. Benítez heard Díaz tell Guzmán that "these Indians complain that you ask for a great deal of gold and silver and they cannot provide so much." Benítez's testimony is in AGI Justicia 337.

88. Simón acted as interpreter. The letter which Licenciado Pérez de la Torre wrote to the king from Guadalajara on November 29, 1537, describing the charges he brought against Guzmán, refers to the cacique as Lucazaque but clearly pertains to the same incident, noting that when the cacique requested more gold and silver to give to Guzmán the other Indians killed him "and his women and children and all the people of his lineage"; see AGI Guadalajara 5, ramo 1, no. 4.

89. The testimony and quotations from Cristóbal de Oñate and Antonio Camacho in this paragraph are in AGI Justicia 337.

90. The quotations are from Guzmán's response to the charges in AGI Justicia 337.

91. On Cortés's presence in the area, see chapter 4.

92. The quotations are from Guzmán's response to the charges in AGI Justicia 337.

93. On the use of slaves in gold and silver mines in New Spain in the first half of the sixteenth century, especially by Cortés, see Jean-Pierre Berthe, "Aspects de l'esclavage des Indiens en Nouvelle-Espagne pendant la première moitié du XVIe siècle," *Journal de la Société des Américanistes* 54, no. 2 (1965), 189–201.

94. Alvarez's testimony is in AGI Justicia 337.

95. The quote is from his letter of March 1545, in which Tejada also stated that "I sentenced the culprits to work in leg irons for those to whom the officials auction them, besides publicly whipping them and shaving [their heads?] in their marketplaces" (AGI Mexico 68, ramo 12, no. 29). He went on to say that the fear inspired by this punishment, especially since many of the offenders were principales, quickly put an end to the practice. "I didn't impose a more rigorous punishment because it [the practice] is very common among these barbarians and also because for them it's a greater punishment to see them serve in irons than [to see them] in the gallows."

96. Both quotes are in Vázquez de Coronado's 1538 letter in AGI Guadalajara 5, ramo 1, no. 5.

97. Alonso López's testimony is in AGI Justicia 337. Martín de Mondragón testified that Alonso López, Guzmán's alcalde, had forty Indians from one of Guzmán's pueblos in the jurisdiction of Guadalajara who were not branded working in the mines and that he had seen another fifty or so naborías working for Guzmán.

98. The mines mentioned possibly were gold mines near Compostela. Gerhard mentions a site by that name that was established in the late sixteenth century but none for the early period.

99. Díaz's testimony is in AGI Justicia 337.

100. On early mining in New Spain, see Ida Altman, "Mexico City after the Conquest," *Hispanic American Historical Review* 71, no. 3 (1991): 422–23.

101. Mondragón's testimony is in AGI Justicia 337.

102. See Hammond and Rey, *Coronado Expedition*, 381–82, charge 21. Vázquez denied the charge but acknowledged that Bracamonte used his encomienda Indians in the mines, although he claimed he was unaware that they were not periodically relieved of their duties. In 1550 Bracamonte's houses at the mines of Tepeguacan were burned during a revolt or raid; see Thomas Hillerkuss, comp. *Documentalía del sur de Jalisco (siglo XVI)* (Zapopan: El Colegio de Jalisco/Mexico City: Instituto Nacional de Antropología e Historia, 1994), 150.

103. Calvo and others, *Xalisco*, 84. Part of this passage is difficult to understand. It may mean that Oñate was moving workers from Xalisco from Culicacan to Huichichila. The Spanish translation of the Nahuatl reads in part as follows: "hay mucho oro aquí en Uitzitzillan [Huichichila], que allá irán todos lo que les estoy pidiendo ochenta varones y mujeres igualmente. Y los que andan allá en Colhuacan [Culicacan] todos vendrán . . . todos andarán juntos allá y acaso yo solo los necesito, acaso no con ellos se van a enriquecer cuando aparezca mucho oro dijo el capitán luego le respondimos, dijimos, porque causa todo eso otra vez nos pides, acaso no algunos andan en Colhuacan . . . no aceptamos entregar todo otra vez."

104. In March 1545 Licenciado Tejada complained that because half the workers in the gold mines were women, "all the gangs have become brothels" (AGI Mexico 68, ramo 12, no. 29); also see Calvo and others' intro. to ch. 2 in *Xalisco*, 50.

105. Simón's testimony is in AGI Justicia 337.

106. See the testimony of Martín Mondragón in AGI Justicia 337; he stated that many people abandoned the mines because of Guzmán's prohibition.

107. These statements appear in questions 100 and 101 of his appeal in AGI Justicia 337.

108. An episode involving accusations of human sacrifice and cannibalism dating from the late 1540s is discussed in chapter 7.

109. Tello, *Crónica miscelánea*, 2:27.

110. See AGI Patronato 60, no. 3, ramo 5. Villanueva stated he had no other legitimate heirs and presumably never married a Spanish woman.

111. Richard Flint writes that Melchor Pérez, who accompanied his father Licenciado Diego Pérez de la Torre to New Galicia and later joined the expedition of Francisco Vázquez de Coronado to New Mexico, first married an Indian woman, with whom he had three daughters, and subsequently married a Spanish woman. He was a vecino of Guadalajara and Compostela in the 1540s and 1550s, later moving to Mexico City and then to Colima. *Great Cruelties Have Been Reported: The 1544 Investigation of the Coronado Expedition* (Dallas: Southern Methodist University Press, 2002), 206.

112. This quote is in Román Gutiérrez, *Sociedad y evangelización*, 39n30; the reference is to AGI Justicia 303, pieza 1, folio 366v. He refers to Alonso López as a vecino of Compostela in 1551, but it is not clear when the scene described actually took place.

113. AGI Guadalajara 46, no. 3.

114. On Pedraza, see also Román Gutiérrez, *Sociedad y evangelización*, 134–35, 145–47, and 151–52.

115. See the letter from Compostela of June 12, 1532, in which Guzmán complained about the Franciscans, saying that, because bishop Zumárraga was the ally of Cortés and opposed the conquest of New Galicia, initially the Franciscan guardian would not send any friars. When a few did arrive, he claimed that they accomplished little and made excessive demands for Indian labor and supplies (Paso y Troncoso, *Epistolario*, 2:151, 172). See also Blázquez and Calvo, *Guadalajara*, 26–27, 246. They point out that Guzmán's feelings about the Franciscans were complex. His older brother had entered the order, and Guzmán made a donation in his will to the Franciscan monastery in Guadalajara (in Castile) where he had a chapel and tomb. Probably the key to his antipathy to the order in New Spain was the Franciscans' close connection to Cortés.

116. See the información of Juan Michel in AGI Guadalajara 41, no. 2, in which Romero testified. He might have been somewhat older than sixty, as in 1547 he testified that he was fifty-five years old, a native of Lucena in Castile who had been in New Spain and New Galicia for twenty-six years; see AGI Justicia 262.

117. See the proceedings of the visita in AGI Guadalajara 5, ramo 4, no. 10. Martínez de la Marcha apparently initiated proceedings against Romero but their outcome is unknown. Román Gutiérrez points out that what seems to have been most troubling was not that Romero moved the people from

Tequila to his encomienda but that he was willing to tolerate the practice of their old customs in return for working for him.

CHAPTER 4

1. Miguel León-Portilla, *La flecha en el blanco: Francisco Tenamaztle y Bartolomé de las Casas en lucha por los derechos de los indígenas, 1541-1556* (Mexico City: Diana, 1995), 141. The quote is from León-Portilla's transcription of Tenamaztle's información in AGI Mexico 205, dated July 1555, prepared while he was in exile in Valladolid, Spain.

2. Carl Sauer notes that Guzmán did not attempt to press farther north where it was thought that Cíbola lay; "it would appear that he was not seriously looking for the Seven Cities, but that he had the intention of cutting across to the Gulf of Mexico to his domain of Pánuco." *The Road to Cíbola*, Ibero-Americana 3 (Berkeley: University of California Press, 1932), 9-10.

3. Ibid., 11-13.

4. See Guzmán, "Memoria," *Cuatro crónicas*, 196-97.

5. The great majority of migrants to New Spain and elsewhere, of course, arrived with much less grandiose expectations and objectives than men like Guzmán, Cortés, or Vázquez. On the merchants, artisans, miners, and other far more numerous if lesser-known individuals who were active in Mexico City after the conquest, see Altman, "Mexico City."

6. Although after the conquest he was in his early forties, Guzmán still might have married, given his concern for family and lineage, had not events so suddenly dashed his ambitions for lasting wealth and political power. The excellent biographical introduction to Blázquez and Calvo's *Guadalajara* includes a quote from a letter written by Bishop Zumárraga, describing how on one occasion García del Pilar helped solicit women for Guzmán and the oidores (25-26). According to Manuel Carrera Stampa, such incidents were common while Guzmán was in Mexico City and the subject of complaints by other members of the clergy as well. He suggests that it is "probable" that "Nuño left one or several illegitimate children," that he took with him a young woman or two on his campaign in New Galicia, and that he acquired other concubines during the campaign. I have found no evidence to corroborate this; given Guzmán's attitude toward Mexico's native people, however, it certainly is possible that he could have had sexual relations with women but formed no affective ties with them or any child he might have fathered. In this regard he would have differed from such other conquistadores as Hernando Cortés or Francisco Pizarro, whose indigenous mistresses are well known and who made provisions for their mixed offspring.

Nuño de Guzmán (Mexico City: Jus, 1960), 39–41, quoted in José María Muriá, dir., *Historia de Jalisco*, vol. 1, *Desde los tiempos prehistóricos hasta fines del siglo XVII* (Guadalajara: Gobierno de Jalisco, Secretaría General, Unidad Editorial, 1980), 277.

7. Quoted in Amaya, *Conquistadores*, 52.

8. Bracamonte's letter is in AGI Justicia 338.

9. On the mines in Guachinango, see AGI Guadalajara 5, ramo 4, no. 10.

10. The letter appears in AGI Guadalajara 5, ramo 1, no. 4. Viceroy Mendoza had called a halt to campaigns of enslavement in 1536.

11. Francisco Vázquez's father was corregidor of Granada in 1515–16 and was close to don Luis Hurtado de Mendoza, the count of Tendilla and marquis of Mondéjar, and the viceroy's older brother, who was captain general of Granada from 1512 to 1564; see Flint, *Great Cruelties*, 272.

12. See Flint, *Great Cruelties*, 271. Another one of Estrada's daughters married Alonso de Avalos, encomendero of the Pueblos de Avalos in Colima, and another married Pedro de Alvarado's brother Jorge de Alvarado. See Sauer, *Colima*, 28.

13. In AGI Guadalajara 5, ramo 1, no. 5.

14. For Vázquez's observations on the use of encomienda Indians for personal service and long-distance transport and of slaves working in the mines, see chapter 3. In the residencia of his term of office in 1544, he himself was charged with committing the same infractions. All quotations in this paragraph are from AGI Guadalajara 5, ramo 1, no. 5.

15. For a useful overview and summary of the changes in legislation regarding early enslavement of Indians and Guzmán's activities within that context, see Adorno and Pautz, *Álvar Núñez*, 3:334–37.

16. Adorno and Pautz write that "with respect to granting slaving licenses, Cortés and others exceeded Guzmán's activity many times over" (*Álvar Núñez*, 3:339). On Guzmán's involvement in the slave trade, see Chipman, "Traffic in Indian Slaves," and Silvio Zavala, *Los esclavos indios en Nueva España* (Mexico City: Colegio Nacional, 1967), 12, 20.

17. The edict of 1534 prohibited the export of slaves from New Spain to the islands and stipulated that women and minors could not be enslaved, although they could be put to work as naborías in private households as "free persons"; see Zavala, *Esclavos indios*, 40–41.

18. See Paso y Troncoso, *Epistolario*, 3:33; the letter was signed by "Alvaro de Bracamonte; Pedro Guzmán de Herrera; Francisco de Villegas; Luis Salido; el Licenciado Diego Nuñez; Pedro Ruiz de Haro escribano, público y del consejo."

19. See testimony of Juan Gallego (AGI Justicia 337). He also claimed it was difficult to take slaves in the valley of Banderas, as the Indians would retreat

to the sierras, from which vantage point they could retaliate against the slave hunters.

20. The letter Guzmán wrote in June 1532 from Compostela has been published in several sources; the copy included in Blázquez and Calvo, *Guadalajara*, has useful annotations. See page 243 for Guzmán's plea to be allowed to take slaves.

21. According to the statement in Guzmán's appeal, he initiated the campaigns only after receiving word of authorization from the Crown: "despues que vino la provision de su mag[estad] para poder hacer esclavos y siendo requerido por toda la gobernacion los hizo y determinando hacerse como por el proceso consta como dicho tiene, fue en persona a los valles de Banderas a los hacer y pacificar la tierra con mucha costa, y por ello dio caballos y ballestas e hilo y herraje y daba muchas raciones de carne y perdio dos caballos que estuvo pasando mucho trabajo por sierras y valles seis meses" (AGI Justicia 337).

22. Ostensibly, when the Spaniards first entered the valley of Banderas, probably at the time of the Francisco Cortés expedition, the people came out to meet them carrying banners—hence the name Banderas; see the letter of Fray Rodrigo de la Cruz of May 1550 in Cuevas, *Documentos inéditos*, 156.

23. Juan Sánchez testified in the residencia that he "saw that they made slaves of certain Indians of the province of the valley of Banderas because they had killed twelve or thirteen Spaniards" (AGI Justicia 337). The 1533 petition and información prepared by the cabildo of Compostela includes the names of some of the men who died; see AGI Guadalajara 46, no. 1.

24. The last slaves recorded in AGI Justicia 338 were taken in December 1536 and January 1537; apparently these were quite small groups. The last entry concerning slaves dates from April 1537, but it is unclear when the slaves actually were captured; it recorded "345 pesos 6 tomines de oro," representing the "quinto de ciertos esclavos en la villa de la Purificación, los cuales enviaron los tenientes de oficiales que en ella residen y no se pone específicamente en esta partida de que se hubieron por no venir clara la razon o se declaran cuando se tome la cuenta a los dichos tenientes de oficiales."

25. Barrón testified in March 1537; see AGI Justicia 337.

26. Sosa's testimony is in AGI Justicia 337.

27. The first list is in AGI Justicia 337; the second is in AGI Justicia 338.

28. In his letter to the king that included the charges against Guzmán, Pérez de la Torre gave the number of slaves that Guzmán had authorized to be taken as 4,570 (AGI Guadalajara 5, ramo 1, no. 4).

29. These slaves were taken in July 1535; see AGI Justicia 337 and 338.

30. Very early the name Jalisco came to be used to refer mainly to central New Galicia, although it could mean the West more generally. Indigenous Xalisco is discussed in chapter 3. What later became known as the Mixton War at

the time was termed the "guerra de Jalisco" or the conquest, reconquest, or pacification of Nueva Galicia. In *Álvar Núñez*, Adorno and Pautz, as do others, frequently use the name "Jalisco" without elaboration, apparently referring to central New Galicia.

31. Ironically the viceroy himself was charged with having invested in an *obraje* (textile workshop) in central Mexico, in which slaves from "Jalisco" (probably meaning New Galicia in general) were employed. See AGI Justicia 259, pieza 3, in which it is alleged that Mendoza "ha tenido y tiene compañia con un Gonzalo Gómez en el obraje de los paños que se hacen en el pueblo de Texcuco donde tiene muchos indios esclavos chichimecas de Jalisco y muchos indios naborias que trabajan en la dicha hacienda y los dichos paños se venden en esta ciudad en una tienda." Mendoza wrote to the (Franciscan?) guardian of Texcoco on January 15, 1544, that he had been informed that Gonzalo Gómez had in Texcoco "muchas indias chichimecas del pueblo de Jalisco" held against their will who are actually free. He instructed the guardian to find out which of them were married in the church and that those who were should be allowed to live with their husbands and the others could go to their own country or anywhere else as free people. He concluded by ordering the guardian to send them to him so that he could "send them to their country with others who are to be sent" (AGN Mercedes, vol. 2, exp. 613). The audiencia's declaration of war in 1541 specifically exempted women from being enslaved; see chapter 6.

32. Zaldívar was supposed to have arrived in New Galicia in 1533, but most likely he was referring to events of 1535, which is when a number of slaves were taken in those pueblos. See Zaldívar's información in AGI Patronato 60, no. 5, ramo 4 (Guadalajara, February 13, 1566). Zaldívar might have been the "Santival" mentioned in the account from Xalisco as being the younger brother of Oñate (see Calvo and others, *Xalisco*, 104–5); confusing a nephew with a younger sibling would not be difficult. Mescala was northeast of Guadalajara, but I have not been able to identify who was the encomendero in the 1530s. According to Gerhard, Bartolomé García was encomendero in 1548 (*North Frontier*, 136). The pueblos mentioned are associated with the beginning of the Mixton War.

33. AGI Justicia 337, question 119, in Guzmán's appeal.

34. AGI Justicia 337.

35. See AGI Guadalajara 46, no. 1. The alcalde at the time was Alvaro de Bracamonte; the regidores were Pedro de Guzmán, Francisco de Villegas, Luis Salido, and Lic. Diego Martínez, all of them close to Guzmán. Given Guzmán's experience of slaving in Pánuco, he certainly did not oppose the practice in principle, and indeed might have been responsible for the cabildo's compiling the testimony as justification for future campaigns.

36. Spaniards adopted the term "Chichimecas" from the Nahuas and used it in New Galicia for the more mobile and less settled groups that lived especially in the sierras. On the use of the term, see Charlotte M. Gradie, "Discovering the Chichimecas," *The Americas* 51, no. 1 (1994): 67–88. See also the discussion of the term in reference to the people of Michoacan in Martínez Baracs, *Convivencia y utopía*, 59–63. Susan Schroeder writes that in Chimalpahin's accounts the term "Chichimecatl" carries "high and positive connotations" and that "generally he uses the term when speaking of the migrant groups that founded the Chalco polities and more particularly the leaders of those groups. 'Chichimeca' thus comes to be a term of great prestige in the context of altepetl history, genealogy, and ruler's titles." *Chimalpahin and the Kingdoms of Chalco* (Tucson: University of Arizona Press, 1991), 172–73. Spaniards, however, most often used the term to refer to groups they viewed as barbarian or savage, and that usage has affected scholars to the present; for example, Peggy K. Liss discusses Viceroy Mendoza's campaign against the "warring seminomadic Chichemecas [*sic*] in northwestern Nueva Galicia in 1541–42, during the Mixtón Wars." *Mexico under Spain, 1521–1556: Society and the Origins of Nationality* (Chicago: University of Chicago Press, 1975), 58.

37. Ulloa's testimony is in AGI Guadalajara 46, no. 1.

38. AGI Justicia 337.

39. I have not been able to identify Aldeanueva. Xalacingo was in the Ameca Valley in an area largely uncontrolled by Spaniards, although it and other surrounding pueblos had been granted to Alvaro de Bracamonte in encomienda. According to Gerhard, "at mid-century the greatly depleted native communities remained largely uncontrolled, most of the survivors hiding out in mountain recesses" (*North Frontier*, 87). The testimony of Juan Navarro, Alonso de Ribera, and Pedro de Ulloa appears in the información of the cabildo in AGI Guadalajara 46, no. 1.

40. See AGI Justicia 262. He did not say when the execution had occurred.

41. Whether Spanish "goods" provided an additional incentive for attacks in these early years is debatable. In a couple of instances Indians were accused of killing pigs rather than driving them off, which would suggest they were not interested in them as food. In the incident involving Xalisco and Acuitlapilco, the items used to lure the "Chichimecs" into the Spaniards' trap were highly prized Mesoamerican goods—gold ornaments and salt—not Spanish ones.

42. Calvo and others, *Xalisco*, 81–82. Like much of this account, discussed in chapter 3, the description of this incident is confusing, all the more so because of the frequent changes of voice and because some parts of the manuscript were missing or unreadable.

43. Ibid., 51.

44. Pérez de la Torre's report and all quotations in this paragraph are in AGI Justicia 337.

45. The manner of execution might have been modeled on the methods of Castile's Santa Hermandad; my thanks to James Boyden for pointing out this parallel (pers. comm.).

46. The letter of September 14, 1544, from Lic. Lebrón de Quiñones appears in AGI Guadalajara 51. The report of the visita by the same appears in AGI Guadalajara 5, ramo 6, no. 13. The oidor stated that he began his visita in October 1551 and ended it in February 1554.

47. AGI Guadalajara, ramo 6, no. 13.

48. Ibid.

49. See the report of Lic. Lebrón de Quiñones in AGI Guadalajara 5, ramo 6, no. 13. Lebrón discussed the case in his letter to Prince Philip of September 14, 1554, written in Taximaroa, Michoacan; see Paso y Troncoso, *Epistolario*, vol. 7, doc. 406. In this letter he mentioned other acts committed by Aguayo, including "ser cruelísmo para los indios como en la visita de una estancia suya que hice me constó que los aperreaba y desnarigaba y cortaba las orejas cuando no servían a su contento" (257). He stated that the oidor Dr. Quesada was a close friend of Aguayo and had reversed his sentence. Lebrón appealed the case to the Council of the Indies. The exact outcome is not known, although clearly Aguayo did not face execution for his crimes, as he wrote a lengthy letter to the emperor on October 25, 1554, accusing Lebrón not only of misbehaving with a number of women, both Spanish and indigenous, but of having contrived to poison the recently arrived juez de residencia, Licenciado Villagar, and his wife; see document 411 in the same volume (272–73).

50. Vázquez's letter is in AGI Guadalajara 5, ramo 1, no. 6.

51. The story of Cabeza de Vaca has had enormous appeal and circulated widely. The year 2007 alone saw the publication of two new books on the subject: Andrés Reséndez, *A Land So Strange: The Epic Journey of Cabeza de Vaca; The Extraordinary Tale of a Shipwrecked Spaniard Who Walked across America in the Sixteenth Century* (New York: Basic Books, 2007), and Paul Schneider, *Brutal Journey: Cabeza de Vaca and the Epic First Crossing of North America* (New York: Owl Books, 2007). There are many editions of the account, in Spanish and in translation. A recent important scholarly publication is the three-volume study by Adorno and Pautz, *Álvar Núñez*. The first volume offers a transcription and translation of the 1542 *Relación* and a biography of Cabeza de Vaca; the second volume focuses on the history and historiography of the Pánfilo de Nárvaez expedition; and the third specifically considers Cabeza de Vaca's *Relación* and its historical context. Given the challenges of

interpretation, it is unlikely that any single scholarly work will settle all the questions that the account raises.

52. Adorno and Pautz suggest that because the major rivers of northwestern Mexico that flow into the coastal plain generally run north-south rather than east-west, "this section of the journey must be envisioned as a series of movements whose orientation was north-south in order to go west" (*Álvar Núñez*, 2:324). The route is important not just geographically but ethnographically as well, in terms of understanding the peoples that the travelers contacted as they gradually descended into Spanish-controlled territory.

53. These groups are known to archaeologists as comprising the Sonora River Culture; see Adorno and Pautz, *Álvar Núñez*, 2:330–31.

54. Ibid., 2:338. At Corazones the men received the extraordinary gift of more than six hundred deer hearts, evidence of the abundant game in the area.

55. Ibid., 2:346.

56. From the translation of the "Relación," in Adorno and Pautz, *Álvar Núñez*, 1:239.

57. Adorno and Pautz, *Álvar Núñez*, 2:349.

58. Ibid., 2:366–67.

59. From the translation of the "Relación," in Adorno and Pautz, *Álvar Núñez*, 1:255.

60. Adorno and Pautz, *Álvar Núñez*, 2:375–83. For their description, drawing on Oviedo, of how this resettlement was accomplished, see pages 378–79.

61. Oscar Hermann Khristian Spate writes that of the ships constructed under Cortés's authority in Zacatula, two burned before they could put to sea "and of the four completed in 1526 two sank and two went with Alvaro de Saavedra for the Molucas in October 1527, sailing from Zihuatanejo." *The Spanish Lake: The Pacific since Magellan*, vol. 1 (Minneapolis: University of Minnesota Press, 1979); http://epress.anu.edu.au/spanish_lake_citation.html (accessed January 24, 2010); the online version lacks page numbers.

62. Adorno and Pautz, *Álvar Núñez*, 3:305–8, 310–12.

63. Ibid., 3:313–15. See also Gerhard, *North Frontier*, 288–89, and Peter Gerhard, "A Black Conquistador in Mexico," *Hispanic American Historical Review* 58, no. 3 (1978): 457–58. The subject of this article, Juan Garrido, was closely connected with Cortés and participated in the ill-fated settlement; see Matthew Restall, "Black Conquistadors: Armed Africans in Early Spanish America," *The Americas* 57, no. 2 (2000): 171–205.

64. See David J. Weber, *The Spanish Frontier in North America* (New Haven: Yale University Press, 1992), 40–41; Adorno and Pautz, *Álvar Núñez*, 3:319–20; and their discussion that follows on "The South Sea in Relation to Mainland Goals" (320–23).

65. Carl O. Sauer, *Sixteenth-Century North America: The Land and the People as Seen by the Europeans* (Berkeley: University of California Press, 1971), 153.

66. On the criticisms of Mendoza, see Ethelia Ruiz Medrano, "Versiones sobre un fenómeno rebelde: La guerra del Mixtón en Nueva Galicia," in *Contribuciones a la arqueología y etnohistoria del Occidente de México*, ed. Eduardo Williams (Zamora: El Colegio de Michoacán, 1994), 365–67.

67. According to Parry, Licenciado Pérez de la Torre "upon his death-bed . . . appointed Cristóbal de Oñate, now a leading *encomendero* and a member of the town council of Guadalajara, to succeed him; but the viceroy . . . rescinded the appointment, and granted the office to an adherent of his own, Francisco Vázquez Coronado" (*Audiencia of New Galicia*, 27).

68. Citing Aiton in *Antonio de Mendoza*, Ruiz Medrano mentions the rebellion of Jocotlan that Pérez de la Torre suppressed, as a consequence of which he died of wounds soon after beginning his term as governor ("Versiones sobre un fenómeno," 357). According to Gerhard in *North Frontier*, there was more than one community by this name (either Jocotlan or Xocotlan) and it is not clear which one was involved.

69. Aiton writes that "the inhabitants were apprehensive that the Coronado expedition would strip the province of its defenders, but at the review of the troops, February 27, 1540, an inspection of the roster showed that only two were citizens of Mexico and two of Guadalajara. The great bulk of the force were newly arrived adventurers attracted by the fame of the entrada" (*Antonio de Mendoza*, 138n1). In contrast, Camilla Townsend writes, for example, that "the majority of the armed Spanish men living in the region [New Galicia] suddenly joined Coronado's expedition to New Mexico." Western Mexico is, of course, peripheral to her main topic. *Malintzin's Choices: An Indian Woman in the Conquest of Mexico* (Albuquerque: University of New Mexico Press, 2006), 179.

70. Some cases are ambiguous. There was, for example, a Juan Navarro who enlisted with the expedition with five horses (Hammond and Rey, *Coronado Expedition*, 91), but whether he was the same Juan Navarro who was Guzmán's criado in Compostela is not certain. Francisco Cornejo, who was a conqueror of New Galicia, claimed to have participated in the expedition to the Tierra Nueva; see Francisco A. de Icaza, *Conquistadores y pobladores de Nueva España: Diccionario autobiográfico sacado de los textos originales*, 2 vols. (Madrid: Adelantado de Segovia, 1923), 2:287–88. In the 1540s he also claimed, however, to have participated in the "última pacificación de la Nueva Galicia"; see Icaza, *Conquistadores y pobladores*, 1:244. Román Gutiérrez writes that "Ruy Gonzalez fue conquistador de Nueva España y Michoacán, luego en la campaña de Nueva Galicia, acompañó a Vázquez de Coronado en la expedición a Cibola, aunque debió regresar mucho tiempo

antes que Francisco Vázquez de Coronado, puesto que acompañó a Mendoza en la pacifiación del Mizton. Recibió escudo de armas por sus servicios y encomiendas bien retribuidas; fue alcalde y regidor de la ciudad de México a partir de 1538" (*Sociedad y evangelización*, 177–78). He might have returned to Mexico City soon after the conquest of New Galicia and never actually was a vecino there.

71. Flint, whose scholarly work on the expedition's participants has helped to clarify the question of their numbers, himself seems to exaggerate them, writing in *Great Cruelties*, that the "departure of the expedition in 1540 . . . had temporarily but dangerously reduced the population of Nueva Galicia, a fact not lost on the native peoples of that ten-year-old province. Within ten months a widespread uprising against Spanish presence and domination in Nueva Galicia was under way. . . . The launching of the expedition to Tierra Nueva, thus, opened the door to a nearly successful challenge to Spanish rule in the whole of the viceroyalty of Nueva España" (536). He also states that "although it has been written that there was no overlap in personnel between the Guzmán entrada and the expedition to Tierra Nueva, in fact, at least a dozen individuals participated in both. More significant still, five of the captains of the expedition to Tierra Nueva had been with Guzmán (Melchior Díaz, Diego de Alcaraz, Juan de Zaldívar, Pedro de Tovar, and Diego López) and the original maestre de campo of the expedition, Lope de Samaniego (appointed directly by the viceroy) had served as a captain under Guzmán" (518). Juan de Zaldívar, the nephew of Juan and Cristóbal de Oñate, in fact did not arrive in New Galicia until after the conquest and was not one of Guzmán's captains.

72. Hammond and Rey, *Coronado Expedition*, 116. Francisco Rojo Loro, a native of Sicily and resident of Compostela, however, apparently enlisted with three horses; see page 100.

73. See Flint's *Great Cruelties*: "Of the thousand-plus Nahuatl-, Tarascan-, and Caxcan-speaking Indians who participated in the expedition to Tierra Nueva, an unknown number remained behind in the Greater Southwest. . . . For instance, during the first few days of the expedition's return trek people from Cibola followed along behind salvaging discarded equipment and welcoming Nahuas and other Indian allies who decided to stay behind. In the Cibola/Zuni area forty years later, the expedition led by Antonio de Espejo found 'Mexican Indians,' and also a number from Guadalajara" (533). He also points out that the Indian allies included "Tecuexes from Zapotlan and the Guadalajara area" (556) and that many of the residents of San Miguel in 1540 were Indians from central Mexico who had been left there when Guzmán's main force turned south and that they too participated in the expedition to New Mexico (569).

74. For a relatively brief summation of events, see Weber, *Spanish Frontier*, 14–17 and 46–49, and Sauer, *Sixteenth-Century North America*, 130–51. For much greater detail, consult the work of Richard Flint and Shirley Cushing Flint. Herbert E. Bolton offers an older, romantic interpretation that downplays Spanish violence and destructiveness; see *Coronado on the Turquoise Trail: Knight of Pueblos and Plains* (Albuquerque: University of New Mexico Press, 1949).

75. Sauer, *Sixteenth-Century North America*, 127.

76. Weber, *Spanish Frontier*, 46.

77. Flint, *Great Cruelties*, 513.

78. Ibid., 550; Sauer, *Sixteenth-Century North America*, 130–34, 138–39.

79. Flint, *Great Cruelties*, 8, 546, 166, 520. The quote from Troyano's testimony is on page 166.

80. Ibid., 8.

81. See Gallego's testimony in AGI Justicia 262. It would appear that he had returned to Purificación before the end of the Mixton War, so he may have gone back to New Galicia in advance of Vázquez de Coronado. He testified that the Indians of one of his pueblos, El Gamochal, had saved some of his estate and cattle and that the Indians of the encomienda belonging to Hernando de Acevedo, another vecino of Purificación and encomendero of Zapotlan, also had warned them and because of that "salvo la persona y parte de su hacienda" (he saved himself and some of his property). This certainly implies that he was in New Galicia at some point during the war.

82. Hillerkuss suggests that Juan de Zaldívar returned for the pacification of Mixton in 1541 and indeed had participated in the defense of Guadalajara in September 1541, but I have not seen any evidence of his presence at those events ("Familia Zaldívar," 25).

83. See Flint, *Great Cruelties*, 251. On the trip to Quivira, see Sauer, *Sixteenth-Century North America*, 146–48. For the información de servicios that Zaldívar executed in Guadalajara in February 1566, see AGI Patronato 60, no. 5, ramo 4. Juan and his younger brother Vicente de Zaldívar were prominent figures in Guadalajara and Zacatecas throughout the remainder of the sixteenth century and allied through kinship and marriage to the descendants of Hernando Cortés and doña Isabel Moctezoma, daughter and heir of Moctezoma, as well as other leading families associated with the northern mines. On these relationships, see Donald E. Chipman, *Moctezuma's Children: Aztec Royalty under Spanish Rule, 1520–1700* (Austin: University of Texas Press, 2005), and the información of Juanes de Tolosa, AGI Patronato 80, no. 5, ramo 1 (my thanks to Don Chipman for lending me his copy of the información and especially for replacing my copy of his fine book, *Moctezuma's Children*, which was lost in Katrina). See also Hillerkuss's

"Familia Zaldívar," which incorporates his extensive genealogical work on the different branches of the family through the seventeenth century.

84. Flint, *Great Cruelties*, 207.

85. In his testimony for the información of Juan de Zaldívar, Pérez stated that he had gone on the journey to Culiacan as "sobre saliente de general y estando en la tierra nueva este testigo fue por soldado en compañia y capitania del dicho Juan de Zaldívar" (AGI Patronato 60, no. 5, ramo 4).

86. According to Flint, "the eleven- or twelve-year-old Pedro de Ledesma knew the future captain general at least seven years before they both sailed for Nueva España in the company of Viceroy Antonio de Mendoza in 1535. From the time of their embarkation for the New World, Ledesma served in Vázquez de Coronado's household, accompanying him to Nueva Galicia . . . in 1538. He was still serving the former governor and captain general in 1545" (*Great Cruelties*, 230).

87. Melchor Pérez and Zaldívar probably remained close. In September 1550 they, together with several other vecinos of Guadalajara, signed a letter complaining of the inconvenience of having to bring silver to Compostela from Zacatecas because of the distance; see AGI Guadalajara 51.

CHAPTER 5

1. León-Portilla, *Flecha en el blanco*, 138, 140, 141.

2. Ibid., 142–43. Note the change in person from first to third, which is typical in accounts and recorded oral testimony from this period, as seen also in the shifts between first-person single and plural (and occasionally third person) in the report from Xalisco (see chapter 3). At the time this deposition was written, Tenamaztle had been in Spain for three or four years. How much longer he lived is not known.

3. León-Portilla, *Flecha en el blanco*.

4. See "Carta de Jerónimo López al emperador," in Archivo Histórico Nacional (hereafter AHN) Diversos, Colecciones, leg. 22, no. 39. López states at the very beginning of his report "primeramente es a saber que el principio del alzamiento de esta provincia fue para no dar los tributos de indios a particulares señores de pueblos que en aquella provincia residen, especialmente a los que viven en la villa de Guadalajara y Compostela." Jerónimo López was a conquistador and longtime vecino and regidor of Mexico City, as well as an encomendero. He wrote a number of reports to the king over the years. He participated in Francisco Cortés's entrada from Colima, accounting for his familiarity with parts of New Galicia.

5. Aiton writes, for example, that "what the Spaniards were facing was a religious revolt from out of the north, with the superstition of the aborigine

fighting against them, not with them, as had been the case in the conquest of Mexico. The new religion promised everything from sensual pleasure to immortality to those who would desert Christianity" (*Antonio de Mendoza*, 140). He adds, however, that "the Indians in encomienda in Jalisco were ripe for rebellion, owing to the harsh treatment they had received from their masters, but no great revolt would have occurred without the incitement of the new religion" (141).

6. See testimony in AGI Justicia 262. Don Pedro, the señor of Tetitlan, was twenty years old when he swore by the cross that "neither he nor those of his pueblo ever received mistreatment from their master nor from any other Christian nor did he know of other pueblos in this province that received bad treatment from their masters or any other Christian; instead, many times they discussed how happy they were" (AGI Justicia 262). Particularly ironic in this light, given the evidence discussed in the previous chapters about the experience of the people of Xalisco under Cristóbal de Oñate, was the testimony of the latter that the Indians were well treated and had they not been, they would have complained to him "as they did in other cases for minor things and the said Indians provided only very light tributes" (AGI Justicia 262).

7. Other indigenous sources for the war almost all originated in central Mexico, not New Galicia. These include pictorial codices (such as the Lienzo de Tlaxcala or the Telleriano Codex) that show battle scenes or incorporate other references to the participation of people from central Mexico in the campaign against the rebels of the West. The most important is the account set down at the behest of don Francisco de Sandoval Acacitli, a ruler of Tlalmanalco in Chalco. García Icazbalceta published the Spanish translation of the original Nahuatl account (which was lost). I have used the version edited by José María Muriá; see Francisco de Sandoval Acacicitli, *Conquista y pacificación de los indios chichimecas*, 2nd ed. (Zapopan: El Colegio de Jalisco, 1996).

8. Román Gutiérrez offers as a tentative explanation the existence of "una creencia religiosa común, de la cual participaban tanto nómadas como sedentarios, y que encuentra su núcleo más fuerte entre los cazcanes y zacatecas" ("Indígenas de Juchipila," 26). This possibility certainly would help account for the rapidity with which an apparent alliance formed between groups that often were at odds.

9. Ruiz Medrano, for example, writes that while Vázquez de Coronado was busy organizing the expedition to the Tierra Nueva, "the Indians of Tlaltenango and Suchipila rose up in a war instigated by the Indians of the north. These last came from the mountains of Tepeque and Zacatecas" ("Versiones sobre un fenómeno," 357). In this she follows Aiton, *Antonio de Mendoza*.

10. Gerhard, *North Frontier*, 110-12.

11. See José López-Portillo y Weber, *La rebelión de la Nueva Galicia* (Mexico City: Colección Peña Roja, 1980), 417. He took this episode from Tello's history.

12. See the report of late 1549 from the justicia and regimiento of Compostela, which states that "los indios Guaynamotas que estaban de paz y venian la dotrina y teniendo por comendero [*sic*] a un español llamado Juan de Arce la mataron y se han alzado y no vienen de paz como solian, tenian dentro en su provincia una iglesia que se dice haber derrocado y aun quemado" (AGI Guadalajara 51). See also the report of the oidores of the audiencia in AGI Guadalajara 5, ramo 3, no. 9. Arce compiled a probanza after the war; see Icaza, *Conquistadores y pobladores*, 2:275. León-Portilla includes (uncritically) the story of Juan de Arce in *Flecha en el blanco*, 49.

13. The *Libro Segundo*, vol. 1 of Tello's multivolume *Crónica miscelánea*, provides an extensive history of the war. It is the most complete early account but highly problematic. Tello, a Franciscan who arrived in Mexico in 1619, consulted (and at times quoted directly from) a range of sources, including some that are no longer in existence. Tello was by no means an uncritical partisan of the Spanish side; he was an admirer of Bartolomé de las Casas and, like Las Casas, condemned Spanish mistreatment of Indians. He was familiar with Las Casas's works, which seem to have influenced him considerably, as well as other histories and chronicles (such as those of Torquemada and Bernal Díaz del Castillo), to which he refers in his own work. Nevertheless he was not a contemporary and could not have interviewed any witnesses to or participants in events that occurred nearly eighty years before his arrival in New Spain. Although most modern historians advise using Tello's history "with caution," Tello nonetheless has exerted considerable influence on the way that the early history of New Galicia, including the war, has been written. Aiton, whose narrative of the war probably is still the best short synopsis in English, closely follows the testimony in the residencia of officials conducted after the war; see *Antonio de Mendoza*, 136-58. He does not use Tello's account, and he critiques or refutes Bancroft's version at various points, although he also at times relies on Bancroft (who probably did use Tello) and fails to give references for certain episodes that seem to appear only in Tello. Brand devotes his appendix B to the problems of using Tello's history and categorically states that his work "should not be used for the preconquest and conquest periods" ("Ethnohistoric Synthesis," 651). Elsewhere in the article, he points out how the errors in Tello have been used by successive historians well into the twentieth century. "The net result, from Tello to J. López-Portillo y Weber, has been an authoritarian pyramiding, each writer contributing some new ornament until the resultant edifice is an historical monstrosity of almost pure fiction accepted as absolutely demonstrated

fact" (634). Tello, nonetheless, continues to be a source for scholars; see, for example, Ruiz Medrano, "Versiones sobre un fenómeno," 356. See also the observations on Tello of Phil C. Weigand and Acelia García de Weigand, *Los orígenes de los caxcanes y su relación con la guerra de los nayaritas: Una hipótesis* (Zapopan: El Colegio de Jalisco, 1995), 42–43. They make the argument that parts of the Tello history actually were additions to the original made by other (unknown) writers, introducing further distortions and inaccuracies; however, they are not explicit about which parts were added.

14. AGI Justicia 259, pieza 3.

15. Martel's testimony and the quotations in this paragraph are in AGI Justicia 261, pieza 3.

16. Martel stated that by informing him of the cacique's activities the naguatatos showed that they wished the cacique ill ("queriendolo mal"), suggesting rivalries or enmities within the pueblo (AGI Justicia 261).

17. Tomás Gil testified that he had heard about the dances from the Indians of his encomienda and of the pueblo of Omitlan because he "traded and went among them and he saw the disturbance and the dance and the devil's talk, all of which they did and acted in front of this witness." Gil explained that at the time of the uprising he had been in his pueblo near the Zacatecas mountains. Since he was there by himself, the Indians were not especially concerned and carried on with their dances. He managed to grab "a very large gourd to the sound of which they did their dance" and broke it, for which he narrowly escaped being killed. "They told him to leave because they were going to rise up in revolt." Martel also mentioned gourds that the so-called *hechiceros* (sorcerers) used to summon people to meet. Gil's testimony is in AGI Justicia 262; Martel's is in AGI Justicia 261, pieza 3.

18. Juan de Zubia testified to having seen Varela "maltratado huyendo" in AGI Justicia 262.

19. AGI Justicia 259, pieza 3.

20. Ibarra's testimony in AGI Justicia 262. In some testimony this man is referred to as López rather than Pérez.

21. Mendoza's response to charges in the residencia, AGI Justicia 259, pieza 3. Calling Indians who served the Spaniards "sodomites" probably was meant to suggest that such service was emasculating.

22. We should recall the differing responses that Spaniards encountered when they reached Tonala during the conquest, when the woman ruler welcomed them, while others—apparently including her close relatives—attempted to repel the Spanish advance.

23. Thomas Hillerkuss identifies Tepetistaque as the modern Cerro el Biznagón. He argues that it had an insufficient water supply and proved too vulnerable to Spanish cannon fire and cavalry attacks to be sustained, thus explaining

why Tepetistaque does not figure in later episodes of the war. He writes that the peñoles chosen had to be high enough for the defenders to be safe from artillery fire and arrows, inaccessible to horses, and with sufficient water and living space and narrow, easily defended entryways. "La guerra de Miztón (1541) a la luz de nuevas fuentes" (paper presented at the Primer Encuentro de Especialistas de la Region Norte de Jalisco, University of Guadalajara, Centro Universitario del Norte, February 22, 2006).

24. His testimony is in AGI Justicia 261, pieza 3. Following the war, mining began in the area but was abandoned in the 1550s. In the mid-eighteenth century a major mining strike occurred there and Tepeque was renamed Bolaños; see Gerhard, *North Frontier*, 71.

25. See Ibarra's testimony in AGI Justicia 262. By choosing Tenamaztle, who consistently is called the brother of the ruler of Nochistlan, to receive the staff of office, Ibarra might have been intervening in an ongoing rivalry between the brothers. The fact that very early Tenamaztle took his people to join the revolt, but his brother apparently did not, suggests that there were disagreements between them, which either purposely or unwittingly might have been exploited by the Spaniards in earlier years.

26. This account and all quotes are from Martel's testimony in AGI Justicia 261, pieza 3.

27. Ibid.

28. Ibarra's testimony is in AGI Justicia 262.

29. The detainees told Ibarra that they had encountered two messengers representing the rulers of Xalpa, Apozol, Juchipila, Mezquituta, and Cuzpatlan, who had informed them that Ibarra and his men had slept in Mecatabasco. The description of events and the quotes in this paragraph come from Martel's testimony in AGI 261, pieza 3.

30. Martel's testimony is in AGI Justicia 261, pieza 3.

31. Ibid.

32. Ibarra does not mention this disagreement with the other men, which is reported by Martel in AGI Justicia 261, pieza 3.

33. Ibarra's testimony is in AGI Justicia 262.

34. Martel's testimony is in AGI Justicia 261, pieza 3.

35. See testimony of don Juan, who in 1547 was "cacique y gobernador" of Juchipila, encomienda de Hernán Flores; he testified through interpreter Bartolomé González de Mendoza: "el dicho capitan Miguel de Ibarra hizo justicia y mato al dicho Xuyteque señor de Juchipila y a don Diego, señor de Xalpa, y a don Martin, señor de Apozol y a Cacil, principal de Apozol y a Coatle, otro principal y otros dos principales de Mizquituta y a otros de otros pueblos que fueron por todos once indios." Alonso, a principal of Apozol, testified that Ibarra "hizo justicia de Xuitecle señor de Juchipila y de don

Diego señor de Xalpa y de Tecajete principal de Xalpa y Coeque principal de Xalpa y de Polacute principal de Xalpa y de don Martin señor de Apozol pueblo deste testigo y de Acucinte principal del pueblo de Apozol y de Coate naguatgato del dicho pueblo de Apozol y de Catule principal de Mezquituta y de Xecul y Coly principales de Mesquituta." The testimony of don Juan and Alonso is in AGI Justicia 262.

36. Zubia's and Ibarra's testimony on this incident is in AGI Justicia 262.

37. Ibarra's testimony is in AGI Justicia 262.

38. Martel's testimony is in AGI Justicia 261, pieza 3.

39. Ibid.

40. According to Pedro de Plasencia, Salinas had written to him for arms and additional men to accompany him to Cuzpatlan, which Plasencia provided (AGI Justicia 262).

41. Juan de Zubia provided some disturbing details of this episode, stating that he had seen clothing of the slain men being sold and that, although the Indians thought to have slain Salinas were at peace, they had never served. He claimed that other Indians had told him that when Salinas and the others arrived they were welcomed and presented with gifts and food to lull them into a sense of security (AGI Justicia 262).

42. Pedro Cuadrado's testimony is in AGI Justicia 261, pieza 3.

43. Juan Hernández de Híjar, the founder of Purificación, offered some interesting testimony regarding long-term plans. He claimed that before Francisco Vázquez de Coronado had organized his expedition, a couple of Spaniards who routinely traded with the Cazcanes and Zacatecas told him that the Indians intended to revolt. He said the men were Francisco Elvira and Alonso Diaz, "and from their tongue this witness, as captain and a man who always worked to know what was going on in the whole country," had found out about the Cazcanes' plans to rebel (AGI Justicia 262). There is no way to assess the veracity of this testimony.

44. Ibarra was encomendero of Nochistlan and a vecino of Guadalajara, while Cristóbal de Oñate lived in Compostela. Since Ibarra lived in much greater geographic proximity to the Cazcan area where the revolt began, he was better positioned than Oñate to deal with the early attacks and confrontations.

45. Gerhard shows the location of Mixton as east of Tlaltenango and northwest of Xalpa (*North Frontier*, 100).

46. Both de la Coruña and de Jesús are used in reference to the same individual who had been guardian in Juchipila; Mendoza referred to him as Martín de la Coruña, but in the información that Román Gutiérrez transcribed from AGI Patronato 181, ramo 1, he is Martín de Jesús; see "Indígenas de Juchipila," 28.

47. Román Gutiérrez, "Indígenas de Juchipila," 27–28. The notary Juan de León wrote this report. Francisco de la Mota, Francisco Delgadillo, Pedro

Cuadrado, Lope de Viana, and Hernando Flores also were present and witnessed it. Francisco de la Mota died in the war; see the 1587 información of his son, Gaspar de la Mota, who was a vecino of Guadalajara, in AGI Patronato 79, no. 2, ramo 9. His mother, Catalina de Mena, apparently long outlived her husband.

48. No one seems to know just why the bishop of Guatemala was present in the area at the time. Most likely he had accompanied Pedro de Alvarado, intending to meet with Mendoza in New Galicia.

49. See testimony of Alonso de Olivares, who arrived with don Luis de Castilla, and his response to question 145 (AGI Justicia 262, pieza 1).

50. See Aiton, *Antonio de Mendoza*, 146–47.

51. Question 147; AGI Justicia 262, pieza 2.

52. See his testimony in AGI Justicia 262.

53. See the testimony in the información of Andrés de Villanueva, in AGI Patronato 60, no. 3, ramo 5.

54. This is the version of events detailed in the información of Andrés de Villanueva, who participated in the siege and in the skirmish with the Indians from Teul; see AGI Patronato 60, no. 3, ramo 5.

55. From question 150, in AGI Justicia 262, pieza 2. In *Antonio de Mendoza*, Aiton judges the date of the battle to have been April 10, 1541. The reports on the number of Spaniards killed differ, varying from nine to thirteen.

56. According to Alonso de Olivares, who was Castilla's alguacil, three or four hours after don Luis de Castilla received the letter from Oñate asking him for help, they left and traveled all night, arriving the next day in Guadalajara (AGI Justicia 262, pieza 1).

57. Ibid., pieza 2. Etzatlan was the site of one of the first Franciscan monasteries and is mentioned in the visitación of 1525, whereas in the visitación "Iztlan" (or Ixtlan) is the pueblo of Ispan. Although in the records of the 1530s it appears as Izatlan, I have used the spelling Etzatlan, which corresponds with modern usage. When the jurisdictions of New Spain and New Galicia were settled, Etzatlan became part of New Spain. In terms of the events and developments of this period, however, it clearly functioned as part of New Galicia, as did Purificación.

58. See Aiton, *Antonio de Mendoza*, 147–49; Ruiz Medrano, "Versiones sobre un fenómeno," 360–61; and AGI Justicia 259, pieza 2.

59. Ruiz Medrano argues that a principal purpose for fighting the war was to take slaves ("Versiones sobre un fenómeno," 371, 375, 376). I would suggest that slave taking was secondary to the much more important consideration of pacifying and stabilizing an area that was beginning to yield possibly significant mineral discoveries. Slave taking held out the possibility of some

rewards for Spaniards who fought in the war; certainly—as Nuño de Guzmán had learned ten years prior to this—there was no other plunder to be had from the Indians of the West.

60. On the relationship between the Cazcanes and Zacatecas, see Weigand and García de Weigand, *Tenamaxtli y Guaxicar*. They write that "the Zacatecas were the less developed and more rural neighbors, living in active symbiosis with the Caxcanes, who were their civilized 'cousins,' inhabitants of the cities. Although frequently they found themselves at war with each other, this in part could reflect as much the conflicts between cities and hinterlands for resources and privileges as matters of territorial conquest. We propose that the Zacatecas and Caxcanes represent an ecological and sociocultural *continuum*" (106; their emphasis).

61. This comes from the testimony of Antón, who after the war was the señor of Tepetatlauca, near Guachinango. He named some of the messengers, who he said were Zacatecas and "made him understand everything . . . until they made him rise up and rebel because he really believed it all" (AGI Justicia 262).

62. AGI Justicia 259, pieza 2.

63. Gerhard mentions a "string of villages in the Ameca and Atenguillo valleys, including Amaxaque, Tepuzuacan, Amatlan, Xalacingo, Istimitique, and Atengoychan," which Guzmán had granted to his protégé and friend Alvaro de Bracamonte (*North Frontier*, 87). This is the area of the future mines of Guachinango. It is not clear to which ethnic group the people of the area, whom Gerhard calls "relatively primitive farmers," belonged (86). He says that in 1545, Atengoychan remained one of the largest of the communities, with 488 tributaries (89).

64. AGI Justicia 262.

65. Ibid. Juan, a naguatato and alguacil of Cuzpantlan, said the same man had come to his pueblo with the messengers.

66. Ibid. At the time he testified, Francisco, whose original name was Tepeche, was a Christian; his testimony was taken via two interpreters, Bartolomé González de Mendoza and Alonso, called an "indio naguatato de Mexico." By this time, evidently many Tecuexe pueblos had rebelled. Alonso Lorenzo, who was interpreter of at least one indigenous language, said that some of the Tecuexes of Tonala also were in cahoots with the rebels. He and some other Spaniards had captured two men from pueblos in the jurisdiction of Tonala, who confessed that some of their people were in the peñol (probably Mixton) "and they were coming from having communicated with them and giving them bows and arrows" (AGI Justicia 262, response to question 133).

67. AGI Justicia 262.

68. In addition to Juchipila and Apozol, churches were reported burned in Aguacatlan, Tequila, and Cuzpatlan. It is probably safe to assume that all the churches in the pueblos that rebelled were destroyed.

69. Don Juan, who was "señor y gobernador" of Iztlan after the war, testified that he had washed "his head and face with the said black ink to remove the baptism and seen them raise tortillas in contempt of the sacrament" (AGI Justicia 262, response to question 154).

70. See AGI Justicia 262, pieza 2, question 153, which reads in part: "mataron muchos cristianos entre los cuales mataron a fray Juan de Esperanza, frayle de la orden de San Francisco, y le quebraron los dientes diciendo ya no nos diras mas palabras de tu Dios con esta boca y asi mismo mataron a fray Antonio de Cuellar, frayle de la dicha orden, guardian de Yzatlan, el cual era lengua de los indios y una de las personas que mas por ellos hacia que habia en toda la tierra y a quien los indios mostraban tener como por padre." Hurtado's testimony also is in AGI Justicia 262. Francisco, the lord of Etzatlan after the war, said that he saw the friars dead, as well as two Christian Indians who served in the church, and he helped to bury them. According to don Pedro, señor of Agualulco, rebels from his pueblo and others from Tequila were responsible for the killings.

71. AGI Justicia 262. After the war Diego Hurtado became encomendero of Cuzpatlan.

72. Don Pedro's testimony is in AGI Justicia 262, response to question 132; don Juan's testimony is in AGI Justicia 262, response to question 137.

73. "Them" is ambiguous here—it could refer to either Tetitlan or Xalisco.

74. Don Cristóbal's testimony is in AGI Justicia 262, response to question 102; Alonso's testimony is also in AGI Justicia 262, response to question 197.

75. Durán's testimony is in AGI Justicia 262, response to question 156.

76. See Gerhard, *North Frontier*, 144.

77. Jerónimo Pérez de Rociniega, a vecino of Compostela, said that because of the warnings many received, he "and the others saved their persons, property, and cattle that they had in the said pueblos" (AGI Justicia 262, response to question 137). His and the other testimony regarding warnings from Indians is found in AGI Justicia 262.

78. The peñol of Nochistlan was located north of the present town, probably the Cerro de San Miguel, according to Thomas Hillerkuss, "La Nueva Galicia entre 1530 y 1550: Un reino insurrecto" (paper presented to the Segundo Encuentro de Especialistas de la Región Norte de Jalisco, University of Guadalajara, Centro Universitario del Norte, March 7, 2007).

79. Aiton, *Antonio de Mendoza*, 149–50.

80. The quote comes from the viceroy's response to the charges in AGI Justicia 262, pieza 2.

81. AGI Justicia 259, pieza 3. Mendoza apparently was criticized by some for leaving central Mexico vulnerable when he left for the campaign in New Galicia. Jerónimo López claimed to have warned the viceroy of an ostensible plot in which Indians from Michoacan met with the governor of Tlaxcala to make common cause and take advantage of the viceroy's absence from Mexico City to assert themselves. López was indignant that when Mendoza was informed of the alleged conspiracy, he made light of it and instituted no inquiries. See "Carta de Gerónimo López al Emperador (Mexico, 20 October 1541)" in García Icazbalceta, *Colección de documentos*, 2:143–44. López wrote to the emperor: "me dijeron e dieron nueva, un vecino de la ciudad de los Angeles, que se dice Gutierre Maldonado . . . que había muy gran mal en la tierra y que están en muy gran peligro toda ella. Preguntado el que era, dijome que se tenía por cosa cierta que los indios de la provincia de Michoacan habían venido a Tascala con embajada, y que era para confederarse a una y dar sobre nosotros y matarnos a todos y alzarse con la tierra. La posibilidad destas dos provincias es tan grande . . . porque se pueden sacar de cada una dellas trescientos mil hombres de guerra, y mucho más" (143).

82. Alvarez stated that Guadalajara had subsequently moved "six or seven leagues toward the city of Mexico." See his testimony in the probanza done by the son of Cristobal de Oñate in 1577 (AGI Patronato 75, no. 1, ramo 3).

83. AGI Justicia 259, pieza 2.

84. Villanueva describes this episode in his deposition in AGI Patronato 60, no. 3, ramo 5. Another story, the oft-repeated tale of the courage and inspirational example of Beatriz Hernández during the siege, comes from Tello, *Crónica miscelánea*, 2:218, and cannot be corroborated in any other independent source. I have found it in no source that does not rely on his history. Beatriz was the wife of Juan Sánchez de Olea. According to Tello, when an attack on the town seemed imminent, and the women and children gathered for Mass began to cry and faint, the governor told them to be quiet. Beatriz addressed the governor, saying that he should concern himself with his duties as captain, and she would lead the women. She took them to the fortified house, encouraged them to be as brave as the men, and assumed the post of guard at the door. The story could be true, or possibly it derives from the decision that was taken not to evacuate the women and children, who surely lived through some frightening times.

85. Diego de Orozco testified that don Pedro Ponce, the ruler of Cuiseo, sent maize to the besieged residents of Guadalajara (AGI Justicia 262). Hernando Martel testified regarding the support of Domingo Ponce, whom he referred to as the gobernador of Cuiseo; he probably is the same person. He stated that Ponce "es muy amigo de españoles y siempre se hallo dende el principio y levantamiento de los naturales de la dicha Nueva Galicia en favor y ayuda

de los españoles. Cuando desbarataron a Cristobal de Oñate y a su gente en el Mixton y se hallo con el con algunos de los suyos y este testigo le tiene por hombre de confianza" (AGI Justicia 261, pieza 3).

86. This figure, offered by Andrés de Villanueva, who was one of the defenders of Guadalajara, seems plausible; see his deposition in AGI Patronato 60, no. 3, ramo 5. Aiton writes that fifty thousand Indians besieged the city, a figure he took from Bancroft (*Antonio de Mendoza*, 151).

87. Letter of Jerónimo López to the king, in AHN Diversos, Colecciones, leg. 22, no. 39. López wrote that Tenamaztle was one of the main leaders in the rebel assault on Guadalajara.

88. See Ruiz Medrano, "Versiones sobre un fenómeno," 361.

CHAPTER 6

1. "Y porque en esta Nueva España se ha alzado y rebelado contra Su Mag. muchos pueblos de indios y conviene a servicio de Su Mag. que yo fuese en persona con mano armada a pacificar los dichos pueblos e indios y hacer castigo y escarmiento en ellas y reducirlos al dominio de Su Mag. y remediar grandes inconvenientes y daños que se podrian recrecer en toda esta Nueva España" (AGI Justicia 259, pieza 3).

2. AGI Patronato 60, no. 3, ramo 5. Guaxacatlan and Cacaluta (probably the other place that appears in the testimony, although the spellings vary quite a lot) both were east of Aguacatlan. Later in the sixteenth century there were mines in the area of Guaxacatlan.

3. See AGI Guadalajara 41, no. 2 (October 1548); the deposition was presented by Diego Vázquez, vecino of Guadalajara, with Juan Michel's power of attorney. Michel also was a vecino of Guadalajara at the time.

4. Iztlan, which was east of Aguacatlan and Xala, was assigned in encomienda to Alonso López by Francisco Cortés. Despite Guzmán's reassignment of encomiendas, López still held Iztlan in the 1540s; see Gerhard, *North Frontier*, 60–61.

5. According to Gerhard, the Aguacatlan Valley is surrounded by "rugged and forested country with several peaks (notably the solitary volcano of Ceboruco). . . . From prehistoric times an important route of commerce and migration between the coast and the central plateau passed through here, climbing the steep barranca walls to the east" (*North Frontier*, 60). This may be the pass to which they were referring.

6. Michel's testimony is in AGI Guadalajara 41, no. 2.

7. Etzatlan (Izatlan) and Iztlan (Ispan) were distinct communities; see chapter 5, note 57, on this.

8. See AGI Guadalajara 41, no. 2.

9. Juan de Alvarado was the son of Garcia de Alvarado, former *comendador*

(commander of a military order) of Montijo, and doña Beatriz de Tordoya. He was from Badajoz and a relative of Pedro de Alvarado but not a sibling (Icaza, *Conquistadores y pobladores*, 2:12–13). He participated in the expedition of Francisco Cortés and subsequently became a vecino of Michoacan.

10. On conditions and developments in central Mexico in the early years following the conquest, see Charles Gibson, *Aztecs under Spanish Rule* (Stanford, CA: Stanford University Press, 1964); Liss, *Mexico under Spain*; Altman, "Mexico City"; Townsend, *Malintzin's Choices*; Warren, *Conquest of Michoacán*; Himmerich y Valencia, *Encomenderos of New Spain*; Ethelia Ruiz Medrano, *Reshaping New Spain: Government and Private Interests in the Colonial Bureaucracy, 1531–1550*, trans. Julia Constantino and Pauline Marmasse (Boulder: University of Colorado Press, 2006); and José Miranda, "La función económica del encomendero en los orígenes del régimen colonial de Nueva España (1525–1531)," *Anales del Instituto Nacional de Antropología e Historia* 2 (1941–46), 421–62.

11. See Altman, "Mexico City." For the roles of Africans in Spanish campaigns, see Restall, "Black Conquistadors."

12. The revolt of the *comuneros*, or *comunidades*, occurred in 1520–21, at the beginning of the reign of the new Habsburg king, the grandson of Ferdinand and Isabel, who was Charles I of Spain and Charles V of the Holy Roman Empire. The rebellion, directed against the new king, was led by members of the middle and upper-middle groups of the towns and cities in north central Castile.

13. Agudelo received a corregimiento from the viceroy in compensation; see AGN Mercedes, vol. 1, exp. 7. See also Icaza, *Conquistadores y pobladores*, 1:251. On don Luis de Castilla, see Icaza, *Conquistadores y pobladores*, 2:7.

14. Ovando was royal governor of Hispaniola from 1502–9. He took with him a very large number of settlers in 1502.

15. See Ida Altman, "The Revolt of Enriquillo and the Historiography of Early Spanish America," *The Americas* 63, no. 4 (2007): 587–614. Gonzalo Martín also appears to have participated in the so-called war of Bahoruco in Hispaniola.

16. Icaza, *Conquistadores y pobladores*, 2:155; Himmerich y Valencia, *Encomenderos of New Spain*, 124.

17. AGI Patronato 56, no. 3, ramo 6.

18. Icaza, *Conquistadores y pobladores*, 1:217–18.

19. See the información of Juan de la Rosa that details the services of his father, Francisco de la Rosa, in AGI Patronato 65, no. 2, ramo 7.

20. AGI Patronato 109, ramo 6.

21. The Crown sent Blasco Nuñez Vela as viceroy to Peru with the charge of enforcing the New Laws, promulgated in 1542–43. This legislation was

designed to limit the privileges of encomenderos and especially targeted the men who had participated in Peru's notorious civil wars; see James Lockhart, *Spanish Peru, 1532–1560* (1968; repr., Madison: University of Wisconsin Press, 1994), 5.

22. AGI Patronato 96, ramo 4.

23. See his información of 1576, in AGI Patronato 74, no. 2, ramo 4.

24. See, for example, Matthew Restall, *Seven Myths of the Spanish Conquest* (Oxford: Oxford University Press, 2003), chapter 2, especially pp. 33–34. For a close examination of the participants in conquests and campaigns in early Peru, see Lockhart, *Spanish Peru*, and *The Men of Cajamarca* (Austin: University of Texas Press, 1972). These seminal works clearly established the varied socioeconomic and occupational background of participants and early settlers; their relative lack of military experience overall; and the patterns by which ambitious men organized subsequent expeditions—often in the hopes of outflanking their rivals—and recruited newcomers, as well as those who failed to garner adequate reward in the form of encomiendas.

25. See the información presented by his son Juan de Nava on his behalf in AGI Patronato 63, ramo 17. In the early 1560s Antonio de Nava claimed to be ninety-five years old, with twelve children and thirty-five grandchildren.

26. See the información executed by his grandson, don Alvaro de Paz, whose maternal grandfather, Gonzalo de Ovalle, also fought in the Mixton War and then lived in Guatemala (AGI Patronato 85, no. 3, ramo 3).

27. AGI Patronato 60, no. 5, ramo 5.

28. The comuneros revolt mainly involved the towns and cities of north central Castile. Little is known about the experience of towns in Extremadura during the conflict, but evidently there were sympathizers of the revolt in the south as well.

29. See Hillerkuss, *Documentalía*, 255–57; see also page 40, note 73, on his marriage to doña Juana de Sosa, the sister of Estrada's successor as treasurer, don Juan Alonso de Sosa. Castilla was the second cousin of doña Ana de Castilla, the wife of the second viceroy, don Luis de Velasco. On Sosa's involvement in mining activities, see also Ruiz Medrano, *Reshaping New Spain*, 85.

30. Himmerich y Valencia, *Encomenderos of New Spain*, 139. He gives the date as 1530.

31. Ruiz Medrano, *Reshaping New Spain*, 111.

32. Hillerkuss, *Documentalía*, 258.

33. On Licenciado Maldonado's ties with Castilla, see Ruiz Medrano, *Reshaping New Spain*, 94–95. He was appointed to the second audiencia in 1530. He often is confused, even in contemporary documents, with the Lic. Francisco Maldonado, who had been his predecessor on Mexico's first audiencia.

Alonso remained on the audiencia during the first part of Mendoza's tenure as viceroy. After the war, in which he took an active part, he was appointed provisional governor of Guatemala and the following year, in 1543, became president of the Audiencia de los Confines established in Guatemala; see Aiton, *Antonio de Mendoza*, 58. He was married to the daughter of Francisco de Montejo. There also was a Francisco Maldonado who held a substantial encomienda in Oaxaca; see Himmerich y Valencia, *Encomenderos of New Spain*, 187. He also was corregidor of Teozapotlan in Oaxaca from 1543 to 1545; see Ruiz Medrano, *Reshaping New Spain*, 112–14. Whether he participated in the Mixton War is not known.

34. Flint, *Great Cruelties*, 33, 271. See the información of 1605 of his grandson don Francisco Pacheco in AGI Patronato 84, no. 1, ramo 6. Pacheco's second wife was doña Juana Colón de la Cueva y de Toledo, the daughter of marshal don Carlos de Luna y Arellano, the very well connected (and controversial) governor of Yucatan.

35. For the story of how this match was effected against the objections of doña María's father, Juan Jaramillo, see Townsend, *Malintzin's Choices*, 178–79. See also an información of Hernando Cortés, in which he makes charges regarding culpability in the seduction of Jaramillo's daughter, in Ciriaco Pérez Bustamante, *Los orígenes del gobierno virreinal en las Indias españolas: Don Antonio de Mendoza, primer virrey de la Nueva España* (Santiago: Universidad de Santiago, 1928), app. 14, p. 178. He implicated Mendoza's mayordomo Agustín Guerrero. Townsend writes that Quesada was from Granada, where possibly he was living before departing for New Spain, but apparently he was originally from Baeza; see the información of his son don Pedro de Quesada in AGI Patronato 76, no. 2, ramo 10. Although Townsend writes that "the war was largely over by the time don Luis got there," if Quesada indeed accompanied Mendoza to New Galicia, a crucial five or six months of campaigning remained before the viceroy declared the war at an end (179). Chapter 8 of Townsend's book focuses on doña María and contains more information on Quesada and their son Pedro, whom don Luis took to Spain to be educated in the mid-1550s. Don Luis returned to Mexico before doña María's death in 1563, but Pedro remained in Spain until 1567. Several years later, he married the daughter of an audiencia judge, Dr. Vasco de Puga.

36. According to Aiton, it was Guerrero's duty to see that the viceroy's "orders were carried out" and that he did so with the aid of Castilla (*Antonio de Mendoza*, 48). For his position as chancellor, see page 62. Cortés claimed that Mendoza also had made Guerrero "contador de rrentas" and "rrecetor de la ynquisición," as well as making Guerrero's nephew the constable of the inquisition; see Pérez Bustamante, *Orígenes del gobierno virreinal*, 177, app., doc. 14, charge 20.

37. Cortés lodged a number of charges against Guerrero; he maintained that "Agustín Guerrero inflicts injuries and mistreatment on many vecinos of Mexico, women, and people who cannot defend [themselves] and defames them and thus they went to fight at the door of Gonzalo Cerezo, a very honorable married hidalgo, and sang to him filthy songs and attacked the house and entered it and insulted him if he would not defend himself" (Pérez Bustamante, *Origenes del gobierno virreinal*, 180–81, app., doc. 14). Gonzalo Cerezo at one time was Cortés's criado and was the inspector of the area conquered by Francisco Cortés in 1525. Cerezo testified that he "did not have good will toward" Guzmán, who "had treated him badly by unjustly holding him prisoner two or three times while he was president of this Audiencia" and that he thought that in this suit, Cortés was right and should win; see *BAGN* 8:554.

38. Aiton, *Antonio de Mendoza*, 55, 72, 122–23.

39. See Ruiz Medrano on Guerrero's role in supplying labor (much of it from Indian captives from the Mixton War) and overseeing the obraje that Mendoza owned in partnership with Gonzalo Gómez in Texcoco (*Reshaping New Spain*, 127–28, 134).

40. See his testimony regarding Guerrero's purchase of captives from the indios amigos in AGI Justicia 258. *Itatzin* means father in Nahuatl, but the word was also used for the higher subordinates and helpers of a ruler (James Lockhart, pers. comm.), so probably the term was used in that sense.

41. On Gómez de Maraver in Oaxaca, see Román Gutiérrez, *Sociedad y evangelización*, 163–64, and Kevin Terraciano, *The Mixtecs of Colonial Oaxaca: Ñudzahui History, Sixteenth through Eighteenth Centuries* (Stanford, CA: Stanford University Press, 2001), 275, 277.

42. On how the bishop rejected a petition from the rulers of Xalisco, see Calvo and others, *Xalisco*, 50. When indigenous leader Tenamaztle turned himself over to the Franciscans in Juchipila, they in turn sent him to Gómez de Maraver, who sent him to don Luis de Velasco, who replaced Mendoza as viceroy in 1552, in Mexico City; see León-Portilla, *Flecha en el blanco*, 90, 98, 119–20. In a 1551 letter to the king, Gómez de Maraver claimed that he "brought to submission to the service of Your Majesty and our Christian religion don Francisco Tenamaztle with other caciques and principales, up to 170 persons of those who . . . had rebelled." The quote is from an excerpt of the letter reprinted in León-Portilla, *Flecha en el blanco*, 119.

43. Román Gutiérrez, *Sociedad y evangelización*, 156–59. He probably was Lic. don Juan de Barrios, member of the order of Santiago and a native of Seville, who at some time was a Franciscan and became archdeacon in the cathedral of Mexico City. He died in late 1546 or early 1547.

44. AGI Justicia 260 (testimony of 1545).

45. Ruiz Medrano, *Reshaping New Spain*, 167–68 and 231n121); see also page 192, where she describes an incident in which Ortiz assisted the Indians of Azcapotzalco to bring their complaints against Tejada before inspector Tello de Sandoval without Tejada's knowledge. The go-between position of these interpreters was ambiguous.

46. See testimony of Alonso de Santa Cruz, in AGI Justicia 262, pieza 1.

47. Pedro Carrasco mentions "don Hernando de Tapia, a son of don Andrés de Tapia Motelchiuhtzin" in "Indian-Spanish Marriages in the First Century of the Colony," *Indian Women of Early Mexico*, ed. Susan Schroeder, Stephanie Wood, and Robert Haskett (Norman: University of Oklahoma Press, 1997), 90. Carrasco's use of *don* is incorrect, as in none of the documents does it appear with Hernando's name. Icaza also calls him "hijo legítimo de Andrés de Tapia, gobernador que fue de la parte de Mexico" (*Conquistadores y pobladores*, 2:158). This Andrés de Tapia, according to James Lockhart, was not born a noble, which might account for why his son was not entitled to the "don." *The Nahuas after the Conquest* (Stanford, CA: Stanford University Press, 1992), 34, table 2.1. On Andrés de Tapia Motelchiutzin and his son Hernando, see Emma Pérez-Rocha and Rafael Tena, *La nobleza indígena del centro de México después de la conquista* (Mexico City: Instituto Nacional de Antropología e Historia, 2000), 39. After being appointed governor of Mexico by Cortés, don Andrés participated in the conquest of Pánuco and accompanied Guzmán to New Galicia, where he died in 1530. Also see figure 5 for his depiction in the Telleriano Codex. Lynn Guitar argues that Hernando was the mestizo son of the encomendero Andrés de Tapia, but the evidence is overwhelming that he was the son of the Andrés de Tapia Motelchiutzin. "Willing It So: Intimate Glimpses of *Encomienda* Life in Early-Sixteenth-Century Hispaniola," *Colonial Latin American Historical Review* 7, no. 3 (Summer 1998): 245–63.

48. See Chipman, *Moctezuma's Children*, 162n36. There is a series of documents regarding financial support for the group in Madrid, including payments for medical expenses for Tapia's wife; see AGI Indiferente General 411, leg. 16; Indiferente General 422, leg. 1; and Indiferente General 1962, leg. 5. In 1535 a royal cedula ordered that Hernando de Tapia be paid five thousand maravedis "pues su compañero Juan habia muerto y los demas regresaban a Indias" (AGI Indiferente General 422, leg. 16).

49. Santa Cruz's testimony referred to her as "una hija de español" (AGI Justicia 261, pieza 1).

50. See Pérez-Rocha and Tena, *Nobleza indígena*, 40.

51. Ruiz Medrano, *Reshaping New Spain*, 167. See also page 181 for Tapia's testimony that the lands that Tejada acquired in Chalco had belonged to Moctezoma.

52. AGN Mercedes vol. 2, exp. 237.
53. Sandoval Acacitli, *Conquista y pacificación*, 20.
54. For the official roster of slaves distributed after the fall of Coyna, see AGI Justicia 259.
55. For more on the epidemics, see Noble David Cook, *Born to Die: Disease and New World Conquest, 1492–1650* (Cambridge: Cambridge University Press, 1998), 97–103.
56. See Ida Altman, "Conquest, Coercion and Collaboration," in Matthew and Oudjik, *Indian Conquistadors*, 163–64.
57. Intro. to Sandoval Acacictli, *Conquista y pacificación*, 9–10. Muriá uses the spelling "Acacictli" but others prefer "Acacitli," which I have used in the text. García Icazbalceta also included the account in his *Colección de documentos*, vol. 2.
58. Taking particular Spanish (or Christian) names at the time of baptism could reflect clientage ties; in this case, we do not know enough about don Francisco to identify any connection he might have had with Bernal Díaz del Castillo or Pedro de Alvarado.
59. Sandoval Acacictli, *Conquista y pacificación*, 14, 30. Regarding the possible deaths of the principales, the meaning of a passage describing their dangerous crossing of a river is unclear (30). In Muriá's transcription it states, "y aun de los Españoles se lo llevó el Rio, y escapó que nó murió, y en Tepanca se ausentaron, y se vinieron Don Diego Quataxochitl, y su hermano mayor Martín Quaxolocatl, anochecieron y no amanecieron, el Quataxochitl hermano menor de el Señor Don Fernando, y el Martín Quaxolocatl hermano mayor de el *dicho* Don Fernando" ("and the river carried off even some of the Spaniards, who escaped and did not die. In Tepanca they left, and don Diego Quataxochitl and his older brother Martín Quaxolocatl came. They went to sleep and did not get up (?), Quataxochitl the younger brother of don Fernando and Martín Quataxochitl, the older brother of the said don Fernando"). The festive reception in Tlalmanalco for don Francisco's return is described on page 41. According to Susan Schroeder, don Francisco de Sandoval Acacitzin was the *tlatquic teuhctli* of Tlalmanalco from 1521–54 (*Chimalpahin*, 92).
60. Possibly Mezquituta.
61. Sandoval Acacictli, *Conquista y pacificación*, 17–18. On don Juan de Guzmán Iztlolinqui, who was installed by Cortés as tlatoani of Coyoacan in 1526, see Rebecca Horn, *Postconquest Coyoacan: Nahua-Spanish Relations in Central Mexico, 1519–1650* (Stanford, CA: Stanford University Press, 1997), 46–49, and other references throughout.
62. Sandoval Acacictli, *Conquista y pacificación*, 24.
63. Ibid., 18.

64. Ibid., 20–21.

65. What is meant by the "Chichimeca song" is not known. It could have been something that don Pedro of Xalpa taught them, or perhaps it was a song in the Chichimec style, or one celebrating the war (and anticipated victory) against the Chichimecs.

66. Sandoval Acacictli, *Conquista y pacificación*, 25–26.

67. For a fuller discussion and comparison of the experience of the Indian allies during Guzmán's and Mendoza's campaigns, see Altman, "Conquest, Coercion and Collaboration."

68. See Gibson, *Aztecs under Spanish Rule*, 156–59, and note 61 of this chapter.

69. AGN Mercedes, vol. 1, exp. 33.

70. See report of Jerónimo López on don Pedro's participation in AHN Diversos, Colecciones, leg. 22 no. 39; and AGN Mercedes vol. 2, exp. 485, in which in October 1543 the viceroy states that don Francisco, now governor of Michoacan, "and other principales there have appeared before me and presented a painting that they say is of the many lands that don Pedro, former governor, sold and alienated that belonged to that jurisdiction."

71. Sandoval Acacictli, *Conquista y pacificación*, 27.

72. See AGI Justicia 262, question 179.

73. See León-Portilla, *Flecha en el blanco*, 47, who quotes from Domingo Francisco Chimalpahin Cuauhtlehuanitzin, *Séptima Relacion*, Ms. Mexicains, num. 74, fol. 204, Biblioteca Nacional, Paris, as follows:

"Año 10-Casa (1541) . . .

"Y cuando se comenzó en Xuchipila, allá fue a sus órdenes el hijo del noble que gobernaba, Tezcatlipopocatzin, habitante del barrio de San Pablo Teopan, en Tenochtitlan. Y también se puso en marcha don Antonio de Mendoza, Visorrey; fue a la conquista de los xuchipiltecas que se había establecido como su señor el que se llamaba Tenamaztle. De todas partes fueron de allí de los pueblos de la tierra para que bien pudieran conquistar a los xuchipiltecas, a todos los chichimecas de Tototlan, de Nuchitlan [Nochiztlan].

"Y allá fueron los hijos de los señores de Amecameca, todavía muchachos; el primero, don Juan de Sancto Domingo de Mendoza Tlacatliltzin, hijo de Quetzalmaca; el segundo, don Lorenzo de Sandoval Ayocuautzin, hijo de Juan de Sandoval Tecuanxayacatzin; el tercero, don Jose de Santa Maria, de Panohuayan que, por linea materna, era nieto del que era el señor Cuauhcececuitzin, señor Tlamaocatl. Llevaron a los nobles; de todas partes de nuestra tierra se fueron."

74. Sandoval Acacitli, *Conquista y pacificación*, 40.

75. This date marks the feast of Saint Michael, the warrior archangel; thanks to Sarah Cline for pointing this out.

76. See testimony of Oñate, in AGI Justicia 259, pieza 3.

77. The exact locations of the peñoles of Coyna (or Coinan) and Acatique are unknown.

78. Mendoza's letter from Coyna referred to "Francisco Maldonado" but in the responses to the charges the reference is to Licenciado (Alonso) Maldonado (Paso y Troncoso, *Epistolario*, 4:44).

79. This detail is surprising. Its inclusion without any comment in Ibarra's testimony, however, suggests that the use of horses by the local principales did not seem unusual to him. Although this was barely ten years after Guzmán's conquest, presumably some Indians in the West already had gained familiarity with—and access to—horses through the labor they performed for Spaniards and perhaps subsequently through raids conducted during the war.

80. Letter from Mendoza to the bishop of Mexico, "de junto a Coyna, 24 de octubre de 1541" (Paso y Troncoso, *Epistolario*, 4:44–45).

81. This document is transcribed and included in the appendix to Pérez Bustamante, *Origenes del gobierno virreinal*, 169–70.

82. See AGI Justicia 259.

83. See AGI Justicia 259, pieza 3, response to charge 39, and the charge in AGI Justicia 262, question 174.

84. See AGI Justicia 262, questions 173, 175.

85. Testimony in AGI Justicia 258; see also charge 98, which alleged that just four or five people had ended up with most of the slaves in "certain peñoles" and later sold them for excessive prices.

86. Beginning in 1551, Dr. Melgarejo, named by the audiencia as "procurador general de los indios de Nueva España," initiated the process of reexamining the status of indigenous slaves being held in central Mexico. Although he reported in detail on his understanding of the legal issues involved, the numbers of people who sued for their freedom, and the progress and disposition of their cases, he did not note precisely where these slaves were being held or by whom (other than more than one hundred who had belonged to Cortés) or their origins. Some of the slaves whose cases were pending seem to have been deposited with third parties who paid them wages, although some of the former slaves so placed ran off, suggesting that their circumstances might not have improved much. Within a decade Melgarejo's efforts freed over three thousand Indian slaves and earned him the bitter enmity of the former slaveholders. Although initially he concluded that slaves from the "guerra de Jalisco" had been taken in just war and thus were not eligible for release, by the late 1550s at least some of those slaves

also had been freed. For Melgarejo's reports, see Paso y Troncoso, *Epistolario*, vol. 6, nos. 335 (p. 123), 337 (pp.123–24), 360 (pp. 208–9); vol. 7, nos. 365 (p. 7), 410 (pp. 270–71); vol. 8, nos. 447 (pp. 128–29), 461 (pp. 182–83); and vol. 9, no. 494 (pp. 102–6). Document numbers 365, 410, 447, and 461 refer specifically to slaves from Jalisco. My thanks to José Cuello for providing these references.

87. AGI Justicia 258.

88. AGI Justicia 262, pieza 1.

89. AGI Justicia 259, pieza 3.

90. Aiton includes this story, which comes from Tello (*Antonio de Mendoza*, 154n35). Its plausibility is diminished because Tello claimed that after Ibarra helped the captives escape, he returned to Guadalajara with the branding iron. If Anuncibay's accusation that Ibarra had the iron in Guadalajara after the war ended is true, Tello possibly conflated the two episodes. All other testimony confirms that Oñate and Licenciado Maldonado were responsible for dividing up the slaves at Nochistlan and paying the royal fifth, and presumably they had the royal branding iron in their possession for that purpose; see, for example, Alonso de Santa Cruz's response to question 189 in AGI Justicia 262, pieza 1.

91. See Francisco de Torres's testimony in 1577 in the información of Hernando de Oñate, the son of Cristóbal de Oñate, in AGI Patronato 75, no. 1, ramo 3.

92. Información of Andrés de Villanueva, in AGI Patronato 60, no. 3, ramo 5.

93. See charge 96 in AGI Justicia 258.

94. AGI Justicia 262, question 179.

95. Ibid., pieza 1.

96. AGI Justicia 258.

97. See AGI Justicia 262, question 180; the testimony of Alonso de Olivares and Alonso de Santa Cruz is in AGI Justicia 262, pieza 1.

98. See AGI Justicia 262, pieza 2, question 182; and AGI Justicia 259, pieza 3.

99. Aiton, *Antonio de Mendoza*, 155.

100. AGI Justicia 259, pieza 3.

101. Ibid., response to charge 39.

102. Weigand and García de Weigand, *Tenamaxtli y Guaxicar*, 138.

103. AGI Justicia 259, pieza 3. He stated that when he was in the area of Tlaltenango, Xalpa, and Apozol "vinieron alguna cantidad de indios de aquellos pueblos y de Mezquituta y Agualera a los cuales recibi aunque eran de los que habían estado encastillados en el dicho Mixton y les mande que estuviesen pacificos en sus casas."

104. Aiton, *Antonio de Mendoza*, 156.

105. See charge 95 (AGI Justicia 258) against the viceroy, which alleged that when he went to New Galicia the people who accompanied him harmed the Indians

who lived in the areas through which they passed, "taking their property and women and children and overloading them and taking them by force to carry things without paying them anything, for which reason some places were depopulated and the Indians went to join the rebels. . . . And when the viceroy found out about it he did nothing to remedy the situation."

106. Mendoza's statement is in AGI Justicia 259, pieza 3.

107. Ibid.

108. The testimony from Durán and Alvarez is in AGI Justicia 262, response to question 187.

109. AGI Justicia 262.

110. Ibid.

111. Ibid., pieza 1.

112. AGN Mercedes, vol. 2, exp. 31.

113. See testimony of Alonso de Villarreal, in AGI Justicia 262, pieza 1.

114. Sandoval Acacictli, *Conquista y pacificación*, 30–31, 33.

115. Ibid., 33, 36.

116. Ibid., 32.

117. Ibid., 36–37.

118. See Aiton, *Antonio de Mendoza*, 154n36, and AGI Justicia 262, the testimony of Francisco Cornejo and Alonso de Santa Cruz.

CHAPTER 7

1. AGI Mexico 68, ramo 12, no. 29. The letter also appears in the appendix to Pérez Bustamante, *Origenes del gobierno virreinal*, 172–73. The governor to whom he referred was Francisco Vázquez de Coronado, whose residencia Tejada carried out.

2. AGI Mexico 68, ramo 12, no. 29.

3. The standard work is Parry, *Audiencia of New Galicia*.

4. The New Laws promulgated in 1542 are best known for the provisions intended to offer some protection and relief for the Spanish Crown's indigenous American subjects by prohibiting Indian enslavement and personal service and curtailing the rights of encomenderos as well as limiting the numbers of encomiendas. For a discussion of the provisions, see Clarence H. Haring, *The Spanish Empire in America* (New York: Harcourt, Brace and World, 1947), 51–53. For an English translation of the text of the laws, see the edition of Las Casas, *An Account, Much Abbreviated*, 93–102.

5. Fray Rodrigo de la Cruz from Aguacatlan wrote in May 1550 that "those Spaniards who have wives in Castile should be made to go for them, and the men who have Indian women should be made to marry or their Indians should be taken from them, because they are all living with Indian women and making a very bad example for the natives" (Cuevas, *Documentos inéditos*, 158).

6. AGI Guadalajara 51. This file contains a series of letters and reports from the town council, the vecinos, and the audiencia.

7. Cuevas, *Documentos inéditos*, 156.

8. AGN Mercedes, vol. 1, exp. 165.

9. Ibid., exp. 277.

10. Ibid., exp. 300, 301.

11. AGN Mercedes, vol. 2, exp. 84.

12. Ibid., exp. 66, 169.

13. AGI Guadalajara 5, ramo 2, no. 8.

14. AGI Guadalajara 51.

15. See AGI Guadalajara 5, ramo 2, no. 8; and AGI Guadalajara 5, ramo 3, no. 9. In September 1550, several vecinos of Guadalajara who were involved in silver mining in Zacatecas complained that it was "a great bother to have to bring the silver to the city of Compostela to pay the quinto and tithe because it is so far" (AGI Guadalajara 51).

16. AGI Guadalajara 51.

17. Ibid.

18. On the founding of the audiencia and duties of the justices, see Parry, *Audiencia of New Galicia*, ch. 2. The dual titles—oidor and alcalde mayor— suggest that their positions combined functions that were exercised by two separate groups of justices in the Mexico City audiencia.

19. Parry, *Audiencia of New Galicia*, 41.

20. Ibid., 47–48. I have used his translation of the excerpt from this letter, which is reproduced in full along with another letter from Gómez de Maraver in Orozco y Jiménez, *Documentos históricos inéditos*, 1:207–28.

21. On the boundary disputes, see Román Gutiérrez, *Sociedad y evangelización*, ch. 5; Hillerkuss, *Documentalía*, ch. 2; and Orozco y Jiménez, *Documentos históricos inéditos*, vol. 1. Gómez de Maraver died intestate and in debt but left a good house near the church in Guadalajara that included a shrine and chapel to Saint Anne, which often was used for processions from the church; see AGI Guadalajara 51.

22. Román Gutiérrez, *Sociedad y evangelización*, 219.

23. Ibid., 237.

24. Cuevas, *Documentos inéditos*, 159.

25. Román Gutiérrez, *Sociedad y evangelización*, 240. He notes that later in the sixteenth century, most of the clergy seem to have taught and preached in Nahuatl.

26. Juan Michel, Juan de Zaldívar, Francisco Delgadillo, Pedro de Ledesma, Rodrigo de Frias, Francisco Cornejo, and Pedro de Plasencia, all longtime residents who would be active in Zacatecas as well, signed the letter (AGI Guadalajara 51).

27. See letter of May 1552 from several Franciscans in the region, in Orozco y Jiménez, *Documentos históricos inéditos*, vol. 5, no. 2, p. 9.

28. AGI Guadalajara 5, ramo 5, no. 11.

29. "The convent and church of Guadalajara . . . are made of adobes and mud [with] a dormitory with ten cells and a thirty-foot-long cloister, and the church is middling and made of adobes with some buttresses of rough uncarved stone and lime to strengthen it and support the heavy beams and timbers that are haphazard. . . . The other monasteries that have been built in this kingdom are as poor and humble as our state and vows require" (Orozco y Jiménez, *Documentos históricos inéditos*, vol. 5, no. 2, p. 9).

30. Cuevas, *Documentos inéditos*, 157.

31. Ibid., 157–58. A letter from Fray Juan Armellones to the king written in Guadalajara in September 1554 echoed de la Cruz's criticisms of the audiencia, emphasizing the discord among the oidores that had made the audiencia virtually dysfunctional but making an exception in the case of Lebrón. He wrote that he had seen him "show much zeal for justice in work and in word and assisting as he can the doctrine and divine religion and favoring the poor and executing justice and the law." For a transcription of this letter, see Román Gutiérrez, *Sociedad y evangelización*, 465, app. 3.

32. In May 1557 the Franciscans wrote that "the Licencidado Lebrón de Quiñones, oidor of the Audiencia Real de Xalisco and His Majesty's inspector has been like a lily among thorns, thoughtful, devout, honest, . . . zealous for justice and that in particular is compassionate regarding the abuses done to the common people, especially against the powerless Indians" and referred to his "kindness and rectitude" (Orozco y Jiménez, *Documentos históricos inéditos*, vol. 5, no. 2, p. 3).

33. See his report in AGI Guadalajara 5, ramo 6, no. 13.

34. Parry writes that Lebrón's "brother Gerónimo had been governor of Santa Marta, where he had shown the same characteristics that Lorenzo was to display in New Galicia—a genius for winning the confidence of the Indians, and a tendency to irritate the Spanish colonists" (*Audiencia of New Galicia*, 41).

35. The basic work on the establishment and development of Zacatecas is Peter J. Bakewell, *Silver Mining and Society in Colonial Mexico: Zacatecas 1546–1700* (Cambridge: Cambridge University Press, 1971). See also Powell, *Soldiers, Indians and Silver*, 4–15; J. Lloyd Mecham, *Francisco de Ibarra and Nueva Vizcaya* (Durham, NC: Duke University Press, 1927), 40–49; and Chipman, *Moctezuma's Children*, 101–8.

36. A transcription of the Tolosa's probanza of 1550 was included in another *información de méritos y servicios* (deposition of merits and services) done in Guadalajara in 1594 by don Juan de Zaldívar Cortés Moctezoma, son of Juan de Tolosa and his wife doña Leonor Cortés, the daughter of Hernando Cortés

and doña Isabel Moctezoma. The informaciones are in AGI Patronato 80, no. 5, ramo 1.

37. Don Francisco testified they were "indios de Bolaños," possibly referring to Toribio de Bolaños, who was encomendero of Tlaltenango, although he also might have meant the area of the Río de Tepeque. He stated that "tuvieron noticia como hacia el norte habian unas minas de metal y que sabian dellas unos indios de Bolaños" (AGI Patronato 80, no. 5, ramo 1).

38. According to Román Gutiérrez, "Mientras Tolosa en su interrogatorio menciona haber recibido la información sobre las minas de Zacatecas de indígenas del pueblo de Quitananque, el cacique don Francisco declaró que Tolosa lo supo de los indígenas de Bolaños, llamado también Tepeque, y de Tenanco. La referencia de Tolosa es totalmente desconocida, quizás porque el pueblo mencionado desapareció rápidamente; Tenanco quizás sea el pueblo de Tenayuca, ubicado al oriente de Juchipila" (*Sociedad y evangelización*, 57).

39. Because Miguel de Ibarra died soon after the discovery of the Zacatecas mines, his early participation is often overlooked; Bakewell, for example, does not mention him. *Silver Mining and Society in Colonial Mexico: Zacatecas 1546–1700* (Cambridge: Cambridge University Press, 1971). Diego de Ibarra, probably his nephew, went on to become a very important early miner there, probably in partnership with Oñate.

40. According to Bakewell, "the establishment of Zacatecas was largely an entrepreneurial and commercial venture undertaken by two settlers of wealth and experience, Cristóbal de Oñate and Diego de Ibarra." "Zacatecas: An Economic and Social Outline of a Silver Mining District, 1547–1700," in *Provinces of Early Mexico*, ed. Ida Altman and James Lockhart (Los Angeles: UCLA Latin American Studies Center, 1976), 201.

41. Oñate held the encomiendas of Culhuacan near Mexico City, assigned to him by Cortés, and Tacambaro in Michoacan, as well as Xalisco and other communities in New Galicia; see Himmerich y Valencia, *Encomenderos of New Spain*, 207.

42. According to Mecham, Diego de Ibarra was a native of Guipuzcoa who arrived in New Spain in 1540. He accompanied the viceroy to the war of pacification in New Galicia and served with his uncle, Miguel de Ibarra (*Francisco de Ibarra*, 42–43).

43. Bakewell writes that Ibarra reportedly supported up to seventy or eighty Spaniards at times and that Oñate "also fed and housed poor people on their arrival" ("Zacatecas," 201–2).

44. On the development of the routes to the mines, see Powell, *Soldiers, Indians and Silver*, ch. 2.

45. See Powell, *Soldiers, Indians and Silver*, 12–14.

46. AGI Guadalajara 5, ramo 4, no. 10.

47. Although Bakewell, in *Silver Mining,* assumes that the number of these houses is equivalent to the number of slaves, that seems unlikely, given the size of the operations at Zacatecas and the presence of both African and Indian slaves; on this see Román Gutiérrez, *Sociedad y evangelización,* 82.

48. AGI Patronato 80, no. 5, ramo 1.

49. See the visita of Lic. Hernando Martínez de la Marcha, in AGI Guadalajara 5, ramo 4, no. 10. Proaño and Martel had been involved in a dispute with Toribio de Bolaños over the possession of the encomienda of the Río de Tepeque. Bolaños claimed that some of the Indians actually were from Tlaltenango and had fled there during the war.

50. AGI Patronato 60, no. 3, ramo 5. Juan de Urbina, who also had been in Zacatecas, testified that the richest mines had been discovered by Villanueva along with his slaves and one of his criados named Juan de Torres. Román Gutiérrez lists Bartolomé García's son Bartolome García Sandi as a priest in the mines of Guaxacatlan and the pueblos de Tequila in 1601, with a salary of two hundred pesos; he was said to speak "buena mexicano y tecuexe" (*Sociedad y evangelización,* 270, cuadro 4).

51. Corral's petition, which includes a copy of the probanza done by Proaño in Guadalajara in 1545, is in AGI Patronato 71, ramo 5. For his holdings in 1550, see AGI Guadalajara 5, ramo 4, no. 10.

52. Bakewell, *Silver Mining,* 29.

53. See his probanza of 1566 in AGI Patronato 60, no. 5, ramo 4.

54. According to Hillerkuss, "Familia Zaldívar," Vicente de Zaldívar y Oñate went to New Spain in 1534, perhaps at the same time as his brother Juan de Zaldívar, but he did not marry for another twenty years. He lived until nearly 1600.

55. See Chipman, *Moctezuma's Children,* 104–7. Doña Catalina de Salazar was the daughter of the royal factor, Gonzalo de Salazar. Cristóbal de Oñate traveled to Mexico in 1527 as the assistant to the accountant Rodrigo de Albornoz and would have become acquainted with his future father-in-law Salazar, who traveled with them, at that time. The two men remained friendly. There is some possibility that doña Catalina's first husband, Ruy Díaz de Mendoza, was still alive in 1535, at the time she left Spain for Mexico to join her parents, traveling in the entourage of her in-law don Antonio de Mendoza. He lived at least until 1572, making her second marriage to Oñate bigamous. She and Cristóbal de Oñate apparently started a romantic relationship in the mid-1540s that produced one or two children. They married at the end of that decade at the mines of Pánuco, in which Oñate had been a leading investor, and had nine children. See Marc Simmons, *The Last Conquistador: Juan de Oñate and the Settling of the Far Southwest* (Norman: University of Oklahoma Press, 1991), 17, 32, and Hillerkuss, "Familia Zaldívar."

56. See Simmons, *Last Conquistador*, 33, 44.

57. Hillerkuss, "Familia Zaldívar." Juan de Zaldívar and his wife doña Marina de Mendoza had nine children. One of their daughters, doña María de Zaldívar Mendoza, married one of the leading miners of Zacatecas, Baltasar Temiño de Bañuelos.

58. AGI Patronato 60, no. 5, ramo 4.

59. This proposal formed part of the deposition of 1566 and indeed probably was the reason that he presented his información de servicios.

60. Ledesma's father-in-law, Melchor Pérez, who also had gone to New Mexico, was a vecino of Colima in 1566 but testified in Guadalajara.

61. AGI Patronato 60, no. 5, ramo 4.

62. According to Gerhard, in 1570 there were only six vecinos at Guachinango and by the early seventeenth century mining had shifted to the west to Ocotitlan and Hostotipac (*North Frontier*, 89).

63. AGI Guadalajara 5, ramo 4, no. 10; see also Hillerkuss, *Documentalía*, 110–11. Part of the visita of Martínez de la Marcha relating to Guachinango is contained in this volume, along with useful notes.

64. AGI Guadalajara 5, ramo 4, no. 10; Hillerkuss, *Documentalía*, 106.

65. See the letter from the oidor Lic. Hernando Martínez de la Marcha to the king written in Compostela in February 1551, in AGI Guadalajara 51. Hillerkuss discusses the continuing violence in several papers, including "Nueva Galicia," and, "La guerra de Miztón de 1541: Causas y consecuencias," paper presented to Antropología e Historia del Occidente de México, Consejo Nacional para la Cultura y los Artes / Instituto Nacional de Antropología e Historia, Zacatecas, December 9, 2007.

66. See Gerhard, *North Frontier*, 92–93.

67. AGI Guadalajara 5, ramo 5, no. 11.

68. Hillerkuss writes that in the decade following the fourth founding of Guadalajara, "a fairly well defined dividing line was established in the canyons of Zacatecas, Jalisco and Nayarit and in southern Durango between the areas dominated by Spaniards and a zone of refuge of those natives who roundly refused to live under the colonial system. Even though occasionally both parties crossed it in peaceful or violent fashion . . . there were no significant confrontations, such as those of 1540 and 1541, or systematic invasions on the part of the Spaniards, so that this undeclared frontier remained quite stable until the beginning of the eighteenth century" ("Miztón de 1541," 1).

69. See, for example, AGI Justicia 237, in which witness Pedro de Plasencia refers to "a Coringa, Indian cacique of the sierras. . . . He brings with him many Indians, robbing those who are at peace and serve." On Coringa, see Lic. Martínez de la Marcha's report in AGI Guadalajara 46, no. 31, and his letter of February 1551 in AGI Guadalajara 51, in which he reported that

Coringa continued to be active in the area between Compostela and Culiacan and had allied with "coras, guainamotas, toconios, tecuales," and "guaxires y guajacatecas."

70. AGI Guadalajara 46, no. 30.

71. See discussion in Román Gutiérrez, *Sociedad y evangelización*, 77–78. Much of the second chapter of Román Gutiérrez's book is devoted to a detailed summary and analysis of the visita of Martínez de la Marcha. In February 1551, having written a detailed report to the king, Martínez de la Marcha noted that Tenamaztle, who was thought to have formed an alliance with Chapuli, was in the custody of the bishop in Guadalajara and that Chapuli was dead (AGI Guadalajara 51).

72. In the testimony of the first two witnesses, the community implicated in the attacks on Tequila and other places is called Talistacan and thereafter Tezol. Gerhard suggests that the "Tezoles" were actually Huicholes (*North Frontier*, 122).

73. This episode is reported in AGI Guadalajara 46, no. 34.

74. Ibid.

75. Ibid.

76. Ibid.

77. A particularly egregious example of intimidation was the effort made by encomendero Cristóbal de Oñate and his mayordomo Domingo de Arteaga to convince the rulers of Xalisco not to testify against them when Licenciado Tejada made his visit to the community in 1545; see Calvo and others, *Xalisco*, 94–95. The narrators of the account described how prior to Tejada's arrival, Oñate and Arteaga met with them secretly and offered to give them cotton mantles every year and cows (probably oxen) for plowing, which they never did, as a reward for their silence and warned them not to complain to Tejada. Don Rodrigo stated that Arteaga threatened to kill him if he did not tell the inspector they were treated well.

78. AGI Guadalajara 46, no. 34.

79. Toribio de Bolaños, who evidently forged friendly relations with some of the Zacateca Indians in the area of the Río de Tepeque mines, harshly criticized Juan de Tolosa in a letter to the king, written in October 1556, in which he referred to "the damages which the said Zacatecas have received with the entradas . . . which Juanes de Tolosa and other persons before have done in the said frontier." See Román Gutiérrez's discussion; he quotes the letter in part (*Sociedad y evangelización*, 93–95). The letter from Bolaños also appears in Paso y Troncoso, *Epistolario*, 8:122.

80. Authorities believed that people living at the peñol were responsible for an attack on Alvaro de Bracamonte's property at the mines of Tepeguacan;

Hillerkuss argues that there was no conclusive proof of their involvement (*Documentalía*, 123).

81. See Hillerkuss's *Documentalía*, which includes both a perceptive analysis and contextualization of the episode and extensive excerpts from AGI Justicia 305, detailing the oidor Licenciado Contreras's attempts to dislodge the people from the peñol and his ultimate decision to attack (122–52).

82. Hillerkuss, *Documentalía*, 127–28.

83. This is the only instance I have seen in the records for early New Galicia in which a woman was called a "nahuatlata," although it is only logical to assume that if there were men who spoke Nahuatl (or languages that were very similar) there were women who did so as well. The feminization of the standard "nahuatlato" is, of course, a Spanish innovation.

84. Hillerkuss, *Documentalía*, 132, 133.

85. Ibid., 134–36.

86. The exact nature of the relationship between the African slaves from the mines and the Indians at Zacatlan is not clear. Given that the Africans were armed with swords and were reported to have participated in the more violent confrontations between the refugees at the peñol and the Spaniards and their Indian emissaries, possibly the Africans had been allowed to join the group in part because of their military capabilities. On the military aspect of the roles and perceptions of Africans in early Spanish America, see Restall, "Black Conquistadors."

87. Hillerkuss, *Documentalía*, 146–51.

88. On Martínez de la Marcha's visita, see Parry, *Audiencia of New Galicia*, 48–54, and Román Gutiérrez, *Sociedad y evangelización*, 89–90. Lebrón's opinions were recorded in a *pesquisa secreta* (secret inquiry) of 1557. Ramírez's letter was written in Poncitlan on April 4, 1551, thus, as Román Gutiérrez points out, he could have known of the events of Martínez de la Marcha's visita only from word of mouth since the report had not yet been completed. In his letter of May 1550, Fray Rodrigo de la Cruz praised Diego Ramírez, who had been "scandalized by the tributes imposed on these poor people." He pleaded with the Crown to authorize Ramírez, together with Lebrón de Quiñones, to remediate the ill treatment of New Galicia's natives (Cuevas, *Documentos inéditos*, 157).

89. Calvo and others, *Xalisco*, 98–103.

90. Ibid., 103. This was the period that epidemics caused substantial mortality throughout Mexico, so disease could have accounted for many of these deaths.

91. AGI Guadalajara 31, no. 2.

92. AGI Guadalajara 5, ramo 4, no. 10.

93. Román Gutiérrez, *Sociedad y evangelización*, 106.

94. Gerhard, *North Frontier*, 91.
95. See the oidores' report in AGI Guadalajara, ramo 3, no. 9. Chapuli and Tenamaztle, who they noted had escaped after being taken prisoner at the peñol of Nochistlan during the war, attracted "muchos esclavos y negros fugitivos."
96. León-Portilla, *Flecha en el blanco*, 13, 21. In November 1552 Viceroy Velasco ordered that Tenamaztle be deported with the next available fleet.
97. Calvo and others, *Xalisco*, 20.

REFELCTIONS ON A VIOLENT HISTORY

1. For comparison, see Susan M. Deeds, "First Generation Rebellions in Seventeenth-Century Nueva Vizcaya," in *Native Resistance and the Pax Colonial in New Spain*, ed. Susan Schroeder (Lincoln: University of Nebraska Press, 1998), esp. 24–25, where she notes that the "revitalizing strain of millenarianism was complemented by a utopian vision in which deserts would yield in abundance and no Spaniards would circumscribe native 'freedoms.'"
2. Slaves could be difficult to control, and their mortality rates tended to be very high. Slaves had to be captured or purchased and then maintained, whereas if the encomienda functioned successfully, Indians would be self-sustaining on their own lands. Furthermore, although slaves were abundant following the conclusion of the war, continuing Spanish access to slaves was far from assured, given the Crown's fluctuating policies on indigenous enslavement.

GLOSSARY

1. "From Nahuatl" indicates that the original Nahuatl term was modified in Spanish usage.

NOTE ON SOURCES

1. Notably, copies of all three of the residencias relating to Nuño de Guzmán, as well as the residencia of Hernando Cortés and the visitación of 1525 conducted after Francisco Cortés's entrada, are in the Scholes collection of the Latin American Library of Tulane University. This is an important collection for the study of early Mexico.
2. *Reshaping New Spain* originally was published as *Gobierno y sociedad en Nueva España* by El Colegio de Michoacan in 1991.
3. See Richard Flint and Shirley Cushing Flint, eds. and trans., *Documents of the Coronado Expedition, 1539–1642: "They Were Not Familiar with His Majesty, Nor Did They Wish to Be His Subjects"* (Dallas: Southern Methodist University Press, 2005); and Richard Flint, *No Settlement, No Conquest: A History of the Coronado Entrada* (Albuquerque: University of New Mexico Press, 2008).

Glossary

adelantado leader granted civil and judicial powers by the Spanish Crown

alcaide warden of a fortress or castle

alguacil mayor chief constable

ajíes chili peppers

alcalde magistrate

alcalde mayor district governor

alcalde ordinario magistrate of the first instance

audiencia high court

ayuntamiento town hall or town council

barranca rocky canyon

braza measurement of approximately six feet

cabecera main pueblo or town

cabildo town or city council

cabildo eclesiástico ecclesiastical council

cacique, cacica indigenous ruler

calpixque tribute or tax collector or receptor; administrator (from Nahuatl)[1]

capitulaciones agreement, contract

carga three or four fanegas

casa house

casa poblada large household establishment

caudillo military leader

Cazonci native ruler of Purépecha (Tarascans)

Chichimecs generic term used by Spaniards for independent Indians considered to be uncivilized

chinampas artificially constructed garden plots near the shores of lakes or canals

ciudad city

comendador commander of a military order

comuneros communities of Castile, specifically those that revolted against Charles I in 1519

contador accountant

continuo member of the Crown's personal guard

contratar to bargain or contract

corregidor governor, district administrator

corregimiento administrative district

criado retainer, servant

cuadra (town or city) block

encomendero holder of an encomienda

encomienda grant of right to extract tribute and labor from a specific group of Indians

entrada expedition of reconnaissance or conquest

estancia subject community; estate

factor royal agent; merchant's agent or representative

fanega dry measure, approximately one and a half bushels

frijoles beans

gobernador governor

guachimontones circular, stepped pyramids

hechicero sorcerer

hombres men

huerta orchard or garden, usually irrigated

indios amigos Indian allies or friendly Indians

información deposition

información de méritos y servicios deposition of merits and services

itatzin father

justicia magistrate, judicial official

lengua interpreter (literally, tongue)

letrado university-trained lawyer

macana wooden sword edged with obsidian

macehual, macegual indigenous commoner (from Nahuatl)

maestre de campo field marshal

manta de la tierra indigenous cotton cloth

matanza slaughter, massacre

mayordomo steward, manager

memoria memoir, account

mitote dance (from Nahuatl)

morador resident

naboría servant, auxiliary

naguatato (nahuatato, nahuatlato) interpreter, Nahuatl speaker (Nahuatl)

obraje textile workshop

oficial de cordonería a maker of rope or lace

oidor judge on high court

penacho feathered headdress

peñol mountainous, fortified stronghold

peso de minas unit of currency worth 450 maravedís

peso de tepuzque unit of currency worth 272 maravedís, also known as
    a peso of common gold

pesquisa secreta secret inquiry

pobre poor

principal Spanish term for an indigenous noble

probanza deposition detailing services to the Crown

procurador deputy, representative

protector de los naturales Spanish official responsible for Indians' welfare

proveedor general general purveyor

quauhtlatoani interim ruler (Nahuatl)

quinto tax, the "royal fifth"

regidor town council member

relación narrative account

repartimiento in this period, term used interchangeably with *encomienda*

requerimiento "requirement"; statement that explained Spain's claims to Indians' allegiance and called on them to acknowledge the sovereignty of the Spanish Crown and the Roman Catholic Church or to suffer the consequences of their refusal

rescatar to conduct uneven or coerced trade or exchange

residencia investigation into an official's conduct in office

Semana Santa Holy Week

señor lord, ruler

señora natural female native ruler

servicio supply and maintenance of a household

solar house lot

tameme (tlameme) porter (from Nahuatl)

tejuelo metal ingot of unspecified size

teniente de gobernador lieutenant governor

tequitlato overseer (from Nahuatl)

tiánguiz indigenous market (from Nahuatl)

tlatoani indigenous ruler (Nahuatl)

tlatol statement or chant (from Nahuatl, *tlatolli*)

tunal nopal cactus

vara de justicia staff of justice

vecino citizen, head of household, neighbor

veedor inspector

visitación, visita tour of inspection or inquiry

Note on Sources

Most of the sources for this history of early New Galicia are well known, and many are readily available. Beginning with Mexican scholar Joaquín García Icazbalceta's publication in the nineteenth century of accounts of the Nuño de Guzmán expedition and other documents relating to the history of early New Galicia, many important records from the period have been reliably transcribed and published and for the most part are quite accessible. Transcriptions of letters and reports have appeared in various collections over the years, including the *Epistolario de Nueva España*, the volumes of documents relating to early ecclesiastical activity compiled by Francisco Orozco y Jiménez, and the *Boletín del Archivo General de la Nación*, as well as in appendices to scholarly studies, such as Ciriaco Pérez Bustamante's study of don Antonio de Mendoza. By now, many important sources relevant to early New Galicia have appeared in more than one collection. The valuable work of scholars based in western Mexico, such as Thomas Calvo and Thomas Hillerkuss, has produced significant additions to the corpus of primary materials on early New Galicia now available in published form.

The residencias of Nuño de Guzmán's governorship of New Galicia and of don Antonio de Mendoza's term as viceroy to a great extent form the core of this history. With the exception of the charges relating to the Mixton War that were brought against Viceroy Mendoza, the residencias are less readily accessible and probably as a result have been less frequently used by scholars.[1] In particular, the residencia of Guzmán's term as governor of New Galicia—one of three conducted of his terms in office as governor of Pánuco, president of the first audiencia of Mexico, and governor of New Galicia—has been underutilized by scholars. This neglect might explain why so little has been written about the earliest

years of Spanish settlement in the West, as there is scarcely any other
documentation still extant. The residencia of Mendoza and the second
audiencia is far lengthier and more complex than that of Guzmán's governorship and is, of course, only partly concerned with the Mixton War
and New Galicia. Ethelia Ruiz Medrano makes extensive use of the entire
residencia in *Reshaping New Spain*, which recently has appeared in English
translation, and for some preliminary work on the Mixton War itself.[2]
Even scholars interested in the Mixton War, however, for the most part
have focused mainly on one part of the residencia—the charges against
Mendoza and his response—and have not devoted much attention to other
testimony, especially that of indigenous witnesses. As a result, Mendoza's
understanding of the causes and progress of the war has had a strong influence on how the rebellion has been described and understood.

Another useful contemporary source that complements letters and
reports from the period and the material found in the residencias are the
probanzas de méritos ("proofs" of merit) and informaciones of Spaniards
who were active in the region. Many of these documents can be found
in the Patronato section of the Archivo General de Indias in Seville.
These depositions and the accompanying testimony, although obviously
presented to cast the activities of the individual responsible for the deposition in a positive light, can be valuable in terms of gaining a personal
perspective on events as well as insight into family background and ties,
social relations, and the politics of the time. Sometimes they bring to light
episodes and interactions that do not appear in other records.

Despite our limited knowledge of the native peoples of New Galicia at
the time of contact, this study has benefited greatly from several sources
that afford an indigenous perspective. The most of important of these are
the reports from Xalisco transcribed and translated by Thomas Calvo and
his colleagues and don Francisco de Sandoval Acacitli's narrative of his
experiences during the Mixton War. In both instances, I have had to rely
on Spanish translations from the Nahuatl (the only version still available
of Sandoval Acacitli's account), meaning that my analysis and translations
are based on texts that are one step removed from the original language
of the accounts. Using the testimony of indigenous witnesses that appears
in the residencias and the visitas that were conducted by the oidores of the
audiencia of New Galicia in the early 1550s can be problematic for reasons
discussed in the book. Here again, although testimony has been filtered
through one or more interpreters, it nonetheless merits examination and

discussion. Last, although the 1525 survey of the southern part of the future New Galicia was conducted by Spaniards, it was based in part on information solicited from indigenous informants. As the most detailed extant description of early New Galicia, it is significant not only for the history of New Galicia but also for that of New Spain more generally.

The secondary literature relating to the early history of New Galicia has grown in recent years and is essential to the present study. Work by Thomas Calvo, Thomas Hillerkuss, José Francisco Román Gutiérrez, and Ethelia Ruiz Medrano has greatly expanded the possibilities for examining aspects of early Spanish-indigenous relations in New Galicia in greater detail. Rolena Adorno and Patrick Charles Pautz's scholarly work on Cabeza de Vaca includes a detailed consideration of the larger context in which the experiences of the survivors of the Pánfilo de Narváez expedition unfolded. The contributions of Richard Flint and Shirley Cushing Flint are of comparable value for understanding the personnel and events of the Francisco Vázquez de Coronado expedition.[3] The archaeological investigations of Phil C. Weigand and his more recent publications written in collaboration with Acelia García de Weigand offering a synthesis of archaeological work on the early societies of western Mesoamerica have contributed much to our understanding of the cultures of the West, as have more recent surveys by Helen Perlstein Pollard and Peter F. Jiménez Betts and J. Andrew Darling. Donald E. Chipman's corpus of work on Nuño de Guzmán, Benedict Warren's study of the conquest of Michoacan, and the work of historical geographers Peter Gerhard and Carl O. Sauer all are fundamental to understanding the context and events of the period and the major figures who dominated this early history. Institutional studies of the early viceroyalty by Arthur Scott Aiton and Ciriaco Pérez Bustamante also remain useful.

Bibliography

Archives

Archivo General de Indias (AGI), Seville

Guadalajara, Audiencia de
Indiferente General
Justicia
Mexico, Audiencia de
Patronato

Archivo General de la Nación (AGN), Mexico City

Hospital de Jesús
Mercedes

Archivo Histórico Nacional (AHN), Madrid

Diversos, Colecciones

Latin American Library of Tulane University, New Orleans

France V. Scholes Collection

Published Sources and Secondary Works

Actas de cabildo de la ciudad de Mexico. Edición del Municipio Libre. 54 vols. (1880–
1916). Mexico City: Bejarano, 1889.

Adorno, Rolena, and Ivan Boserup. *New Studies of the Autograph Manuscript of Felipe Guaman Poma de Ayala's Nueva corónica y buen gobierno.* Copenhagen: Museum Tusculanum Press, 2003.

Adorno, Rolena, and Patrick Charles Pautz. *Álvar Núñez Cabeza de Vaca: His Account, His Life, and the Expedition of Pánfilo de Narváez.* 3 vols. Lincoln: University of Nebraska Press, 1999.

Aiton, Arthur Scott. *Antonio de Mendoza: First Viceroy of New Spain.* New York: Russell and Russell, 1927.

———. "Coronado's First Report on the Government of New Galicia." *Hispanic American Historical Review* 19, no. 3 (1939): 306–13.

Altman, Ida. "Conquest, Coercion and Collaboration: Indian Allies and the Campaigns in Nueva Galicia." In Matthew and Oudjik, *Indian Conquistadors,* 145–74.

———. "Mexico City after the Conquest." *Hispanic American Historical Review* 71, no. 3 (1991): 422–23.

———. "The Revolt of Enriquillo and the Historiography of Early Spanish America." *The Americas* 63, no. 4 (2007): 587–614.

Altman, Ida, and James Lockhart, eds. *Provinces of Early Mexico.* Los Angeles: UCLA Latin American Studies Center, 1976.

Amaya, Jesús. *Los conquistadores Fernández de Híjar y Bracamonte.* Guadalajara: Gráfica, 1952.

Anawalt, Patricia Rieff. "Ancient Cultural Contacts between Ecuador, West Mexico, and the American Southwest: Clothing Similarities." *Latin American Antiquity* 3, no. 2 (1992): 114–29.

Bakewell, Peter J. *Silver Mining and Society in Colonial Mexico: Zacatecas 1546–1700.* Cambridge: Cambridge University Press, 1971.

———. "Zacatecas: An Economic and Social Outline of a Silver Mining District, 1547–1700." In *Provinces of Early Mexico,* edited by Ida Altman and James Lockhart, 199–229. Los Angeles: UCLA Latin American Studies Center, 1976.

Baus de Czitrom, Carolyn. *Tecuexes y cocas: Dos grupos de la región Jalisco en el siglo XVI.* Serie Etnohistoria. Colección Científica 112. Mexico City: Instituto Nacional de Antropología e Historia, 1982.

Berthe, Jean-Pierre. "Aspects de l'esclavage des Indiens en Nouvelle-Espagne pendant la première moitié du XVIe siècle." *Journal de la Société des Américanistes* 54, no. 2 (1965): 189–209.

Blázquez, Adrián, and Thomas Calvo. *Guadalajara y el nuevo mundo: Nuño Beltrán de Guzmán; Semblanza de un conquistador.* Guadalajara: Institución Provincial de Cultura, 1992.

Bolton, Herbert E. *Coronado on the Turquoise Trail: Knight of Pueblos and Plains.* Albuquerque: University of New Mexico Press, 1949.

Brand, Donald D. "Ethnohistoric Synthesis of Western Mexico." In *Archaeology of Northern Mesoamerica*. Part 2, vol. 11, edited by Gorden F. Ekholm and Ignacio Bernal, 632–56. *Handbook of Middle American Indians*. Austin: University of Texas Press, 1971.

Calvo, Thomas. *La Nueva Galicia en los siglos XVI y XVII*. Zapopán: El Colegio de Jalisco, 1989.

Calvo, Thomas, Eustaquio Celestino, Magdalena Gómez, Jean Meyer, and Ricardo Xochitemol. *Xalisco: La voz de un pueblo en el siglo XVI*. Mexico City: Centro de Investigaciones y Estudios Superiores en Antropología Social / Centro de Estudios Mexicanos y Centroamericanos, 1993.

Carrasco, Pedro. "Indian-Spanish Marriages in the First Century of the Colony." In *Indian Women of Early Mexico*, edited by Susan Schroeder, Stephanie Wood, and Robert Haskett, 87–103. Norman: University of Oklahoma Press, 1997.

Carrera Stampa, Manuel. *Nuño de Guzmán*. Mexico City: Jus, 1960.

Chavero, Alfredo. *El Lienzo de Tlaxcala*. 1892. A facsimile of the first edition. Mexico City: Cosmos, 1979.

Chipman, Donald E. *Moctezuma's Children: Aztec Royalty under Spanish Rule, 1520–1700*. Austin: University of Texas Press, 2005.

———. *Nuño de Guzmán and the Province of Pánuco in New Spain, 1518–1533*. Glendale, CA: Clark, 1967.

———. "The Traffic in Indian Slaves in the Province of Pánuco, New Spain, 1523–1533." *The Americas* 23, no. 1 (October 1966): 142–55.

———. "The Will of Nuño de Guzmán: President, Governor and Captain General of New Spain and the Province of Pánuco, 1558." *The Americas* 35, no. 2 (October 1978): 238–48.

Chuchiak, John F., IV. "Forgotten Allies: The Origins and Roles of Native Mesoamerican Auxiliaries and Indios Conquistadores in the Conquest of Yucatan, 1526–1550." In Matthew and Oudjik, *Indian Conquistadors*, 175–225.

Clendinnen, Inga. "Disciplining the Indians: Franciscan Ideology and Missionary Violence in Sixteenth-Century Yucatán." *Past and Present* 94 (February 1982): 27–48.

Cline, Sarah. "The Spiritual Conquest Reexamined: Baptism and Christian Marriage in Early Sixteenth Century Mexico." *Hispanic American Historical Review* 73, no. 3 (1993): 453–80.

Cook, Noble David. *Born to Die: Disease and New World Conquest, 1492–1650*. Cambridge: Cambridge University Press, 1998.

Cuatro crónicas de la conquista del reino de Nueva Galicia. Guadalajara: Instituto Jalisciense de Antropología e Historia, 1960.

Cuevas, Mariano, comp. *Documentos inéditos del siglo XVI para la historia de México*. Mexico City: Museo Nacional de Arqueología, Historia y Etnología, 1914.

De Bry, Theodor. *Americae pars quinta*. Frankfurt: privately printed, 1595.

Deeds, Susan M. *Defiance and Deference in Mexico's Colonial North: Indians under Spanish Rule in Nueva Vizcaya*. Austin: University of Texas Press, 2003.

————. "First Generation Rebellions in Seventeenth-Century Nueva Vizcaya." In *Native Resistance and the Pax Colonial in New Spain*, edited by Susan Schroeder, 1–29. Lincoln: University of Nebraska Press, 1998.

Flint, Richard. *Great Cruelties Have Been Reported: The 1544 Investigation of the Coronado Expedition*. Dallas: Southern Methodist University Press, 2002.

————. *No Settlement, No Conquest: A History of the Coronado Entrada*. Albuquerque: University of New Mexico Press, 2008.

Flint, Richard, and Shirley Cushing Flint, eds. and trans. *Documents of the Coronado Expedition, 1539–1642:"They Were Not Familiar with His Majesty, Nor Did They Wish to Be His Subjects."* Dallas: Southern Methodist University Press, 2005.

Foster, Michael S., and Phil C. Weigand, eds. *The Archaeology of West and Northwest Mesoamerica*. Boulder, CO: Westview, 1985.

Francis, J. Michael. *Invading Colombia: Spanish Accounts of the Gonzalo Jiménez de Quesada Expedition of Conquest*. University Park: Pennsylvania State University Press, 2007.

Fuentes, Patricia de, ed. and trans. *The Conquistadors*. Norman: University of Oklahoma Press, 1993.

García Icazbalceta, Joaquín. *Colección de documentos para la historia de Mexico*. 1858–66. 2nd ed. 2 vols. Mexico City: Porrúa, 1971.

Gerhard, Peter. "A Black Conquistador in Mexico." *Hispanic American Historical Review* 58, no. 3 (1978): 457–58.

————. *The North Frontier of New Spain*. 1982. Princeton: Princeton University Press, 1993.

Gibson, Charles. *Aztecs under Spanish Rule*. Stanford, CA: Stanford University Press, 1964.

Gradie, Charlotte M. "Discovering the Chichimecas." *The Americas* 51, no. 1 (1994): 67–88.

Guitar, Lynn. "Willing It So: Intimate Glimpses of *Encomienda* Life in Early-Sixteenth-Century Hispaniola." *Colonial Latin American Historical Review* 7, no. 3 (Summer 1998): 245–63.

Guzmán, Nuño de. "Memoria." In *Cuatro crónicas de la conquista del reino de Nueva Galicia*, 163–99. Guadalajara: Instituto Jalisciense de Antropología e Historia, 1960.

Hammond, George P., and Agapito Rey, eds. *Narratives of the Coronado Expedition, 1540–1542*. Glendale, CA: Clark, 1940.

Haring, Clarence H. *The Spanish Empire in America*. New York: Harcourt, Brace and World, 1947.

Harkness Collection in the Library of Congress: Manuscripts concerning Mexico. Selected transcriptions and translations by J. Benedict Warren. Washington, DC: Library of Congress, 1974.

Hassig, Ross. *Aztec Warfare: Imperial Expansion and Political Control.* Norman: University of Oklahoma Press, 1988.

Hillerkuss, Thomas, comp. *Documentalia del sur de Jalisco (siglo XVI).* Zapopán: El Colegio de Jalisco / Mexico City: Instituto Nacional de Antropología e Historia, 1994.

———. "La familia Zaldívar y su red de parentesco durante los siglos XVI y XVII." *Revista del Seminario de Historia Americana* 6, no. 4 (Winter 2006): 7–38.

———. "La guerra de Miztón (1541) a la luz de nuevas fuentes." Paper presented at the Primer Encuentro de Especialistas de la Región Norte de Jalisco, University of Guadalajara, Centro Universitario del Norte, February 22, 2006.

———. "La guerra de Miztón de 1541: Causas y consecuencias." Paper presented to Antropología e Historia del Occidente de México, Consejo Nacional para la Cultura y las Artes / Instituto Nacional de Antropología e Historia, Zacatecas, December 9, 2007.

———. "La Nueva Galicia entre 1530 y 1550: Un reino insurrecto." Paper presented to the Segundo Encuentro de Especialistas de la Región Norte de Jalisco, University of Guadalajara, Centro Universitario del Norte, March 7, 2007.

Himmerich y Valencia, Robert. *The Encomenderos of New Spain, 1521–1555.* Austin: University of Texas Press, 1991.

Horn, Rebecca. *Postconquest Coyoacan: Nahua-Spanish Relations in Central Mexico, 1519–1650.* Stanford, CA: Stanford University Press, 1997.

Icaza, Francisco A. de. *Conquistadores y pobladores de Nueva España: Diccionario autobiográfico sacado de los textos originales.* 2 vols. Madrid: Adelantado de Segovia, 1923.

Jiménez Betts, Peter F., and J. Andrew Darling. "Archaeology of Southern Zacatecas: The Malpaso, Juchipila, and Valparaiso-Bolaños Valleys." In *Greater Mesoamerica: The Archaeology of West and Northwest Mexico,* edited by Michael S. Foster and Shirley Gorenstein. Salt Lake City: University of Utah Press, 2000.

Kellogg, Susan. "Households in Late Prehispanic and Early Colonial Mexico City: Their Structure and Its Implications for the Study of Historical Demography." *The Americas* 44, no. 4 (1988): 483–94.

Kelly, Isabel. *The Archaeology of the Autlán-Tuxcacueso Area of Jalisco. Part 1: The Autlán Zone.* Iberoamericana 26. Berkeley: University of California Press, 1945.

Las Casas, Bartolomé de. *An Account, Much Abbreviated, of the Destruction of the Indies.* Edited by Franklin Knight. Translated by Andrew Hurley. Indianapolis: Hackett, 2003.

Leonard, Irving A. *Books of the Brave: Being an Account of Books and of Men in the Spanish Conquest and Settlement of the Sixteenth-Century New World.* Berkeley: University of California Press, 1992.

León-Portilla, Miguel. *La flecha en el blanco: Francisco Tenamaztle y Bartolomé de las Casas en lucha por los derechos de los indígenas, 1541–1556.* Mexico City: Diana, 1995.

Liss, Peggy K. *Mexico under Spain, 1521–1556: Society and the Origins of Nationality.* Chicago: University of Chicago Press, 1975.

Lockhart, James. *The Men of Cajamarca.* Austin: University of Texas Press, 1972.

———. *The Nahuas after the Conquest.* Stanford, CA: Stanford University Press, 1992.

———. *Spanish Peru, 1532–1560.* 1968. Madison: University of Wisconsin Press, 1994.

López-Portillo y Weber, José. *La conquista de la Nueva Galicia.* Mexico City: Talleres Gráficos de la Nación, 1935.

———. *La rebelión de la Nueva Galicia.* 1935. Mexico City: Colección Peña Roja, 1980.

Martínez Baracs, Rodrigo. *Convivencia y utopía: El gobierno indio y español de la "ciudad de Mechuacan" 1521–1580.* Mexico City: Instituto Nacional de Antropología e Historia / Fondo de Cultura Económica, 2005.

Matthew, Laura E. "Whose Conquest? Nahua, Zapoteca, and Mixteca Allies in the Conquest of Central America." In Matthew and Oudjik, *Indian Conquistadors,* 102–26.

Matthew, Laura E., and Michel R. Oudjik, eds. *Indian Conquistadors: Indigenous Allies in the Conquest of Mesoamerica.* Norman: University of Oklahoma Press, 2007.

Mecham, J. Lloyd. *Francisco de Ibarra and Nueva Vizcaya.* Durham, NC: Duke University Press, 1927.

Miranda, José. "La función económica del encomendero en los orígenes del régimen colonial de Nueva España (1525–1531)." *Anales del Instituto Nacional de Antropología e Historia* 2 (1941–46): 421–62.

Morales, Francisco, OFM, "The Native Encounter with Christianity: Franciscans and Nahuas in Sixteenth-Century Mexico." *The Americas* 65, no. 2 (October 2008): 137–59.

Muriá, José María, dir. *Historia de Jalisco.* Vol. 1, *Desde los tiempos prehistóricos hasta fines del siglo XVII.* Guadalajara: Gobierno de Jalisco, Secretaría General, Unidad Editorial, 1980.

"Nuño de Guzmán contra Hernan Cortes, sobre los descubrimientos y conquistas en Jalisco y Tepic, 1531." *Boletín del Archivo General de la Nación* 8, no. 4 (1937): 365–400, 541–76.

Orozco y Jiménez, Francisco. *Colección de documentos históricos inéditos y muy raros, referentes al arzobispado de Guadalajara.* 5 vols. Guadalajara: Trimentral Ilustrada, 1922–26.

Ortelius, Abraham. *Theatrum Orbis Terrarum.* Antwerp: privately printed, 1579.

———. *Culiacanae Americae.* Antwerp: privately printed, 1592.

Pagden, Anthony, trans. and ed. *Hernán Cortés: Letters from Mexico.* New Haven: Yale University Press, 1986.

Parry, J. H. *The Audiencia of New Galicia in the Sixteenth Century.* Cambridge: Cambridge University Press, 1948.

Paso y Troncoso, Francisco del, comp. *Epistolario de Nueva España, 1505–1818.* 16 vols. Mexico City: Antigua Librería Robredo de José Porrúa e Hijos, 1939–42.

Pérez Bustamante, Ciriaco. *Los orígenes del gobierno virreinal en las Indias españolas: Don Antonio de Mendoza, primer virrey de la Nueva España.* Santiago: Universidad de Santiago, 1928.

Pérez-Rocha, Emma, and Rafael Tena. *La nobleza indígena del centro de México después de la conquista.* Mexico City: Instituto Nacional de Antropología e Historia, 2000.

Pollard, Helen Perlstein, "Recent Research in West Mexican Archaeology." *Journal of Archaeological Research* 5, no. 4 (December 1997): 345–82.

Powell, Philip Wayne. *Soldiers, Indians and Silver: North America's First Frontier War.* Tempe: Center for Latin American Studies, Arizona State University, 1975. First published 1952 by University of California Press.

Quiñones Keber, Eloise. *Codex Telleriano-Remensis: Ritual, Divination, and History in a Pictorial Aztec Manuscript.* Austin: University of Texas Press, 1995.

Radding, Cynthia. *Wandering Peoples: Colonialism, Ethnic Spaces and Ecological Frontiers in Northwestern Mexico, 1700–1850.* Durham, NC: Duke University Press, 1997.

Razo Zaragoza, José Luis, comp. *Crónicas de la conquista del reino de Nueva Galicia.* Guadalajara: Instituto Jalisciense de Antropología e Historia, 1963.

Reséndez, Andrés. *A Land So Strange: The Epic Journey of Cabeza de Vaca; The Extraordinary Tale of a Shipwrecked Spaniard Who Walked across America in the Sixteenth Century.* New York: Basic Books, 2007.

Restall, Matthew. "Black Conquistadors: Armed Africans in Early Spanish America." *The Americas* 57, no. 2 (2000): 171–205.

———. *Maya Conquistador.* Boston: Beacon, 1998.

———. *Seven Myths of the Spanish Conquest.* Oxford: Oxford University Press, 2003.

Riley, Carroll L. "Mesoamerican Indians in the Early Southwest." *Ethnohistory* 21 (Winter 1974): 25–36.

Román Gutiérrez, José Francisco. "Los indígenas de Juchipila alrededor de 1540–1547." *Estudios Jaliscienses* 23 (February 1996): 21–29.

———. *Sociedad y evangelización en Nueva Galicia durante el siglo XVI.* Zapopán: El Colegio de Jalisco / Instituto Nacional de Antropología e Historia / Universidad Autónoma de Zacatecas, 1993.

Romero de Solís, José Miguel. *El conquistador Francisco Cortés: Reivindicación de un cobarde.* Colima: Archivo Histórico del Municipio de Colima, 1994.

Ruiz Medrano, Ethelia. *Reshaping New Spain: Government and Private Interests in the Colonial Bureaucracy, 1531–1550.* Translated by Julia Constantino and Pauline Marmasse. Boulder: University of Colorado Press, 2006.

———. "Versiones sobre un fenómeno rebelde: La guerra del Mixtón en Nueva Galicia." In Williams, *Contribuciones,* 355–78.

Sandoval Acacictli, Francisco de. *Conquista y pacificación de los indios chichimecas.* 2nd ed. Edited by José María Muriá. Zapopán: Colegio de Jalisco, 1996.

Sauer, Carl O. *Colima of New Spain in the Sixteenth Century.* Berkeley: University of California Press, 1948.

———. *The Road to Cíbola.* Ibero-Americana 3. Berkeley: University of California Press, 1932.

———. *Sixteenth-Century North America: The Land and the People as Seen by the Europeans.* Berkeley: University of California Press, 1971.

Schneider, Paul. *Brutal Journey: Cabeza de Vaca and the Epic First Crossing of North America.* New York: Owl Books, 2007.

Schroeder, Susan. *Chimalpahin and the Kingdoms of Chalco.* Tucson: University of Arizona Press, 1991.

Schroeder, Susan, Stephanie Wood, and Robert Haskett, eds. *Indian Women of Early Mexico.* Norman: University of Oklahoma Press, 1997.

———. ed. *Native Resistance and the Pax Colonial in New Spain.* Lincoln: University of Nebraska Press, 1998.

Simmons, Marc. *The Last Conquistador: Juan de Oñate and the Settling of the Far Southwest.* Norman: University of Oklahoma Press, 1991.

Soto de Arechavaleta, María de los Dolores. "El primer censo neogallego: *Treslado de una vesitación . . . de 1525.*" In Williams, *Contribuciones,* 341–53.

Spate, Oscar Hermann Khristian. *The Spanish Lake: The Pacific since Magellan.* Minneapolis: University of Minnesota Press, 1979. http://epress.anu.edu.au/spanish_lake_citation.html (accessed January 24, 2010).

Tello, Antonio. *Crónica miscelánea de la sancta provincia de Xalisco: Libro Segundo.* Vol. 1. Guadalajara: Gobierno del Estado de Jalisco / Universidad de Guadalajara / Instituto Jalisciense de Antropología e Historia / Instituto Nacional de Antropología e Historia, 1968.

Terraciano, Kevin. *The Mixtecs of Colonial Oaxaca: Ñudzahui History, Sixteenth through Eighteenth Centuries.* Stanford, CA: Stanford University Press, 2001.

Townsend, Camilla. *Malintzin's Choices: An Indian Woman in the Conquest of Mexico.* Albuquerque: University of New Mexico Press, 2006.

"Visitacion que se hizo en la conquista, donde fue por capitan Francisco Cortes." In "Nuño de Guzman contra Hernan Cortes, sobre los descubrimientos y conquistas en Jalisco y Tepic, 1531." *Boletín del Archivo General de la Nación* 8, no. 4 (1937): 556–76.

Warren, J. Benedict. *The Conquest of Michoacán: The Spanish Domination of the Tarascan Kingdom in Western Mexico, 1521–1530.* Norman: University of Oklahoma Press, 1985.

Weber, David J. *The Spanish Frontier in North America.* New Haven: Yale University Press, 1992.

Weigand, Phil C. "Evidence for Complex Societies during the Western Mesoamerican Classic Period." In *The Archaeology of West and Northwest Mesoamerica*, edited by Michael S. Foster and Phil C. Weigand, 63–69. Boulder, CO: Westview, 1985.

Weigand, Phil C., and Acelia García de Weigand. *Los orígenes de los caxcanes y su relación con la guerra de los nayaritas: Una hipótesis.* Zapopán: Colegio de Jalisco, 1995.

———. *Tenamaxtli y Guaxicar: Las raíces profundas de la Rebelión de Nueva Galicia.* Zamora: Colegio de Michoacán / Guadalajara: Secretaría de Cultural de Jalisco, 1996.

Williams, Eduardo, ed. *Contribuciones a la arqueología y etnohistoria del Occidente de México.* Zamora: Colegio de Michoacán, 1994.

Zavala, Silvio. *Los esclavos indios en Nueva España.* Mexico City: Colegio Nacional, 1967.

Index

319